Troubleshooting and Repairing Compact Disc Players

Other Books by the Author

Build Your Own Test Equipment
Illustrated Home Electronics Fix-It Book
Microwave Oven Repair, 2nd Edition
Radio Receiver Projects You Can Build
Troubleshooting and Repairing Audio Equipment, 2nd Edition
Troubleshooting & Repairing Audio and Video Cassette Players & Recorders
Troubleshooting and Repairing Camcorders
Troubleshooting and Repairing Solid-State TVs, 2nd Edition

Troubleshooting and Repairing Compact Disc Players

2nd Edition

Homer L. Davidson

TAB Books

Division of McGraw-Hill, Inc.

New York   San Francisco   Washington, D.C.   Auckland   Bogotá
Caracas   Lisbon   London   Madrid   Mexico City   Milan
Montreal   New Delhi   San Juan   Singapore
Sydney   Tokyo   Toronto

Trademarks   3 3113 01428 8940

Optimus   Tandy Corp.
Realistic   Tandy Corp.
Technics   Panasonic Corp.

© 1994 by **TAB Books.**
TAB Books is a division of McGraw-Hill, Inc.

pbk   2 3 4 5 6 7 8 9 10   DOH/DOH   9 9 8 7 6 5 4
hc   1 2 3 4 5 6 7   8   9   DOH/DOH   9 9 8 7 6 5 4

Library of Congress Cataloging-in-Publication Data

Davidson, Homer L.
    Troubleshooting and repairing compact disc players / by Homer L.
Davidson.—2nd ed.
        p.   cm.
    Includes index.
    ISBN 0-07-015669-7 (h)   ISBN 0-07-015670-0 (p)
    1. Compact disc players—Repairing.   I. Title.
TK7881.75.D38   1994
621.389'32—dc20   93-38578
                                                   CIP

Acquisitions editor: Roland S. Phelps
Editorial team: Andrew Yoder, Managing Editor
                Melanie Holscher, Editor
Production team: Katherine G. Brown, Director
                 Rose McFarland, Desktop Operator
                 Linda L. King, Proofreading
                 Joann Woy, Indexer
Design team: Jaclyn J. Boone, Designer
             Brian Allison, Associate Designer
Cover design: Stickles Associates, Bath Pa.
Illustrations: Bender & Bender, Waldo, Oh.   0156700
Cover copy writer: Michael Crowner   EL1

I dedicate this book to several consumer electronics technicians
—Tom Krough, Tom Rich, and Glen Jochims.

Contents

13 Troubleshooting methods and service hints *385*

Acknowledgments

WITHOUT THE HELP OF MANY ELECTRONIC TECHNICIANS AND THE DIFFERENT manufacturers, this book would never have been printed.

To the manufacturers who gave me encouragement and the permission to use valuable service data, I owe a great deal of thanks: Joe B. Cagle of Alpine Corp., H. Kushida of Denon America Inc., William E. Berg and Harry F. Fouds at Matsushita Engineering and Service Co., Walt Herrin and Gordon W. Remala of Mitsubishi Electric Sales America Inc., Philip Kistner of NAP Consumer Electronics Corp., Valerie Young and Ted White at Onkyo Corp., Barry W. Smith of Pioneer Electronic Corp., Lynn Haley and Leon R. Schultz of Radio Shack, J.W. Phipps at RCA Consumer Electronics, Fred Walstrom of Sony Corp., and Jan Nesmith of Yamaha Electronics Corp., USA.

Material relating to Technics Compact Disc player taken from *Technics Service Manual*, 1985, Matsushita Electric Corp. of America. Used with permission.

Introduction

THE COMPACT DISC (CD) PLAYER HAS COME A LONG WAY IN THE PAST FIVE YEARS. The little rainbow-colored disc has brought a clear, crisp, noise-free reproduction of music to our ears. The digital music source can now be reproduced with more depth, greater detail, and more imaging than ever before. This new digital-to-analog technology has brought to us the ultimate in glorious sound.

Like any electronic and mechanical device, the compact disc player can break down. The purpose of this book is to provide practical service data to help make CD repairs much easier. It can help the beginner, intermediate, or experienced electronics student or practicing technician to further their knowledge with compact disc servicing methods. You can go as far as you want to with easiest or the most difficult repairs. Troubleshooting and repairing the compact disc players has opened up another new field in consumer electronic maintenance.

This book contains 14 chapters, beginning with the basic CD principles and ending with schematic diagrams of home, auto, and portable compact disc players. Chapter 2 explains how to clean and care for the compact disc. The laser pickup assembly is described thoroughly in chapter 3. How to troubleshoot the low-voltage power supply is given in chapter 4. Chapters 5 and 6 describe the signal circuits and the servo system in the CD player. What can happen to the motors and control circuits is given in chapter 7. Chapter 9 discusses the critical electronic CD player adjustments and why they are made. Servicing the portable CD player is described in detail in chapter 11, while chapter 12 covers the auto compact disc player. The most important chapter in this book, chapter 13, tells you how to do the many troubleshooting methods and service hints. Each circuit drawing is comprised of actual CD circuits found in popular models.

There are many different service problems related to today's electronic devices. Sometimes in electronic servicing, you cannot actually see the defective electronic component, so you must use test instruments to guide you through the circuit to locate the defective part. The compact disc player is no different, because the laser beam that is essential for operation cannot be seen with the naked eye. For this reason, extreme caution must be exercised while servicing or working around the laser beam. Always keep a disc loaded on the turntable when servicing to prevent eye damage.

One of the most important tools you will need to troubleshoot the compact disc player is the schematic diagram. Over eleven different compact disc player manufacturers have provided valuable service literature and schematics for this book. You cannot successfully service the compact disc player without a schematic diagram. It is just as important as a voltmeter or oscilloscope. The manufacturers provide needed service information, and this book would never have been written without their help.

Compact disc players are loaded with special components, such as surface-mounted parts, critical large-scale integration (LSI) and integrated circuit (IC) processors, optical lens-and-laser assemblies, and special motor components. You must obtain these parts through the CD manufacturer, a manufacturer's service depot, or the manufacturer dealer handling the CD players. Very few universal parts are found in the compact disc player. Always replace these special components with that of the original part number. Again, all parts should be listed in the manufacturer's service literature for that brand and model number.

All chapters in the second edition have been expanded with the latest CD information, charts, and photos. The boom-box CD player is included with optical, signal processing, servo section, and troubleshooting data. How the automatic CD changer operates in both the tabletop and auto units, special CD circuits, carousel and turntable loading and playing operations.

Discover how the automatic changer operates from the trunk of the car, with latest changer features, and how to troubleshoot the CD changer. Look for new motor problems with the new elevator, magazine, eject, up and down motors are added besides the regular motor circuits and service problems.

The latest CD features and many circuits add to the excitement of CD repair. You will find actual troubleshooting tips and data throughout the newly added pages of troubleshooting and repairing the CD player.

Servicing the compact disc player can be fun. Servicing any electronic product provides something new and exciting—another hill to climb. Tackling the "tough dog" CD player can be a challenge with a reward of satisfaction when you repair one of the more difficult servicing problems. Tomorrow that tough repair will become easy, and so it progresses each day in the exciting field of electronics.

1
Basic CD principles

THE BEST NEW SOUNDS IN AUDIO TECHNOLOGY ARE PRODUCED BY THE COMPACT disc player. What you hear is pure music—no hissing, no scratching, no harshness, no popping—nothing except pure music with depth and wholeness. Compact discs harbor a greater dynamic range with richer bass and highs from high-fidelity analog recordings.

Music can be reproduced on a compact disc to sound almost identical to the original sound. The CD is quite small compared to the phonograph record and the disc has a hole in the center like a record, but there is no comparison to the final result of 70 minutes of music. Music reproduced by the compact disc player has opened up a new field in pure sound.

Four basic types

There are four basic compact disc players found today in consumer electronics: the home, car, portable, and combination CD players. CD changers are used in the home and car CD players (Fig. 1-1). The auto CD changer is found in the trunk area.

1-1 The Denon DHC-500 car CD changer fits in the trunk of the car and can be operated with dash controls.

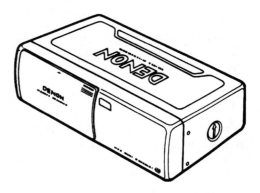

Home CD player

The home or tabletop CD component is powered by the ac power line and looks somewhat like a cassette player (Fig. 1-2). They are available in front or top-loading. Some automatic disc players can play several discs, like a stackable phonograph (also available in the car CD player). The following is a list of specifications for the Pioneer PD-7010:

- Type: Compact disc digital audio system
- Usable discs: Diameter: 120 mm; thickness: 1.2 mm
  Playing time: 60 minutes (or more)
  Linear speed: 1.2 to 1.4 m/sec
- Signal format: Sampling frequency: 44.1 kHz
  Sampling bit number: 16-bit linear
  Transmission rate: 4.3218 Mb/sec
  Modulation system: EFM
- Laser used: Semiconductor laser; wavelength = 780 nm
- Power requirements: HEM model: 220 Vac, 50–60 Hz
  HB model: 240 Vac, 50–60 Hz
  KU, KC models: 120 Vac, 60 Hz
  S, S/G models: 110/120/220/240 Vac, 50–60 Hz

1-2 The home CD player has a headphone jack or line output jacks for a stereo amplifier.

Auto CD player

The car compact disc player is just now achieving considerable popularity and is being factory installed in several new automobiles. The car player can plug into the existing sound system, into an AM/FM cassette player with CD input jack, or it can be mounted separately. The new in-dash models could include an AM/FM tuner and CD player in one unit.

The auto CD player is front loaded (with a slot in the front panel). The Sony CDX-A10 Disc Jockey CD player offers a remote controlled 10-disc changer that turns your car into a jukebox. A separate Sony XT10 AM/FM tuner can be used with the Disc Jockey auto player, but the Disc Jockey must be used with an outboard amplifier. Other CD changers are available that fit in the trunk and are operated by remote control from the front seat of the car. The following is a specification list for a popular car model.

Alpine Model 5900

System	Compact disc digital audio system
Laser	Semiconductor laser (780 nm)
Spindle speed	200 rpm to 500 rpm (CLV)
Number of channels	2
D/A conversion	16-bit linear
Frequency response	5 to 20,000 Hz ± 3 dB
Harmonic distortion	0.008% (1 kHz)
Dynamic range	90 dB (1 kHz)
Signal-to-noise ratio	85 dB
Wow and flutter	Below measurable limit
Sampling frequency	44.1 kHz
Quantization	16-bit linear
Modulation	EFM
Power supply	14 Vdc (negative ground)
Current drain	1.2 A (playback)

Denon Car CD Auto Changer DCH-500 (Fig. 1-3)

System	Compact disc digital audio system
Laser diode properties	Material GaAlAs
	Wavelength (780 nm)
	Emission duration-continuous
	Laser output power-less than 40 μp
Frequency response	5–20,000 Hz
Dynamic Range	90 dB
Distortion	0.005%
Wow and flutter	Below measurable limit
Outputs	Line output
Current drain	800 ma (CD playback)
	1.5 A during disc loading or eject
Power supply	14 Vdc

Portable CD player

Most portable players are used with a pair of stereo headphones. In some portable players, a set of stereo line output jacks can be plugged into the outside amplifier. You can operate the player from a battery pack or an ac power adapter. Some manufacturers provide a 12-Vdc line cord so that the portable player can be used in the car. Specifications follow for a popular portable CD player.

(1) CASE SECTION

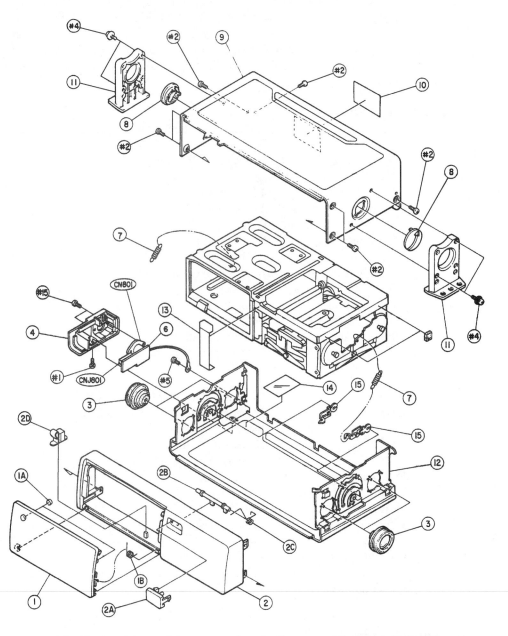

1-3 The breakdown of the case section of a Denon car CD changer DCH-500.

Sony Model D-14

System	Compact disc digital audio system
Laser diode properties	Material GaAlAs
	Wavelength 780 nm,
	Emission duration continuous Laser output
	Max. 0.4 mW
•Spindle speed	200 rpm to 5 rpm (CLV)
Number of channels	2
D/A conversion	16-bit linear
Frequency response	20 to 20,000 Hz
Harmonic distortion	Less than 0.008% (1 kHz)
Dynamic range	More than 90 dB (1 kHz)
Channel separation	More than 85 dB (1 kHz)
Wow and flutter	Below measurable limit
Sampling frequency	44.1 kHz
Quantization	16-bit linear
Modulation system	EFM
Power requirements	9 Vdc alkaline batteries, six size
	C nickel-cadmium rechargeable
	batteries (Sony NP-11), ac power adapter
	120 Vac/60 Hz, or Sony DCC-120A
	car battery cord

Combination CD player

Now the CD player can be purchased as part of a portable AM/FM MPX cassette "boom box." Also, several models have been introduced with the tabletop stereo. Furthermore, with the present day TVs operating with total stereo sound, you might see the compact disc player built right into TV cabinets within a few years.

Realistic CD-3304 Boom-Box CD Player

Sampling frequency	44.1 kHz
Quantization	16-bit linear/channel
Transmission bit	4.3218 Mb/sec.
Transmission clock	8.46 MHz
Error correction	CIRC C1, C2 double conversion
Pickup	Optical pickup-object lens drive
Wavelength	780 nm
Tracking system	3 beam tracking servo type
Digital filter	2 fold over sampling type
Analog filter	3 order active filter
D/A converter	R-2R ladder type
Output voltage	Nominal 0.95 V
Distortion	0.05%
Frequency response	0 dB—18 kHz

Required test equipment

You need several test instruments to troubleshoot and make the necessary alignment adjustments in the compact disc player. Most of these test instruments are already common to the average electronic technician's service bench (Fig. 1-4).

1-4 A Sharp boom-box player, model QT-CD7GY, has a combination AM-FM MPX radio, cassette and CD player in one unit.

- Dual-trace oscilloscope
- Optical power meter
- Digital multimeter
- Low-frequency AF oscillator
- Signal generator
- Capacitance meter
- Frequency counter
- Test discs
- Special tools, filter adjustment circuits, manufacturers special jigs, wrist strap, etc.

The optical power meter, test discs, special tools, filter circuits, and special jigs purchased from the manufacturer for special adjustments are probably the only devices that the already established repair shop might not have (Fig. 1-5).

Special tools such as a grating tool, feeler gauge, or special screwdrivers might be needed for some adjustments. The focus and tracking, loop gain harness, and special manufacturer circuits can be hand made. Special manufacturers jigs, monitor devices, and test cables can be purchased for certain tests required by the manufacturer. Although each manufacturer might require a certain test disc, the most common ones used are the YEDS7, YEDS18, and SZZP1014F (Fig. 1-6).

1-5 An oscilloscope, digital multimeter, and schematic diagram usually used to service most CD players.

ADJUSTMENT	TEST INSTRUMENTS
Laser output	Laser optical power meter
Grating adjustments	Test Disc
	Digital multimeter
	Oscilloscope
RF Signal - HF level - jitter	Oscilloscope
EF Balance	Oscilloscope
Focus lock and spindle lock	Test Disc
	Oscilloscope
Focus gain - tracking gain	Test Disc
	Digital multimeter
	AF oscillator
Tracking offset and	Digital multimeter
Focus offset	Oscilloscope
VCO - PLL	Frequency Counter
	Oscilloscope

1-6 CD player adjustments and the correct test instruments.

Safety precautions

For continued protection of the customer and service technician, several safety precautions must be followed. Always make a leakage current check after repairs. Keep your eyes at least 30 centimeters away from the optical laser beam. Replace crucial safety parts identified by the safety symbol ▲ with originals. Do not alter the design or circuitry of the CD player to where it could result in injury or property damage. Remove all test clips and shorting devices around interlocks after repairs. Keep a conductive mat under test equipment and the CD player while servicing.

Leakage current check

With the ac plug removed from any source, connect an electrical jumper across the two ac plug prongs. Place the instrument ac switch in the ON position. Connect one lead of an ohmmeter to the ac plug prongs tied together and touch the other ohmmeter lead in turn to each push button control, exposed metal screw, metalized overlay, and each cable connector. If the measured resistance is less than 1.0 MΩ or greater than 5.2 MΩ, an abnormality exists that should be corrected before the instrument is returned to service.

Leakage current hot test

Measure leakage current to a known earth ground (water pipe, conduit, etc.) by connecting a leakage current tester between the earth ground and all exposed metal parts of the CD player. Plug the ac line cord of the player directly into the 120-V power outlet and turn the ac switch on (Fig. 1-7). Any current measured must not exceed 0.5 mA.

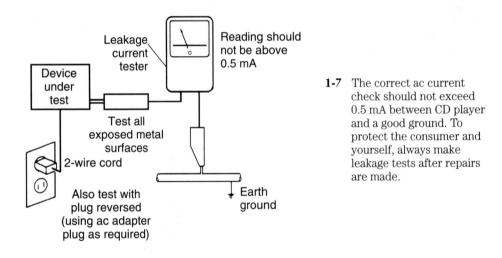

1-7 The correct ac current check should not exceed 0.5 mA between CD player and a good ground. To protect the consumer and yourself, always make leakage tests after repairs are made.

Laser beam protection

Be careful when working around the CD player to avoid laser beam radiation exposure. You can damage your eyes if you stare at the bare optical lens assembly while the player is operating, so keep your eyes away from this area. The laser beam warning label is usually fastened to the back of the laser optical assembly citing danger (Fig. 1-8). Always keep a disc on the spindle while servicing any CD player. Remember, the laser beam is not visible like that of an LED or pilot light.

Servicing protection methods

Many ICs and especially the laser diode assembly are critical components that are sensitive to static electricity or high voltage, so be careful around them. Remove excess solder with an antistatic suction-type solder iron or solder braid. Replace the sensitive devices and solder with a low-wattage soldering iron; the battery-operated

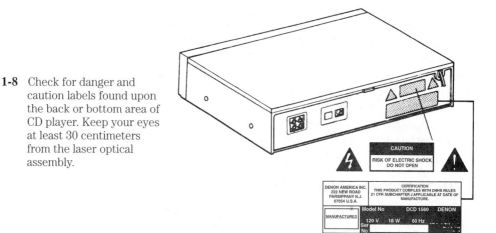

1-8 Check for danger and caution labels found upon the back or bottom area of CD player. Keep your eyes at least 30 centimeters from the laser optical assembly.

solder iron is ideal. Clip the metal part of the iron to the CD chassis to ground it. Wear a protective arm band and also clip it to the chassis (Fig. 1-9). Use a conductive metal sheet or mat under the CD player and test equipment to keep all units at the same ground potential.

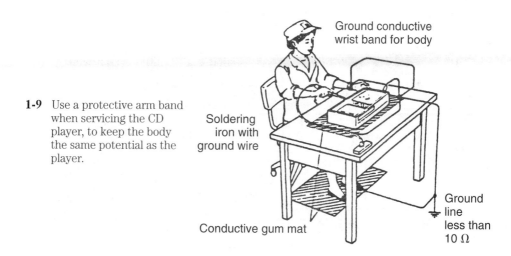

1-9 Use a protective arm band when servicing the CD player, to keep the body the same potential as the player.

Comparison tests

You might find the same chassis and circuits in different players of different names, but they are made by the same manufacturer. Sometimes the circuits are the same, except the components are slightly different and are mounted in different places. In others, the part number might be different but can be replaced with the same component. After servicing several of these CD players, troubleshooting will become easier.

Comparison tests can be made between two chassis if both units are the same. If you are having problems with one particular CD player and have another just like it on hand, compare the scope voltage and resistance measurements with the good one. Comparison tests can be made on a certain circuit or component of different makes when a schematic is not available.

Always write down the voltage and scope waveforms on the schematic for future reference after making repairs. Circle the defective component on the diagram and possible trouble for future reference. A lot of the troubles in CD players repeat, like in TVs. Sometimes it is wise to mark down the various scope waveforms of an IC input and output (for example, a new or good player). This practice not only acquaints you with the various circuits, but it is also good for future reference when a service problem occurs.

Front panel controls

Simply understanding exactly how to operate the various compact disc players could save a lot of service time and problems. The front panel controls might be named differently, but they operate in the same manner (Fig. 1-10). Improper operation of these controls could make a service problem more difficult than it really is. After servicing several CD players, operation control comes automatically. Refer to Fig. 1-10 for front panel operation of a Pioneer PD-7010 CD player.

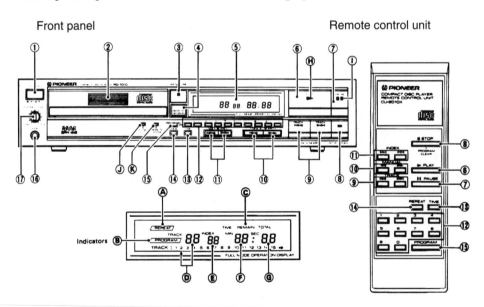

1-10 Have a thorough understanding of the front panel controls before servicing.

POWER switch

Simply press this switch to turn the unit off and on. All power to the CD player is controlled by the power switch. Always turn the CD player unit off when not in use.

Disc tray

When power is turned on and the OPEN/CLOSE switch is pressed, the disc tray opens outward. To close the tray, either press the OPEN/CLOSE switch again, or push the tray in manually (some players have pressure switches that engage the tray motor to close it automatically).

OPEN/CLOSE switch

Press to open or close the disc tray. The disc tray alternately opens and closes each time the switch is pressed.

Remote control signal sensor

The remote control sensor is located behind the front panel. It picks up the transmitted signal from the remote control transmitter and feeds it to the remote circuits.

Indicators:

REPEAT Lights during repeat play.

PROGRAM Lights after tracks are programmed.

TIME/REMAIN/TOTAL Switches alternate each time the TIME key is pressed as follows:

TIME: Indicates the track number, index number, and playing time (min-sec).

REMAIN: Indicates the number of the current track, index number, and the playing time (min-sec) remaining to the end of the disc.

TOTAL: Indicates the total number of tracks and total playing time (min-sec) of the loaded disc.

TRACK Indicates the number of the track currently playing or being programmed. The bottom row of digits indicates the number of tracks on the disc (number of tracks programmed during programmed playback). The digits decrease each time a track ends. The arrow lights if there are over 15 tracks.

INDEX Indicates the index numbers dividing a single track into sections.

MIN Indicates the time (minute units) of a track or remaining time on a disc.

SEC Indicates the time (second units) of a track or remaining time on a disc.

PLAY Lights during playback.

PAUSE Lights during the PAUSE mode (playback has been temporarily interrupted).

DISC Lights when a disc has been loaded properly.

REMOTE CONTROL Lights when a command signal is received from the remote control unit.

PLAY key Press to begin playback. Also releases the player from the PAUSE mode. All systems are go when the PLAY button is pressed. The disc motor starts to spin and the pickup head assembly starts to read from the loaded disc. The play indicator should light.

PAUSE key Press to temporarily interrupt playback. When pressed again, the player is released from the pause mode. Although the disc motor continues to spin, the laser assembly does not move. Do not leave the player in the pause mode for a long period of time.

STOP/CLEAR key Press to stop playback. When pressed, all operations stop. The disc stops spinning and the laser assembly is turned off. Also, when the player is in the stop mode, press this key to cancel memorized contents of programmed play (CLEAR function).

TRACK SEARCH key   The track search button is also known as the "track up" or "track down" search key. When the player is in the normal PLAY, PROGRAMMED PLAY, or PAUSE mode, these keys are pressed to perform search for a desired track.

FORWARD or TRACK UP   When pressed once, the disc playback advances to the beginning of the next track. When pressed continuously, the disc playback moves to the beginning of succeeding tracks on the disc (during programmed playback, it moves to the beginning of the next programmed track).

REVERSE or TRACK DOWN   When pressed once, the disc playback returns to the beginning of the currently playing track. When pressed continuously, the disc playback moves further in reverse to the beginning of previous tracks on the disc (during programmed playback, it returns to the beginning of the previously programmed track).

MANUAL SEARCH keys   These keys are pressed to perform fast forward and fast reverse when the player is in the play or pause modes. The function operates only during the time the keys are held depressed. If the keys are held for three seconds or more, the speed increases. During programmed play, the player will enter the pause mode before moving to the next (or previous) track.

FAST FORWARD   The disc spins forward at a high rate of speed to locate the desired music (if the end of the disc is reached, the player enters the pause mode).

FAST REVERSE   The disc is spinning at a rapid rate in the reverse direction (if the beginning of the disc is reached, the player enters the pause mode).

INDEX SEARCH keys   When the player is in the PLAY or PAUSE mode, these keys are used to search for divisions (index numbers) within individual tracks. When pressed, the player returns the disc to the previous index number, or it advances it to the next index number. This function cannot be used in the programmed playback mode.

FORWARD   Advances to the next index number.

REVERSE   Returns to the previous index number.

NUMBER keys   (1 through 0) Use these keys to designate track numbers during playback.

When memorizing tracks for programmed play, press the number keys corresponding to the numbers of the desired tracks in the desired playback order (press number keys, then program key).

To begin playback from a designated track, press the number keys corresponding to the number of the track (press number keys, then PLAY key).

To confirm the playing time of a track, press the number keys corresponding to the number of the track (press number, then TIME keys; the time will be displayed for about 3.5 seconds).

TIME key   Press this key to change the display mode of the time indicator. Each time the key is pressed, the display mode changes alternately in the order TIME, REMAIN, TOTAL (for details regarding the contents of the displays, see the section on indicators).

REPEAT key Press to perform repeat playback.

When pressed during the normal playback mode, all tracks on the disc are played back repeatedly.

During programmed playback, the programmed tracks are played back repeatedly in the programmed order.

PROGRAM key (PGM MEMORY) Use to memorize desired programs for programmed playback. After designating a desired track number with the number keys, press the PROGRAM key to memorize the track. Tracks will be programmed in the order memorized.

PHONES TERMINAL When using headphones, plug the phones into the jack.

PHONES LEVEL control Use to adjust the sound volume when listening with headphones. Sound volume increases as the control is rotated clockwise. Not all CD players have headphone jacks or volume controls.

Removing transport screws

The CD player optical mechanism is protected from excessive vibration or rough handling during shipment with one or more *transit* or *transport* screws. These screws hold the pickup assembly in position and if not removed the player might shut off and not operate. Look for these screws (and any labels identifying them) on the bottom of the chassis (Fig. 1-11). Simply loosen the screw so the mechanism is free. Some screws fall out while others cannot be completely removed. If the screws are removed, tape them to the back of the chassis with masking tape. You should replace these screws (or tightened them if they were not completely removed) when you take the player in for repair or when you move it.

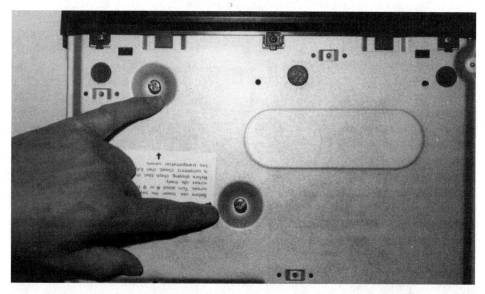

1-11 Remove transport screws before operating the CD player. These screws hold the optical assembly in position during transportation.

Check for tight transport screws when the player won't operate. A lot of CD players have been brought into the shop or taken back to the dealer for repairs with the transport screws still in place. A Phillips or straight screwdriver can usually be used to loosen these screws (Fig. 1-12).

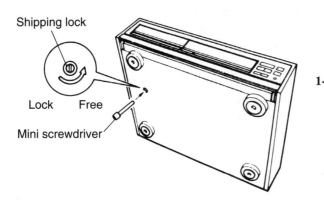

1-12 Remove the transportation screws or rotate the shipping lock on the bottom side of the CD player.

Removing covers

Always remove the power cord from the receptacle before removing covers. Most CD players have two metal setscrews on each side of the top cover. Remove these screws so that the top cover can be pulled off to reveal the insides of the CD player (Fig. 1-13). The front edge of the top cover might have a lip that sticks under the plastic front panel, so be careful not to damage the front panel.

In some players, the bottom cover can be removed to get at the printed wiring and components mounted on the bottom side of the board, while in other units the

1-13 Remove the top cover to get at the electronic or mechanism assemblies.

large board is bolted to a solid bottom plate. The latter means the circuit board or mechanism assembly must be removed to get to the bottom side of the printed circuit board (PC board). CD players with bottom covers are much easier to service than those with a solid bottom. In these cases, simply remove the entire outside cover or wood cabinet to get at the chassis.

For example, see Fig. 1-14 for the disassembly procedure for the Denon DCC-9770 auto compact disc player and AM-FM MPX radio. Figure 1-15 shows how to disassemble the different covers, handle assembly, front panel assembly, and CD mechanism unit.

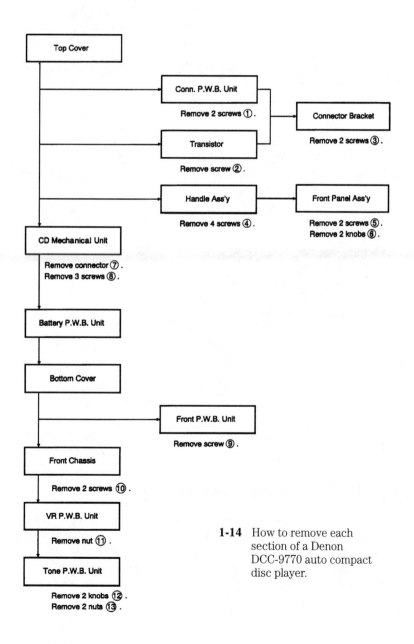

1-14 How to remove each section of a Denon DCC-9770 auto compact disc player.

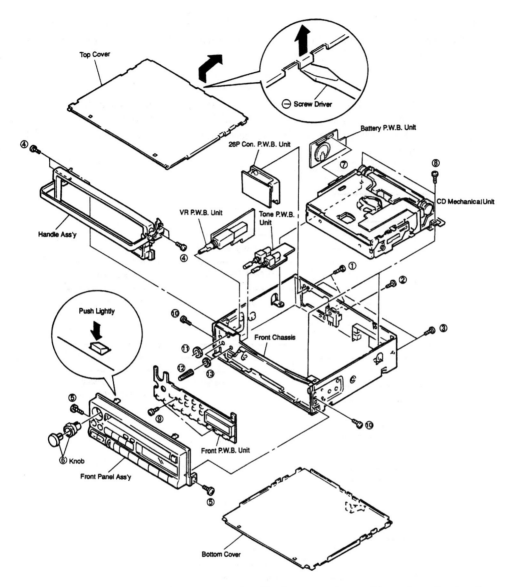

1-15 How to remove the different covers, handle, front panel assembly, and mechanism in a Denon DCC-9770 auto CD player.

Portable CD cover removal

Before disassembling the unit, spread a soft rubber mat or cloth on your workbench to avoid scratches and grease stains. Take out any compact discs and all batteries, and then turn off the power switch and unplug the ac adapter. Do not use a material that is likely to cause static electricity because transistors and ICs can be easily damaged. Place all screws and small parts in a cup or container for reassembly. Reassemble in reverse order.

Remove the battery cover and batteries (Fig. 1-16). Remove the four screws (A) holding the bottom cabinet and lift off the cover. Then remove the top cabinet and pull out the connector from the CD main PC board (Fig. 1-17).

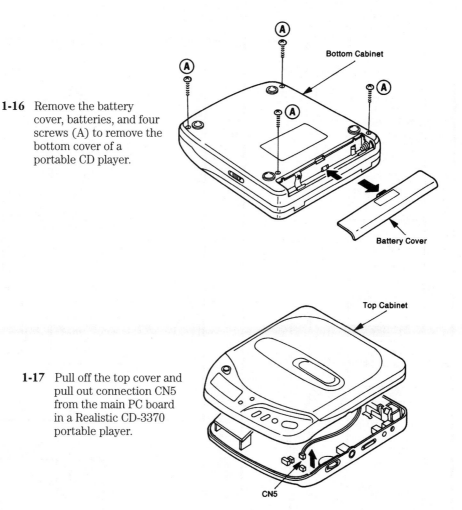

1-16 Remove the battery cover, batteries, and four screws (A) to remove the bottom cover of a portable CD player.

1-17 Pull off the top cover and pull out connection CN5 from the main PC board in a Realistic CD-3370 portable player.

The block diagram

Begin troubleshooting procedures with the block diagram. Upon checking the block diagram, you can quickly isolate the defective section(s) in the CD player. You can see where the signal path goes from section to section (Fig. 1-18). The block diagram can further be broken down to show several blocks of one particular section. A partial block diagram might include the internal operation of a servo LSI processor (Fig. 1-19). Not only does the block diagram illustrate how the different sections are tied together, it can be used to tell how the circuits operate in the CD chassis.

BLOCK DIAGRAM

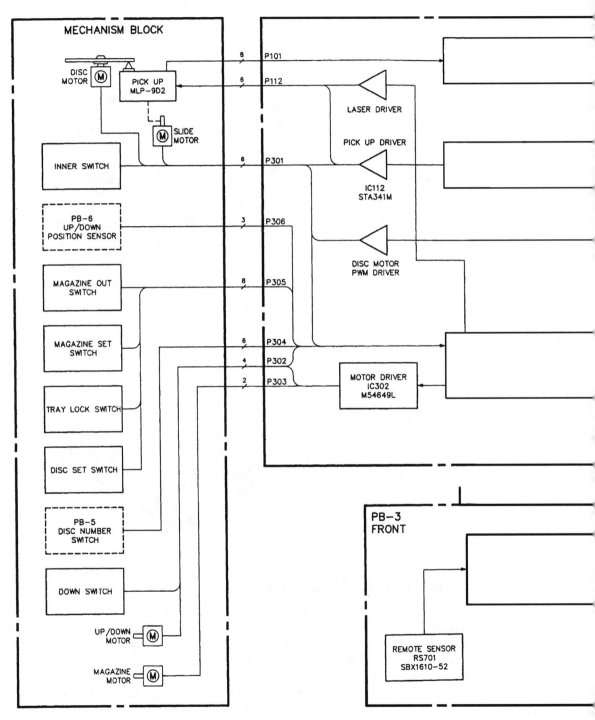

1-18 A block diagram of a Mitsubishi M-C4030 auto changer compact disc player.

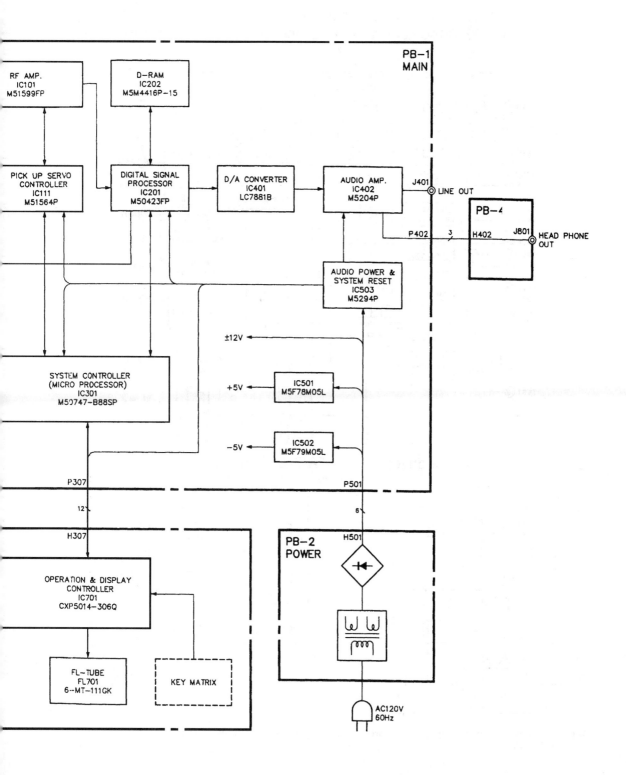

IC block diagrams and descriptions
CXD2500AQ (digital signal processor)

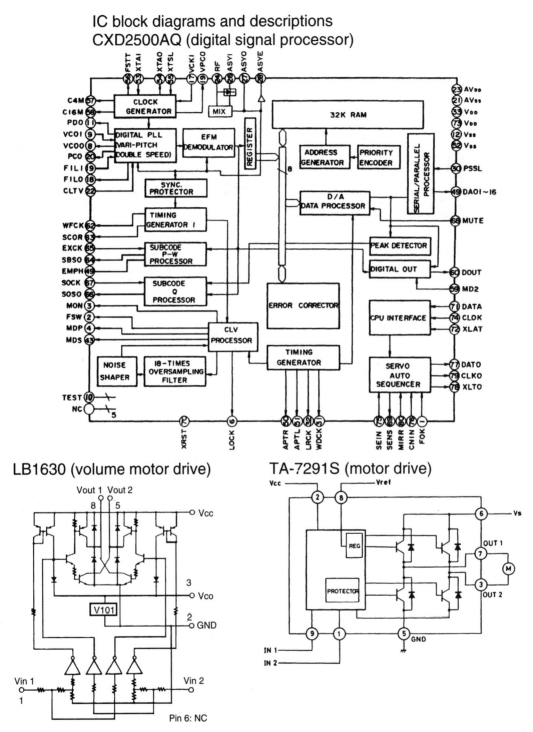

LB1630 (volume motor drive)
TA-7291S (motor drive)

1-19 IC block diagrams of digital signal processor and motor drive circuits in the Onkyo DX-C909 and DX-C606 CD players.

Location of components

The parts layout, exploded view, and photos make it easier to locate a possibly defective component after determining the likely problem area on the block diagram. A wiring diagram is shown in Fig. 1-20 that illustrates how the various boards are tied together. An exploded view of the mechanism helps when replacing the various parts in the correct sequence (Fig. 1-21). Remember, the manufacturers service literature is absolutely essential in servicing CD players. Besides the schematic and wiring diagrams and the electronic and mechanical parts layouts, the service literature includes crucial component numbers for ordering or obtaining the correct part (Table 1-1).

Schematic breakdown

The first look at a schematic diagram of the compact disc player might appear complicated, but if you break the schematic down into various sections, servicing becomes more systematic. For instance, if the loading motor is not operating, go directly to the servo or system control IC and trace the signal back to the driver and loading motor (Fig. 1-22). Each functional problem can be circuit traced using the same logic.

A lot of the manufacturers have the different circuits drawn in various colors so they stand out. Others use a variation of dotted lines to separate the various circuits. Most CD schematics have arrows or a thick color path of arrows indicating the signal path throughout the various stages (Fig. 1-23). Critical voltages are found on the schematic or listed separately in a voltage chart. Some schematics have voltages listed in red or green. If not, mark them directly on the diagram before you start servicing procedures. After locating a defective component, circle it and draw a line out to the side to the margin area to record the service problem.

Locating the suspected component on the PC board chassis might be difficult if a parts layout diagram is not handy. Sometimes the components are labeled and others are not (Fig. 1-24). The electronic components are often mounted on one board and the mechanical parts are located on another assembly (Fig. 1-25). Small components such as transistors, capacitors, resistors, and diodes might be difficult to locate because many are not individually marked. If you do not have a service manual, you must trace out wiring and components, which takes up a lot of valuable time.

Chips and more chips

In addition to the optical pickup assembly, there are many IC processors, CPUs, and LSI components that must be handled with care, not only in testing but also during removal and replacement of the many terminal leads attached to the chip. Some have from 40 to 80 different terminal connections (Fig. 1-26). After the defective IC has been located, be careful not to damage the printed wiring while removing it.

The LSIs and IC components perform many CD player operations. The digital signal processing LSIs can integrate up to 13 or more different digital functions in a single chip. ICs handle many other functions, such as optical focusing, transport servo control, tracking, pulse width modulation and digital-to-analog conversion.

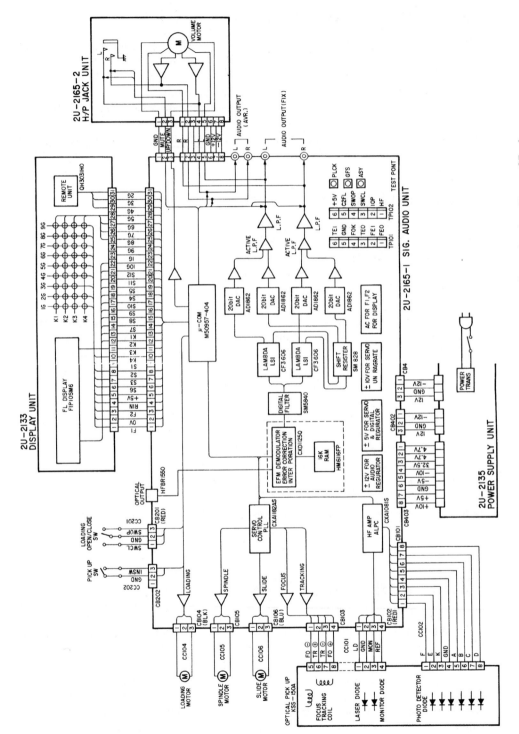

1-20 A wiring diagram shows you how the various circuits are tied together in a Denon CD player.

CDP MECHANISM EXPLODED VIEW

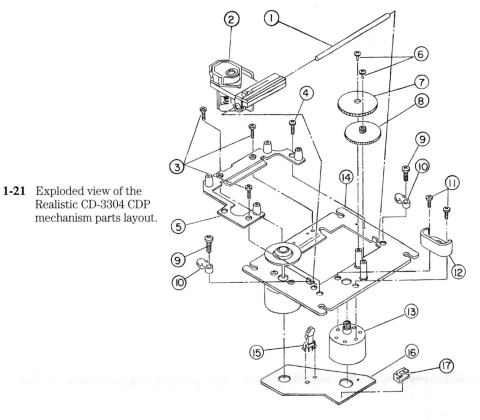

1-21 Exploded view of the Realistic CD-3304 CDP mechanism parts layout.

Table 1-1. CDP mechanism parts list

Ref. No.	Description	R/S Part No.	Mfr's Part No.
1	Shaft slide		88A-0001
2	Device optical		88A-0002
3	Screw 2×6		88A-0003
4	Screw 2×4		88A-0004
5	Chassis holder		88A-0005
6	Screw M1.7×3		88A-0006
7	Gear (A)		88A-0007
8	Gear (B)		88A-0008
9	Screw STP 2.6×8		88A-0009
10	Screw shaft		88A-0010
11	Screw + P2×4		88A-0011
12	Cover gear		88A-0012
13	Slide motor ass'y		88A-0013
14	Spindle motor ass'y		88A-0014
15	Leaf switch		88A-0015
16	Motor PCB		88A-0016
17	Connection pin		88A-0017

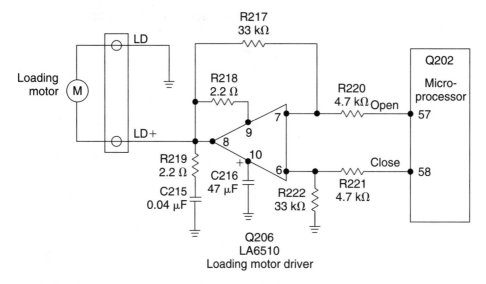

1-22 Loading motor circuits of an Onkyo DX-909 CD player with Q206 as motor driver.

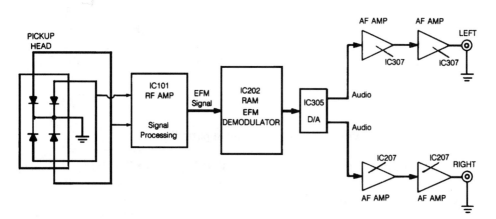

1-23 Follow the signal path arrows in most CD players for easy troubleshooting.

The large-scale integrated (LSI) and central processing unit (CPU) components should be handled with kid gloves, so to speak. Remove the solder around the leads with a solder sucker or solder wick. Heat the area by laying the wick material along the row of terminals. Slide the wick along as the solder is melted. Now, remove the solder from the same row of the other side. A solder sucker that fits over an IC terminal is quick in removing solder from around pins, but it will not remove excess solder where several pins are soldered together at a grounded area. Do not keep the soldering iron on one area for any length of time to avoid lifting the wiring. Remember, ICs are sensitive to static electricity. Keep them in the foil or static boxes until ready to install.

Surface-mounted components

Like the latest TV chassis, some of the CD chassis have surface-mounted components soldered directly to the board wiring. The surface-mounted parts can be resistors, capacitors, transistors, or ICs (Fig. 1-27). You might also see LEDs with a compact, thin, leadless type of structure. These components are mounted flat on the board and then soldered to the wiring.

There are many different surface-mounted devices found in the CD player. Some have over five different kinds of ICs. The SMD IC components might have gull type flat terminals with over 80 connecting flat terminals (Fig. 1-28). Be very careful not to short out when you take voltage measurements on these terminals with test probes. Often, terminal number one is indicated with a dot on top or numbers stamped upon the PC board. See Fig. 1-29.

The surface-mounted transistor might appear in a chip form with flat contacts at one side, top and bottom, or on both sides. You might find more than one transistor inside one chip (Fig. 1-30). The same applies to fixed diodes and LED SMD parts. Two or more fixed diodes might be found in one component. These transistors and diodes can be tested like any regular diode or transistor.

Because many surface-mounted devices have similar shape and size, it is quite difficult to identify them at a glance. The resistors appear as round, flat, leadless devices. The ceramic capacitor is a flat, solid device with the terminal connections at the outside, tinned ends. Always obtain these parts from the manufacturer, because they mount perfectly. If they are not obtainable, you might be able to secure these universal components from large electronic wholesalers or mail-order firms. The resistor has a number for identification with lines at the ends, while the ceramic capacitor has a line at the top with a letter of the alphabet and number (Fig. 1-31). Transistors and diodes are often identified with two letters.

By referring to the manufacturer's cross-reference table, you can identify the transistor or diode. However, each manufacturer might have its own type of transistors. Check Fig. 1-32 for the marking of surface-mounted resistors and capacitors found in the Sylvania FDD104 player.

Handling the chips

Clip devices are not heatproof or shockproof. These devices are made of ceramic or plastic molding, and they should not be subjected to direct shock. Install the chip flat onto the printed circuit board. Do not apply unnecessary stress to the chip. When soldering two terminals of the chip, do one at a time. Sometimes, when one terminal is soldered, another unsoldered terminal might try to lift up. If this is the case, do not try to push down the lifted terminal using the tip of the soldering iron. You could crack the chip or break the terminals.

Soldering should be done rather quickly. Do not apply high temperature to any chip for a long period of time, because they cannot withstand rapid heating or cooling. Do not heat the chip itself, only the terminals. Try to reduce the amount of solder you use when soldering, because any excess could affect the necessary flexibility of the chip bending against the board.

Main P.C. boards

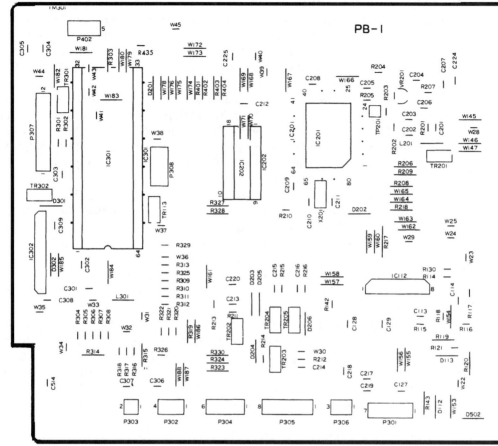

Headphone P.C. board (PB-4)

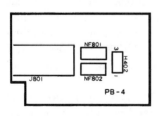

Disc no. switch P.C. board (PB-5)

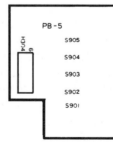

1-24 The main PC board layout of parts to easily locate the correct component in Mitsubishi M-C4030 CD player.

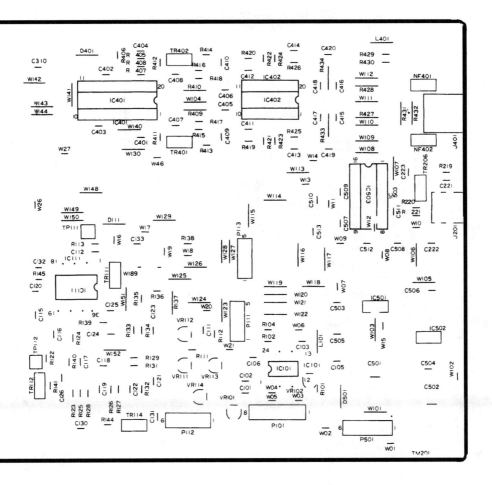

Photo-coupler P.C. board (PB-6) Jumper P. C. board (PB-7)

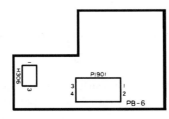

CD main printed circuit board
(bottom view)

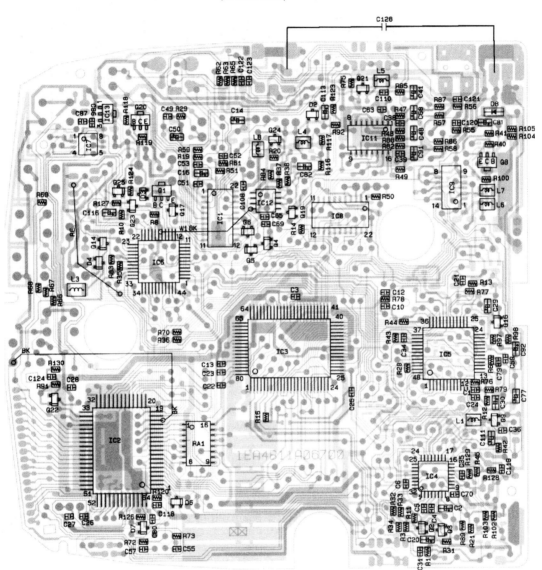

1-25 A close up view showing most of the top-mounted parts on top side of the PC wiring with SMD components underneath.

Always use a low-wattage soldering iron (30 watts or less) when soldering chips. The diameter of the iron tip should be about 2 mm. The temperature of the soldering iron should be less than 280° Celsius. Clean excess solder from the board with solder wick.

1-26 Notice the large IC mounted on top and SMD components underneath of the PC board in a Magnavox CDC-552 changer.

When mounting the chip to a PC board, set it as close as possible to the surface of the board. Do not apply unnecessary pressure to make the chip lie flat on the board surface, but try to keep the distance between the chip and board less than 0.5 mm. Do not solder a connecting wire to the chip before soldering to the board. Do not mount the chip upside down or vertically, always horizontally. Dismounting and mounting chips are shown in Fig. 1-33.

Removing IC or processors

Regular IC components with terminals pressed through the slots in the PC board and soldered on the foil side can easily be removed with a soldering iron and solder mesh or wick material. Run the solder wick with iron on top, down each side of the row of pin terminals. Likewise go down the other side of the same row of pins. Remove all excess solder. Carefully inspect each terminal to see if solder is around the small pin. Flick the pin terminal with screwdriver blade or pocketknife, to make sure the pin is loose and free. Carefully pry up the IC part and try not to damage the PC wiring.

The gull-type terminals of surface-mounted components can be removed in the same manner. Afterwards clean up the PC wiring for flat terminal mounting. Do not replace any SMD parts that have been unsoldered and removed from the PC board, even if tests are normal. Electronic-controlled soldering stations are ideal when removing and replacing SMD and IC components.

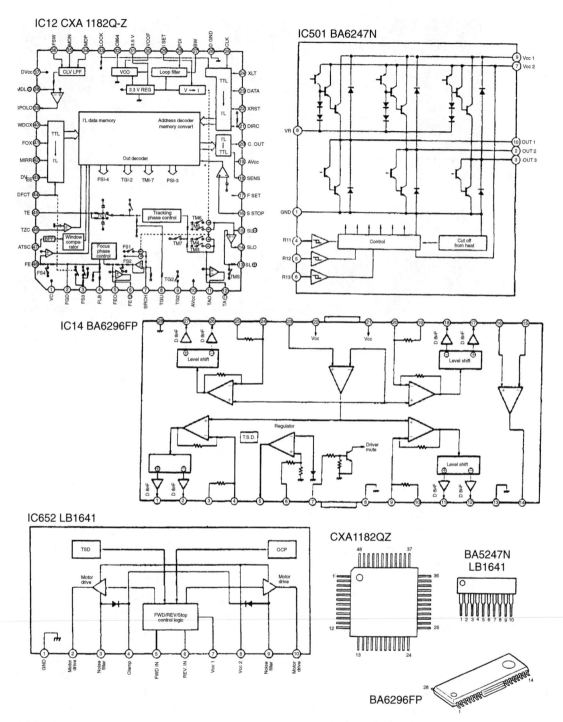

1-27   The various ICs, processors, and LSI components with internal circuits in the Denon DCH-500 changer.

● Terminal guide of IC's, transistors and diodes

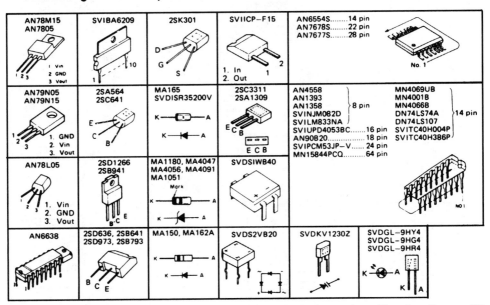

1-28 Locating the correct terminals of transistors, ICs, diodes, and rectifiers in a Quasar CD player.

Op amp

There are many integrated-circuit operational amplifiers (op amps) found in the compact disc players. The IC op amp is a very high-gain directly coupled differential amplifier with two separate inputs—one positive and one negative (Fig. 1-34). The op amp can amplify both ac and dc signals. When a signal is applied to the positive (*non-inverting*) terminal, the phase or polarity remains the same at the output terminal. On the other hand, the output signal is shifted 180° when signal is applied to the negative (*inverting*) terminal. Notice separate positive and negative bias voltages are applied to the IC. Several separate op amps can be integrated in one component.

Op amps are found in motor circuits, D/A converters, de-emphasis, tracking error, servo loops, focus error, VCO control, audio, and many other circuits within the CD player (Fig. 1-35). You find op amps in many other functional IC, LSI, and CPU processors. Op amps can operate in a feedback, inverter, noninverter, comparator, add, or amplifier circuit.

Double-sided boards

In many of the compact CD players with only one large PC board, you might find wiring and components on both sides of the board. Usually, the LSI, CPU, or IC components mounted underneath the board are surface-mounted parts. These compo-

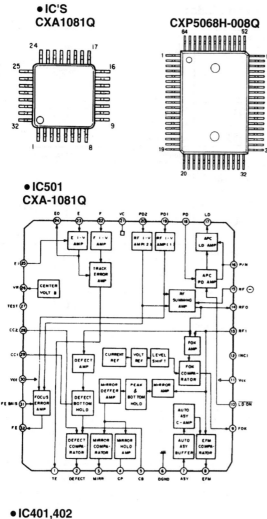

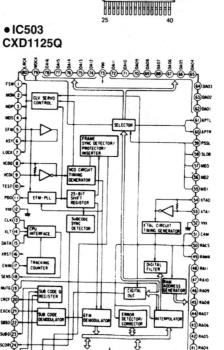

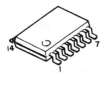

1-29   Surface-mounted ICs with gull-type terminals in a Denon AM/FM MPX DCC-9770 CD player.

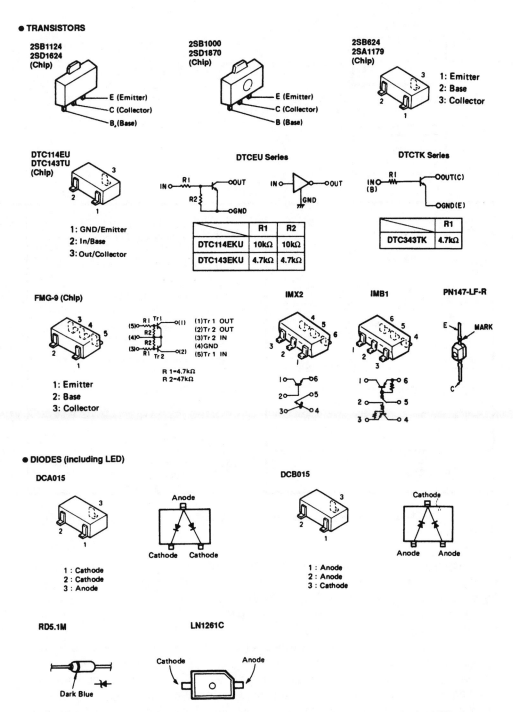

1-30 Surface-mounted transistors, diodes, and LEDs in the Denon car radio and CD player.

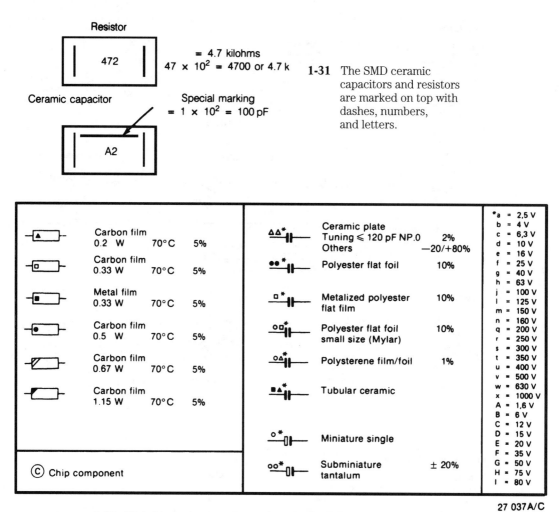

1-31 The SMD ceramic capacitors and resistors are marked on top with dashes, numbers, and letters.

Resistor

= 4.7 kilohms
$47 \times 10^2 = 4700$ or 4.7 k

Ceramic capacitor

Special marking
$= 1 \times 10^2 = 100\,pF$

A2

Carbon film 0.2 W	70°C	5%	
Carbon film 0.33 W	70°C	5%	
Metal film 0.33 W	70°C	5%	
Carbon film 0.5 W	70°C	5%	
Carbon film 0.67 W	70°C	5%	
Carbon film 1.15 W	70°C	5%	

© Chip component

Ceramic plate Tuning ≤ 120 pF NP.0 Others	2% −20/+80%	
Polyester flat foil	10%	
Metalized polyester flat film	10%	
Polyester flat foil small size (Mylar)	10%	
Polysterene film/foil	1%	
Tubular ceramic		
Miniature single		
Subminiature tantalum	± 20%	

a	= 2,5 V
b	= 4 V
c	= 6,3 V
d	= 10 V
e	= 16 V
f	= 25 V
g	= 40 V
h	= 63 V
j	= 100 V
l	= 125 V
m	= 150 V
n	= 160 V
q	= 200 V
r	= 250 V
s	= 300 V
t	= 350 V
u	= 400 V
v	= 500 V
w	= 630 V
x	= 1000 V
A	= 1,6 V
B	= 6 V
C	= 12 V
D	= 15 V
E	= 20 V
F	= 35 V
G	= 50 V
H	= 75 V
I	= 80 V

27 037A/C

1-32 Flat chip resistors and capacitors in the Sylvania FDD104 CD player.

nents lay flat and solder directly to the wiring. In some chassis, the single-sided wiring board has components mounted on both sides of the board, so if you are having special difficulty locating a component, look under the chassis (Fig. 1-36). However, most IC component outlines are shown on the top side of the board. Locate the manufacturers parts layout section.

Double-sided wiring presents various service problems in troubleshooting the chassis. If test points are not provided on the top side of the chassis, the board must be removed and turned over to get at the various surface-mounted components. Cracked wiring and surface-mounted element connections can break loose if the board has the opportunity to warp or sag. You might have to make various voltage and signal tests on components on the top side that feed through to the suspected component underneath.

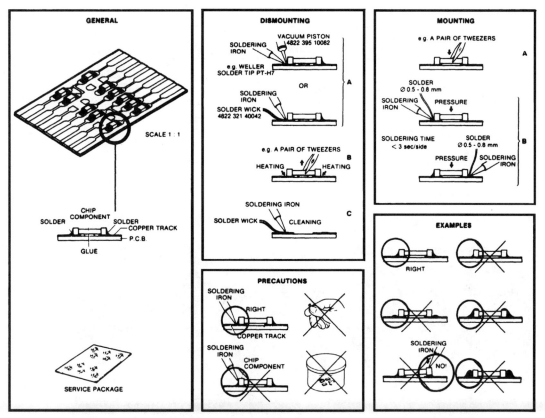

1-33   Removing and installing SMD parts in the Yamaha YCD1000 auto CD player.

1-34   The dual operational (op) amp has a positive and negative input with two amps in one component. You might also find some quad-capacitors (op amp) in portable CD players.

IC12 dual-operated AMP

Where to lubricate

Many CD player movable components never need to be lubricated. Small motors are often lubricated once at the manufacturer, which lasts for the life of the player. For a squeaking noise, a drop of light oil on the motor bearing might stop it.

Plastic gears and bearings throughout the player often require light grease on the teeth and bearings. A binding plastic clamper gear on a plastic bearing might

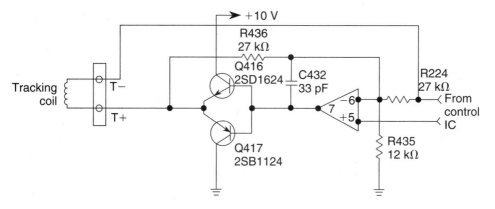

1-35 The op amp drives two driver transistors to control the tracking coil.

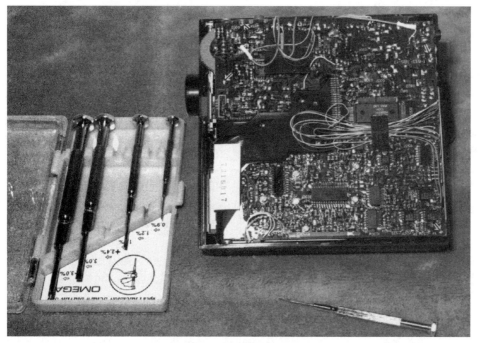

1-36 SMD components are found on the PC wiring side in a portable CD player.

need light grease or oil (Fig. 1-37). Sliding areas under the plastic gear assembly should have a light grease coating. If dirty, clean the slide rails and chassis surface where the pickup assembly slides back and forth. Remove the old grease with alcohol and a cloth before installing a new laser pickup assembly. Apply Morton #380 grease to the side rails. Dry or gummed-up tray sides and mechanism base can prevent or cause intermittent tray operation. Clean off and apply light grease to the track teeth and plastic sliding areas. Check Figs. 1-37 and 1-38 for areas to lubricate within the mechanical section of the CD player.

Application Points for Grease and Adhesive

Item	Points to apply grease
KF96H; 10,000 CS (Shin-etsu-kagaku)	• Engagement portion of Holder ass'y and Toggle spring.
G-501 (Shin-etsu-kagaku)	• Fitting portion of feed shaft and bushing. • Sliding portion of right edge of PU base and upper side of mechanism base.
G311S (Kanto-kasei)	• Gear engagement portion. • Engagement portion of tray and mechanism base. • Top of cam on the under side of main gear in loading section. • Boss of Lever. • Lever portion of mechanical base. • Spindle portions of gears and pulleys.

Adhesive

Item	Points to apply adhesive
LOCTITE #460	• Joining the spindle motor shaft and turntable together.

Note: If the specified greases and adhesives are not available, consult your nearest JVC dealer.

1-37 Lubricating grease and oil data show where to oil and grease moving parts in the CD player.

Safety interlocks

The *safety interlocks* are provided so the operator or service personnel are not exposed to any laser radiation that can damage your eyesight. Never look directly at the laser lens assembly while servicing the CD player. Just remember to keep your eyes away from this assembly. Also make sure a playing or test disc is in the tray at *all* times.

The laser outputs are controlled by the injection or cut off of the constant voltage source to the laser diode at pin 29 (LS) of IC401 (Fig. 1-39), and also by Automatic Laser Power Control Circuit. When pin 29 is in "H" (high) level, the laser emits the beam. When pin 29 is in "L" (low) level, the laser does not emit the beam.

Pin 29 is set in high level when the unit is loaded with the disc and is reading the index signals or is in PLAY mode. When the unit reads the index signals and the following two conditions are met, the laser emits the beam:

- When the loading limit switch (SW101) is set in the "CL" side (the disc tray is closed).
- The pickup is located at the area of the minimum internal circumference.

After the above conditions are met and the index signals have been read, the laser emits the beam when the following two conditions are met:

- When the PLAY key (SW404) or that of the remote control transmitter is pressed.
- When the play display is on.

Other interlock safety circuits and switches are activated when the tray is loading and unloading. The interlock switch is open (disabling the laser) when the tray is out, and it is closed with the disc loaded when the tray is in (turning on the laser

11-(1) Application Points for Grease

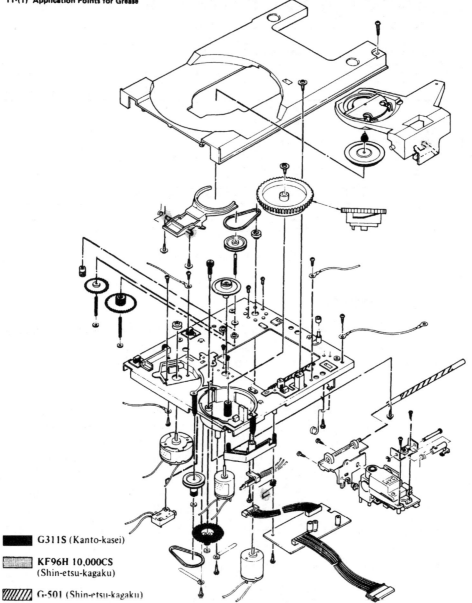

G311S (Kanto-kasei)

KF96H 10,000CS
(Shin-etsu-kagaku)

G-501 (Shin-etsu-kagaku)

1-38 The areas to be lubricated within JVC's XL-V400B mechanism.

beam). In other players, the laser beam is not turned on unless a disc is placed on the spindle (Fig. 1-40). With the tray empty the light emitted by an LED can shine on a phototransistor and shut down the laser assembly. When a disc is mounted on the spindle, it blocks the LED light from striking the phototransistor and turns the laser beam on (Fig. 1-41).

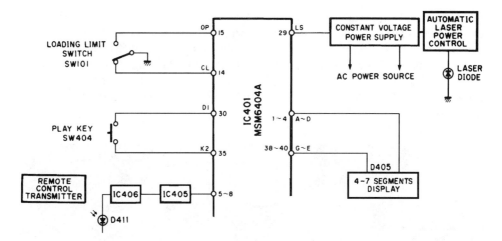

1-39 The interlock protection circuit found in Yamaha CD-3 player.

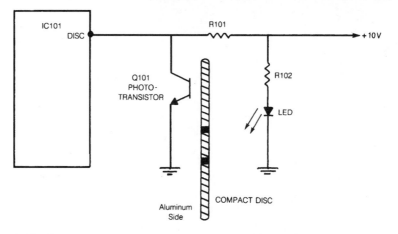

1-40 In the RCA RP-7901 portable CD player, the laser beam will not turn on until the top lid is closed on interlock switch.

1-41 When a disc is not on the spindle, the LED strikes the photo transistor (Q101) and shuts-down laser beam.

If the disc motor starts to run with the tray open or no disc is loaded on the spindle, suspect a bent or damaged interlock switch or a defective LED/phototransistor circuit. Check the phototransistor and LED with a meter. The LED can be checked like any ordinary diode (Fig. 1-42). Always remove the shorting pin or piece of plastic that holds the interlock switch engaged after servicing the portable CD player, but remember, do not look at the lens assembly if the disc spindle is rotating with no disc in position.

1-42 LEDs can be checked with the diode test of digital multimeter.

2

The compact disc

THE COMPACT DISC LOOKS SOMEWHAT LIKE THE 45 RPM RECORD, EXCEPT IT HAS A silvery surface and no grooves (Fig. 2-1). The CD has an outside diameter of 120 mm (less than 5 inches) with an inside hole of 15 mm. Just a little over one hour of music fits on a CD.

Rather than grooves and a pickup stylus, the little silver CD has a laser beam to pick up the recording. The CD starts out at an inside diameter speed of around 500 rpm and slows down to approximately 200 rpm, while the 45 rpm speed is constant. Instead of starting the recording at the outside edge, like the phonograph record, the CD disc is read from the center outward.

2-1 The compact disc is only 120 mm in diameter with a large 15-mm center hole.

Record versus disc

In the conventional phonograph record, the stylus (needle) rides through a groove that has been "coded" with varying amplitudes that correspond to the sound signal. The compact disc, however, has a track of microscopic indentations called *pits*, rather than a groove (Fig. 2-2). These pits and the space between the pits are the encoded digital representation of the original analog audio information. The high density information on these tracks is read by a laser pickup device that has no physical contact with the surface of the disc.

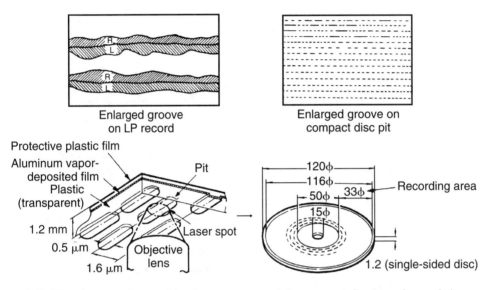

Enlarged groove on LP record

Enlarged groove on compact disc pit

2-2 The phonograph record has large grooves and the compact disc is made up of pits.

Digitizing the music signals eliminates both deterioration of the signals through the recording and playback process as well as the mechanical restrictions (physical wear). Also, with incorporating a high density and high fidelity that could not be achieved with conventional systems, it is now possible to reproduce a sound far superior to the limits attainable by analog systems.

The phonograph record contains two channels of information—one channel on each side of the groove. Because only one stylus must pick up both channels of information, there is a great amount of crosstalk between channels. With the compact disc method of recording, right and left channel information are in serial sequence. Channel separation is extremely good, which is important for accurate stereo reproduction.

The original audio signal is a smoothly changing (analog) waveform that is sampled at a 44.1-kHz rate (Fig. 2-3). No information is lost when the analog audio signal is converted to a digital pulse train as long as the sampling rate is at least two times the highest frequency to be reproduced. The sampled audio is converted to 1's and 0's using 16 bits of resolution. This provides 65,536 possible voltage level repre-

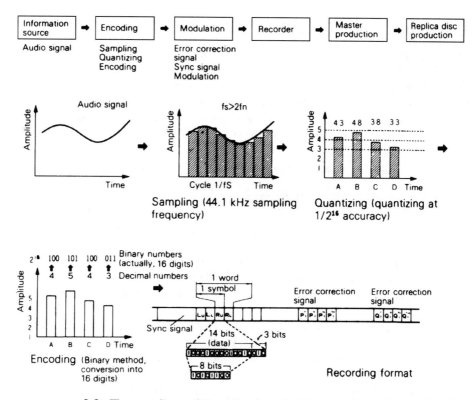

2-3 The encoding and recording format of the compact disc.

sentations. The dynamic range of the system using 16-bit resolution is greater than 90 dB. Because some sampled voltage levels might fall between two steps of the 65,536 combinations, the voltage level is rounded off to the closest 16-bit level.

On records, the amplitude of the sound grooves where a loud sound is reproduced is large. Also, the fluctuations in the low-frequency music components are greater than those of the high-frequency components. With compact discs, however, all the information is pulse coded and incorporated into digital signals (combinations of 0's and 1's).

A very complex encoding scheme is used to transform the digital data to a form that can be placed on the disc. Each 16-bit word is divided into two 8-bit symbols. These symbols are arranged in a predetermined sequence with error correction, sync, and subcode information added. The subcode is used to store index and time information. This information is then modulated by a process known as eight-to-fourteen-bit modulation (EFM). The 8-bit data is changed to 14-bit data through the use of a ROM-based IC. The EFM reduces the disc system's sensitivity to optical system tolerances in the disc player. The three merging bits added to each word (now 17 bits) contain sync and subcode data. This encoded data is recorded onto the discs as a series of small pits of varying lengths. During the playback process, the laser pickup reads the transition between the pit and the mirror—the *island*—not the pit itself.

Compact disc construction

The compact disc is composed of three layers of different materials. A clear plastic material contains the musical information with tiny pits and islands of digital information (Fig. 2-4). A reflective coating of aluminum or silver is applied over this. The reflective coating can be applied with a vacuum coating or ion-sputtering method. Next, a protective layer of acrylic resin is applied over the reflecting coating for protection. The music label is applied to the plastic side.

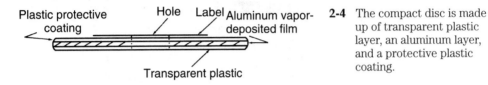

2-4 The compact disc is made up of transparent plastic layer, an aluminum layer, and a protective plastic coating.

Hence, the shiny disc contains the true-fidelity reproduction of music on the "rainbow" reflection side. When loaded in a CD player, the rainbow side is always face down and the aluminum side (with the label is on top), because the laser pickup is underneath the loaded disc.

Although reproduction of disc software has been the biggest drawback to CD player production because most CDs were manufactured overseas, the future of CD software is much brighter. Today, a great number of CD pressing plants have opened up in the United States in Indiana, Alabama, Wisconsin, and Maine. Currently, there are five more CD pressing plants preparing to begin manufacturing. With millions turned out each year, the true sound of music is here to stay.

The compact disc is a delicate piece of recording and must be handled with extreme care. Small pinholes in the aluminum coating can cause *dropout*, or errors in playing. Although these small pinholes are difficult to see, hold the disc up to a strong light and take a peak. The disc label might obstruct some holes, but return the disc if you can see several pinholes.

Handling

Hold the compact disc by the edges (Fig. 2-5). Do not touch or scratch the rainbow side (opposite the label). Some players can play through a smear of fingerprints, but don't take any chances. Remember, the side of the disc with the rainbow reflection is the side containing the audio information, so keep it clean. Do not stick paper or adhesive tape to the label side, and don't write on it.

Keep the compact discs free of dirt and dust. To clean a record, you wipe it with a circular motion. Do not try to clean off the CD with this method. When fingerprints and dust adhere to the disc, wipe it with a soft cloth starting from the center out (Fig. 2-6). Excessive dust in the player can gum up the disc drive and delicate mechanism. This prevents any scratches from covering a large area of corresponding data bits. Do not go around the disc in a circular motion. If it is difficult to remove the smudges, wipe off with a cloth moistened with clear water. Discs can become scratched the more they are wiped clean, just like a pair of eyeglasses. Excessive

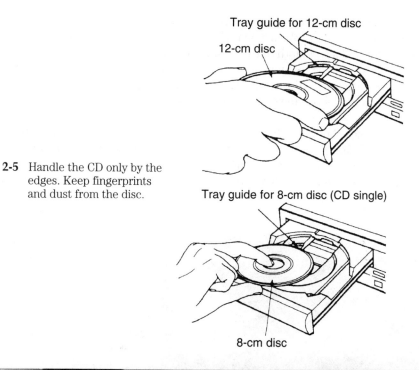

Tray guide for 12-cm disc

12-cm disc

2-5 Handle the CD only by the edges. Keep fingerprints and dust from the disc.

Tray guide for 8-cm disc (CD single)

8-cm disc

2-6 Wipe the CD with a soft cloth from center toward the outside edge.

cleaning of dust can even help grind particles into the soft plastic. If it's not visibly dirty, leave it alone. You can blow off dust with a can of photo dust spray. Do not clean the disc with benzene, alcohol, thinner, record cleaner, or antistatic agents. Like record cleaners, there are many different types of disc cleaners on the market. Some might do more harm than good, so you have to be the judge and jury. Some of these units clean in a circular motion and should be avoided. Make sure the commercial CD cleaner wipes outward on the disc surface. However, simply cleaning the disc with water and a soft cloth does a respectable job.

The CD disc must be handled and stored with care for long-lasting music reproduction. If the disc warps, the laser beam will not track properly. Avoid bending the discs. Scratches on the playing side can cause the disc to drop out and automatically shut off.

Compact discs should not be exposed to excessive cold, heat, or high humidity. If a disc is left outside in the winter, let it warm up to room temperature before playing it. The disc can become brittle when it is subjected to cold. Excessive heat can warp a disc and cause a CD player to shut down. Keep discs in their plastic cases (Fig. 2-7).

2-7 Return the disc to its case after playing.

If the disc is brought from a cold environment to a warm room, dew might form on the disc. Wipe off any dampness with a soft dry cloth before inserting the disc into a player.

Store compact discs in a location protected from direct sunlight, humidity, and extreme temperatures. There are many compact disc storage containers on the market. Discs can be stored vertically or horizontally, provided they are kept in their cases. With proper care and cleaning, the compact disc should last for 10 years or longer.

Ten compact disc do's and don'ts

1. Do not allow fingerprints, oil, or dust on the surface of the compact disc. If the signal surface is dirty, wipe it off with a soft, dry cloth.
2. Do wipe and clean CD discs from the center to outside edge.
3. Do not use water, benzene, thinner, record sprays, electrostatic proof chemicals, or silicone treated cloth to clean disc.

4. Always use care when handling disc to prevent damaging the surface, in particular when you are removing a disc from the case.

5. Do not bend discs.

6. Do not apply heat to compact discs.

7. Do not enlarge the hole in the center of the disc.

8. Do not write on a disc and do not attach any labels to it.

9. Condensation will form on the disc surface if it is brought into a warm room from a cold area, such as outdoors in the winter. Do wait until the condensation disappears.

10. Don't try to dry CD discs with a hair dryer or outside heat.

CD disc cleaners

There are many different CD cleaning methods including a wet and dry CD cleaner. A dirty lens can cause the CD to skip and distort. This type of cleaner is a digitally encoded CD with a built-in ultra fine brush that will safely clean the optical lens of a CD player. It removes dirt, dust, and smoke from the lens in less than ten seconds.

A CD cleaning kit can quickly remove fingerprints and smudges from CDs. These kits come with a fluid in a spray bottle, a lambskin wiper, a cleaning cloth and a hard brush. The automatic motorized chamois cleaning system provides true radial cleaning and it automatically stops when finished. The automatic cleaner can be used wet or dry with a kit of cleaning fluid. The automatic cleaner operates from four AA batteries.

A compact disc polish system cleans and polishes compact discs, and it protects them from dust and fingerprints. These systems prevent CD skipping because they contain a special antistatic formula. See Fig. 2-8.

2-8 There are several different cleaning kits upon the market to keep the CD free of dust and dirt.

Loading the disc

Although most CD players have front loading, a few models use top loading. The following paragraphs explain how to load each type of player.

For a front-loading unit, connect the output cables to the amplifier and plug in the power cord. Press the POWER button and make sure the display is lighted. Push the OPEN/CLOSE button and the loading drawer will slide out. Place the disc on the tray with the label up, and press the OPEN/CLOSE button again to prepare the player for play.

With a top-loading unit, notice that a top side keeper goes over the disc and rotates with disc in a portable or boom-box player (Fig. 2-9). Push down the top cover or lid until it locks into position.

2-9 The boom-box CD player is loaded at the top. Close and lock the top cover.

With a tray-mounted player, the disc tray must be ejected (open) to load the disc. Place the disc in the slotted area and push the close button to take the disc inside a home- or auto-type CD player. All discs should be loaded in the auto changer type player before closing or pulling the tray into the CD changer. After playing, press the disc button once to select the next compact disc for playback. Press the button repeatedly to select a desired disc as indicated on the display.

The test disc

There are many different test discs on the market for correcting alignment and other adjustments (Fig. 2-10). Most manufacturers have their own test disc, or they recommend one for alignment procedures. See Chart 2-1. These adjustments can also be made with a regular musical disc if you are very familiar with that selection. The

2-10 The CD test disc is used for alignment and adjustment of the EFM signal, PLL free run, EF balance, grating, tracking offset, focus gain, focus offset, tracking gain, and tracking offset recheck.

test disc is used to make EFM RF signal, grating, track offset, focus gain, and tracking gain adjustments. Some manufacturers use a regular disc to make the required test adjustments. Follow each manufacturer's special alignment and other adjustments in the manufacturer's service literature. Most test discs range in price from $9.00 to $50.

Chart 2-1. A list of various CD players with manufacturer recommended test discs.

Make	Model	Test disc
Denon	DCH-500	CA-1094
Goldstar	GCD-616	YEDS-7 (Sony)
Magnavox	FD1040	NAP-4822-397-30085
Onkyo	DX-200	YEDS-18 (Sony)
Panasonic	SL-P3610	SZZP1014F
Pioneer	PD-7-10	YEDS-7 (Sony)
Quasar	CD8975W	SZZP1014F
Realistic	14-529	YEDS-43 (Sony)
Sanyo	CP-500	800104
		400088
		400067
Sony	CDX-5	YEDS-1
		YEDS-7
		YEDS-18
		YEDS-43
Sylvania	FDD104	NAP-4822-397-30085
		NAP-4822-397-30096

Sony YEDS-1 demo test disc

The YEDS-1 stereo CD test disc contains 16 different music selections consisting of classical, jazz, and modern music. It contains a wide range of bass, percussion, and high notes throughout the various selections.

Phillips CC test set

A two-set CD test disc is available at the NAP Consumer Electronics Corporation. It consists of a single audio-frequency test. One disc supplies audio signals for the CD technician to use to measure the performance of the CD player. The other contains a variety of simulated defects as fingerprints, dust, and scratches. Very fine lines represent fingerprints, dust is represented by large black dots, and scratches are simulated by interruptions in the reflective information layer. The set (17165500-40) costs $89.95.

The ultimate test CD disc

A test disc for alignment and adjustment of CD players can be purchased from local or mail order electronic firms. The Ultimate test disc gives a choice of volume levels, frequency responses, noise levels, resonance, phasing, and tracking tests on auto or home CD players.

In this test disc there are 99 different tracks with sine waves of different frequencies, varying from 20 Hz to 20 kHz and sweeping left and right from 20 Hz to 20 kHz. The silicone track test counts from 1–99. The track test counting starts at 50–99. The test disc part is 80-505 and sells for $8.99 from:

MCM Electronics
650 Congress Park Dr.
Centerville, OH 45459-4072

3

The laser pickup assembly

THE LASER PICKUP ASSEMBLY IS A CRITICAL AND DELICATE ASSEMBLY THAT SHOULD be handled with care. The laser assembly can be dangerous to the eyes, so either keep a disc on the turntable or cover the laser optical lens with a piece of metal foil. Keep your fingers and tools away from the optical lens assembly. Always follow the manufacturer's procedures when replacing a laser pickup assembly.

There are basically two different types of laser pickup assemblies. Several of the compact disc players employ the *arc* or *swing-out arm mechanism*, such as the Magnavox FD1040 and the Sylvania model FDD104. Others use the *slide* or *sled mechanism* that glides along metal rods straight out from the center of the disc (Fig. 3-1).

The optical laser pickup assembly consists of the objective lens, focus-tracking coils, collimating lens, beam splitter, semitransparent mirror, photodetectors, monitor, and laser diode. The basic optical pickup block diagram shown in Fig. 3-2 illustrates four photodetectors (A, B, C, D), two tracking photodetectors (E and F), the focus and tracking coils, monitor diode (MD), and laser diode (LD).

Photodetector diodes

The photodetector diodes sense the EFM signal from the disc and pass it on to the RF amplifiers. Besides supplying the EFM signal, the photodetector diodes (A, B, C, D) provide a tracking error signal. Because the EFM signal is very weak, a preamp is connected to the photodetector diodes. In some pickup assemblies, the photodetector diodes are called *HF sensors*.

The tracking control photodetector diodes (E and F) provide a tracking error signal so that the error control circuits help keep the beam on track. The tracking error circuit generates an error signal if the laser beam spot moves away from the center pits. This error signal is used to ensure that the beam spot correctly tracks the line of pits. The tracking photodetectors are called *tracking sensors* in some players.

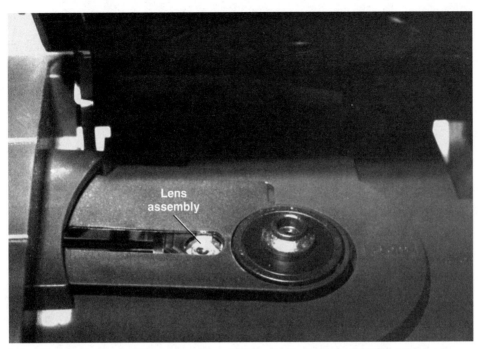

3-1   The laser lens assembly moves outward while playing with the SLED or slide motor assembly in the CD player.

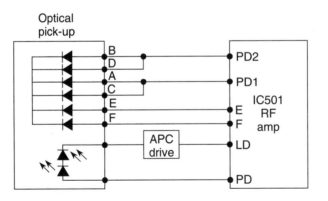

3-2   The optical pickup assembly contains the laser diode, photodetector, tracking and focus error diodes.

The laser diode

The laser diode emits a beam of light that is accurately aimed at the pits on the disc surface. Although the semiconductor laser beam is fairly weak compared to other laser systems, you should never look directly at the optical lens while working on the CD player. Also remember that the laser diode is very susceptible to the effects of static electricity. Use extreme care when removing and installing a pickup assembly.

The laser diode optical output is also beamed onto a monitor diode that is built into the optical pickup. The light source current generated as a result is fed back to the minus input of the operational amplifier to maintain the laser output power at a constant level. In the Denon DCD-1800R pickup, there is a laser protection diode with reverse polarity across the laser diode (Fig. 3-3). Although most pickup assemblies have the auto power control (APC) circuits on the main chassis, the Pioneer PD-7010BK player, covered in the next chapter, has the APC IC located on the pickup assembly (Fig. 3-4).

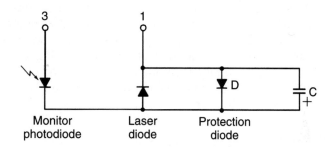

3-3 The Denon DCD-1800R player has a laser-protection diode across the laser diode.

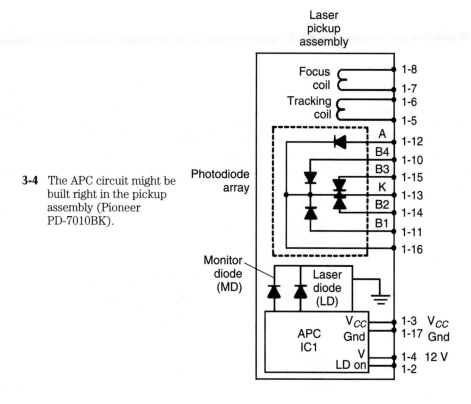

3-4 The APC circuit might be built right in the pickup assembly (Pioneer PD-7010BK).

Realistic CD-3370 laser pickup mechanism

Although it appears to be smooth and shiny, the surface of the compact disc is covered with tiny pits that represent digital information stored on each disc. Each pit is approximately 0.5 microns wide; a disc can hold up to 2.5 billion pits. As the laser beam scans the pits on the surface of the disc, the rise and fall of the beam over a pit is detected as a binary "1," while no change in the beam on a smooth area is detected as a "0." The laser beam must focus precisely on the pits to accurately read the disc. Several control systems are used to maintain disc reading accuracy.

The laser pickup uses four main photo diodes, A–D, to detect the laser light reflected from the disc and to check the focus of the lens (Fig. 3-5). Two additional diodes, E and F, are placed on either side of the main diodes to check for proper tracking. Finally, there are the laser diode LD and a diode PD for monitoring laser beam power.

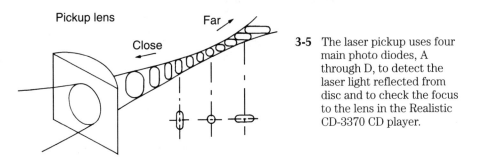

3-5   The laser pickup uses four main photo diodes, A through D, to detect the laser light reflected from disc and to check the focus to the lens in the Realistic CD-3370 CD player.

The main diodes are arranged in a square (Fig. 3-6). Changes in the magnitude of the laser reflection, strong (nonpitted area) and weak (pitted area), are detected and converted to digital signals. Focus adjustments are done by differently processing the outputs of the A-C and B-D diode pairs by RF IC amplifier. When the laser is properly focused, the signals from the diodes pairs should be exactly the same and cancel each other out. Otherwise, a focus error signal is generated at the output of the RF amplifier.

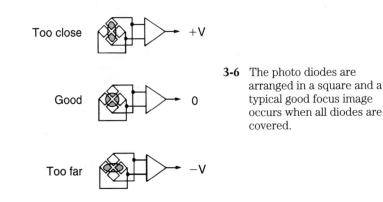

3-6   The photo diodes are arranged in a square and a typical good focus image occurs when all diodes are covered.

An astigmatic focusing method is used for this player. As the lens gets too close to the disc, the reflection becomes vertically longer, increasing the signal from the A-C diode pair. As the lens gets farther away from the surface, the reflection becomes horizontally longer, increasing the signal from the B-D diode pair. The error signal generated by the RF IC amp is fed to the servo processor, which generates a servo control signal. The servo control signal is fed to the driver IC, which energizes the focus coil. This moves the pickup actuator, adjusting the positions of the lens until correct focus is achieved.

The optical section

Optical pickups can have either one or three beams. Although there is very little difference in the sound output of the player, most incorporate the three-beam system, which is slightly more complicated in design. The semiconductor laser light source has a wavelength from 750 to 850 nm.

The path of the laser beam and arrangement of the optical elements in the Pioneer PD-5010BK optical system are shown in Fig. 3-7. The semiconductor laser emits a beam of light with a wavelength of 780 nm. It is barely within the range of visibility. The beam is produced from an extremely small point and has an elliptical distribution. It is dispersed in a conical shape.

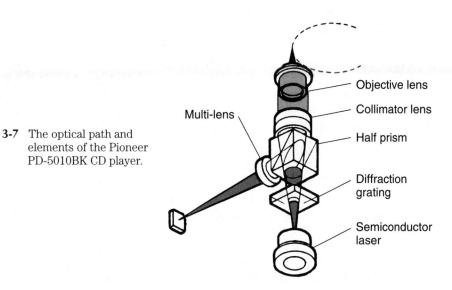

3-7 The optical path and elements of the Pioneer PD-5010BK CD player.

Objective lens

Collimator lens

Multi-lens

Half prism

Diffraction grating

Semiconductor laser

To produce the beam used to detect tracking error, the beam is passed through a diffraction grating that splits the beam into three separate beams—the primary beam (zero order) and two side beams (±1 order). A small amount of higher order elements are also produced, but these are lost and not used. Next, the beams are passed through a half prism where 50 percent of the energy is lost.

The *collimator* lens produces a completely collimated (parallel) beam. The diameter of the collimated beam is large enough to cover the movement of the objective lens. The beam is then condensed to a spot with an extremely small diameter by the objective lens before it is radiated to the disc. Part of the beam is then reflected back from the disc, diffracted, and routed back through the objective lens to be re-collimated and condensed.

When this beam reaches the half prism, 50 percent passes through the grating and returns to the laser diode. The other 50 percent is reflected by the prism to the multiple lens that has the functions of both a concave and cylindrical lens. This beam then goes to the photodiode alley where an electrical signal with a strength proportional to the intensity of the beam is produced.

The optical path of the compact disc can be compared to that of the video disc player. The first feature is that the outgoing path is a straight line, so no auxiliary parts are needed to alter the light path. This way, overall tolerances can be minimized. The development of the double-shaft activator for use in the parallel drive method allows the objective lens unit to be reduced in size. This makes it possible to maintain very satisfactory performance while using compact optical parts.

The second feature is the half prism. In the video disc player optical system, the outgoing and incoming light paths are separated by a ¼ wavelength panel and polarizing beam splitter. The primary reasons the half prism can be used in a CD player, but not in a video disc player, are:

- Although a semiconductor laser diode is much smaller than an HeNe laser, it nevertheless has a fairly high optical power output. Therefore, the energy loss caused by the half mirror is not a problem.

- Both video and compact discs tend to polarize light because they are made of a resin-based material that is not perfectly flat. In video discs, the amount of polarization is carefully checked against an established standard. In compact discs, the limitation is not very strict. Because of the lack of a strict standard, CD players normally use an extremely accurate ¼-wavelength plate. In actual use, however, this plate cannot function properly due to polarization of the laser beam caused by the disc. A half prism, on the other hand, is not at all affected by polarization of the laser beam. Consequently, a very stable optical path can be made.

Another feature of this optical system is the use of a parallel drive unit that allows optimum utilization of the objective lens at all times. As is shown in Fig. 3-8, the beam from the laser diode is converted into a completely collimated beam by the collimation lens. The parallel drive unit causes the objective lens to move parallel and perpendicular to the beam. Therefore, the optical path is usually not affected by movement of the objective lens within the collimated light cluster.

Still another feature of the optical section is the use of a multiple lens. This lens prevents the focusing point depth on the photodiode from becoming too shallow, a problem that has appeared as optical sections have become more compact. It is an effective way to permit lowering of the installation accuracy required by the photodiode. This multiple lens is cylindrical with the functions of a concave lens. Previously, there were two beams and both a concave and cylindrical lens. In this pickup, however, one lens performs both functions, thereby allowing a further reduction in size.

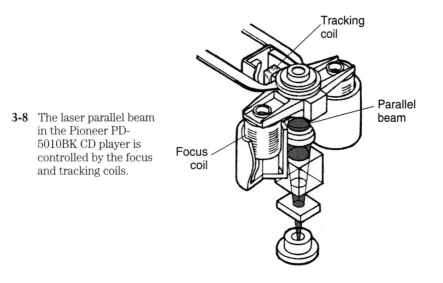

3-8 The laser parallel beam in the Pioneer PD-5010BK CD player is controlled by the focus and tracking coils.

When designing the optical section of a CD player, the most important concern is accommodating any differences between various compact discs. To do this, it is desirable to have a very short wavelength. The wavelength used is 780 nm because this is the shortest wavelength possible today with mass-produced pickups.

Laser action

To reproduce signals encoded as a series of tiny pits, players use a laser beam spot of approximately 1.6 micrometers in diameter. By rotating the disc and shining the laser beam on the series of pits, an *optosensor* (photodetector) detects the presence or absence of the pits within a fixed period of time. The changes in the reflected light correspond to the recorded signals.

The source of the laser beam is a laser diode with a 780-nm wavelength and a 3-nw optical output (Fig. 3-9). The beam from the laser diode is divided into three beams. The three beams pass through a half mirror, become a parallel beam through the collimator lens, get refracted by a prism, pass through the object lens, and focus on the disc. The light focused on the disc reads the disc data and is reflected. It then passes back through the objective and collimator lenses, through the half mirror and the flat concave cylindrical lens, then the beam strikes the photodetector. To be in line with the vertical fluctuations and the aberrations of the disc, the object lens moves up, down, left, and right so that the series of pits on the disc are always in focus.

Differences in one- and three-beam lasers

Both the one- and three-beam lasers use the objective lens, collimator, laser, and photodiodes. The one-beam system can have a semitransparent mirror and optical wedge besides those components mentioned above. The three-beam system can

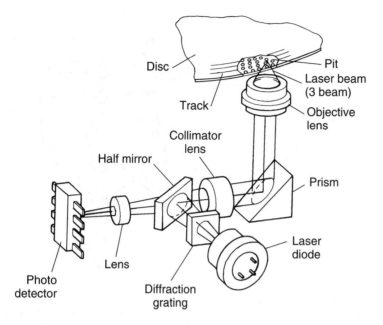

3-9   Laser beam operation in a three-beam pickup assembly of the RCA MCD-141 CD player.

have a subbeam, quarter-wave plate, polarized beam splitter, diffraction grating, and cylindrical lens besides those elements common to both systems. All of these components are located in the optical pickup section. Nevertheless, very little difference in sound is noticeable between the two systems.

Focus and tracking coils

The focus and tracking coils are located close to the optical lens. The beam from the laser must be focused on the disc surface at all times. There must be precise tracking as the disc rotates.

The focus and tracking coils within the pickup can be checked for continuity with an ohmmeter (Fig. 3-10). You might notice a shift in the optical lens when making resistance measurements. Both resistance measurements should be very low. In the RCA MCD-141 player, the focus coil measures 30 Ω, and the tracking coil 10 Ω .

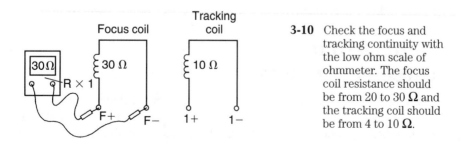

3-10   Check the focus and tracking continuity with the low ohm scale of ohmmeter. The focus coil resistance should be from 20 to 30 Ω and the tracking coil should be from 4 to 10 Ω.

In a Radio Shack CD-1000 model, the focus coil has a total of 20 Ω, and the tracking coil 4 Ω. A focus coil that reads less than 10 Ω and a tracking coil that reads less than 1 Ω could have shorted turns. Infinite ohms indicates the coils, lead wires, or socket connections are open. Both coils are controlled from the servo-control IC.

The focus and tracking coil can be checked with a C or D flashlight battery (1.5 V). Locate on the schematic diagram the focus and tracking coil terminal connections on the laser assembly. Remove the terminal leads for the test, writing down which was which. Place the battery across the tracking coil, and if normal, the optical assembly will move in a horizontal tracking direction (Fig. 3-11). Reverse the leads of the battery and it should move in the other horizontal direction if the tracking coil is normal. Now, place the battery across the focus coil terminals and the optical or activator assembly should go up or down. Reversing the battery polarity and the optical assembly should make it move in the opposite direction. If any one of the coils is open or shorted, the activator assembly will not move when tested with the 1.5-V battery.

3-11   The movement of the focus and tracking coil can be checked with a 1.5-V flashlight battery. You can assume that the coils are functioning if they move and begin to search when player is first turned on.

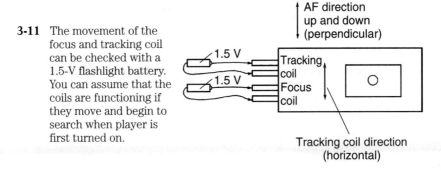

The beam from the laser pickup must remain focused on the disc surface to accurately read the information. When the focus on the pits is no longer precise, the focus servo moves the object lens up or down to correct the focus. Under this system, when a beam is irradiated through the cylindrical and convex lenses, the beam is elongated and then becomes a perfect circle. When the laser beam is reflected from the disc, it is directed to the cylindrical lens by the prism and then to the optosensor (photodetector) where it is split into four and forms a perfect circle (Fig. 3-12).

Latest optical systems

Besides all of the laser and photo diodes, focus and tracking coils, the pickup optical block assembly might have the spindle drive IC and SLED and spindle motor assembly (Fig. 3-13). Notice the focus, tracking, and Sled components are driven from IC14 in a Denon DCH-500 trunk changer.

In an Onkyo compact disc table model DX-C909 changer, the focus and tracking coils, SLED, and spindle motors are driven from IC102 (Fig. 3-14). The focus/tracking, SLED servo, and comparator IC101 takes the signal directly from the optical pickup assembly. You will find in the latest CD circuits that IC components can serve several different functions.

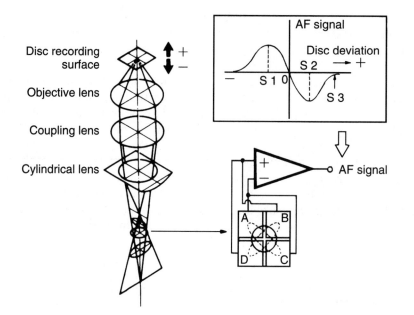

3-12   How the perfect circle beam is focused within the RCA MCD-141 auto focus assembly.

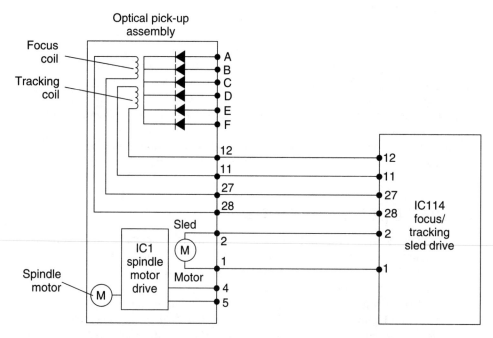

3-13   The spindle drive IC and motor with SLED motor are found upon the optical pickup assembly in the Denon DCH-500 CD player.

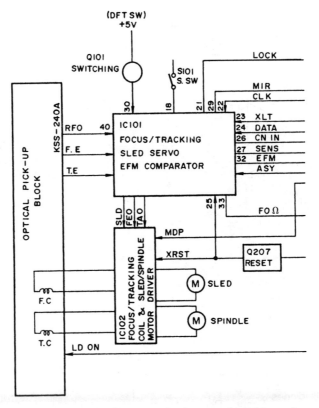

3-14 One IC (IC102) drives the focus and tracking coils, SLED and spindle motors in an Onkyo DCD-C909 CD player.

Pickup transport systems

Pickup transport systems take the optical pickup assembly from the center to the outer edge of the compact disc. One system uses the arm or arc movement where the optical pickup system travels in a semicircle to the outside of the disc. This action is controlled by a pickup motor. The optical pickup focus and tracking coil are mounted on the radial tracking arm (Fig. 3-15).

The other type is the *sled* (or slide) motor and gear assembly that moves the pickup across the disc on a rail or rod assembly. The sled assembly is now found in more CD players than the swing arm assembly.

Laser head connections

The laser diode is powered from a 5-V source or through the automatic power control (APC) circuits. The monitor diode is controlled by the APC circuits. The signal from the four photodetector diodes feeds to the preamp of EFM IC component (Fig. 3-16). The output of the tracking sensor or diodes feed to the tracking error amps in-

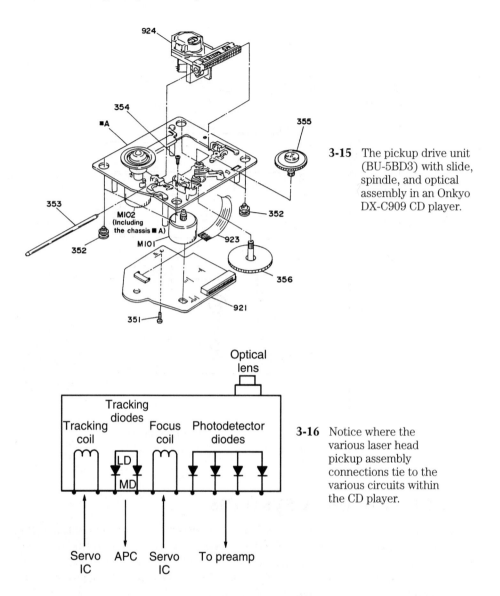

3-15 The pickup drive unit (BU-5BD3) with slide, spindle, and optical assembly in an Onkyo DX-C909 CD player.

3-16 Notice where the various laser head pickup assembly connections tie to the various circuits within the CD player.

side the RF and tracking amp IC. The focus and tracking coils are controlled by the servo control IC, or in some models, one large RF servo IC.

Testing the laser assembly

Weak or improper tracking of the optical pickup assembly could be caused by components outside the assembly, improper voltage sources, or a defective laser assembly. The laser diode light assembly can be checked with voltage and current measurements, light meters, or a homemade indicator. The commercial optical power meter or simulator should be used for critical laser diode adjustments. Voltage and current measurements can be taken across a fixed resistor in the laser diode circuits, but not directly on the laser diode. The homemade indicator simply indicates whether the laser diode is emitting a beam to the disc. Never look directly at the optical assembly when making these tests. Do not take diode or resistance measurements on the diode terminals.

The commercial light meter or simulator slips underneath the flapper or clapper assembly over the optical lens assembly instead of the compact disc. If the laser beam assembly is not emitting, look for a laser beam interlock assembly. This laser interlock is usually an LED/phototransistor combination located above the compact disc. When the disc is not in place, the LED provides light to the phototransistor and shuts down the laser beam circuits. Place a piece of cardboard or paper between the LED and hole of the phototransistor (Fig. 3-17). Check the interlock switch when the clapper or flapper assembly is removed and the turntable or laser assembly are not working. The optical power meter or simulator can be purchased at manufacturer distributors. The service life of the laser diode could have expired if the meter indication was less than 0.1 mW. Also, when the EFM output is extremely low, the service life of the laser diode has probably expired.

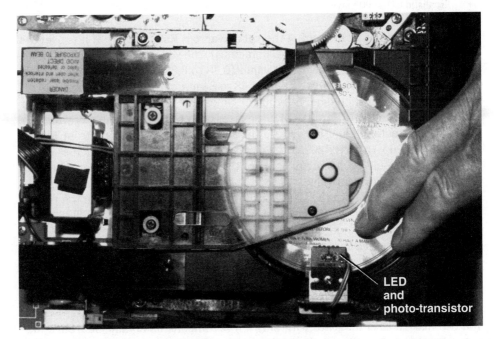

3-17 Cover the LED/photo transistor, between LED and hole, with a piece of cardboard or paper to represent a disc so that the laser head can be tested.

Accurate voltage and current measurements within the laser circuits are the best way to tell if the laser diode has become weak. Actually, the current of the laser diode is taken by a voltage measurement across a fixed resistor in the laser drive emitter transistor circuit (Fig. 3-18). In this Realistic CD-1000 compact disc player, the laser unit is normally driven with a current of 40 to 70 mA. Check this

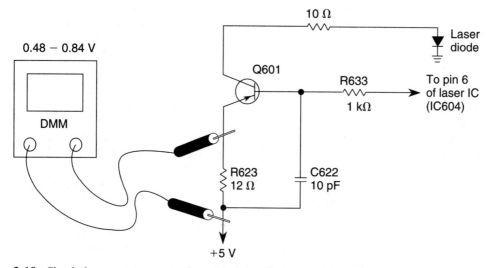

3-18   Check the correct current value of the laser diode with DMM probes across R623 in the Realistic CD-1000 player.

laser driving current by measuring the voltage across R623 (12 Ω). If it is over 100 mA, the laser unit could be defective. Remember, the voltage across the fixed resistor is less than 1 V. Here, the current value (0.48 to 0.84 V) across R623 is normal. The voltage value of 0.48 to 0.84 V equals 48 to 84 mA of current (a safe level).

The laser output should not be adjusted unless the laser pickup assembly or circuit is replaced. In the RCA MCD-141, the laser current can be checked by measuring the voltage across R209 (Fig. 3-19). The laser diode current ranges from 40 to 80 mA (0.48 to 0.96 V) across R209. If the current is over 120 mA (1.44 V across R209), the laser diode could be defective. Look for the current label on the pickup head assembly for correct current value.

The electric current of the laser is usually indicated on the label on the pickup. For the Akai Model CD-M88T, connect a voltmeter between TP2 and TP3 on the servo PC board and measure the voltage (Fig. 3-20). The electric current of the laser equals the voltage measured divided by 10. If the electric current of the laser exceeds 10 percent of the recommended value, replace the pickup assembly.

Infrared detector/indicator

You can make a laser indicator with only a few components obtainable from a local parts distributor or Radio Shack. See Fig. 3-21.

Q1 is an infrared photodetector (276-142) that picks up the laser beam light and activates the buzzer and LED when infrared is detected. Wire terminal 2 (collector) directly to the piezo buzzer and wire terminal 1 (emitter) to the ON/OFF switch. Terminal 3 is not used. The infrared emitter diode and detector comes as a pair, but only the photodetector is used in this small indicator.

The piezo buzzer (273-065A) was chosen because of its size and pleasant tone. The buzzer operates on 3 to 20 Vdc and has an operating frequency of 2.8 kHz. The

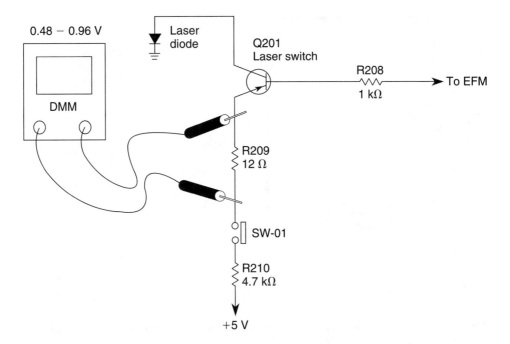

3-19 Check the normal current across R209 (0.48–0.96 V) in the RCA MCD-141 player.

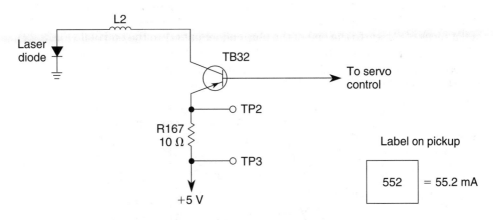

3-20 Measure the operating current of the laser diode across resistor R167 at test points TP2 and TP3 in an Akai CD-M88T player.

positive pin (+) is marked on the case and must be connected to the positive side of the 9-V battery or in series with the flashing LED.

The blinking red LED (276-036C) combines an MOS integrated circuit driver and red LED within a plastic LED housing. Because the resistance of the MOS driver transistors limits the current through the LED, no external current-limiting resistor is necessary. The typical supply voltage is 2.5 to 3 Vdc with a blinking rate of 2.0 Hz. Connect the longest (positive) lead of the LED to the positive battery terminal.

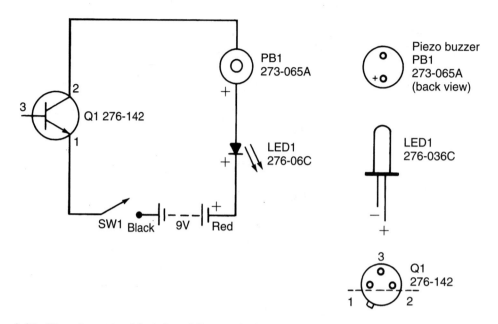

3-21   The schematic of the infrared detector/indicator with all components wired in series of the infrared laser diode tester.

All components are wired in series. The 9-V battery supplies power to Q1, PB1, and the LED. This little tester fits into a plastic project box-sized 3¼" × 2" × 1". Add a flat piece of plastic to the end of the box, and mount Q1 to the end of it (Fig. 3-22). Cement the piezo buzzer to one end of the box and the LED to the other. The photodetector should fit under the flapper or clamper assembly and directly over the optical lens assembly.

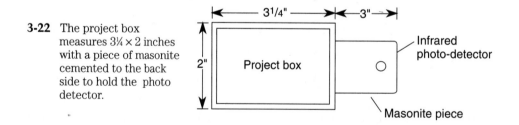

3-22   The project box measures 3¼ × 2 inches with a piece of masonite cemented to the back side to hold the photo detector.

The infrared indicator can be tested by holding it directly under the sun's rays or under a regular light bulb. The buzzer should sound off intermittently and the LED should flash. The stronger the infrared, the greater the output from the indicator. The infrared detector/indicator is also used to test remote transmitters as in chapter 10. This small indicator only indicates that the laser diode is operating from the optical lens assembly but it does not indicate how much current the laser diode is pulling.

Laser diode optical light meter measurements

Laser diodes usually have a wavelength of 765 to 850 nm with a continuous wave. Measure the laser power output over the optical lens assembly. Although the wavelength and power of each laser diode varies with each manufacturer, the range should be between 765 and 850 run. The maximum or minimum laser output should be listed within the manufacturer's service literature. The laser diode properties and output of several CD players are listed in Fig. 3-23.

CD Player	Diode Material	Wavelength	Laser Output (maximum)
Onkyo DX-200	GaAs/GaAlAs	780 nm	0.4 mW
Mitsubishi DP-107	Ga-Al-As	765-795 nm	0.4 mW
Sanyo CP-660		775-830 nm	0.7 mW
Yamaha	Ga-Al-As	760-800 nm	0.5 mW
Pioneer PD-7010		780 nm	0.26 mW

3-23 The laser diode material, wavelength, and laser output current of several CD players.

Cleaning the optical lens

Before troubleshooting the optical activator or sensor assembly, clean the lens area. The optical lens could have become stained or tarnished with cigarette or cigar smoke. Excessive dust can cloud up the optical lens to the point where the laser beam can't reach the compact disc. Be careful not to apply too much pressure when cleaning the optical lens or you can damage the lens assembly (Fig. 3-24).

Clean the lens with lint-free cotton or cleaning paper for camera lenses moistened with a mixture of alcohol and ether. Cleaning solution for cameras is ideal. Wipe the lens gently to avoid bending the supporting spring. Blow excessive dust from the optical lens with a can of dust spray available in camera departments.

Protection of laser diodes

Laser diodes are so sensitive to such pulsive electrical noises as static voltage or surge current that their reliability can be decreased or destroyed. Take precautions against any kind of static voltage potential in addition to electrically grounding the workbench and test equipment. Do not attempt to check the laser diode by applying multimeter or scope probes directly to the laser terminals. Do not apply voltage with a poorly made voltage source or with temporary contact pins or clips.

3-24 The laser lens and diode assembly is located directly underneath the CD disc with spindle motor to one side.

Some laser diode assemblies have a shorting metal bar to neutralize any static electricity. Although a shorting bar is used to establish contact with the laser diode leads during shipment, it can lose its conductivity due to vibrations during transportation or oxidation. Take sufficient precautions even when the shorting bar is on. Make sure that the optical laser unit is not handled with the shorting metal removed nor left near appliances that emit high-frequency surge voltages. For storing the unit, be sure to short the laser diode leads with the shorting metal (or by soldering the leads together) and place in a conductive container.

When removing the laser diode assembly, turn down the optical output (work current) and turn off the power. Short the laser diode leads with the shorting metal (or by soldering the leads), and remove the laser assembly connections. To install the laser assembly, make the right connections, remove the short circuit or bar, turn on the power, and then adjust the optical output. Always replace the whole optical laser assembly— not just the laser diode inside the optical assembly. Follow the manufacturers' procedure for removing and installing a new optical laser pickup or block assembly.

Handling the pickup assembly

Use extreme care when removing and replacing the pickup assembly. Be careful not to touch the terminals of the semiconductor laser or those that are attached to the board by hand or with a tool. New laser pickup assemblies come in a conductive bag.

Keep strong magnets (such as speakers or TV focus magnets) away from the pickup assembly, because some pickups have a magnet within the assembly. Leave all adjustment set screws alone on the pickup. These are adjusted at the factory. Readjusting a pickup set screw could damage both the pickup and assembly. Do not adjust any semifixed variable resistor on the laser assembly; they are also factory adjusted.

Defective laser assembly-shutdown

When the RF or EFM signal is not found at the digital or servo control IC, the turntable motor might start up, focus and tracking coils will begin to search, and then the whole chassis will shut down. Sometimes the chassis shutdown occurs so fast it's impossible to trace the EFM signal at the output of RF amplifier IC. You can't tell if laser assembly or the RF IC is defective.

To eliminate shutdown, determine if a separate RF amp IC is used or only one IC is found to control the focus and tracking coils, spindle and SLED motors, and the optical assembly. If a separate RF amp IC and servo IC is used, remove the low-voltage source (VCC) pin from the servo IC and PC wiring. Simply use solder wick or mesh and iron to remove excess solder around pin terminal (Fig. 3-25). Now, the servo loop is disconnected and you can check the RF or EFM waveform from the optical pickup assembly or RF IC, without chassis shutdown.

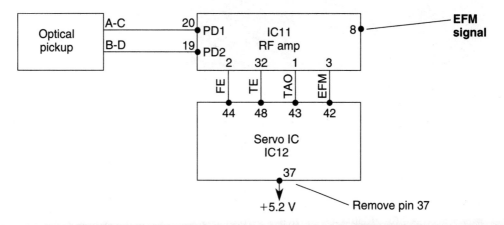

3-25 Remove supply voltage pin 32 (VCC) on the servo IC to prevent chassis shutdown so that the EFM waveform can be seen at RF amp (pin 8).

Replacing the pickup laser assembly

Pull out the ac power cord. Make sure the power is off before attempting to remove the different components necessary to get at the laser pickup assembly. The pickup is usually located under the flapper or clamper assembly (Fig. 3-26). In some players, the disc tray must be removed. Remove the bottom cover of the disc player. Some disc player chassis set right down into the cabinet and do not have a removable bottom cover. If you do not have the manufacturer's removal procedure at hand, write down the removal sequence for each component for easy replacement. After replacing the pickup assembly, make the laser current adjustments, if provided by the manufacturer.

Here are three different procedures for removing and replacing the laser pickup, taken from the respective service literatures:

Denon DCD-2560 pickup removal

Detach the laser pickup assembly KSS-151A housing assembly, then remove 6 screws (B) (Fig. 3-27). Remove 2 screws (A), unsolder 2 portions (B), and detach

3-26 The laser pickup assembly is located under the flapper assembly in the Sanyo tabletop CD player.

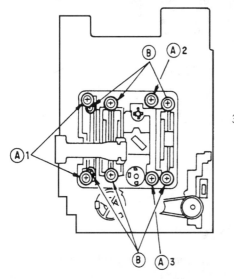

3-27 Remove six screws (B) to detach the laser pickup assembly in the Denon DCD-2560 player.

the speed detector coil (Fig. 3-28). The pickup laser assembly must be removed from the loader frame assembly (Fig. 3-29).

Panasonic SL-P3610 laser removal

Material relating to Technics compact disc player was taken from *Panasonic Service Manual* 1985 Matsushita Electric Corporation of America.

1. Pull out the connector (CN101, CN102) of the optical servo PC board (Fig. 3-30).
2. Remove the bracket setscrew (1).
3. Remove the guide rail retainer setscrew (2) and pull out the laser pickup from the two guide rafts. The pickup must be readjusted when it is replaced or fitted after removal.

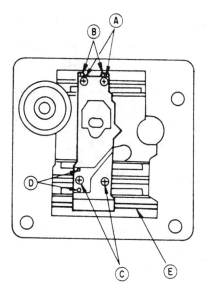

3-28 Remove screws (A) and unsolder two portions (B) to detach the speed detector coil.

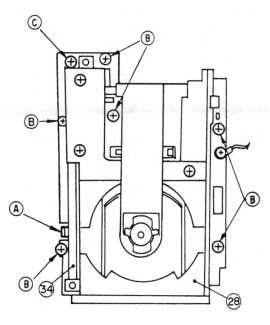

3-29 Remove pickup assembly KSS-151A of the Denon DCD-2560 player from loader frame assembly.

RCA MCD-141 laser assembly removal

1. Follow the procedure for removing the top cover, front panel, and loading mechanism.

2. Turn the loading motor mechanism over, being careful not to damage the flexible flat cable.

3. Remove four (4) screws holding the laser assembly to the load mechanism chassis. *Caution:* when replacing the laser assembly, be certain to completely

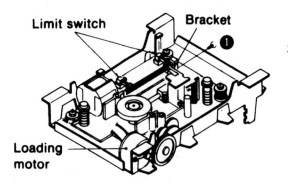

3-30   In a Panasonic SL-P3610 player, you must remove the bracket setscrew (1) and guide rail retainer setscrew to pull out the laser pickup from the two guide rails.

reassemble the laser assembly into the disc drawer mechanism before attempting to test or confirm proper operation. Handle the laser assembly with care. Use an electrostatic (wrist type) ground strap. The flexible flat cable pins should be wrapped with a conductive material to prevent electrostatic damage.

Simply reverse the procedure when installing a new optical pickup. Leave the new assembly in the conductive envelope until the old unit has been removed. Disconnect the old cable from the pickup. Remove the shorting pin from the new pickup and reconnect the pickup cable to the new assembly within seconds to prevent damage to the laser pickup. Some manufacturers recommend applying Morton grease #380 to the optical pickup guide rails after installation. After replacing the pickup assembly, make laser current and alignment adjustments.

Realistic CD-3370 portable laser removal

Remember, laser diodes are extremely susceptible to damage from static electricity. Even if a static discharge does not ruin the diode, it can shorten its life or cause it to work improperly. When replacing the pickup, use a conductive mat and a grounded soldering iron to protect the laser diode from static discharge.

Remove the two screws (C) holding the rack gear and rack plate spring. Loosen, but do not remove, screw (D) holding slide shaft (A). Pull out shaft (A) (Fig. 3-31 and Fig. 3-32).

3-31   Remove two screws (C), which hold the rack gear and push slide shaft (A) out in a Realistic CD-3370 CD player.

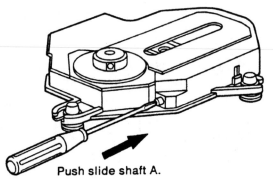

Push slide shaft A.

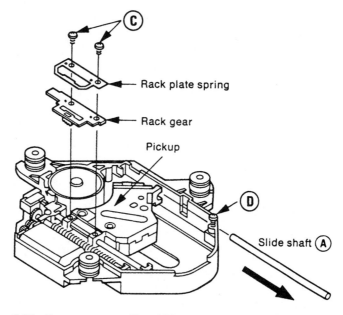

3-32 Remove screws (C and D) to remove rack plate assembly and shaft (A) in Realistic CD-3370 CD player.

Remove screw (E) holding the plate shaft spring. Take out the pickup. Then, pull out slide shaft (B) (Fig. 3-33). Gently, remove the laser pickup. Disconnect the wire connector and desolder and remove the shorting pad. After replacing the new pickup, adjust the focus offset and E/F balance.

3-33 Remove the screw (E) and pull out slide shaft (B) in the Realistic CD-3370 portable player.

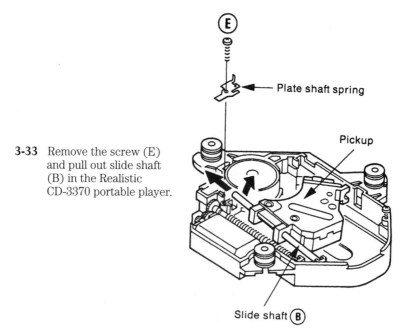

4

Low-voltage power supply circuits

THE LOW-VOLTAGE POWER SUPPLY IS ONE OF THE MOST IMPORTANT CIRCUITS IN the CD player because without adequate or proper voltage, very few circuits can operate. Most electronic technicians first verify that the dc voltages in the power supply are correct before proceeding to the suspected section (Fig. 4-1). Extremely low voltages can indicate a defective power supply, or a leaky component in the voltage source could be overloading.

In addition to improper voltages, a malfunctioning power supply can produce excessive hum if there is a defective filter or regulator feeding the voltage source of the audio circuits. Erratic relay operation could result from improper capacitor filtering. Finally, improper filtering of the dc sources can lower the dc voltages applied to the various sections of the CD player.

A digital multimeter (DMM), oscilloscope, and digital capacitance meter can locate most defective components in the low-voltage power supply. Of course, the VOM or VTVM can serve to take voltage measurements as the digital multimeter. But besides critical voltage measurements, a DMM with a diode/transistor test helps when testing leaky diodes and regulator transistors. Overloaded circuits can be tested with the milliampere current range of the DMM. Use the oscilloscope waveform of the different voltage sources to indicate poor filtering. Finally, the digital capacitance meter is used to check for a possibly open filter capacitor.

The block diagram

The low-voltage power supply provides the various dc output sources (Fig. 4-2). Besides voltages, the diagram can indicate zener diode and transistor regulation. A typical block diagram shows bridge, half-wave, or full-wave rectifiers. Notice the bridge rectifier is one diode symbol in the center of the diamond with the cathode terminal pointing toward the positive voltage source. The various transformer terminals are

4-1 The electronic technician checks the different voltage sources of the low-voltage power supply to determine if correct voltages are present.

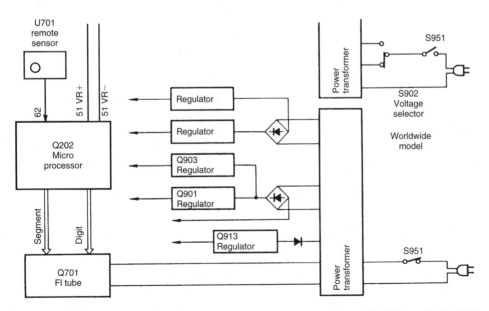

4-2 The block diagram of the low-voltage power supply in an Onkyo DX-C909 and DX-C606 CD player.

tied to the bridge half-wave rectifiers and fluorescent display tube. With the block diagram, you can quickly locate the possible improper voltage source.

The main low-voltage power supply circuits

After locating the suspected low-voltage source with the correct symptom and block diagram, proceed to the main schematic diagram. The low-voltage circuits are tied directly to the other circuits in the main schematic or there might be a separate power supply circuit (Fig. 4-3). Here the various voltage sources are shown and where they are supplied to the various sections of the CD player.

Many of the manufacturers have the various dc and ac voltage sources in red ink. Notice the location of the actual ac voltages from the transformers as applied to the bridge and diode rectifiers on Fig. 4-3. The input and output voltages are located on the regulator components. Other manufacturers do not list voltages on the main schematic, but they can be found on a voltage chart of ICs and transistors (Fig. 4-4).

Sometimes the dc voltages are drawn with red ink and boxes are used to help signal trace the various voltage sources (Fig. 4-5). A boxed red voltage might indicate the actual voltage measurement with no signal input. A solid red line indicates the positive B+ power supply, while the dotted red line indicates the negative B- power supply. The signal path might be traced with a halftone path.

The power transformer

The ac power transformer in the CD players is quite small compared to a TV transformer (Fig. 4-6). Usually, it is the only transformer found on the chassis. The power transformer is mounted on the chassis, while the other power supply components are mounted on the main PC board.

Because the CD player is made for many different countries, the primary winding must be adjustable to accommodate a range of power line frequencies, currents, and voltages. A multi-voltage model would have an ac hookup of 120/220/240 V at 50 to 60 Hz. Various ac voltage taps are switched on the ac transformer primary winding (see Fig. 4-7). Notice when different input voltages are used, the protection fuse must change in amperage. In the United States, most systems use 120 V at 60 Hz.

The primary winding in other models might be wired directly into the circuit, or different taps on the power transformer can be changed. In the Magnavox FD1040 model, the transformer ac connections are changed for the various input ac voltages (Fig. 4-8). In case of adaptation to 110 V or 127 V, the glass fuse (F1) on the main filter PC board must be changed from 200 mA to 400 mA. The ac input transformer connections of an Onkyo DX-C606 CD player for the countries of Switzerland, Sweden, the United Kingdom, and Australia are shown in Fig. 4-9.

The transformer secondary can have three or more separate windings providing ac voltage to bridge, full-wave, and half-wave rectifiers. The centertap of each winding might be the ground terminal of the bridge circuits, which divides the positive

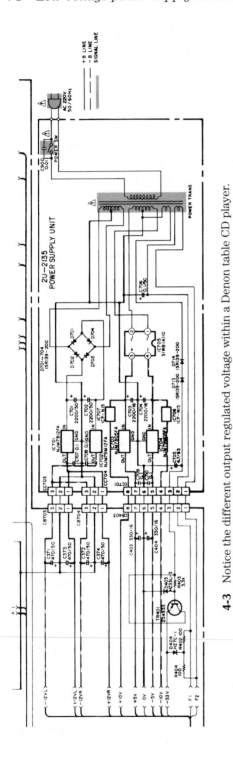

4-3 Notice the different output regulated voltage within a Denon table CD player.

Regular transistor	Q603			Q604			Q602		
Terminal number	D	S	G	E	C	B	E	C	B
Voltage at play mode	−5.3 V	−9.2 V	−9.2 V	5 V	8.8 V	5.1 V	−5 V	−9 V	−5.6 V

Regular transistor	Q606			Q607		
Terminal number	D	S	G	E	C	B
Voltage at play mode	13.5 V	9.5 V	9.5 V	−16.7 V	−26 V	−17.1 V

4-4 A voltage chart of regulator transistors.

Shows dc voltage to the chassis with no signal input.

4-5 Some schematics have the dc voltages in red, solid lines denote B+ voltages, and dotted lines denote B– voltages.

Indicates positive (B+) power supply.

Indicates negative (B–) power supply.

Indicates signal path.

4-6 The ac power transformer is mounted upon a separate PC board within the boom-box CD player.

and negative power sources. In some models, three different voltage sources are produced from one secondary transformer winding (Fig. 4-10).

CD boom-box power circuits

The low-voltage power supply within the compact disc player might have a conventional bridge rectifier with large filter capacitor input. The cassette tape motor might

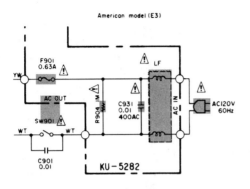

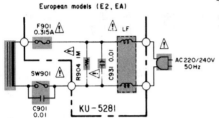

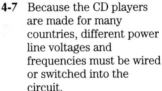

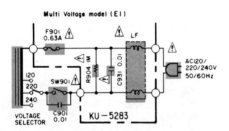

4-7 Because the CD players are made for many countries, different power line voltages and frequencies must be wired or switched into the circuit.

have transistor and zener diode regulation. A separate transistor and zener diode regulation can be found for radio and preamp audio cassette head circuits (Fig. 4-11).

Besides transistor and diode regulation in the regular low-voltage circuits, you might find a separate transistor and zener diode voltage regulation within the CD circuits. The regulated +10-V source is fed directly to the driver ICs of spindle and SLED motors, to driver ICs of tracking and focus coils.

The voltage regulated +5-V source feeds the rest of the circuits in the CD section. You might find a separate transistor regulator feeding +1.5 V to the laser diode of optical assembly (Fig. 4-12). The failure of the zener diode or transistor regulators might prevent CD operation in the various compact disc circuits. Low or no voltage can occur with an open or leaky transistor or zener diode.

Bridge rectifier circuits

The bridge rectifiers can be in the form of one component or four separate diodes, and they number 2 or 3 per low-voltage power supply. In Fig. 4-13, six duodiode

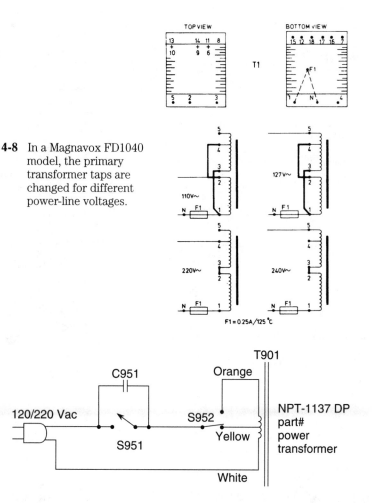

4-8 In a Magnavox FD1040 model, the primary transformer taps are changed for different power-line voltages.

4-9 The primary winding of T901 has a 120- and 240-V switch for American or foreign operation in the Onkyo DX-C606 CD player.

components form the bridge rectifiers and are mounted on the main PC board (Fig. 4-14). If one diode is leaky, it could open the line fuse. Two diodes are frequently faulty in a defective power supply. The whole bridge component must be replaced if one diode is leaky, but if four separate diodes compose the bridge circuit, replace only the leaky diodes.

Look for a shorted or leaky diode, voltage regulator transistor, or zener diode if the line fuse opens. Sometimes the line fuse opens because of flashover from a transistor or IC circuit; however, when the fuse is replaced, the player operates normally. A change in power line voltage can cause the line fuse to open. Suspect a defective component in one of the different voltage sources if the fuse keeps blowing with a normal low-voltage power supply.

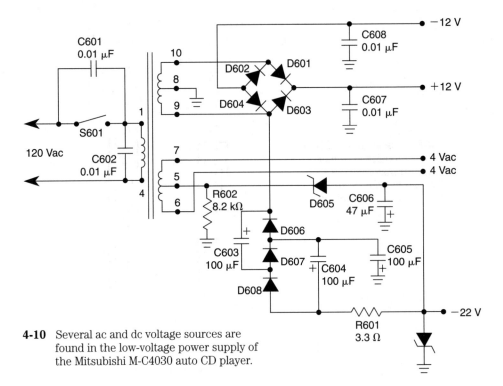

4-10 Several ac and dc voltage sources are found in the low-voltage power supply of the Mitsubishi M-C4030 auto CD player.

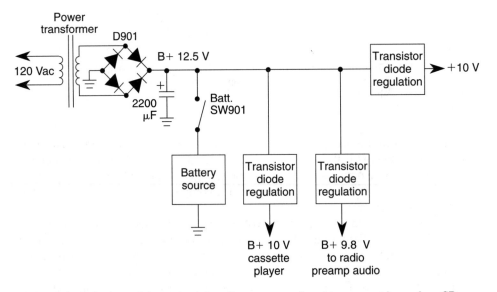

4-11 A block diagram of the various dc voltage sources found in a recent boom-box CD-cassette player.

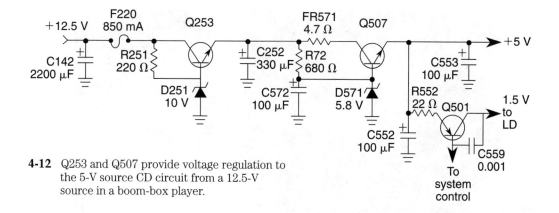

4-12 Q253 and Q507 provide voltage regulation to the 5-V source CD circuit from a 12.5-V source in a boom-box player.

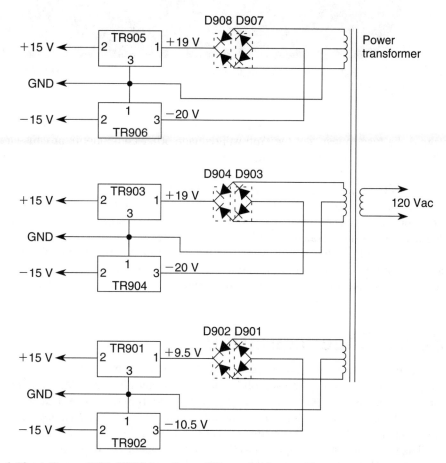

4-13 A Denon DCD-1800R has three different bridge rectifiers than a Sharp QT-CD7GY boom-box player.

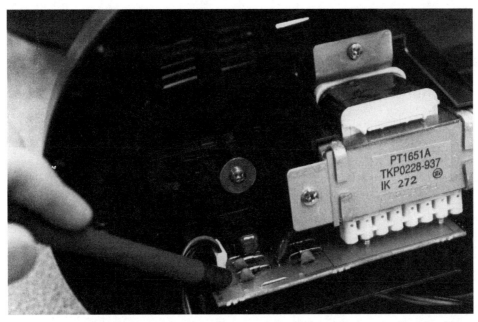

4-14   The dc low-voltage circuit has single diodes for bridge rectifiers with two sets of duo-diodes in each.

Always replace the fuse with the same amperage and voltage. Never wrap tin foil around the fuse to just "get by." You will damage other components or cause a fire with this method or larger amperage fuses. Some models have the fuse on a separate PC board.

Check the low-voltage diodes if the fuse keeps blowing. Remove one end of the diode for accurate tests. A normal diode indicates a low measurement in only one direction. A leaky (nearly shorted) diode shows a low reading in both directions. Remove the anode or transformer lead (~) of the bridge circuit (if all diodes are in one component), using solder wick and iron to remove the terminal from the board. In duodiode rectifier components, remove the common terminal that is tied to the circuit board for tests. If in doubt, remove the entire diode assembly from the circuit.

Zener diode regulation

The zener diode can be used by itself or with a transistor in voltage regulation circuits of the low-voltage power supply. Usually, the zener diode regulates a higher dc voltage to the display tube (Fig. 4-15). The ac voltage from the power transformer is rectified by D713 and D714 in the Denon tabletop CD player. Notice a negative voltage is taken from the anode terminal of D713 and D714.

The negative voltage is applied to the base terminal of TR401 with zener voltage regulation of D403. The negative 33 V is taken from the emitter pin of a pnp transistor (TR401). Notice C706 has a positive terminal connected to common ground.

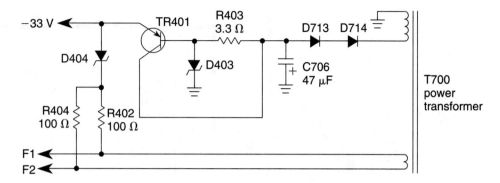

4-15 The high negative voltage source for the display section contains transistors and zener diode regulation in a Denon table CD player.

When replacing or shunting an electrolytic capacitor in the negative power supply, connect the common positive terminal to ground.

Zener diodes have a tendency to overheat, producing leakage or an open circuit. When the diode becomes leaky, the voltage applied to the circuit is lowered. Overheated diodes can be detected if you see burned or white marks on the body of the diode. Check the zener diode like any low-voltage diode with the diode test of the DMM. Remove one end of the diode for leakage test. The leaky zener diode shows a low measurement in the normal direction and a higher resistance with reverse test leads. Replace the leaky diode if a measurable resistance is found in both directions.

Transistor regulation circuits

Power transistors can be used by themselves or in combination with a zener diode for critical voltage regulation. There can be two to thirteen voltage regulator transistors in the CD player power supply. In the RCA MCD 141 power supply, only two transistors (Q702 and Q701) are the basic transistor regulators (Fig. 4-16). The –5- and + 5-V regulated dc sources are taken from the emitter terminals of Q701 and Q702. Zener diodes ZD702 and ZD703 provide voltage regulation for the 10-V sources and also provide a reference voltage at the base of Q701 and Q702.

Besides full-wave bridge rectifier circuits, the transistor-zener diode regulator circuits can be tapped from the one transformer winding that supplies ac voltage to the bridge circuit. Here half- or full-wave rectification is employed with transistor-diode regulation (Fig. 4-17). The –27 voltage source is regulated with Q331 and D316. Zener diode D316 provides a fixed reference voltage at the base of Q331. A –40.7 V is applied to the collector terminal with an output of –27 V at the emitter terminal of regulator Q331. The high –27 voltage source supplies working voltage for microprocessor IC802 of the display and system control IC in the JVC XL-V400B player.

Regulator transistors have a tendency to open or leak. When the regulator opens, there is no output voltage at the emitter terminal. The output voltage reads much lower if the regulator transistor becomes leaky. A leaky regulator transistor

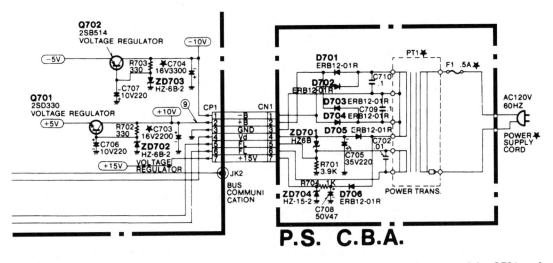

4-16 Transistor regulation is used throughout the power sources in many different models. Q701 and Q702 regulate the negative and positive 5-V sources in the RCA CD141 player.

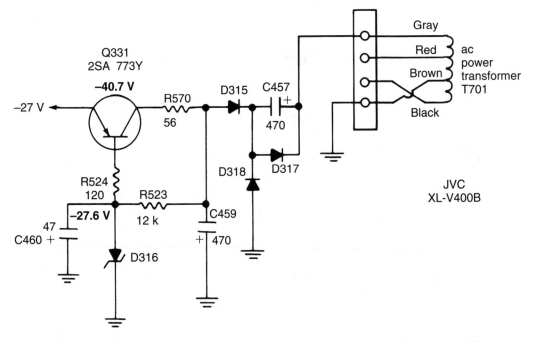

4-17 Diodes D317 and D318 provide full-wave rectification with the ac tap off voltage of the power transformer winding. The negative 27-V source supplies voltage to the microprocessor IC (IC802) in a JVC XL-V400B model.

can damage the zener diode ties to the base circuit. Check all diodes and transistors in a defective voltage source.

Suspect a leaky voltage regulator transistor if improper voltage is read at a given voltage source. Quickly check the transistor in the circuit with a transistor tester or the transistor test of the DMM. Remove the base terminal for correct leakage tests. If in doubt, remove the regulator transistor from the board.

When the transistor is bolted to the chassis or heatsink, remove the solder from all terminals with iron and solder wick. Then check the transistor for open or leaky conditions. If the output voltage is intermittent, replace the suspected regulator transistor. Regulator transistors might run warm after several hours of operation, but they should not be too hot to touch.

IC voltage regulators

Some units use a combination of transistors, zener diodes, and ICs for the needed regulator voltage shapers. In Fig. 4-18, the bridge rectifier circuits provide an input of 10 V at terminal 1 of IC701 and IC702 with a −26.4 V at IC704 and +25.2 V at IC703.

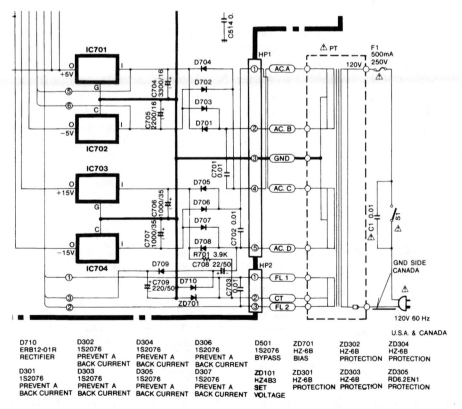

D710	D302	D304	D306	D501	ZD701	ZD302	ZD304
ERB12-01R	1S2076	1S2076	1S2076	1S2076	HZ-6B	HZ-6B	HZ-6B
RECTIFIER	PREVENT A	PREVENT A	PREVENT A	BYPASS	BIAS	PROTECTION	PROTECTION
	BACK CURRENT	BACK CURRENT	BACK CURRENT				
D301	D303	D305	D307	ZD101	ZD301	ZD303	ZD305
1S2076	1S2076	1S2076	1S2076	HZ4B3	HZ-6B	HZ-6B	RD6.2EN1
PREVENT A	PREVENT A	PREVENT A	PREVENT A	SET	PROTECTION	PROTECTION	PROTECTION
BACK CURRENT	BACK CURRENT	BACK CURRENT	BACK CURRENT	VOLTAGE			

4-18 IC regulation in the low-voltage sources of the Realistic CD-1000 player.

An IC voltage regulator can become leaky and produce a lower output voltage. If leaky, the IC regulator feels very warm. Measure the input and output voltages on the IC regulators (Fig. 4-19). If the IC is leaky, the output voltage is very low and the input voltage (pin 1) is somewhat lower. If open, no voltage is measured at the output terminal and a higher than normal input voltage is at pin 1. If the output voltage source is low after replacing the IC or transistor regulator, suspect a leaky component tied to the voltage source.

	IC701	IC703
I	10.0V	25.2V
G	–	–
O	5.0V	1.5V

	IC702	IC704
I	– 11.7V	– 26.4V
G	–	–
O	– 5.0V	– 15.0V

4-19 Check the input and output voltages of the IC regulator to determine if it is defective. The low-voltage source could indicate a leaky IC regulator.

dc-dc converter

You might find a dc-dc converter in the low battery-operated CD portables or auto receivers. In the Realistic CD-3370 portable CD player, the player can be operated from an external ac power source or from two small batteries. The rechargeable nickel-cadmium batteries can be charged by the ac adapter by turning on charge switch (SW10).

The dc-dc converter output terminals, pins 4, 5, 29 (IC6), supplies the power circuitry with +4 V and the dc-dc converter (IC12A) supplies the player circuitry with +5 V, converted from the dc supply (2.0–4.0 V) (Fig. 4-20). Notice that IC6 converts the real low-battery voltage to a +4 V, and IC12A to +5 V. Before supplying the audio circuitry, the dc-dc converter output is filtered by C7, and C8 to eliminate ripple.

To detect a low-battery condition, IC9D compares the battery voltage with a 2.1-V reference. When the battery voltage falls below the reference voltage, IC9D outputs a low signal to the microprocessor, which then displays a low-battery indicator on the LCD (Fig. 4-21).

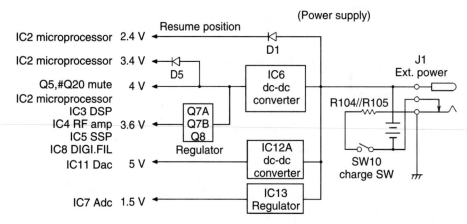

4-20 The block diagram of Realistic portable CD-3370 low-voltage circuits with two separate dc/dc converters, IC6 and IC12A.

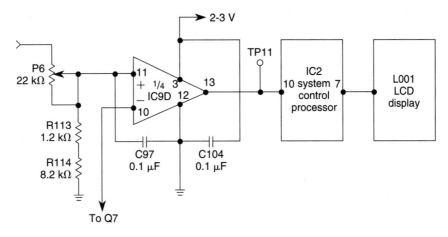

4-21 The low-battery detection circuit in a Realistic CD-3370 CD player.

Auto CD regulation circuits

Several different voltage sources can be found in the auto CD players and changers. The battery 12.8-V source can be fed to several transistor, IC, and zener diode voltage regulator components. In the Denon DCH-500 changer, low-voltage circuits contain several 4.8, 4.9, 5, 7.2, and 9-V sources are derived from the 12.8-V car battery (Fig. 4-22).

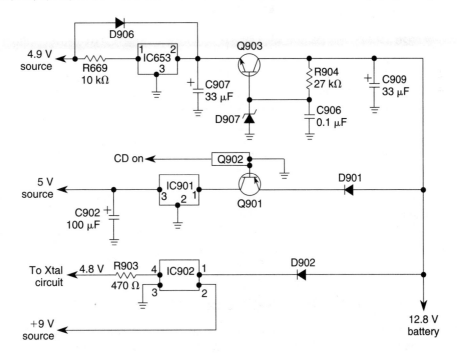

4-22 Transistor, IC, and zener diode regulation within the Denon DCH-500 auto CD changer.

The 4.8-V source is fed to a crystal control signal processor (IC13), through the D902 diode to a 12.8-V battery source. Also, the 9-V source feeding IC13 and the motor drive IC652, is found at pin 3 of IC902. The 5-V source at pin 3 of IC901 regulator with Q901 and Q902 as transistor regulators, and CD ON terminal 2 of system control IC601. The 4.9-V source feeds to system control IC601 from IC653 and the Q903 voltage regulator from the 12.8-V line.

Overloaded power supply circuits

Unplug the suspected component in the lower than normal voltage source if any other components in the power supply seem normal. If the regulated voltage increases, a leaky IC, transistor, diode, or capacitor is pulling down the voltage source within the connecting circuits. Suspect a leaky regulator IC, transistor, or zener diode if the voltage remains low after disconnecting the power source.

Locate what sections of the CD player are powered with the low-voltage dc source on the schematic diagram (Fig. 4-23). Take a low-ohm resistance measurement. If the measurement is under 150 Ω, you can assume a leaky component is lowering the voltage unless a dc motor is in the same circuit. Pull out each plug-in cable component with the ohmmeter attached as a monitoring device. If the resistance goes up at once, you have located the section with the leaky component.

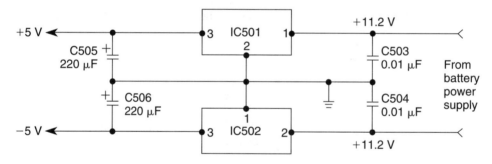

4-23 A typical IC-regulated positive and negative voltage source within the low-voltage circuits.

Keep on checking each component in the overloaded circuit until the defective component is located. Take the ohmmeter probe and a resistance measurement of major components, such as transistors and IC terminals tied to the same low-voltage source. As you approach the leaky component, the resistance should be lower than at the common low-voltage source terminal.

The low-voltage sources

There are many different low-voltage sources in the CD player. For example, in a Mitsubishi DP-107 low-voltage power supply, there are negative and positive 5- and 10-V sources from one bridge circuit (Fig. 4-24). Positive and negative 12- and 13-V

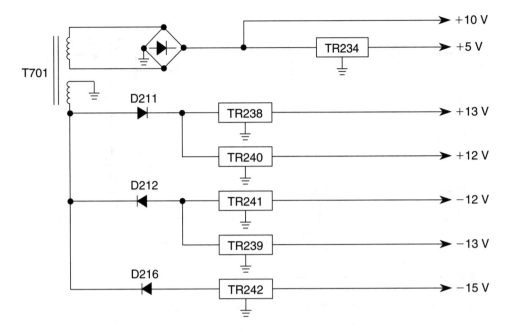

4-24   Several different voltage sources are found in the low-voltage power supply of a Mitsubishi DP-107 CD player.

sources are taken from another transformer winding with half-wave rectification. A
–15-V supply feeds digital and analog IC circuits from the same transformer winding.

In an Onkyo DX-200 player, there are two separate +5 and –5 voltage sources (A
and B). A positive and negative 15 V is from the same power supply source (Fig.
4-25). The +5 and –5 voltage source (B) is taken from another bridge circuit. From
the same bridge rectifier source (B), the 10-V sources are tapped off. A separate
–28-V source feeds the fluorescent tube indicator circuit. Remember, one defective
voltage source can disable more than one function in the disc player. Doublecheck
the power supply schematic.

Filter capacitor problems

Besides causing hum in the sound, a defective filter or decoupling capacitor can produce erratic or shorted conditions. A shorted electrolytic capacitor can keep blowing
the main fuse or destroy the bridge rectifiers (Fig. 4-26). Sometimes a leaky filter capacitor runs warm. A suspected leaky capacitor can be checked with the ohmmeter.
Discharge the suspected capacitor and take a resistance measurement across the capacitor terminals (Fig. 4-27). Because the main PC board containing the low-voltage
components is mounted at the bottom of the metal chassis, voltage and resistance
measurement on the suspected capacitor is very difficult. Locate a component or
test point on the chassis for a quick capacitor check. You might save a lot of service
time by not removing the PC board to find the electrolytic capacitor. If the test indi-

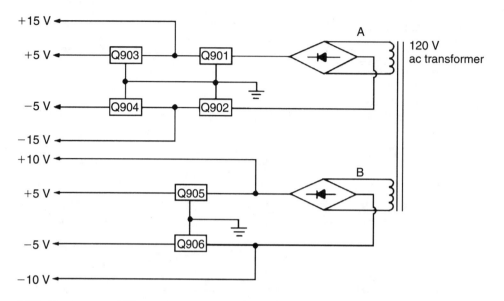

4-25 Two separate 5-V sources are used in the power supply circuits of an Onkyo DX-200 CD player.

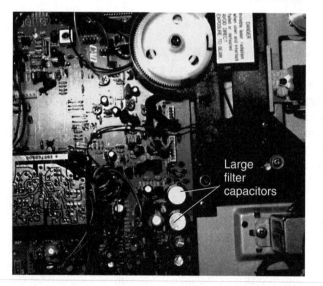

4-26 Locate the low-voltage power supply circuits with the largest electrolytic capacitors on main PC board.

cates that the capacitor is shorted, remove the PC board from the bottom of the metal chassis and remove the capacitor.

The defective filter capacitor might not be leaky, but it could have dried up or lost capacitance. Check the suspected capacitor in the circuit with a digital capacitance tester. These low-priced capacitance meters are very handy in locating defective capacitors. A leaky or shorted capacitor shows a low resistance or no measurement at all. Here a normal decoupling capacitor (33 μF) measures 34.9 μF in the circuit (Fig.

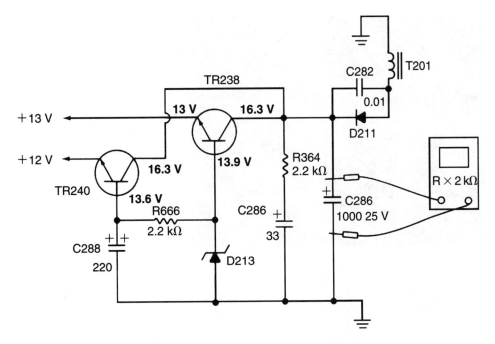

4-27 Discharge the electrolytic capacitor with a test clip before taking resistance measurements across the capacitor terminals.

4-28). Replace the dried-up capacitor when it measures 5 µF less than normal. Remove the capacitor, if in doubt, for the accurate capacity measurement.

Adequate filtering of each power voltage source can be checked with the scope (Fig. 4-29). High ripple content can indicate an open or dried-up filter capacitor.

4-28 A small digital capacity tester will check out those small electrolytic capacitors for loss of capacitance.

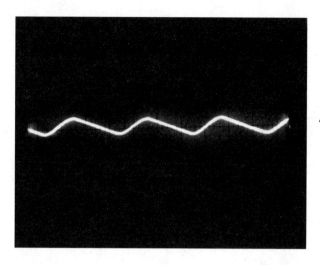

4-29 Check the low-voltage source for high-ripple waveform with the scope.

Compare the waveform with the other positive or negative voltage source. For instance, if the +5-V source has higher ripple than the –5-V source, suspect a defective capacitor within the +5-V power source.

The main filter capacitors in the low-voltage source are 1000 µF or above. Turn off the power, discharge the voltage source, and clip another electrolytic across the suspected one. Never shunt another capacitor across the suspected one with the power on, or you could damage ICs and transistors. Replace the defective capacitor with the same capacitance and voltage or one with higher capacity.

Never replace a filter capacitor with a lower voltage. The capacitor with lower voltage will overheat and could blow up. A 1000-µF, 25-V electrolytic capacitor could be replaced with a 2200-µF, 25-V type without any problems, provided there is adequate mounting room. Likewise, a 33-µF, 16-V decoupling capacitor can be replaced with a 47-µF, 16-V without any complications in the low-voltage power supply.

Universal capacitor replacement

Most electrolytic filter capacitors can be replaced with universal types found on the service bench. Of course, the physical size of a larger replacement takes up a lot more room, if the capacitor has a higher capacity and voltage rating. Always, replace with a higher voltage and capacity rating when the exact capacitor cannot be located. These radial-type leads can be mounted higher up with reinforced leads or insulated spaghetti placed over each terminal for self support and insulation. Make sure the capacitor terminals are tight so that the capacitor will not flop around (Fig. 4-30).

Lightning damage

The power transformer and bridge rectifier components are at the highest risk when lightning strikes the outside power line. Power-line outage can cause the fuse to open. If the power lines are whipped together, 220 Vac can enter the CD chassis and

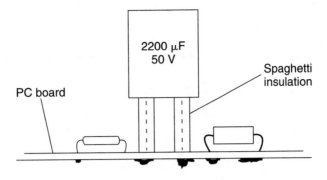

4-30 Large universal capacitors can be elevated above small components if not enough room is available to mount them on the chassis.

damage the power transformer, fuse, ON/OFF switch, or power supply components. A direct lightning strike can damage the CD player beyond repair. So, be sure to make a complete estimate of all damaged parts before ordering parts. Sometimes, when the ac power switch is off and lightning strikes, the charge jumps the switch and knocks out the power transformer. If very little visual damage is noticeable, most of the damage is probably contained within the power supply circuits.

Checking the ON/OFF switch

The ON/OFF switch in the CD player can be pushed on or off and rotated. The switch might be located towards the front or extreme rear of the player, mounted on a separate PC board (Fig. 4-31). You might find a long plastic rod that activates the ON/OFF switch. While in the boom-box CD player a rotary function switch on the front panel, turns on the player. In the Onkyo DX-C606 table CD player, the ON/OFF switch (S951) is operated from the front and connected to a separate power supply PC board (Fig. 4-32).

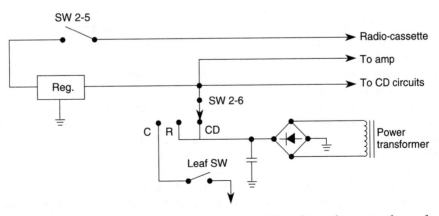

4-31 SW2-6 switches in the voltage source to the CD, radio, and cassette player of a boom-box CD portable.

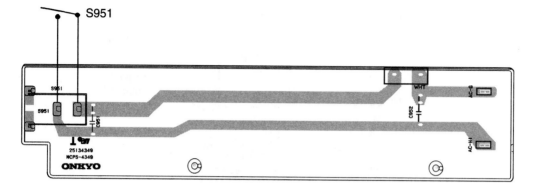

4-32 You might find the on/off switch (S951) connected to a separate power supply circuit PC board.

The defective ON/OFF ac switch can cause erratic or impeded operation. Most ac power switches are located in the primary winding circuit of the power transformer. A few CD players have the primary winding of the power transformer connected directly to the power cord with the turn-on switch in the dc circuits. A dirty ON/OFF switch can prevent normal contact operation. Spray cleaning fluid down into the switch area and work the switch back and forth to clean the contacts. Replace an ON/OFF switch that shows erratic or no operation.

Locate the defective ON/OFF switch by clipping across the switch terminals with a short clip lead. The player should come on, because it is now plugged into the power line. The ON/OFF switch can also be checked by taking an ac voltage measurement across the switch terminals. Replace the switch if 120 Vac is measured across the switch terminals with the switch in ON position. These switches must be replaced with originals, because they solder directly to a separate PC board.

Replacing the power transformer

Power transformers pop, crack, or overheat if they have shorted windings or overloaded diodes. Remove the secondary leads from the circuit and plug in the power cord, checking the transformer for excess heat. If the transformer still runs very hot, replace it. In this case, the transformer has shorted windings. Suspect shorted or leaky diodes if the transformer operates cool and the fuse does not blow when the transformer is disconnected.

The primary winding of the transformer could be open from lightning damage or shorted diodes (Fig. 4-33). If the replaced fuse is too large or tin foil has been wrapped around the fuse, suspect an open primary winding with leaky bridge rectifiers or diodes. Check the primary winding of the transformer with the 200-Ω range with the switch on. Shorted coil windings often occur in the secondary winding instead of the primary. The primary winding usually opens with shorted or leaky rectifiers.

Before removing the defective transformer, mark down the color code of each lead and where it goes. Some manufacturers label the transformer wires on the schematic while others do not. Cut the terminal leads ½ inch from the soldered joint.

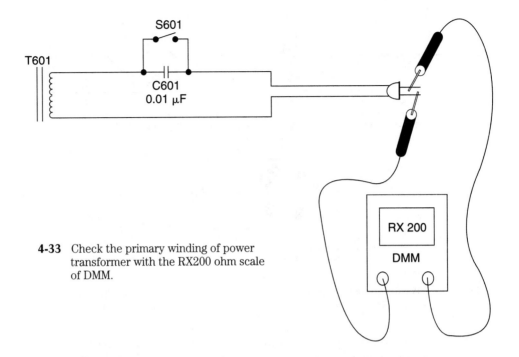

4-33 Check the primary winding of power transformer with the RX200 ohm scale of DMM.

Then you can identify where each lead goes in replacing the transformer. Remove one lead at a time and solder on the new transformer wire. Whenever possible, replace the defective transformer with the original part number. Transformer replacement in the CD player is not as costly as the TV chassis.

Universal replacement parts

To prevent long delays in CD repairs, universal components can be used in many areas of the player. The bridge rectifiers, with one complete or two different components, can be replaced with universal bridge parts (Fig. 4-34). If neither one is available, single diodes of the same amperage and voltage ratings can be installed. Replace the diodes with single 3-A diodes when current readings are not known. Make sure the diode polarity is correct with the ac symbol (~) connected to the power transformer windings. Wire and solder all diode leads together, leaving four long leads to go through the bridge rectifier mounting holes.

Regulator transistors and zener diodes can be replaced with universal replacements. Cross reference the transistor and diodes for universal replacement. If the part number is not available, look up the operating voltage of the zener diode. The part number often provides the zener diode voltage. For instance, an MTZ13C zener diode operates at 13 V. If in doubt about the wattage, replace with a 5-W zener diode. It's best to have one with higher wattage than a small one that could overheat.

Replace the IC regulator, the power transformer, and the ON/OFF switch with the exact part number.

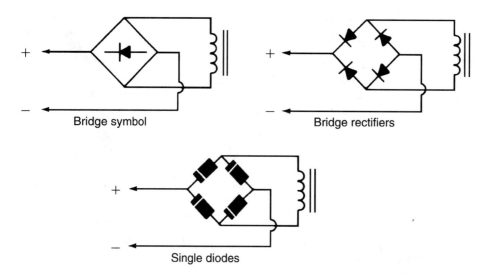

Bridge symbol   Bridge rectifiers

Single diodes

4-34   Bridge rectifiers in one component can be replaced with separate 2.5-A silicon diodes.

All filter and bypass capacitors can be replaced with universal parts. Replace with the correct voltage and capacity. The capacitor can have a higher capacity but not a lower working voltage. Make sure there is adequate room for mounting. Sometimes filter capacitors are mounted with the transformer on a separate PC board that is bracketed to the side of the metal cabinet.

Quick low-voltage test points

Inspect the line fuse before taking any voltage measurements. Check the voltage at each voltage source. Follow the schematic and locate the transistor, IC, or zener output regulator (Fig. 4-35). Each output voltage can be checked from the emitter terminal of the regulator transistor (1). Measure the collector voltage to locate a defective regulator transistor. Now check the input and output voltage at the IC regulator (2).

Go directly to the positive terminal of the bridge rectifier when locating a low- or no-voltage source (3). Check the voltage across the main filter capacitors, if accessible. Measure the voltage on each single diode in the bridge circuit. A higher positive voltage indicates that the B+ voltage is feeding the regulator circuits. Check the ac voltage applied to the bridge circuit with no dc output voltage (4).

Dead chassis

Check the line fuse and ON/OFF switch for a completely dead chassis. Take a quick + voltage measurement at the positive terminal of the bridge rectifier or main filter capacitor. Do likewise with single diodes in the bridge circuit. Measure the ac applied to the bridge rectifier circuit. Suspect a defective power transformer if no ac voltage

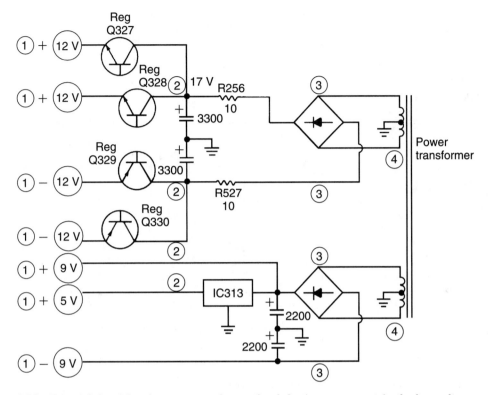

4-35 Take 1-2-3 quick voltage tests to locate the defective component in the low-voltage power supply.

is reaching the bridge circuits. If dc voltage is found at the bridge rectifier but not at the collector terminal of the regulator transistors or input terminal of the IC regulator, look for an open fuseable (10-Ω) resistor. Some power supplies have a fuseable raster between bridge rectifiers and regulation transistors.

Suspect an open or leaky transistor or IC regulator with correct input voltage and low or no voltage at the emitter terminals. Check both the regulator transistor and zener diode for open or leakage condition. When checking the regulator transistor out of the circuit for leakage tests, visually inspect the small bias and isolation resistors. Carefully check for correct resistance of each resistor. Likewise, take a resistance measurement across the small decoupling and filter capacitors. If in doubt, check the capacitor with a digital capacitance meter.

Dead Magnavox portable CD player

The batteries were removed and tested in a Magnavox CD9510BK01 portable CD player. Very low voltage was found at pin 1 of K001 power supply unit. Zero voltage was found at pins 6 and 7. Q1, Q3, and Q7 tested normal. IC TL145IC was found defective in the K001 power supply (Fig. 4-36).

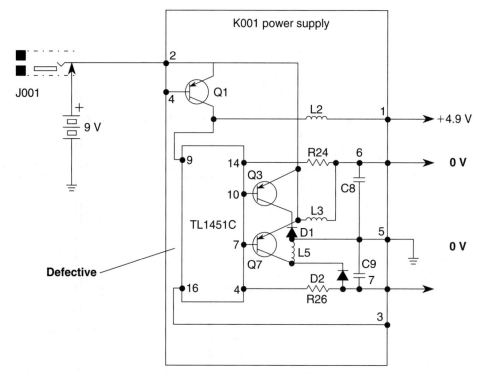

4-36 The dead Magnavox portable CD player CD9510BK01 was caused by a defective IC in the K001 power supply.

Immobile tray (no loading)

When the disc tray will not move, suspect a defective loading circuit, motor, or improper dc voltage. Locate the loading motor plug-in cable or wires. Measure the voltage at the motor terminals when the load button is pressed. Now check the power supply voltage feeding the loading motor drive circuits. Often, the voltage is a positive and negative 12, 10, or 9 volts. Both + and – voltages must be applied to the output driver transistors or ICs of the motor drive circuits.

Inspect the schematic and trace the voltage sources to the low-voltage power supply. Measure the voltage at the dc source. Low or no voltage indicates problems within the low-voltage source. If the regulated low voltage is normal, suspect loading problems within the loading drive motor circuits.

Erratic Magnavox CDC552 loading

The five-disc changer tray seemed to operate erratically in a Magnavox CDC552 CD changer. Usually, the erratic condition seemed to occur before the tray was completely extended. The loading tray motor voltage was normal throughout loading and unloading of changer tray assembly. No doubt this was a mechanical problem.

The tray was released and inspected. A careful inspection of the plastic tray guide system seemed normal. Finally, after a closer inspection when the tray hung up, a couple of long wires were clinging to the bottom of the tray, just before it reached the outward position. These wires were disturbed and not properly replaced when the main chassis was serviced (Fig. 4-37).

Five CD disc
changer rack or tray

4-37 Improperly replaced wires caused the Magnavox loading tray to hang up in a CDC522 changer.

No disc rotation

Improper voltage applied to the spindle motor circuits can prevent the disc from rotating. Measure the voltage at the spindle motor with the disc loaded. Follow the schematic and check what voltage source is feeding the spindle motor servo circuits. A 12- or 10-V negative and positive voltage frequently is used to feed the spindle servo output drive transistors. If correct voltage is found at the dc power supply, check the servo drive circuits.

Power supply troubleshooting chart

In Chart 4-1, a typical low-voltage power supply troubleshooting chart shows how to locate the defective components in a JVC XL-V400B CD player. This same troubleshooting procedure can be used in most low-voltage power supplies. Compare the block diagram with the JVC XL-V400B power supply schematic in Fig. 4-38.

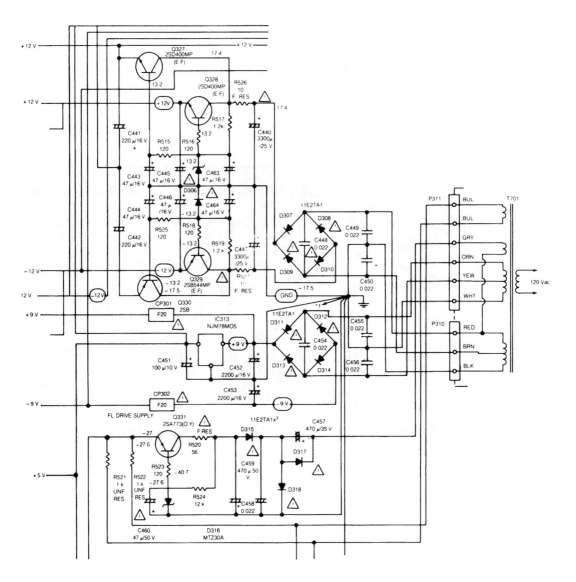

4-38 Compare the troubleshooting chart in Chart 4-1 with the various components in the low-voltage schematic of a JVC XL-400B player.

Chart 4-1. Here is the low-voltage power supply troubleshooting chart for the JVC XL-V400B CD player.

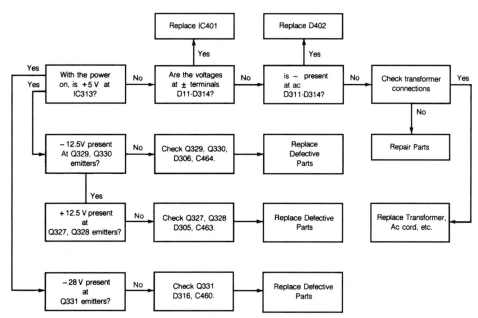

5
The signal circuits

THE SIGNAL CIRCUIT CONSISTS OF A PREAMP, SIGNAL PROCESSING LSI (LARGE-SCALE integration) chip, phase-locked loop (PLL), random-access memory (RAM) and digital-to-analog (D/A) converter. In some models, one LSI component might handle most signal processing circuits except the D/A converter stage (Fig. 5-1). In others, the preamp, tracking, automatic focus, and signal processing circuits are located in one large IC. Although two LSI components might do the work of the signal circuits in lower priced compact disc players, several different LSI and IC components are used in the most expensive models.

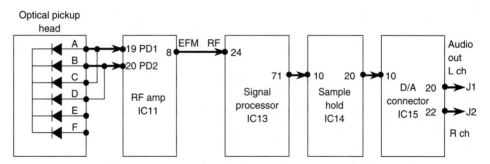

5-1 The signal starts at the photodetector diodes to pin 19 and 20 of RF amp (IC11), with EFM output at pin 8 and fed to pin 24 of signal processor IC13.

The signal from the photodetector diodes is very weak and must be amplified before it can be used by the signal processor. The preamp stage is sometimes located with the servo circuits. In the Realistic CD-3304 portable compact disc player, the RF amp, track error, focus error, mirror hold, APC, FOK amp, FOK comparator, and EFM comparator are all found in the RF amp (IC4) (Fig. 5-2). Besides these signals,

105

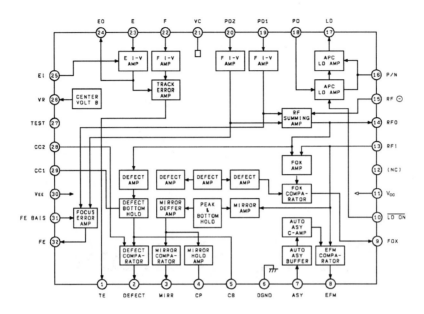

5-2 An internal block diagram of the RF amplifier (IC4) in the Realistic CD-3370 CD player.

the APC (automatic power control) circuits, sometimes located in the pickup head or in RF amp IC and on the main PC board, are covered in this chapter.

The signal circuit block diagram

The block diagram is useful in determining how the different stages and circuits are tied together. Use the block diagram to locate the problem area. Then, with the correct waveform, voltage, and resistance measurements, you can find the defective component. The signal from the signal circuits might also tie into the servo or system control circuits.

Figure 5-3 shows the Realistic CD-3770 portable CD player block diagram. The RF signal from the four photodetector diodes and tracking diodes is fed into RF amp (IC4). Besides tracking and auto focus offsets circuits, a signal is fed from RF amp IC4 to the servo control IC5. The amplified RF circuit is fed from the RF IC to digital signal processor IC5. Q9 provides laser driver signal for the laser diodes.

The EFM signal is fed from RF IC4 from pin 8 to pin 5 of the digital signal processor (IC3). The EFM signal of RF amp IC4 can be checked at pin 8 or RF signal at test point TP1. When the EFM or RF signal is not present here, suspect a defective RF amp (IC4) or optical pickup assembly (Fig. 5-4). If the signal is missing from the RF amp to the servo signal processor or servo IC, the chassis will automatically shut down.

The EFM signal is fed to pin 5 of IC3 and the output signal of IC3 is fed to the digital filter IC8 (Fig. 5-5). The D/A converter (IC11) separates the digital signal to analog left and right stereo channels. Q12 and Q13 provide audio mute circuits of the line output jack (J2).

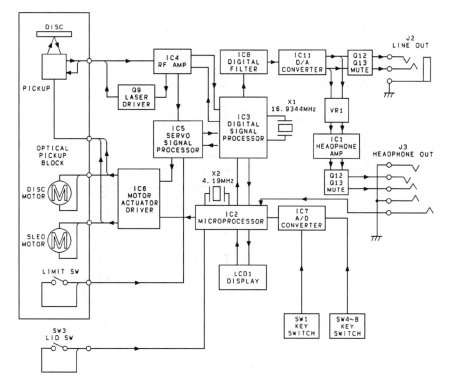

5-3 A complete block diagram of a Realistic CD-3370 portable CD player.

5-4 The EFM waveform signal at pin 8 of the RF amp (IC4) and fed to the digital signal processor (IC3).

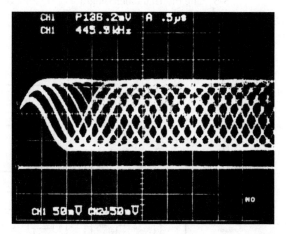

The Yamaha CD-3 signal block diagram is shown in Fig. 5-6. The HF amplifier and preamp circuits are amplified with a separate IC101, TR101, and TR102. The HF amplifier feeds to the ALPC and IC207. Besides the VCO, clock regeneration, and EFM signal circuits, IC207 provides servo control to tracking, focus, feed, and loading motors. The EFM signal is fed directly to the signal processor IC209. The RAM IC208 and VFO oscillator circuits are tied into IC209. The signal output from the dig-

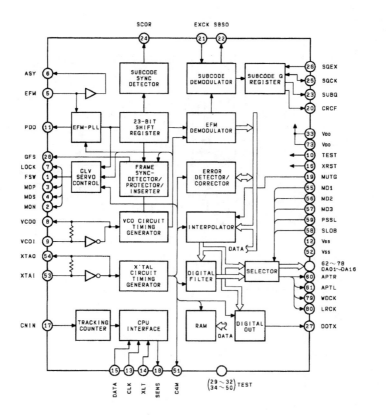

5-5 The internal block diagram of the digital signal processor (IC3).

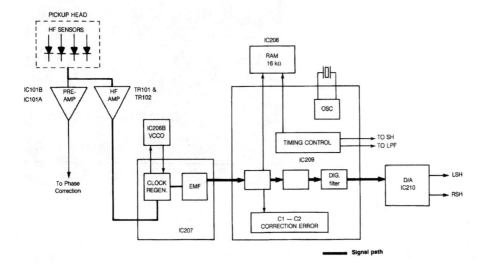

5-6 The signal path in a Yamaha CD-3 player goes from the four HF sensors to the HF pre-amp, EFM in IC207, and through signal processor IC209 and D/A converter IC210.

ital filter network of IC209 feeds to the D/A converter. IC210 converts the signal to analog or audio. Remember, when more than one function is defective, try to isolate the problem to one component or low-voltage power source. Check the block diagram and schematic to locate the defective component.

Realistic CD3304 RF amp

The RF1-V amps, 1 and 2, are converted to voltage from the signal circuit of pin photodetector diodes connected to PD1 and PD2 through a 58-kΩ equivalent resistance (Fig. 5-7). The photo diode current PD1 and PD2 are fed from the optical assembly to pin 7 and 8 of op amps inside the RF amplifier IC501. The RF sum of A+B+C+D is found at output (RFO) pin 2. The EFM or RFO eye pattern can be checked on pin 2.

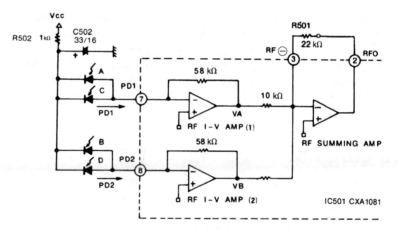

5-7 The RF PD1 and PD2 op amp preamp in IC501 of a Radio Shack CD-3304 player.

Denon DCH-500 changer signal circuits

The RF signal from A-C, B-D are photodetector diodes PD1 and PD2 at pins 19 and 20 of the RF amp (IC11). The RF signal is fed two separate op amps inside IC11 (Fig. 5-8). The 11 to 14 modulation (EFM) is found at pin 8 and the RF signal is fed to pin 24 of signal processor (IC13).

The digital analog signal path of IC13 output pins 34 and 35 are fed to digital analog converter (IC301). This analog or audio signal output is found at the right channel (RO and R ON) at pins 23 and 25 with the left audio channel output (L ON and LO) at pins 18 and 20.

The dual audio line amp (IC101) feeds the stereo audio signal to each right and left line output jack terminals 5 and 9, respectively. Q101 and Q102 provide audio muting of the left and right channels. A +5-V source is fed to IC101 (pin 8 with pin 4 at common ground).

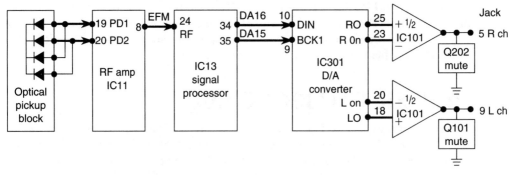

5-8 The signal path of a Denon DCH-500 CD auto changer.

LSI and IC signal processors

The large-scale integrated (LSI) and other IC signal processors are fragile and must be handled with care. The processors in the signal circuits have many terminals and can be surface-mounted or regular (Fig. 5-8). Remember, besides carrying the RF or high frequency, the LSI or IC processors might be tied into other circuits. The processor itself can be individually replaced or exchange the whole LSI PC board depending on the manufacturer and size of the board. Always replace the LSI or IC processor with the exact part number.

Replacing LSI or IC signal processors

After determining that the signal processor is defective with scope tests and voltage measurements, remove and replace it. The regular IC component exchanges like any other IC (Fig. 5-9).

The larger chips might be a little more difficult to remove. Make sure the soldering iron has a flat, angled tip and is grounded. Check to see how the IC is mounted and mark the numbers on the board. Now, remove the IC by cutting each terminal. Remove the remaining leads and solder from the board with the iron and wick.

Prepare to mount the new IC by straightening each terminal (Fig. 5-10A). Apply flux to the printed wiring on the board where the solder will go—about 2.5 mm wide (Fig. 5-10B). Be careful to apply only a minimum amount of flux so you don't smear it on unwanted areas.

Carefully align the printed wiring with the IC's leads and solder each corner to hold the IC flat and in position (Fig. 5-10C). Doublecheck the terminal numbers for correct mounting.

Apply flux to the areas on the IC's leads where solder goes. Be careful not to get flux on the root portion of any lead or on the body of the IC. Apply flux to only the portion where the flat leads of the IC connect to the wiring (Fig. 5-10D).

Place the flat soldering iron tip on the junction, and feeding very thin solder to the joint, move the iron slowly in the direction of the arrow (Fig. 5-10E). Move the iron at the rate of approximately 1 cm in 5 seconds. Make sure a clean fillet of solder

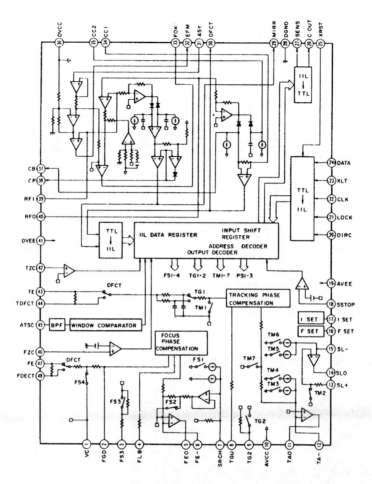

5-9 Large-scale integrated (LSI) processors can have over 80 terminals. In this case, the Denon DCH-500 signal processor (IC13) has over 48 terminals.

forms on each lead, as soon as the flux melts. Moving the iron too quickly can result in loose solder or poor connections. Be especially careful when soldering the first lead (where loose soldering most likely forms). When the soldering is finished, check each terminal with a magnifying glass.

Surfaced-mounted RF and signal components

Surfaced-mounted devices (SMDs) are found in many CD portables in the RF and signal path components. These small transistors, ICs, processors, diodes, resistors, and capacitors are very difficult to locate even with a part layout diagram. They are found on the PC wiring side (Fig. 5-11). The values of resistors and capacitors can

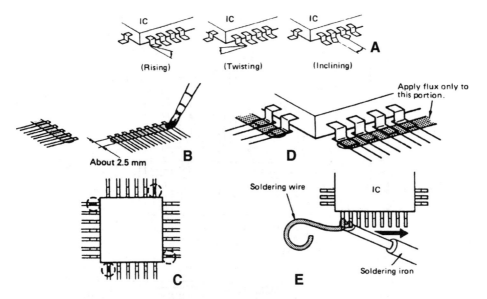

5-10 Steps for replacing surfaced-mounted devices, LSI, or IC processors in the CD player.

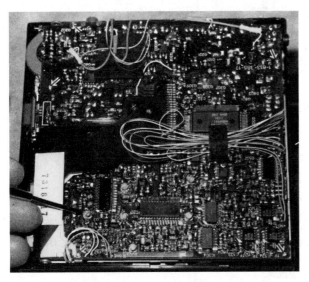

5-11 Small surfaced-mounted devices (SMD) transistors, IC, LSI, diodes, resistors, and capacitors in the portable CD player.

be numbered on top of the miniature devices. You might need a magnifying glass to identify the resistance or capacity numbers.

The RF or HF sensor preamp

The radio frequency (RF) or high frequency (HF) circuits pick up the weak signals from the HF sensor or photodetector and amplify the signal to a level that can be used by the signal processor. The preamplifier might work in conjunction with the servo IC. The preamp might also be used for detecting and correcting errors for focus and tracking.

The RF preamp can operate from a separate IC, transistor, or a combined IC processor component (Fig. 5-12). The RF preamp is located between the pickup head and the LSI or IC signal processor. Here, the HF signal from photodetector diodes A/C and B/D are capacitor-coupled through C102 and C103 to preamp transistors TR101 and TR102. The output signal is coupled from the emitter terminal of TR102 through C107 to the HS terminal of servo 1 board.

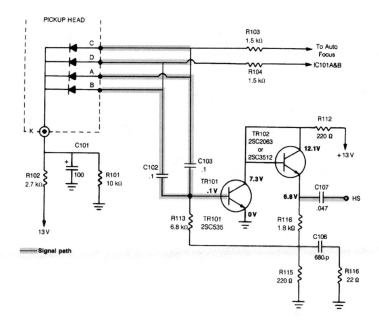

5-12 You might find RF transistors in the preamp circuits instead of IC components. Here, TR101 and TR102 in a Yamaha CD-3 player are the preamp transistors connected to the pickup head.

Because the RF preamp IC has many different circuits, it is wise to know what terminals go to the different circuits. The RF input from the photodetector diodes connect to terminal 2 and the EFM output at terminal 20, which ties to the EFM input terminal of the signal processor (Fig. 5-13). The positive power source connects to terminal 24. Improper signal at terminals 2 and 20 with low or no voltage at terminals 24 tells you what circuits are defective. The various pin numbers of the RF amplifier in an Onkyo DX-200 CD player are given in Fig. 5-14. An "eye" test pattern at pin 20 or the designated "eye test point" can indicate the RF signal from the head pickup and out of the RF preamp is normal.

In the Onkyo DX-200 RF amp circuit, the RF amp, focus OK circuit (FOK), MIR (mirror detector circuit), and EFM waveform rectifier are in IC Q101 (see Fig. 5-15). The RF signal is taken from the detector diodes (A, B, C, and D) and fed to terminals

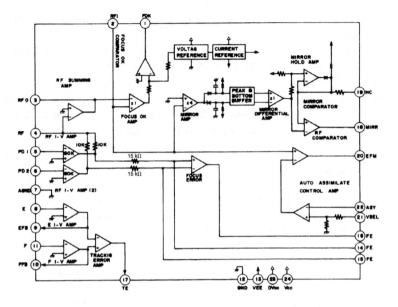

5-13 A large IC component (CX-20109) is in the RF amplifier of an Onkyo DX-200 CD player front end.

1. Focus OK output
2. RF input
3. RF summing amp output
4. RF summing amp inversion input
5. RF I-V amp (1) inversion input
6. RF I-V amp (2) inversion input
7. Ground of small signal analog system
8. EI-V inversion input
9. EIV amp output
10. FIV amp output
11. FI-V amp inversion input
12. Ground
13. Negative power supply
14. Focus error amp input
15. Focus error amp inversion input
16. Focus error amp output
17. Tracking error amp output
18. Mirror output comparator output (Active at H)
19. Mirror hold capacitor connection terminal
20. EFM output comparator output
21. Terminal for reference input level setting of auto assimilate control amp
22. Auto assimilate control input
23. EFM comparator system power supply
24. Positive power supply

5-14 The various pin numbers of the Onkyo DX-200 player IC indicates the input and output circuits connected to the RF amp IC.

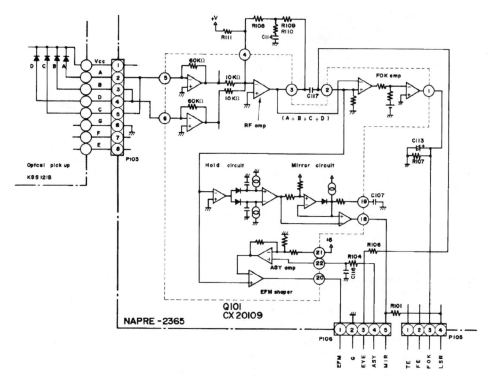

5-15 IC (Q106) of an Onkyo DX-200 preamp and RF circuits also include the FOK, MIR, and EFM waveform rectifier circuits within one component.

5 and 6 of Q101. In addition to amplifying the RF signal ($A + B + C + D$) obtained from the photodetector, the RF amplifier is also used in equalization of the signal. By using R108 through R110 and C114 in the RF operational amplifier negative feedback loop (between pins 3 and 4 of Q101) to boost frequency components above 1 MHz and to advance the phase, eye (eye pattern) TP209 jitter components are suppressed. When the laser diode, servo systems, and disc are normal, the value of eye (TP209) is 1.1 ± 0.2 (VP-P) shown in Fig. 5-16.

Denon DCC-9770 CD changer RF path

In the Denon DCC-9770 CD changer, the RF path begins at A-C, B-D, and fed to PD1 and PD2 on pins 19 and 20 of the RF amp IC501. Inside IC501 the RF signal is amplified with an EFM output signal at pin 8. This EFM signal is then fed to the signal processor (Fig. 5-17).

Besides amplifying the RF signal, IC501 provides detect, focus, tracking, and mirror signals to the servo control IC502. When the MIRR signal is missing, the servo control IC might shut down the whole CD operation (pins 3 and 42). The focus error gain signal adjustment is found between pins 32 and 45 to keep the focus on all four photodetectors. A tracking gain adjustment is found between pins 1 and 45 to keep the optical assembly on track.

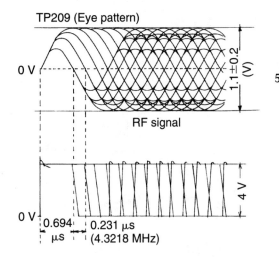

TP209 (Eye pattern)

0 V

1.1 ± 0.2 (V)

RF signal

4 V

0 V

0.694 μs

0.231 μs
(4.3218 MHz)

5-16 The eye pattern of an Onkyo DX-200 player is taken from test point TP-209. A clear-cut diamond shape in the center of the waveform indicates good RF signal from the pickup and RF stages.

Signal processor or modulator

The signal processor or modulator IC usually contains the clock generator, EFM, data luch, data concealment mute, digital filter, timing control, osc, subcode modulation, CLV servo, servo system control, and error connection circuits. Besides the internal circuits, the VCO, disc motor control, RAM, and system control circuits are tied to it (Fig. 5-18). The RF or HF signal is fed into the signal processor IC with the timing control and is sent to the D/A converter and servo control circuits.

The interleaving and EFM signals are processed with the signal processor or modulator. This interleaving method is standard, determined when the discs are manufactured. The disc during playback returns the signals to the original state in accordance with this method. The interleaving data is memorized inside the RAM IC and the data are recalled in exactly the same sequence of the original signals.

The signal processor might be a separate IC, LSI processor, or it could be combined with other circuits. The PLL IC circuit tied to the signal processor basically consists of an 8.6436-MHz VCO (voltage-controlled oscillator). Often, the RAM and PLL or VCO circuits are in separate IC components that are tied to the signal processor IC.

In the Realistic CD-1000 signal processor circuit, in combination with both the data strobe circuit and the section that detects and corrects the errors as soon as the data signals are demodulated, this circuit compensates when the sync signal is missing, and it identifies 1s and 0s. It is composed of circuits that control the whole signal processor circuit and a RAM control circuit, entering the data once into the random access memory and rearranging it (Fig. 5-19).

The rearrangement of the signals, as performed by this circuit, is particularly effective with a high signal loss. The continuous stream of audio signals is thrown into disarray, adroitly rearranged (interleaved) and entered into the disc. In the reproduction system, these signals are restored by a method that is the reverse of that used to throw them into disarray. In order to restore the signals, the data is memorized inside the RAM and then recalled in exactly the same sequence of the original

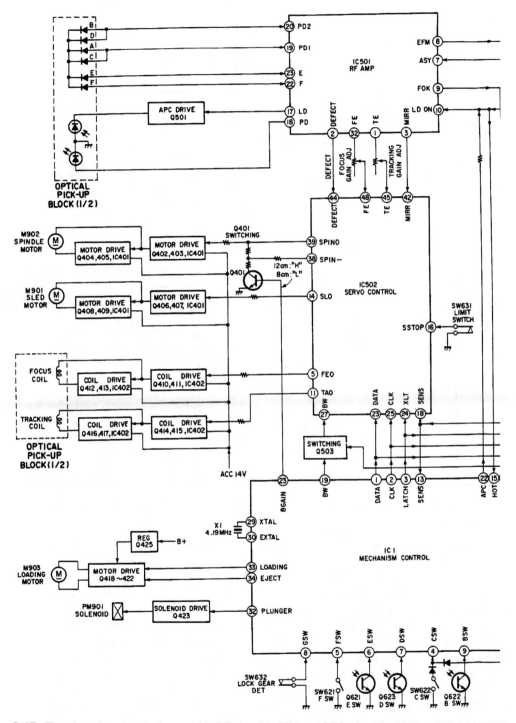

5-17 The photodetector diodes provide RF signal to PD1 and PD2, pins 19 and 20, of RF amp IC501 in a Denon DCC-9770 CD changer.

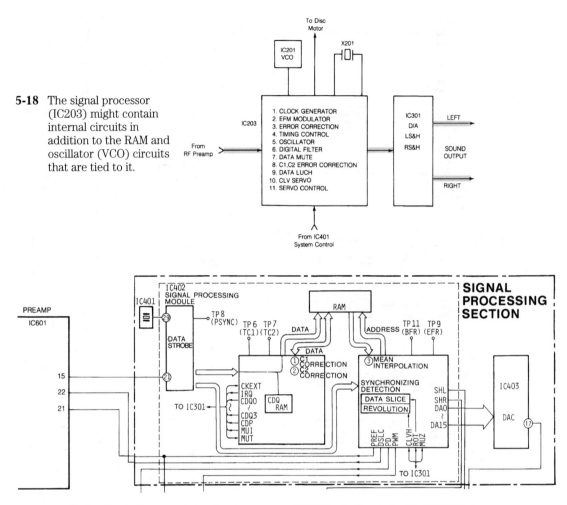

5-18 The signal processor (IC203) might contain internal circuits in addition to the RAM and oscillator (VCO) circuits that are tied to it.

5-19 Block diagram of the signal processor (IC402) of a Realistic CD-1000 CD player.

continuous stream of signals. Even if there is a high signal loss, the sequence of the signals is dispersed at random, so the signals before and after those that were lost are still present when the sequence is restored. Hence, original signals can be compensated for. This interleaving method is determined when the discs are manufactured and the disc reproduction equipment returns the signal to its original state.

In the RCA MCD-141 Signal Processor, along with the preamplifier circuit, the signal processing circuits can compensate for high signal loss by identifying the signals through the process of interleaving. The encoded disc is recorded during production with a predetermined sequence of digitized audio information, but it is out of normal sequence due to the interleaving process (Fig. 5-20).

When the disc is decoded or played back, this digitized audio information is restored to a normal sequence by taking the interleaving process and reversing it. This reversing process of interleaving is done by IC402 (signal processor/IC403 RAM) and the information is recalled in exactly the same sequence as the original audio infor-

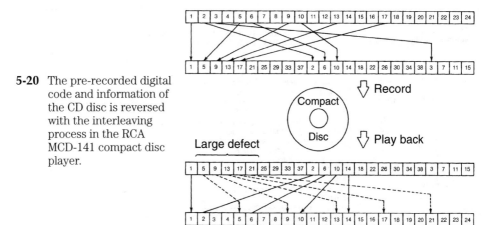

5-20 The pre-recorded digital code and information of the CD disc is reversed with the interleaving process in the RCA MCD-141 compact disc player.

mation. Even if there is a high signal loss, the rearrangement of these signals, dispersed at a predetermined scrambled pattern, allows the signal (before and after the signals having been lost) to be present when the sequence is restored. The end result is that the original lost signals can be compensated for.

The RCA signal processor IC402 is shown with terminal connections in Fig. 5-21 with the correct pin numbers and various functions listed in Fig. 5-22. This pin identification chart is valuable to determine the input and output signals tied to the signal processor IC402. IC402 has a total of 80 pins.

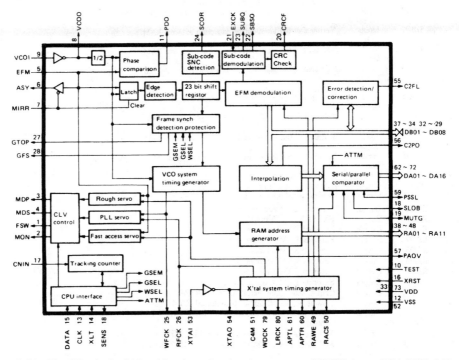

5-21 The IC terminal identification of a signal processor (IC402) in an RCA MCD-141 CD player.

Pin Number	Pin Symbol	Input Output	Functions of Disc Motor, CLV Servo/ EFM/PLL/ERM Demodulation
1	FSW	Output	Time constant selection of disc motor output.
2	MON	Output	Disc motor on/off control output.
	MDP	Output	Disc motor drive output. Rough control in CLV-5 mode and phase control signal in CLV-P mode.
4	MDS	Output	Disc motor drive output. Speed control signal in CLU-P mode.
5	EFM	Input	EFM input signal from preamplifier IC.
6	ASY	Output	Preamplifier IC slice level control output.
7	MIRR	Input	Mirror input from preamplifier IC.
8	VCOD	Output	VCO output F = 8.6436 MHz.
9	VCOI	Input	VCO input.
10	Test	Input	Test terminal.
11	PDO	Output	PLL phase comparison output.
12	VSS	—	Ground.
13	CLK	Input	Serial data transmission. Clock input from microprocessor.
14	XLT	Input	Latch input from microprocessor.
15	Data	Input	Serial data input from microprocessor.
16	XRST	Input	System reset input rest at ''L.''
17	CNIN	Input	Tracking pulse input.
18	SENS	SENS	Output Servo status output according to the serial data from microprocessor.
19	MUTG	Input	Muting input.
20	CRCF	Output	Result of CRC clock of sub-code Q ID output.
21	EXCK	Input	Clock input for subcode serial output.
22	SBSO	Output	Subcode serial output.
23	SUBQ	Output4T-SSubcode Q output.	
24	SCOR	Output	Subcode sync SO + S1 output.
25	WFCK	Output	Write frame clock output.
26	RFCK	Output	Red frame clock output Xtal system 7.35 KHz.
27	GTOP	Output	Frame sync protected status indication output.
28	GFS	Output	Frame sync locked status indication output.
29	DBO8	Input/Output	Terminal of the input/output data from external RAM (MSB).
30	DBO7	Input/Output	Terminal of the input/output data from external RAM.
31	DBO6	Input/Output	Terminal of the input/output data from external RAM.
32	DBO5	Input/Output	Terminal of the input/output data from external RAM.
33	VDD	-	+5 V.
34	DBO4	Input/Output	Terminal of the input/output data from external RAM.
35	DBO3	Input/Output	Terminal of the input/output data from external RAM.
36	DBO2	Input/Output	Terminal of the input/output data from external RAM.
37	DBO1	Input/Output	Terminal of the input/output data from external RAM (LSB).
38	RAO1	Output	External RAM address output (LSB).
39	RAO2	Output	External RAM address output.
40	RAO3	Output	External RAM address output.
41	RAO4	Output	external RAM address output.
42	RAO5	Output	EXTERNAL RAM address output.
43	RAO6	Output	External RAM address output.
44	RAO7	Output	External RAM address output.
45	RAO8	Output	External RAM address output.
46	RAO9	Output	External RAM address output.
47	RA10	Output	External RAM address output.
48	RA11	Output	External RAM address output.
49	RAWE	Output	Chip enable signal output external RAM
50	RACS	Output	Chip select signal output to external RAM.
51	C4M	Output	1/2 frequency division output of Xtal F = 4.2336 MHz.
52	VSS	-	Ground.
53	XTAI	Input	Xtal oscillation circuit input, F = 8.4672 MHz.
54	XTAO	Output	Xtal oscillation circuit of output, F = 8.4672 MHz.

5-22 RCA pin number identification chart and functions.

55	C2FL	Output	Correction status output. Set to "H" when presently impossible to correct.
56	C2PO	Output	Error flag output of C2 pointer, synchronized with audio data output.
57	RAOV	Output	Overflow and underflow output of RAM for absorbing jitter of $\pm$ 4 frame.
58	SLOB	Input	Mode select input of audio data output. Serial out at low level. Two's complement output at low level.
59	PSSL	Input	Mode select input of audio data output. Serial output at "L."
60	APTR	Output	Control output for compensating aperture "H" at RCH.
61	APTL	Output	Control output for compensating aperture "H" at LCH.
62	DAO1	Output	Output error correction status in C1 (C1F1).
63	DAO2	Output	Output error correction status in C1 (C1F2).
64	DAO3	Output	Output error correction status in C2 (C2F1).
65	DAO4	Output	Output error correction status in C2 (C2F2).
66	DAO5	Output	UGFS output.
67	DAO6	Output	WFCK reversed output.
68	DAO7	Output	WFCK/4 output.
69	DAO8	Output	RFCK/4 output.
70	DAO9	Output	VCO/2 output, F = 4.3218 MHz.
71	DA10	Output	LRCK reversed output.
72	DA11	Output	Strove signal, F = 176.4 KHz.
73	VDD	-	+5V.
74	DA12	Output	LCH serial data enable signal.
75	DA13	Output	RCH serial data enable signal.
76	DA14	Output	C210 reversed output, F = 2.1168 MHz.
77	DA15	Output	Bit clock output, F = 2.1168 MHz.
78	DA16	Output	Audio signal serial data output.
79	WDCK	Output	88.2 kHz strove signal output.
80	LRCK	Output	44.1 kHz strove signal output.

5-22 Continued.

Realistic CD-3304 EFM comparator

The EFM comparator changes RF signal into a binary value. As the asymmetry generated due to variations in disc manufacturing cannot be eliminated by the ac coupling alone, the reference voltage of EFM comparator is controlled utilizing the fact that the generation probability of 1,0 is 50% each in the binary EFM signals (Fig. 5-23).

As this comparator is a circuit SW type, each of the H (high) and L (low) levels does not equal the power supply voltage, requiring feedback through a CMOS buffer. R532, R528, and C546 form a low-power filter (LPF) to obtain (*VCC* + *DGND*)/2 V.

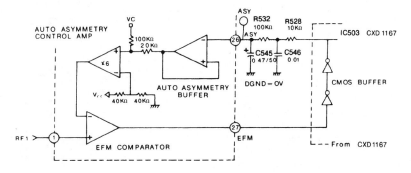

5-23 The EFM comparator changes RF signal into a binary value in a Realistic CD-3304 CD chassis.

Other RF circuits

Besides the RF or HF circuits, the RF preamp and RF processor IC can contain the auto focus (AF), 8- to 14-bit modulation (EFM), focus error (FE), focus OK (FOK), mirror detector (MIR), and tracking error circuits. Because these circuits relate to the RF processor circuits, they are described in the following sections.

In the Onkyo DX-200 EFM waveform rectifier circuit, there is a binary conversion of the RF signal following input to the comparator. Because asymmetry in the RF signal about the X axis cannot be eliminated simply by ac coupling, EFM-signal dc components must be fed back after rectification to control the slice level. (The asymmetry is generated as a result of various factors in the manufacturing of compact discs and results in loss of dc balance.)

The EFM output (pin 20 of Q101) obtained by rectifying the RF signal by the comparator is converted to CMOS in Q303 to become the ASY (asymmetry) signal. The low-frequency components of this signal are fed back into 22 of Q101 via R104 and C116 (Fig. 5-24). The voltage of this pin 22 is approximately 2.5 V (5/2) when operation is normal.

The Pioneer PD-9010 EFM comparator serves to convert the RF signal into a signal with two values. Problems caused by disc asymmetry cannot be dealt with by ac

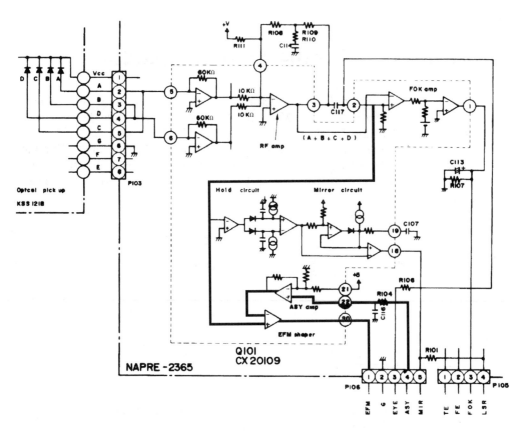

5-24 The EFM output is taken from pin 20 of Q101 in an Onkyo DX-200 CD player.

linkage alone. Therefore, the EFM comparator reference voltage is controlled by using the fact that a 1.0 occurrence probability becomes 50% for each of the two EFM signals.

Because this EFM comparator is a current-switch type unit, the H and L levels do not reach that of the power supply voltage (Fig. 5-25). It is therefore necessary to apply feedback through a CMOS buffer. Components R25, R90, C22, and C60 make up the low-pass filter needed to obtain + 2.5 Vdc. If FC is 500 Hz or more, leakage of the reduced component of EFM becomes serious, resulting in a worsening of the block error rate. This system has two stages. In one, $R_{25} = 100$ kΩ and $C_{22} = 0.47$ μF, so $FC = 3.4$ MHz. In the other, $R_{90} = 10$ kΩ and $C_{60} = 0.01$ μF, so $FC = 1.6$ kHz.

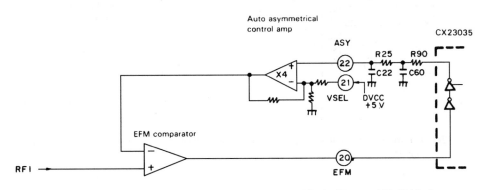

5-25 The EFM comparator output is taken from pin 20 of a Pioneer PD-9010 player.

AF (auto focus) and focus error circuits

The beam from the laser pickup must remain focused on the disc surface to accurately read the information. When the focus on the disc strays, the focus servo moves the object lens up or down to correct the focus. Under this system, when a beam is irradiated through a combination of the cylindrical and convex lenses, the beam is elongated and then becomes a perfect circle. When the laser beam is reflected from the disc, it is directed to the cylindrical lens by the prism and then to the optosensor (photodetector) where it is split into four, forming a perfect circle. These outputs from the four optosensing elements are supplied to the error signal amplifier, and a zero output is produced. The focus error circuit is designed to detect changes in the distance to the disc and thereby ensures that the laser beam spot is kept in proper focus on the reflecting surface of the disc.

In the Onkyo DX-200 focus error circuit, the changes in the laser beam focus are achieved by what is called the *astigmatic method*. This method uses the fact that the shape of the laser spot reflected from the disc into a six-part photodiode in the pickup varies according to the distance from the disc. These changes are due to the action of a cylindrical lens.

The A, B, C, and D photodiode light source currents undergo a diagonal subtraction in three operational amplifiers in Q101, resulting in the generation of a focus error (FE) signal (Fig. 5-26). Figure 5-27 summarizes the FE signal changes at different distances from the disc reflecting surface.

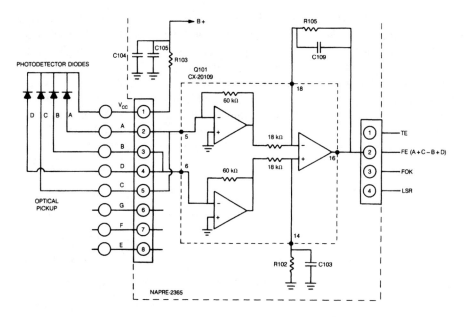

5-26 The focus error signal (FE) is taken from pin 2 of Q101 in an Onkyo DX-200 CD player.

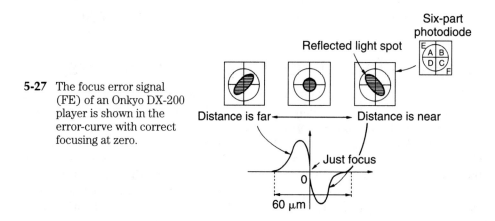

5-27 The focus error signal (FE) of an Onkyo DX-200 player is shown in the error-curve with correct focusing at zero.

Figure 5-28 shows the *Pioneer PD-7010 (BK)* focus error amp. The difference between the outputs of the two RF 1-V amps ($B_2 + B_4$, and $B_1 + B_3$) is computed and output ($B_1 + B_3 - B_2 - B_4$). When $R_{27} = R_{36}$, the *FE* output voltage (low frequency) is:

$$VFE = \frac{R_{27}}{15 \text{ k}\mu} \times VA - VB$$

$$= \frac{R_{27}}{15 \text{ k}\mu} \times (IPD_2 - IPD_1) \times 60 \text{ k}\Omega$$

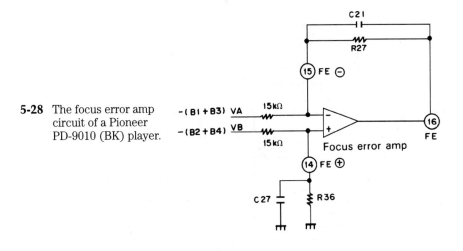

5-28 The focus error amp circuit of a Pioneer PD-9010 (BK) player.

Capacitors C21 and C27 are needed to prevent leakage of the EFM component into the focus error output. Due to the gain setting, $R_{27} = R_{36} = 100$ kΩ, and $C_{21} = 27 = 56$ pF. That means $FC = 28.4$ kHz. For the output at pin 16, a 5 V (p-p) output in form of an "S" curve results.

Figure 5-29 shows the RCA MCD-141 auto focus (AF) circuit. The output from the four optosensing elements $A_1 + A_3$ and $A_2 + A_4$ are supplied to the error signal amplifier, and a zero output is produced. If the beam is shifted upward or downward with respect to the focusing position of the object lens, the beam is elongated when entering the optosensing elements, and signals $(A_1 + A_3, A_2 + A_4)$ corresponding to the shift are sent to the error signal amplifier (IC004, pins 3, 4 as in Fig. 5-29). They are converted to a voltage signal and amplified. The resultant output voltage $(A_1 + A_3$ minus $A_2 + A_4)$ (IC004, pin 9) is returned to the focus lens activator circuit through the servo IC101, pins 20 (input) and 21 (output), where the object lens of the activator through a focus coil drive circuit (Q101, Q102), is moved up or down. The reference voltage for this circuit is established by R010 (auto focus offset). The activator in this circuit acts like a speaker with the object lens as the speaker cone.

See Fig. 5-30 for the Realistic CD-1000 auto focus detection. In order for the focus lens to be focused at all times at a ±1 μM accuracy with discs that fluctuate in the vertical direction, a focus servo is employed so the signals can be picked up accurately from the disc. When the focus fades, the focus servo functions to move the objective lens up or down promptly to correct the focus. *Astigmatism* is used for focus shifting.

Under this system, when a beam is irradiated on to a combination of the cylindrical lens and convex lens, the beam shape that forms after the beam has passed through the cylindrical lens changes from an ellipse in the height direction to a perfect circle and again to an ellipse in the width direction, in sequence. When the laser beam is reflected from the disc, it is directed to the cylindrical lens by the prism and then to the optosensor, which is split into four. Each optosensing element forms a pair and is electrically connected. When the objective lens is positioned properly with respect to the disc surface, the laser beam directed to the optosensor forms a perfect

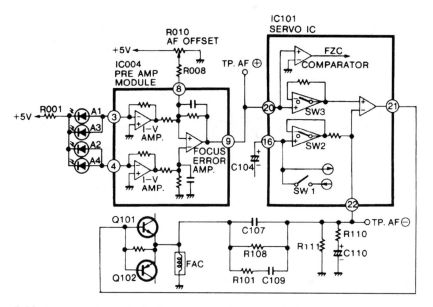

5-29 The auto focus block diagram in the RCA MCD-141 compact disc player.

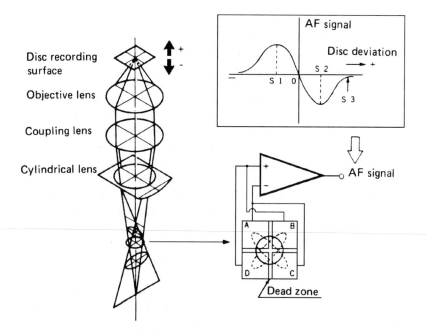

5-30 Here, the AF (auto focus) signal detection curve is shown in a Realistic CD-1000 player.

circle, and when the output of the four optosensing elements is supplied to the error signal amplifier, "0" is produced. If the disc shifts upward or downward with respect to the focusing position of the objective lens, the beam is turned into an ellipse that enters the optosensing elements, and a signal corresponding to the shift is output to the error signal amplifier. This output is returned to the lens drive activator.

The lens drive *allenvator* largely resembles the mechanism of a speaker, although instead of the cone, there is the objective lens. This lens is moved upward and downward by a drive section that resembles the voice coil in a speaker. In fact, audio speaker technology was used in the creation of this mechanism, and highly precise error tracking characteristics are produced as a result.

Figure 5-31 shows the Onkyo DX-200 FOK (focus OK) circuit. The FOK circuit generates a signal that is used to judge when the laser spot is on the reflecting surface of the disc.

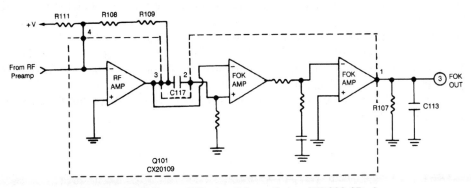

5-31 The FOK (focus OK) circuit in an Onkyo DX-200 CD player.

The dc level of the RF signal is compared with a reference voltage. If the dc level is higher than the reference voltage (which means that the light source generated by the reflected beam is greater than the reference level), the comparator is activated and a high output is obtained from pin 1 of Q101. Resistor R111, connected to pin 4 of Q101, determines the bias used in adjusting the FOK reference level. The FOK output is applied to the microcomputer where it is used in disc identification, focus adjustment timing, and detection of disc flaws.

The Pioneer PD-5010 BK focus OK circuit makes the timing window for switching on the focus servo from the focus search mode (Fig. 5-32).

The threshold value V_{TH} of the focus OK comparator is set so that it is reversed when $V_G = -0.4$ V. Therefore, the focus OK comparator is reversed when $V_{RFO} = V_C = 0.4$ V. The threshold value of this comparator is stable due to the accuracy of the reference voltage within the IC.

Capacitor C28 determines the time constants for the EFM comparator, mirror-circuit high-pass filter, and focus OK amp low-pass filter. This makes it possible to prevent worsening of the block error rate caused by the RF envelope loss when scratches and other disc damage is encountered. In this system, 0.0047 μF is used as the optimum value for C28, which results in $F_C = 3.4$ kHz. The RF offset current is unnecessary.

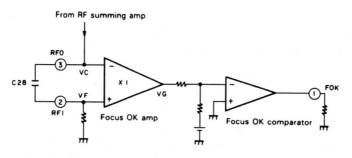

5-32 The FOK (focus OK) circuit in a Pioneer PD-5010 CD player.

In the Onkyo DX-200 the MIR detector circuit is used in detection of the mirror portion of the disc between tracks and outside the lead-out tracks, and it is also used to detect disc flaws (Fig. 5-33). The differential output obtained by peak and bottom holding of the RF signal envelope is compared with a signal that is held by an even larger time constant (determined by C107). If the differential output drops below ⅔ of the hold signal, the comparator is activated to obtain a high-level MIR output (from pin 18 of Q101). This output is passed to the microcomputer and the PLL circuit (pin 7 of Q303) and is used in counting tracks and in switching the PLL to open loop if a disc flaw is detected.

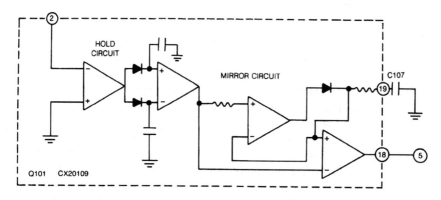

5-33 The MIR (mirror detector circuit) in an Onkyo DX-200 CD player.

For the Pioneer PD-9010 (BK) mirror circuit, after amplifying the RF1 signal, peak and bottom hold occur. For peak hold, the time constant is such that the 30 kHz transverse can also be followed. For bottom hold, the time constant is such that the rotation cycle envelope fluctuations can be followed (Fig. 5-34).

The dc-restored envelope signal is obtained by performing differential amplification of these peak/bottom hold signals. By comparing this signal with that held by peak hold at ⅔ of the peak level using the large time constant, the mirror output is obtained. In other words, mirror output is "L" when over a track (row of pits) and "H" when between tracks. Furthermore, "H" is also output when a defect is detected. The time constant for mirror hold must be sufficiently larger than the transverse signal.

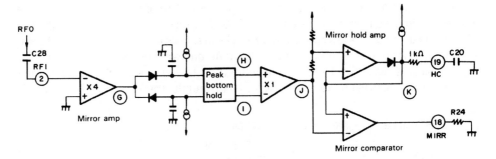

5-34 The mirror circuit in a Pioneer PD-9010 (BK) player.

Realistic CD-3304 auto focus

The focus OK circuit (FOK) generates a timing window to look on the focus servo from a focus search status. Pin 1 will receive the high-pass filter (HPF) output from an RF signal of pin 2, the low-pass filter (LPF) output (opposite phase) for the focus OK amplifier output (Fig. 5-35).

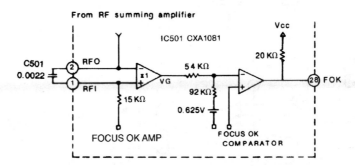

5-35 The focus OK circuit (FOK) in a Realistic CD-3304 compact disc player.

The focus OK circuit output is inverted when $V_{RFI} - V_{RFO} = -0.37$ V. C501 is for determining the time constants of high-power filter (HPF) in the EFM comparator and mirror circuits as well as low-power filter (LPF) in the focus OK amplifier.

Tracking error circuits

The tracking error circuit generates an error signal if the laser beam spot moves away from the center of the pits. This error signal is used to ensure that the beam spot correctly tracks the line of pits. The tracking error circuits are inside the RF preamp or signal processor IC.

For the Onkyo DX-200 tracking error circuit, the mechanism divides the laser beam into three separate beams—a main beam and two auxiliary beams on either side of the main beam. These three beams are arranged at a slight angle (0.88°) to the line of pits in what is known as the *three-beam method*.

If the beam tends to move away from the pits, as indicated in Fig. 5-36, the degree of reflection in the auxiliary beams changes depending on the direction of the shift. The reflected auxiliary beams are converted into electric signals by the E and F detectors at both ends of the six-part diode, and the mutual differences are obtained as a tracking error (TE) signal (Fig. 5-37). The circuit includes three operational amplifiers. The E and F detectors are balanced by variable resistor R114, and the tracking offset is cancelled.

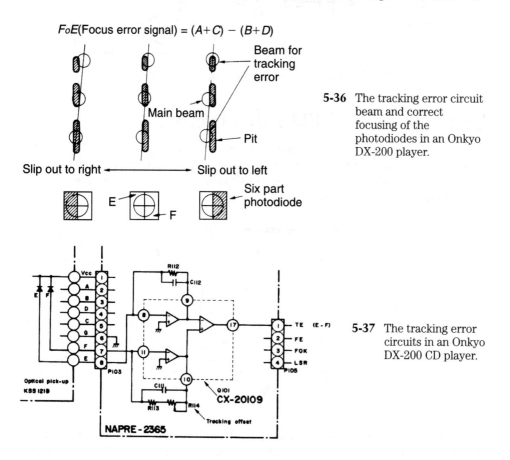

FoE(Focus error signal) $= (A+C) - (B+D)$

5-36 The tracking error circuit beam and correct focusing of the photodiodes in an Onkyo DX-200 player.

5-37 The tracking error circuits in an Onkyo DX-200 CD player.

For the Pioneer PD 7010 (BK) tracking error amp, the current of the side-spot pin diode that is input at E and F undergoes IV conversion at the E and F IV amps (R_{28} and R_{29} + VRS) in the following manner (Fig. 5-38):

$$3\,VE = IA\,R_{28}$$
$$VF = IC\,(R_{29} + VR_5)$$

Then, the difference between the two IV amps is calculated at the tracking error amp to produce the output $(E - F)$. The gain of the tracking error amp for 11 (21 dB) is:

$$VTE = (VE - VF) \times 11 = (IA - IC) \times R_{28} \times 11$$

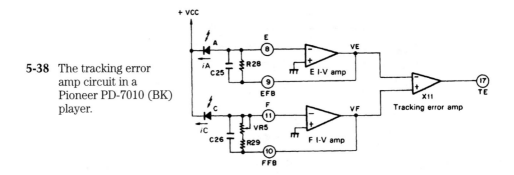

5-38 The tracking error amp circuit in a Pioneer PD-7010 (BK) player.

Capacitors C25 and C26 are required to prevent leakage of the EFM component into the tracking error output. The gain setting makes $R_{28} = R_{29} + VRS = 150$ kΩ, and $C_{25} = C_{26} = 47$ pF. Here, $FC = 22.6$ kHz.

$R_{29} + VR_5$ includes adjustment VR. This is tracking error balance for the purpose of obtaining a dc-balanced tracking error signal. It is needed primarily to perform the tracking jump properly. The output of pin 17 is a 4 V (p-p) tracking error signal.

See Fig. 5-39 for the RCA MCD-141 tracking error circuit. The laser pickup must track the groove of pits at all times. Because the grooves are only 1.6 micrometers between centers, a very precise method of reading them is necessary. The MCD-141 uses a three-spot laser system. The main spot is used to maintain proper focus and retrieve the digital information. The two subspots are used to maintain tracking.

The subspots are generated by passing the laser beam through a glass diffraction grating where the same light is seen a number of times. The subspots, positioned before and after the main laser spot, are aligned by shifting them slightly to the left or right. When the beams are reflected from the disc surface, the two subspot laser beams fall on two optical sensors (B1 and B2), and the output from these detectors is applied to pins 5 and 6 of IC004.

These signals pass through a full-wave rectifier circuit and are converted to an amplified voltage signal. The tracking error output voltage (B1 minus B2) exits IC004 at pin 11 and is sent to the servo IC101 (pin 13) through the tracking gain adjusts (R126). The output voltage from the IC101 (pin 27) provides the necessary connection voltage for the tracking coil drive circuit (Q105, Q106) to position the main laser spot. The reference voltage for this circuit is established by R020 (TR offset adjust).

Figure 5-40 shows the Realistic CD-1000 tracking error detection system. The laser spot must track the series of pits accurately at all times, regardless of the disc's eccentricity. This particular unit uses an extremely accurate tracking mechanism known as a "three-spot" system. As shown in the figure, this system makes use of two subspots, obtained by passing the main laser beam through a glass diffraction grating, which are positioned before and after the main laser spot. They are aligned by shifting them slightly to the left and right. After the laser spot has been reflected

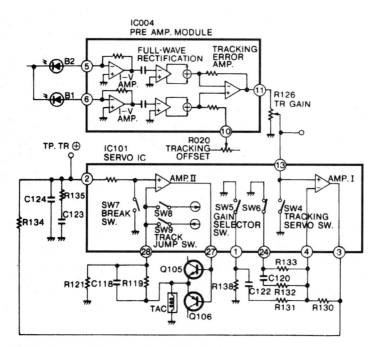

5-39 The tracking error circuit block diagram in the RCA MCD-141 CD player.

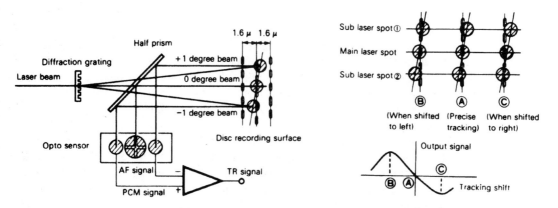

5-40 The tracking error detection and how it connects the beam in a Realistic CD-1000 player.

by the disc surface, it is passed to the optosensor. However, the reflected light of the two subspots is detected first, converted into electricity, and it then enters the error signal amplifier. Any shift, no matter how slight, is translated into a difference in the input to the amplifier. This error output difference enters the servo circuit to move the objective lens to correct the position of the main laser spot. Thanks to this system, the tracking servo is extremely precise.

Realistic CD-3304 tracking error circuits

$E\mathrm{I} - V$ amplifier and $F\mathrm{I} - V$ amplifiers are connected to voltage from the signal current of pin photo diode connected: E and F. The E and $F\mathrm{I} - V$ amplifiers output voltage is,

$$VF = iF \times 403 \text{ k}\Omega, \text{ and}$$
$$VE = iF \times (260 \text{ k}\Omega + RA) \ (Rb + 22 \text{ k}\Omega) + (Ra + 260 \text{ k}\Omega).$$

The tracking error amplifier is the difference between the $E\mathrm{I} - V$ amplifier output and the $F\mathrm{I} - V$ amplifier output, this output is (EF).

$$VTE = (Ve - Vf) \times 3.2$$
$$= (iE - iF) \times 1290 \text{ k}\Omega$$

APC circuits

The purpose of the APC (auto power control) circuit is to keep the laser diode optical output at a constant level. The APC circuit is located in the laser head assembly or on the PC board (Fig. 5-41). The APC circuit consists of transistors or an IC component.

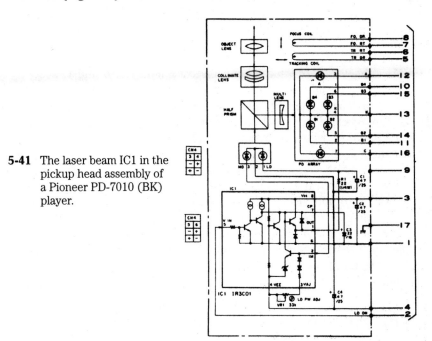

5-41 The laser beam IC1 in the pickup head assembly of a Pioneer PD-7010 (BK) player.

See Fig. 5-42 for the *Onkyo DX-200* APC circuit. When the LSR laser ON/OFF control signal from the microcomputer (P105, pin 4) is changed to low level, Q102 is turned off via D102 and R118, and Q104 is turned on to supply a current to the laser diode. Current *I*LD is obtained from the following equation:

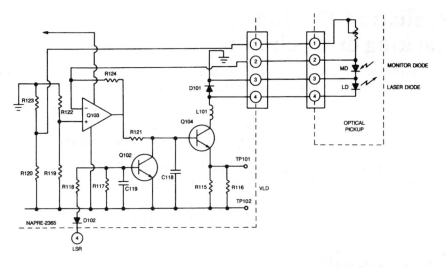

5-42   The APC (auto power control) circuit connects to the monitor and laser diodes in an Onkyo DX-200 optical head assembly.

$$ILD = \frac{VLD}{\left(\dfrac{R_{115}}{R_{116}}\right)} = VLD\left[\frac{(V)}{21.5}\right]$$

where VLD is the voltage measured between test points TP101 and TP102.

The ILD value lies in the 50- to 80-mA range when the laser diode is normal. The ILD value for each pickup is set prior to delivery from the factory and is indicated as a three-digit number below the lot number on the pickup spindle motor. (For example, a figure of 691 indicates a current of 69.1 mA.) A measured current that differs from this value by more than 10% (at 25° Celsius) indicates that the laser diode has probably deteriorated. Because the laser diode is very susceptible to the effects of static electricity, switch the CD player power off before connecting a digital voltmeter across TP101 and TP102 to measure VLD. After the measurement has been completed, again switch the power off before disconnecting the voltmeter.

The laser diode optical output is also beamed on to a monitor diode built into the optical pickup. The light source current generated as a result is fed back to the minus input of the Q103 operational amplifier to maintain the laser output power at a constant level.

Defect circuits

In the Realistic CD-3304 CD player the RFI signal bottom, after being inverted, is held with two time constants, one long and one short. The short time constant bottom hold is done for a disc mirror defect more than 0.1 msec. The long time constant bottom hold is done with the mirror level prior to the defect. By differentiating this with a capacitor coupling and shifting the level, both signals are compared to generate the mirror detect detection signal (Fig. 5-43). The defect signal at pin 21 of RF amp (IC501) is fed to pin 2 of the analog signal processor IC502.

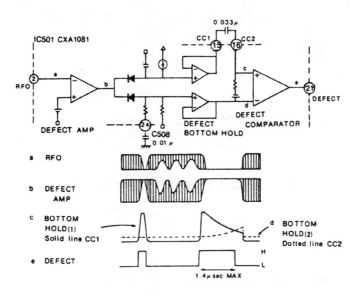

5-43 Operation of the defect circuit in the Realistic CD-3304 player.

Realistic CD-3304 mirror circuits

This circuit, after amplifying the RFI signal, holds the bottom and peak. The peak hold is done with a time constant able to track down a 30 kHz traverse and the bottom hold. This is done with a time constant able to track down envelope fluctuations in the revolving cycle (Fig. 5-44).

With the differential amplification of this peak and bottom hold signals, H and I, the envelope signal J (demodulated to dc) is obtained. Two-thirds of the peak value of the signal J is held with a large time constant for the signal K. When K is compared with J, a mirror output is obtained.

That is, the mirror output gives "L" on the disc track, "H" between tracks (mirror section) and also "H" in the defect section. The time constant for the mirror hold must be sufficiently larger than that of the traverse signal.

Sanyo CP500 chassis shutdown

In a Sanyo CP-500 CD player the laser diode lights up, the focus and tracking coils began to search, then chassis shutdown. The scope probe was connected to pin 20, to determine if the RF-preamp IC101 was providing an EFM signal (Fig. 5-45). The RFO eye pattern can be checked at test point TP1 (RF) or terminal 3. Often, the servo IC will shut down the chassis when the EFM signal is not present at the RF IC amp.

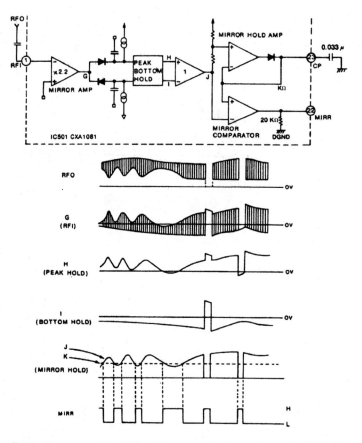

5-44 The operations of the mirror circuits in a mirror circuit in the Realistic CD-3304 CD player.

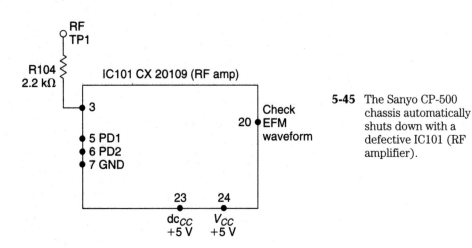

5-45 The Sanyo CP-500 chassis automatically shuts down with a defective IC101 (RF amplifier).

Again the chassis was fired up, with no sign of EFM waveform at IC101. The supply voltage was normal at pins 23 and 24 (+5 V). The +5-V source was good to the PD1 and PD2 diodes. Because the laser diode was emitting a beam, measured with an infrared checker, and normal voltages, IC101 was replaced. The original part number was used (CX20109), restoring the chassis shutdown symptom.

RF and EFM waveforms

You know the optical pickup assembly and RF amp are functioning with RF or EFM waveforms at the RF or preamp IC. When these waveforms are missing, suspect a defective laser optical assembly or RF amp IC. The HF signal (RF signal) waveform is found at test point HF or pin 2 of RF amp (IC501) in a Realistic CD-3304 player (Fig. 5-46).

The FM signal (EFM) on pin 27 of IC501 is shown in Fig. 5-47 during normal play.

$\left(\begin{array}{l}\text{0.5 V / div.}\\ \text{500 mS / div.}\end{array}\right.$

———————— 0 V

5-46 The eye pattern waveform at test point HF or pin 2 of the Radio Shack CD-3304 CD player.

$\left(\begin{array}{l}\text{2 V / div.}\\ \text{500 mS / div.}\end{array}\right.$

———————— 0 V

5-47 The FM signal waveform at pin 27 of IC501 in the Realistic CD player.

6
The servo system

THE SERVO SECTION PROVIDES SIGNAL AND POWER TO THE FOCUS AND TRACKING coil drive, slide or sled motor drive, spindle servo, tray motor drive, track jump, and search circuits. In some models, the loading or tray motor is controlled by the system control circuits. The servo circuits can be included in one or two large LSIs, or a combination of LSI, IC, and transistor circuits (Fig. 6-1). Some of the servo control circuits might be combined within the signal processor LSI (Fig. 6-2).

IC12 CXA1182Q-Z

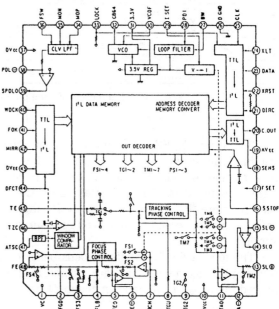

6-1 The servo IC can be conventional or surfaced-mounted to the PC board.

CXA1182Q Terminal Function

Terminal No.	Terminal Symbol	Terminal Function
2	FGD	In case of reducing higher range gain of focus servo, connect a capacitor between this terminal and terminal number (9).
3	FS3	Shifts higher range gain of focus servo by FS3 ON/OFF.
4	FLB	Terminal for external time constant to increase lower range of focus servo.
5	FEO	Focus drive output.
6	FE(−)	Reverse input terminal for focus amplifier.
7	SRCH	Terminal for external time constant to make focus search waveform.
8	TGU	Terminal for external time constant to shift higher range gain of tracking.
9	TG2	Terminal for external time constant to shift higher range gain of tracking.
11	TAO	Tracking drive output.
12	TA(−)	Reverse input terminal for tracking amplifier.
13	SL(+)	Non-reverse input terminal of sled amplifier.
14	SLO	Sled drive output.
15	SL(−)	Reverse input terminal of sled amplifier.
16	SSTOP	Terminal for limit switch ON/OFF to detect disc innermost circle.
17	FSET	Terminal to compensate peak in focus tracking phase, and for setting Fo in CLV LPF.
18	SENS	Terminal to output FZC, AS, TZC, SSTOP, BUSY by command from CPU.
20	C. OUT	Terminal to output signal for track number count.
21	DIRC	Terminal is used at the time of 1 track jump. A 47 kΩ pull up resistor is included.
22	XRST	Reset input terminal. Resets at "L".
23	DATA	Serial data input from CPU.
24	XLT	Latch input from CPU.
25	CLK	Serial data transfer clock input from CPU.
27	BW	Terminal for external time constant of loop filter.
28	PDI	Input terminal of PDO for CXD1125 phase comparator.
29	ISET	Delivers a current to set the height of focus search, track jump, and sled kick.
30	VCOF	Resistance value between this terminal and terminal (37) is nearly in proportion to VCO free-run frequency.
32	C864	Output terminal of 8.64 MHz VCO.
33	LOCK	Reckless drive protection circuit activates at "L". A 47 kΩ pull up resistor is included.
34	MDP	Terminal to connect MDP terminal of CXD1125.
35	MON	Terminal to connect MON terminal of CXD1125.
36	FSW	Terminal for external LPF time constant of CLV servo error signal.
38	SPDL(−)	Reverse input terminal for spindle drive amplifier.
39	SPDLO	Spindle drive output.
40	WDCK	Clock input for auto-sequence. Normally applied 88.2 kHz.
41	FOK	FOK signal input terminal.
42	MIRR	MIRR signal input terminal.
44	DFCT	Defect signal input terminal. Defect measure circuit activates at "H".
45	TE	Tracking error signal input terminal.
46	TZC	Tracking zero cross comparator input terminal.
47	ATSC	Input terminal of ATSC detecting window comparator.
48	FE	Focus error signal input terminal.

6-2 The terminal functions of each pin of IC12 shown in Fig. 6-1.

When the TE, FE, DEF, and mirror circuits are not completed from the RF amplifier, the servo control IC might shut down the whole operation. When the CD player comes on and then shuts down at once, make sure the EFM or RF waveform is found at the RF amp. Make sure the tracking and focus coils began to search before the chassis shut down. Besides these signals, the servo control IC cannot function without proper voltage source (*VCC*) from the low-voltage power supply.

The focus gain, focus offset, focus balance, tracking gain, tracking offset, and tracking balance adjustments are located in the servo system. (These adjustment procedures are given in detail in chapter 9.)

Block diagram

The block diagram of any compact disc player indicates what circuits are controlled by the servo IC (Fig. 6-3). Here in a Mitsubishi M-C4030 player, the servo pickup system is fed signals to and from the RF amp IC101, and then operates the focus, tracking, slide, and disc motor assemblies. While in the Sanyo CP-500 CD player, IC201 provides focus, tracking, and SLED servo control directly from IC201.

BLOCK DIAGRAM

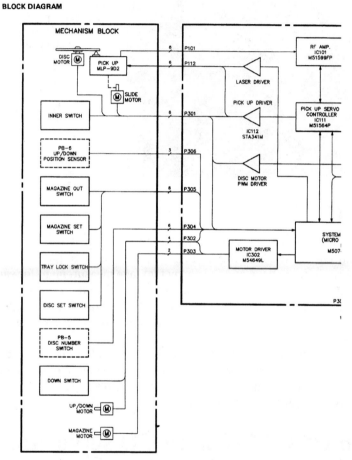

6-3 The block diagram showing pickup servo controller IC111, which provides the signal to laser and pickup driver IC112.

The focus, tracking, and Sled servo IC201 accepts the TE and FE signals from the RF IC101 (Fig. 6-4). The tracking output signal (TAO) drives transistors Q204 and Q205 to the tracking coil winding. FEO from pin 21 of IC210 drives three transistors Q201, Q202, and Q203 to the focus coil winding. The slide motor output signal (SLO) drives transistors Q206 and Q207 to the SLED motor winding.

6-4 The location of a servo IC, which provides drive to TE and FE coils in a Sanyo CP-500 player.

Servo IC

The servo IC is frequently one large component with up to 60 terminals, depending on how many circuits the IC controls (Fig. 6-5). The different pin numbers identify what circuit ties into each pin and the correct voltage measurement for each. Terminals 21 and 22 control the focus drive coil, and pins 27 and 28 control the tracking drive coil assembly. Terminals 23, 24, and 25 control operation of the slide motor assembly circuits. The internal circuits of IC-101 are shown in Fig. 6-6 and the pin voltages are depicted in Fig. 6-7.

Use extreme care when working around these large LSI or IC servo components. Be careful not to short together pins when taking voltage measurements or test waveforms. Always use a small soldering iron when replacing a servo IC component to avoid overheating and damaging the IC.

Denon DCC-9770 auto CD servo circuits

The tracking error (TE) signal taken from pin 1 of RF amp IC501 through tracking gains control to pin 45 on servo IC502. The tracking coil output (TAO) is fed from pin 11 of IC502 to coil drive IC402, Q414, Q415, Q416, and Q417 to the tracking coil (Fig. 6-8). Notice there are two sets of transistors driving the negative and positive leads of the tracking coil.

The focus error (FE) signal is taken from pin 32 of RF amp IC501 through gain control and to pin 48 of servo control IC502. The focus gain output signal (FEO) from pin 5 feeds the focus coil driver IC402, Q410, Q411, Q412, and Q413. Again

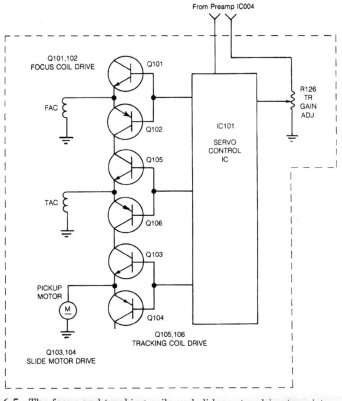

6-5 The focus and tracking coils and slide motor drive transistors
are controlled by IC101 in the RCA MCD-141 player.

each positive and negative focus coil terminals are driven with separate IC and transistors in this automatic changer.

The spindle and SLED motors are controlled by the servo control IC502 through the various ICs and transistors motor drivers. The loading motor is driven by driver Q418 through Q422 from loading and eject signal of the mechanism control IC1.

Denon DCH-500 servo circuits

The tracking error (TE) signal is taken from pin 1 of the RF amp IC11 and fed through the tracking gain control RV13 to pin 45 of the servo control IC12. The tracking output signal from pin 111 of IC12 is fed to pin 10 of focus, tracking, and SLED drive IC14. Notice that one large driver IC (IC12) provides drive voltage for the SLED motor, focus, and tracking coils (Fig. 6-9).

The focus error signal (FE) is taken from pin 32 of RF amp (IC11) and is fed through the focus gain control RV14 to pin 49 of servo control IC12. In turn the focus error output (FEO) signal on pin 5 of IC12 is fed to pin 25 of the focus error driver IC14.

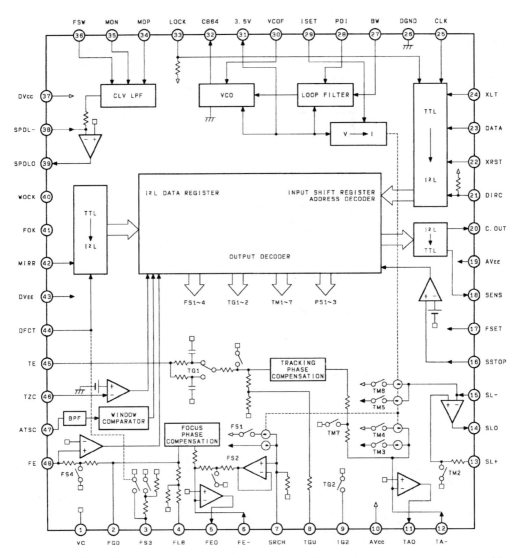

6-6 The IC5 block diagram of the servo signal processor and terminal connections in a portable CD player.

IC PIN NUMBERS DC VOLTAGES																				
Ref. No.	DEVICE	1	2	3	4	5	6	7	8	9	10	11	12	13	14	15	16	17	18	19	20
IC5	CXA1272Q	1.8V	0.9V	N.C.	1.8V	1.8V	1.8V	1.8V	1.8V	1.8V	3.6V	1.8V	1.8V	1.8V	1.8V	1.8V	3.6V	0.7V	3.6V	0V	0V
		21	22	23	24	25	26	27	28	29	30	31	32	33	34	35	36	37	38	39	40
		3.8V	3.6V	1.6V	3.6V	1.6V	0V	1.8V	1.8V	0.7V	3.4V	3.5V	0.1V	3.6V	2.0V	3.6V	3.6V	3.6V	2.0V	2.0V	N.C.
		41	42	43	44	45	46	47	48	49	50	51	52	53	54	55	56	57	58	59	60
		N.C.	1.8V	0V	1.8V	1.8V	1.8V	1.8V	1.8V	—	—	—	—	—							

6-7 The actual voltage measurements upon each pin of the IC5 servo processor.

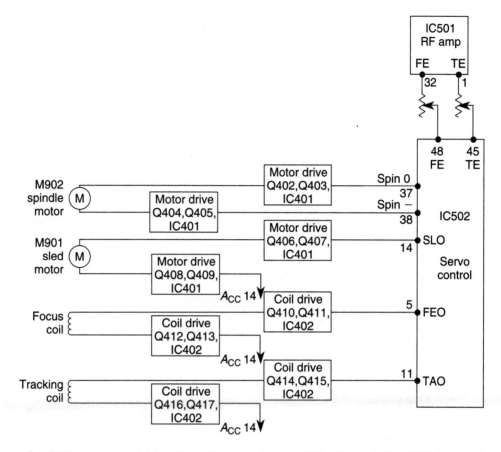

6-8 IC502 servo control drives the various transistors and ICs of the spindle, SLED, focus and tracking coils in a Denon DCC-9770 player.

The SLED or slide motor signal is sent from pin 14 of the servo control IC12 to pin 3 of the SLED drive IC14. The SLED voltage is fed from pins 1 and 2 of IC14 SLED driver to the motor terminals. Often the spindle motor and disc motor is controlled through a common driver IC501, from the control system IC601.

Mitsubishi M-C4030 auto changer servo circuits

The slide motor signal is fed from the pickup servo control IC111. The slide signal is sent to a common driver IC112, which also drives the laser and disc motor circuits. The disc motor signal is actually controlled by the digital signal processor IC201. The up/down motor and magazine motors are controlled through driver IC302 from the system control IC301 (Figs. 6-10 and 6-11).

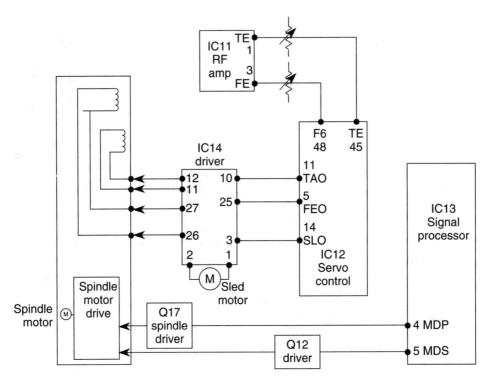

6-9   Servo control IC12 provides drive for IC14, which drives the focus tracking and SLED motor in a Denon DCH-500 CD changer.

IC111: M51564P PICKUP SERVO.

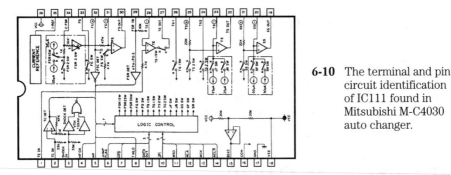

6-10   The terminal and pin circuit identification of IC111 found in Mitsubishi M-C4030 auto changer.

Realistic CD-3304 boom-box servo circuits

In the Realistic boom-box CD servo circuits, the focus error (FE) is taken from pin 19 of the RF amp IC501 through a focus gain control to pin 6 of the servo LSI IC502 (Fig. 6-12). The tracking error (TE) signal is taken from pin 20 of RF amp IC501 through tracking gain control to pin 3 of servo LSI IC502. The focus error output (FEO) is fed from pin 11 to IC506 driver and to the focus coil winding. Likewise the tracking error output (TEO) is fed from pin 17 to driver IC506 and to the tracking coil winding.

Pin No.	NAME	Function Block	Input/Output	Function
1	TE IN	Pre. Amp input	I	Tracking error signal input
2	TC IN	Pre. Amp input	I	Track cross signal input
3	SHOCK IN	Pre. Amp input	I	SHOCK detection circuit input
4	HF OK	Pre. Amp input	I	HFOK signal input
5	MR	Pre. Amp input	I	Disc mirror detection signal input
6	JUMP F	Micro computer I/O	O	TS OFF·JFJR·BRAKE output (JUMP Mode)
7	HFD	Micro computer I/O	O	MR input = "1" and Track servo loop off HFD = "1"
8	T·HLD	TRACK SERVO	I	TS 1 SW direct control
9	DATA OUT	Micro computer input	O	Internal status output
10	JP1	Micro computer input	I	1 track jump control signal input
11	MSD	Micro computer input	I	Micro computer serial data transfer clock
12	MLA	Micro computer input	I	Micro computer serial data latch
13	MCK	Micro computer input	I	Micro computer serial data transfer
14	ACLR	Micro computer input	I	Internal register flip-flop all clear
15	BIAS	Power	O	Vcc/2 Bias power output
16	COM	Power	I	COMMON ± Power → GND, one level power → BIAS
17	GND	Power	I	GND pin
18	VEE	Power	I	Minus power, one level power → GND
19	SS OUT	SLIDE SERVO	O	Operational amplifier SS output
20	SS ⊖	SLIDE SERVO	I	Operational amplifier SS invert input
21	SS ⊕	SLIDE SERVO	I	Operational amplifier SS non-invert input
22	TS OUT	TRACK SERVO	O	Operational amplifier TA output
23	TS ⊖	TRACK SERVO	I	Operational amplifier TA invert input
24	TG 2	TRACK SERVO	—	Track gain change switch TG 2 output
25	TS ⊕	TRACK SERVO	I	Operational amplifier TA non-invert input
26	TG 1	TRACK SERVO	—	Track gain change switch TG 1 output
27	TE OUT	TRACK SERVO	O	Operational amplifier TE output
28	TE ⊖	TRACK SERVO	I	Operational amplifier TE invert input
29	FSR IN	FOCUS SERVO	I	Focus research voltage level detector input
30	FS OUT	FOCUS SERVO	O	Operational amplifier FA output
31	FS ⊖	FOCUS SERVO	I	Operational amplifier FA invert input
32	FS ⊕	FOCUS SERVO	I	Operational amplifier FA non-invert input
33	FG	FOCUS SERVO	—	Focus gain change switch FG output
34	C·FSR	FOCUS SERVO	—	Focus search wave form time constant condenser
35	I·REF	FOCUS SERVO	I	Connect current setup resistor
36	VCC	Power	I	PLUS power

6-11 Each pin function of servo IC111 of Mitsubishi M-C4030 changer.

Notice two separate driver op amps of IC506 are fed to the focus coil and two separate drivers to the tracking coil. Driver IC506 provides four op amps and ¼ of each is applied to the different terminals of focus and tracking coils.

The spindle and slide motors are controlled by the servo control LSI (IC502) with the spindle signal at pins 21 and the slide motor output at pin 20 of IC502. IC507 provides four op amps that drive the negative and positive terminals of each motor.

The focus servo circuits

The purpose of the focus servo circuit is to keep the laser beam spot correctly focused on the pits of the disc surface. The focus zero cross (FZC) circuit detects the focus error signal and is used with the FOK circuit to determine the focus adjustment timing. The focus search circuit shifts the object lens up and down to find the correct focus point. The signal from the servo processor controls the focus drive IC or transistors tied to the focus coil.

See Fig. 6-13 for the Onkyo DX-200 focus servo circuit. The focus servo circuit is used to ensure that the beam is always correctly focused on the disc. This is done with the feedback of the FE (focus error) signal that makes the object lens respond to fluctuating perpendicular disc movements.

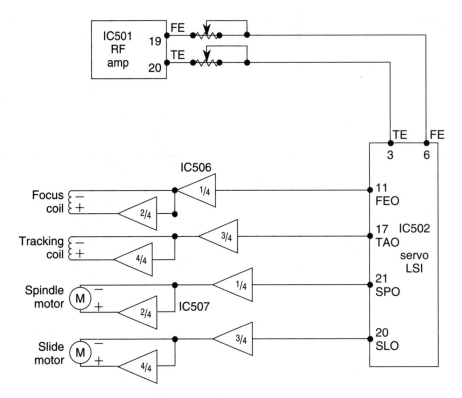

6-12 The servo LSI in a Realistic boom-box CD player provides drive to the focus, tracking, spindle and slide motor.

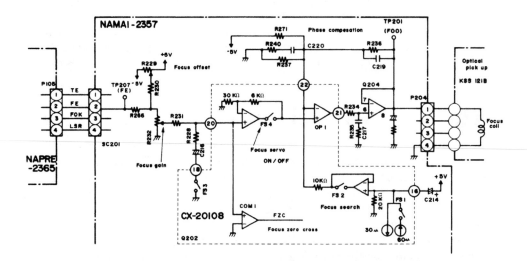

6-13 The focus servo control circuits in the Onkyo DX-200 player.

Referring to the figure, when the FE input from pin 2 of P-201 is passed to the R229 variable resistor, a dc offset voltage is added before the signal is applied to the R-232 gain regulator and pin 20 of Q202. Although this pin is connected to ground via R-228, C216, pin 18 of Q202, and switch FS3, this FS3 is on during accessing operations. The high-frequency components in the FE signal are attenuated by about 10 dB to suppress mechanical noise.

The FE signal applied to pin 20 of Q202 is passed via the servo ON/OFF switch FS4 in Q202 and the phase compensating operational amplifier OP1 to appear at the pin 21 output. Then, after the current level is increased by the Q204 driver, the signal is passed from P204 to the focus drive coil in the optical pickup to control perpendicular object lens movement.

The Onkyo DX-200 focus zero cross (FZC) circuit detects when the focus error (FE) signal reaches 0 V and is used together with the focus OK (FOK) circuit in determining the focus adjustment timing.

The FE signal applied to pin 20 of Q202 is also passed to a comparator COM1 in the IC to form the FZC signal that is subsequently passed to the IC's larger section (Fig. 6-14). When the FZC output signal receives an instruction from the microcomputer, it passes from pin 5 (sense) to the microcomputer.

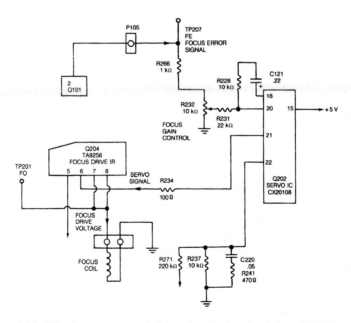

6-14 The focus servo and drive circuits for the Onkyo DX-200
Disc player.

See Fig. 6-14 for the Onkyo DX-200 focus search circuit. Because the FE signal can only be obtained when it is within ± 30 µM of the focus point, a focus search circuit is required to shift the object lens up and down in the beginning to find the focus point before closing the servo loop for stabilized focus servo operation.

FS2 and FS4 are off when the lens is stationary and the focus drive output is kept at the bias voltage of approximately 0.35 V by R271. When an instruction is received from the microcomputer, FS2 is switched on and FS1 is switched on and off every 500 ms, resulting in the repeated charge and discharge of C214. Consequently, a 1-Hz delta wave signal is applied to the focus coil to move the object lens up or down in search of the focus point.

The focus adjustment timing circuit is outlined in Fig. 6-15. When the delta wave signal is applied by the driver to the focus coil and the focus point is reached, the FOK signal is changed to high level and the FZC (sense) signal is changed to low. The microcomputer generates an instruction for switching the focus servo on at that time, turning FS2 off and FS4 on to close the loop. The dotted lines in Fig. 6-15 indicate the waveforms when the servo loop is not closed.

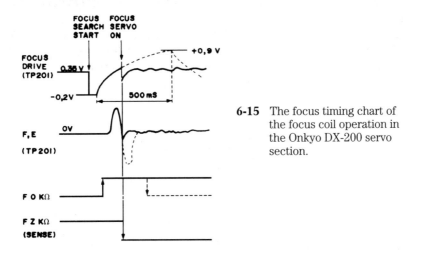

6-15 The focus timing chart of the focus coil operation in the Onkyo DX-200 servo section.

Figure 6-16 shows the Pioneer PD-9010 (BK) focus servo loop. Servo control is performed using two LSIs (CX-20109 and CX-20108) configured around a system control CPU (Fig. 6-16). Each LSI is connected to the CPU by a data bias. All controls use the serial data from the CPU. The primary servo control systems of the CD player are the focus, tracking, and spindle servo systems.

The purpose of the focus servo loop is to control the distance between lens and disc to keep the laser beam focused on the pits on the disc surface (Fig. 6-17). When the focus servo does not lock, focus is attempted one more time. If the result is still unsatisfactory, focus-in operation stops (Fig. 6-18).

The system starts when you load a disc. The laser diode emits a beam. The focus start-up data is being supplied from the output system control IC12 (PD-3037). The lens forcibly moves down and then up (internally processed by IC6). See Fig. 6-19.

The related signals are as follows when the zero cross is located during the lens movement:

SENS output Goes to focus lock after generation. When the zero cross is detected using the SENS output, the disc sets the LED lights and the focus servo loop is closed.

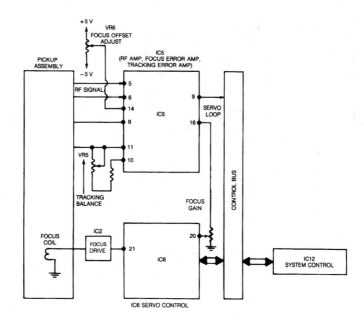

6-16 The focus servo block diagram of a Pioneer PD-9010 (BK) control system.

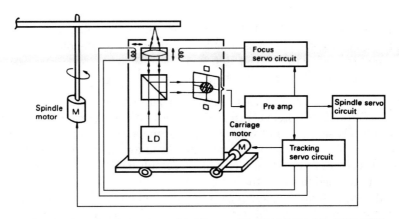

6-17 The focus loop circuit used in Pioneer PD-9010 (BK), PD-7010 (BK), and PD-5010 (BK) players.

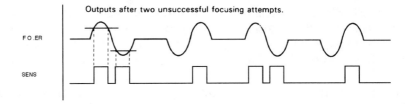

6-18 The focus loop output attempt chart used in the Pioneer PD-9010 (BK) player servo section.

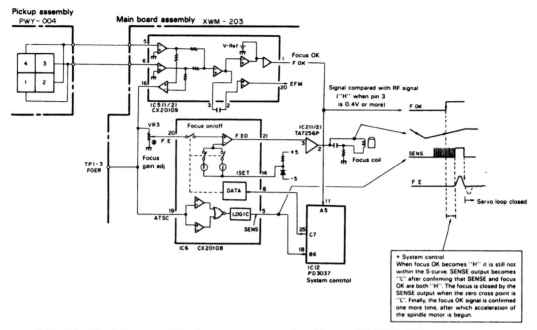

6-19 The block diagram of the focus servo system in a Pioneer PD-9010 (BK) servo section.

Focus OK output (H level) If the system control does not confirm the existence of this output, focus lock is inhibited. Furthermore, this output is checked again before proceeding to the next step.

Focus error signal Generates the zero cross (S-curve).

Refer to Fig. 6-20. The focus servo system begins with a serial data output, supplied by the CPU (IC12 system control), that goes to pin 8 of servo IC6. The internal circuitry of IC6 is shown in Fig. 6-20. The pin terminal connection and where each circuit goes are shown in Fig. 6-21. The signal used for up and down movement of the focus lens comes from output terminal pin 21 of IC6 (Fig. 6-19). This focus error signal goes to IC2 and finally to the focus coil.

The RF output from the pickup goes to pin 5 and pin 6 of IC5 (CX-20109). The RF signal is compared at the FOK circuit and the FOK signal output goes from pin 1 of IC5 to pin 11 of the CPU (IC12). If the RF signal becomes larger than the FOK circuit comparator level, FOK output goes to the CPU (IC12).

When the CPU receives the FOK signal, the trailing edge of the sense signal is used for the FO-ER (focus-error) signal at zero cross point. If the sense output becomes H (high), data to close the focus servo loop at the trailing edge goes from the CPU to pin 8 of IC6. When focused at the zero cross point of the FO-ER signal, the data from the CPU causes the internal circuitry of IC6 to close the focus servo.

Remember, for the focus coil assembly to operate successfully, an RF signal from the preamp or servo IC must exist at the servo focus IC. The computer (CPU IC) requires a focus OK signal, and the focus servo IC requires a data signal from

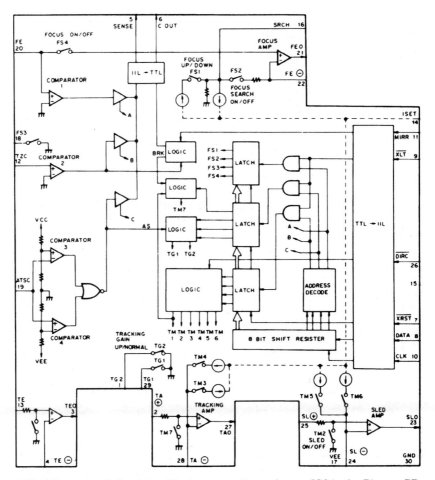

6-20 The internal circuitry with pin connections of servo IC6 in the Pioneer PD-9010 (BK) player.

the system control (CPU IC). Likewise, a focus-error signal from the servo focus IC is fed to the corresponding focus drive IC or transistors and to the focus coil itself (Fig. 6-22).

Realistic CD-3304 focus servo system

The focus servo system receives an FE (focus error) signal from the RF amp IC501. The FEO (focus error output) and focus error signal can be checked at test points, FEO and FE. The focus error adjustment is made with VR502, on pin 6 of servo IC502. The focus output signal at pin 11 drives focus actuator driver IC506 (Fig. 6-23).

When FS3 is switched on, the high-frequency gain can be reduced by forming a low-frequency time constant through the capacitor connected across pins 2 and 3, and the internal resistor.

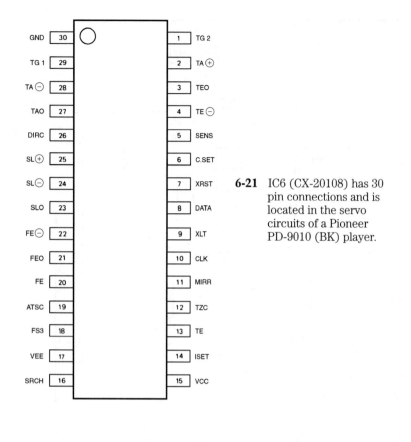

6-21 IC6 (CX-20108) has 30 pin connections and is located in the servo circuits of a Pioneer PD-9010 (BK) player.

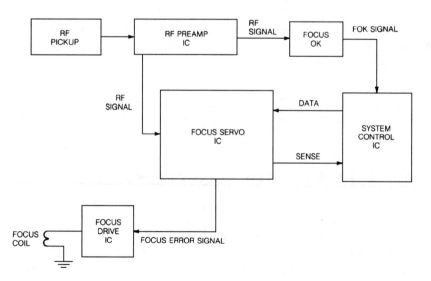

6-22 Here is a typical block diagram of the focus servo system found in most compact disc players.

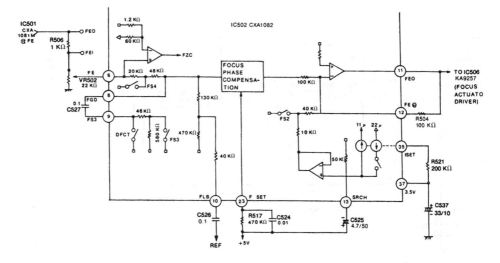

6-23 The focus servo system circuits in the Realistic CD-3304 boom-box CD player.

The capacitor (C526) across the pin 10 and ground (GND) has a time constant to raise the low frequency usually to playback condition. The peak frequency of the focus phase compensation is inversely proportional to the resistor connected to pin 23 (about 1.2 kHz when the resistor is 510 kΩ).

The focus search peak becomes ± 1.1 Vp-p with the above constant. The peak is inversely proportional to the resistor connected across the pins 35 and 37. However, when this resistor is varied, the peaks track jump and SLED kick also vary.

Focus coil drive circuits

The signal from the servo IC to the focus drive circuits can be a combination of ICs and transistors or simply an IC drive circuit (Fig. 6-24). The input RF signal from the pickup diodes goes to the servo IC and in turn the focus error signal goes to an op-amp IC that drives two transistors in push-pull operation. The focus coil drive transistors can be separate transistors or a two-in-one envelope as in the Yamaha CD-3 player. In the RCA MCD-141 chassis, the servo IC101 directly drives two separate transistors. Their commonly tied emitter terminals go directly to the focus coil winding located in the pickup assembly (Fig. 6-25).

Tracking servo system

The purpose of the tracking servo system is to control the laser beam spot directly in the center of the pit track laterally or horizontally. The tracking coil assembly movement is horizontal, where the focus coil assembly moves closer or further. The tracking error signal from the RF amp or preamp IC goes to the servo control IC that in turn drives a tracking coil drive IC or transistor (Fig. 6-26). The tracking driver IC or transistors provide voltage to the tracking coil assembly located in the optical pickup assembly (Fig. 6-27).

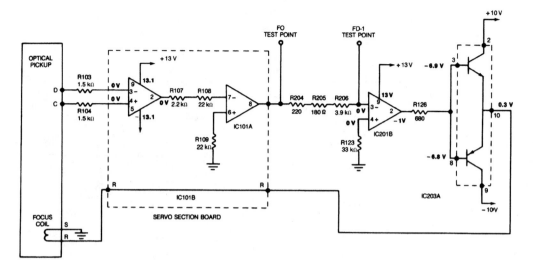

6-24   The servo focus error drive circuits within the Yamaha CD-3 servo system.

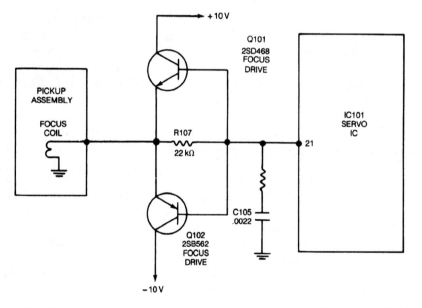

6-25   Servo IC101 drives two focus transistors Q101 and Q102 in the RCA MCD-141 focus error drive circuits.

The Onkyo DX-200 tracking servo circuit is shown in Fig. 6-28. The tracking error (TE) input from pin 1 of P201 is posed to the R226 variable resistor for gain adjustment before being applied to pin 13 of Q202. The signal passes via a phase-compensating operational amplifier (OP4) to pin 3 and then to pin 2 to be passed through another phase-compensating operational amplifier (OP2). The output from pin 27 then passes to the optical pickup tracking coil by driver Q204 to drive the object lens.

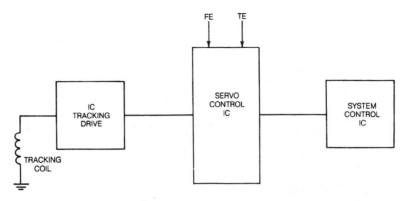

6-26 A typical block diagram of the tracking servo system within the compact disc player.

6-27 Here, two tracking transistors drive the tracking coil in a Sanyo CP-660 model.

The purpose of R262, R263, C228, and C229 (located between pins 2 and 3 of Q202) is to switch the gain for the high frequency by pin 1 switch TG2. The frequency response can be switched by TG1 in combination with C227 connected to pin 1. These switching circuits are activated as a result of track kicking and track accessing in order to stabilize the tracking servo. TM1 is the servo ON/OFF switch.

The same figure shows the Onkyo DX-200 tracking zero cross (TZC) circuit. The TZC circuit generates the timing for switching the tracking servo on and off, following a track-kicking action or when the number of tracks is counted together with the MIR signal during track accessing. The low-frequency components in the TE signal are removed by C215 and R225 before the signal is applied to the COMP2 compara-

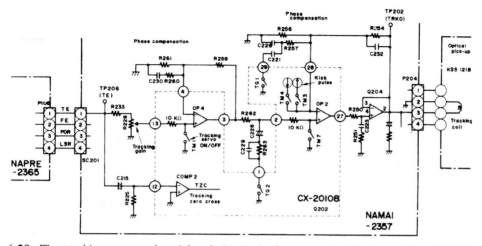

6-28 The tracking servo and peripheral circuits in the servo circuits of an Onkyo DX-200 player.

tor from pin 12 of Q202. Then, in response to an instruction from the microcomputer, the output passes from pin 5 (sense).

The Onkyo DX-200 track kick circuit is used when the laser beam skips to a relatively close pit track (from 1 to 100 tracks away) during track accessing and cue/review mode operations. Basically, this skipping is achieved by applying kick and brake pulses to the tracking coil with the tracking servo loop open.

TM1 switches on to cut the servo loop at the same time the negative/positive current source switches TM3 and TM4 (connected to the negative input of OP2 in Q202) on and off. Following a track kick, TG2 switches off and TG1 switches on to stabilize the dynamic characteristics of the servo loop (Fig. 6-28). At the same time, the TZC and MIR signals are monitored, and the servo loop switches on and off for better system-initiating performance (by suppressing generation of vibration in the tracking system). The timing for all these operations is determined by microcomputer instructions.

The Pioneer PD-7010 (BK) tracking servo circuit is shown in Fig. 6-17. The purpose of the tracking servo loop is to control horizontal alignment of the CD pickup so that the laser beam is accurately aimed at the pits on the disc surface (Fig. 6-29). On-and-off switching of the tracking servo occurs during track jump and search to locate the desired point on the disc. For proper start-up conditions, the correct focusing signal (FOK) must be available and the spindle motor must be turning.

When the FOK (focusing signal) is confirmed by the system control, acceleration of the spindle motor begins, and the "start tracking" data is at the output (Fig. 6-29). The RF and tracking error (TE) signals come from the pickup. The RF signal is then used to produce the MIRR signal. When RF exists, this signal is "L" (low). When RF does not exist, the MIRR signal is "H" (high). This provides the indispensable data needed to close tracking. (The MIRR signal is also used for judgement of the outer edge mirror and track count during search and jump.)

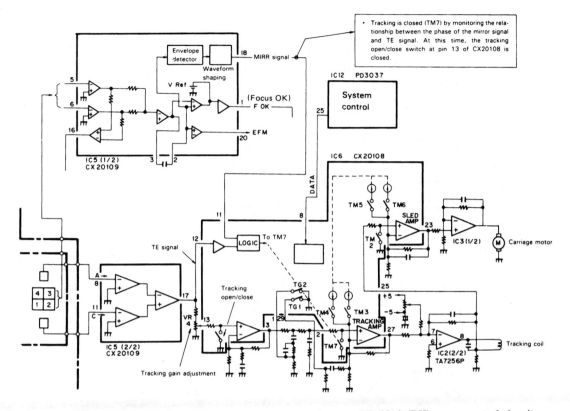

6-29 A block diagram of the tracking servo circuits in a Pioneer PD-9010 (BK) servo control circuit.

The system control indirectly knows that tracking has begun because when the RF signal exists, the MIRR signal is low, and the GFS is locked.

Both focus and tracking operations are performed by the servo IC6 (CX-20108), a 30-pin flat package. Extreme care must be used when replacing and installing a new CX-20108 servo IC. To improve servo performance with regard to disc scratches and other disc defects, a discrete defect correction circuit is included.

The spindle motor is located within the servo loop. The purpose of the spindle servo loop is to control disc rotation speed so that constant linear velocity (CLV) is maintained. (Disc speed is gradually lowered as the pickup moves from the inside of a disc to the outside as the disc is played.) The servo controls the spindle rotation speed to maintain the frame synch encoded in the disc pits at 7.35 kHz. A proper focusing signal (FOK) must be present before the spindle motor will start.

When the focus OK signal is confirmed by the system control, spindle acceleration is triggered for an interval of .300 ms. When tracking has begun and the PLL is locked, IC9 (CX-23035) generates an "H" GFS signal. This GFS signal tells the system control that the tracking and spindle servo loops are locked.

The PD-9010 (BX) Pioneer braking mode circuit is shown in Figs. 6-31 and 6-32. The brake mode circuit exists to make the smooth closing of tracking possible when the pickup and disc are moving in relation to each other. The directions of pickup and disc movement are detected using the phase relationship between the envelope and tracking error (at RF). Switching is conducted in such a way that the accelerating side of the tracking error is cut. Consequently, only the decelerating side is used. This operation, called the *brake mode*, is shown in Figs. 6-30 and 6-31 and can be controlled externally.

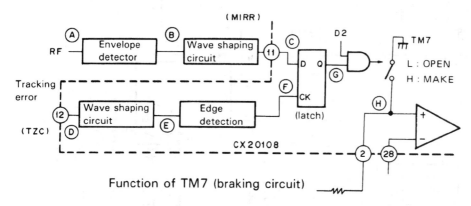

6-30   The braking circuit functions in Pioneer's PD-9010 (BK) servo control section.

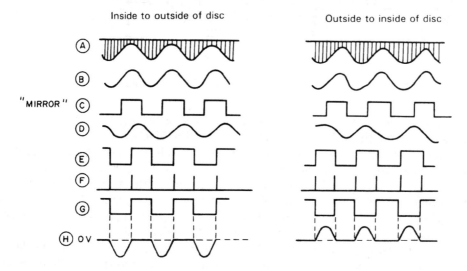

6-31   The braking mode operation waveforms in the Pioneer PD-9010 (BK) servo section.

The brake mode is used to close tracking after focusing. By doing this, smooth focus closing is possible even for tracks (line of pits) whose distance to the pickup is varying greatly due to disc eccentricity, warping, and other factors.

There are two gain settings for normal disc play: the nominal gain setting and the higher gain setting for track jump. The main loop consists of a one-stage fixed low-range gain compensator, a one-stage fixed high-range phase compensator, a one-stage switching high-range phase compensator, and a two-stage high-range noise-cut filter.

As shown in the diagram, there are two low-range and two high-range stages at the normal gain setting and two low-range and one high-range stages at the high-gain setting. Figure 6-32 shows the circuit configuration of this section. For normal gain, both TG1 and TG2 are on; for the high gain, both TG1 and TG2 are off.

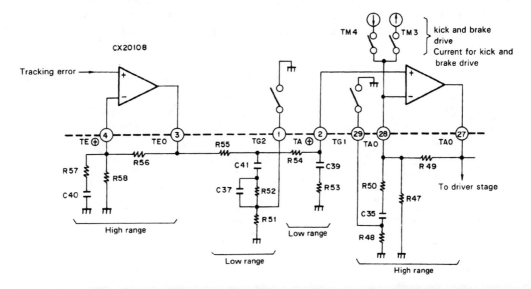

6-32 Pioneer PD-9010 (BK) high- and low-range kick brake operation circuits.

The drive supply current is 22 μA. Therefore, in this system, the output voltage of pin 27 is the voltage obtained when this current reaches the resistance between pins 28 and 27 (9.1 kΩ). In this case, the output voltage is 200 mV. This becomes the kick-and-brake drive voltage (output voltage at pin 27). This output voltage is then used for current drive of the tracking actuator in the final driver.

The Pioneer PD-9010 (BK) defect processing circuit of Fig. 6-33 detects disc defects (scratches, dirt, etc.) and switches the focus servo loop equalizer to improve

6-33 Pioneer's PD-9010 (BK) defect processing waveforms.

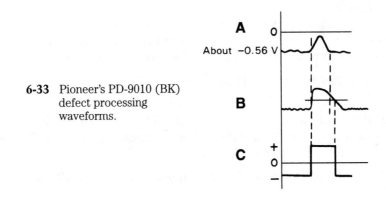

"playability" when such defects are encountered. Waveform (A) is the output of the leading beam of the three-beam tracking pickup. It is obtained from the preamp. This output changes in the manner shown on the right when a defect is encountered.

The output is amplified at IC7 2/2 and ends up as shown in diagram (B) due to a capacitor that extends the drop-off in the output (Fig. 6-34). By routing this output through a comparator, output (C) becomes correct from the beginning of the defect period to the point where the 2.4 ms time constant component is extended (after the defect period has ended). The focus servo equalizer switches by this procedure. Equalizer switching is executed by switching the transistors of Q2 and Q3 on using (C) output.

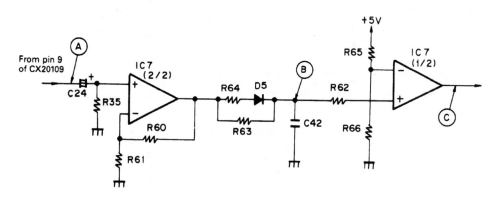

6-34   Defect processing circuit of the Pioneer PD-9010 (BK) servo circuit.

Realistic CD-3304 tracking servo system

The tracking error (TE) signal is fed from the RF amp IC501 to pin 3, through a reference adjustment of VR-503. This TE signal can be checked at test point TEO. The output signal at pin 17 goes to the tracking actuator IC506 and then to the tracking coil (Fig. 6-35).

The capacitor across pins 14 and 15 has a time constant to lower the high frequency when TG2 is switched off. The tracking phase compensation peak frequency is inversely proportional to the resistor connected to pin 23 (about 1.2 kHz when the resistor is 510 kΩ).

For a track jump in the FWD (fast forward) or REV (reverse) duration TM3 or TM4 are set ON. At this time, the peak voltage fed to the tracking coil is determined by TM3 and TM4 current values and the feedback resistor from pin B. That is:

Track jump peak voltage = *TM3 (TM4) current value × feedback resistor value.*

The FWD or REV sled kick is done by setting TM5 and TM6 to ON. At this time, the peak voltage added to the SLED motor is determined by TM5 or TM6 current value and the feedback resistor from pin 21.

SLED jump peak voltage = TM5 (TM6) current value × feedback resistor value.

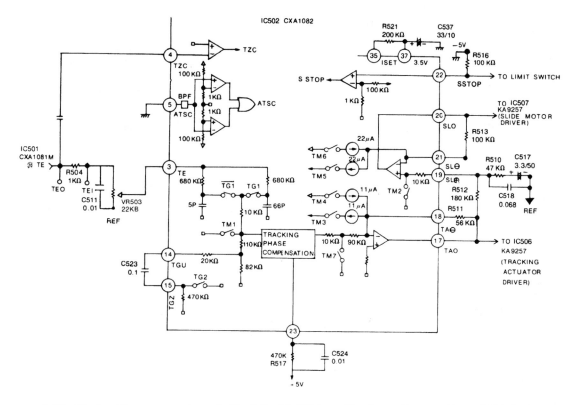

6-35 The tracking servo system of a Realistic CD-3304 combination radio, cassette, and CD player.

Each SW current value is determined by the resistor connected to pin 35 and 37, when the resistor is set at about 120 kΩ.

TM3 or TM4 ± 1.1 µa and TM5 or TM6 is ± 22 µA. This current value is almost inversely proportional to the resistor variable within a range of about 5 to 40 µA for TM3. S Stop is the on/off detection signal for the limit SW of the SLED motor innermost circumference.

Tracking coil drive circuits

The tracking coil drive circuit receives a signal from the servo IC and goes to the tracking coil transistors or ICs (Fig. 6-36). The servo IC can directly drive the drive transistors, or a drive IC could exist between them. In some models, the tracking coil is driven with two transistors inside an IC (Fig. 6-37). The tracking coil is located inside the optical pickup assembly.

Slide or carriage motor circuits

The slide, sled, feed, or carriage motor assembly is also operated from the same servo IC in most CD players. In a Mitsubishi DP-107 servo circuit, the servo IC207

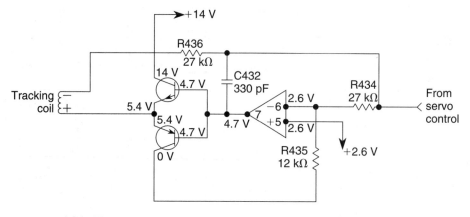

6-36 The tracking coil drive circuits in a Denon DCC-9770 CD player.

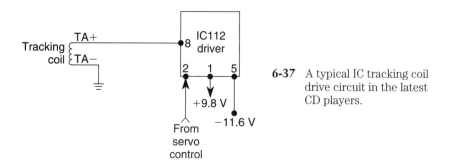

6-37 A typical IC tracking coil drive circuit in the latest CD players.

provides signal to op amp IC205B, which drives IC204B. The feed motor is con-nected to pin 6 of the drive IC204B (Fig. 6-38). (The feed or slide motor operation is given in detail in chapter 7.)

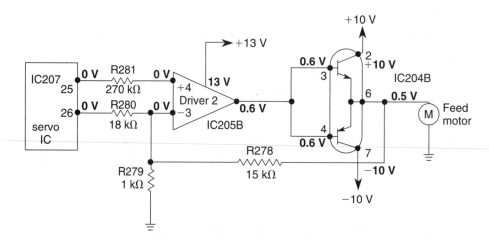

6-38 The feed motor circuit controlled by IC207 servo controls in the Mitsubishi DP-107 compact disc player.

Realistic boom-box servo and LPF circuits

The 200-Hz low-power filter (LPF) is formed with capacitor C542 (0.033 µF) and a 20-kΩ resistor connected to pin 42 and the secondary low-power filter (LPF) is formed with the built-in LPF (Fc up to 200 Hz within 510 kΩ for pin 23), and the carrier component of the CLV servo error signals MDS and MDP is eliminated (Fig. 6-39).

In the constant linear velocity (CLV) –S mode, F_{SW} becomes L (low) and pin 42 low-power filter (LPF) F_c lowers, strengthening the filter VCC (+5 V). F_c does not vary with power supply voltage fluctuations.

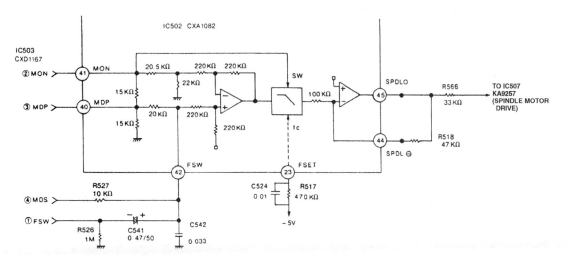

6-39 The spindle servo and low-power filter (LPF) in a Realistic CD-3304 boom-box player.

Servo problems

Determine if the CD player display lights are on and whether the spindle or disc motor is operating after the player shuts down. Notice if the focus and tracking coil assemblies began to search or move before shutdown. Check for FE, TE, and mirror signals from the RF amp IC. Does the RF amp have a constant EFM waveform before or after shutdown? Suspect a defective RF amp or optical system without an EFM or RF signal. Sometimes the EFM waveform can be taken before the player shuts down, indicating the optical pickup and RF amp is normal.

Suspect a defective focus circuit if neither the focus nor the motors operate. Check the tracing circuits when the tracking coil fails to operate. Test for TE and FE waveforms from servo IC to driver ICs or transistors. Measure the positive and negative supply voltage applied to the servo IC and driver IC or transistors. Check for a supply voltage at VCC pin of servo IC.

With correct EFM and RF waveforms, normal supply voltage, and no focus or tracking signal, suspect a defective servo IC. Disconnect servo voltage supply pin (VCC) to prevent shutdown and then check EFM waveform, TE, and FE signals at the RF amp to servo IC. Doublecheck the operation of spindle or SLED motor before deciding to remove and replace the Servo IC.

Check the focus and tracking drive ICs or transistors when adequate focus and tracking drive signals are present. Suspect a common driver IC when the focus and tracking coil, and SLED motor does not operate, fed from the same driver IC or combination IC and transistors. Check each drive transistor with a transistor in-circuit tester.

Take all voltage measurements with each circuit functioning and when no disc is in position. Compare these measurements with the manufacturers. Of course, the disc interlock must be shunted, to operate without a disc moving. Make sure the optical lens is covered or keep your eyes away from the lens while taking measurements. Suspect an open or defective focus and tracking coil if drive voltage is present.

7

The various motors and control circuits

THERE ARE THREE BASIC MOTORS FOUND IN THE TABLETOP CD PLAYER. USUALLY, the CD boom-box player has top loading, which eliminates the loading motor. The auto CD changer might have four or more motors while the tabletop changer might have up to five different motors (Fig. 7-1). You might find only two motors in the portable or combination CD and cassette player.

The tray or loading motor pushes out and pulls in the CD tray when the open/close switch is engaged. (A top-loading CD player has no loading motor.) A disc, spindle, or turntable motor rotates the CD disc at a variable speed, somewhat like the phonograph motor. Sometimes the disc or turntable motor is called the spindle motor. Although the phono motor operates at a constant speed, the disc motor travels faster at the beginning and slows down as the laser assembly moves toward the outside rim of the CD. The slide or sled motor moves the laser from the center to the outside of the CD on sliding rods (Fig. 7-2). Some players have a pickup motor that travels in a radial or semicircle fashion.

Tabletop changer motors

You might find a slide, disc, up/down, magazine, and loading motor within the tabletop changer (Fig. 7-3). The two new motors are the up/down and magazine motors. The up/down motor assists in loading and playing of disc while the magazine motor rotates the turntable (carousel) or changes the different discs for playing. The magazine motor can be referred to as a turntable motor. The up/down and magazine motors can operate directly from a dc source or from motor driver IC. In the Onkyo DX-C909 carousel player, the carousel, tray or loading, and chucking motors operate from microprocessor (system control) Q202 (Fig. 7-4).

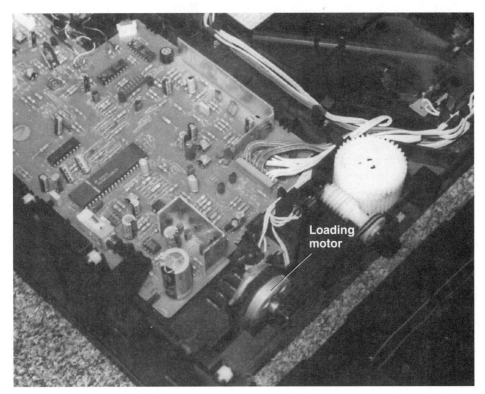

7-1 The belt-driven loading motor of a Magnavox CD CDC522 player moves the turntable tray in and out for loading and unloading.

7-2 The sled motor moves the laser assembly upon a sliding rod from center to outside rim of disc.

7-3 The table-top automatic disc changer can have a slide, disc, up/down, magazine, and loading motors.

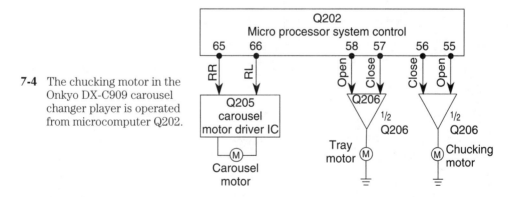

7-4 The chucking motor in the Onkyo DX-C909 carousel changer player is operated from microcomputer Q202.

Realistic CD-3370 portable CD motors

The CD-3370 portable CD player uses two motors: A sled motor that moves the laser pickup over the disc, and a spindle motor that rotates the disc (Fig. 7-5). A servo control circuit is used to control each motor.

A tracking servo signal is used to move the pickup horizontally. If the position of the pickup is out of the tracking control range set by the tracking coil, a dc compo-

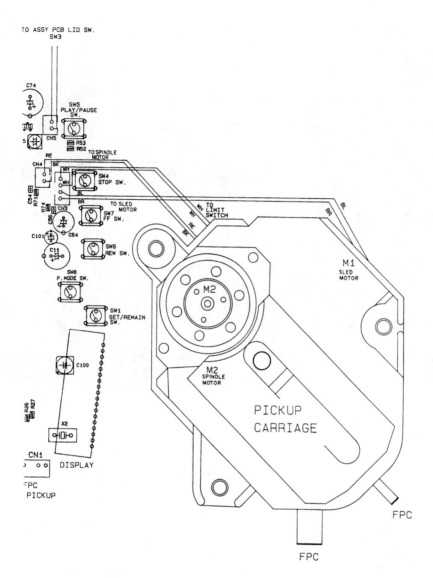

7-5 The Realistic CD-3370 portable player has a sled and spindle motor on one assembly.

nent appears on the tracking servo signal, pin 11 (TAO), of the servo signal proces-sor IC5. The dc component is amplified and appears on pin 14 (SLO). It is then fed to pin 1 of IC6 to drive the sled motor, which brings the pickup to within the line tracking control range (Fig. 7-6). The sled motor stops when the dc component be-comes zero, and the line tracking control regains control of the tracking.

When searching for a track or disc, the servo controller (IC5) applies a positive (at +) or a (at −) dc voltage to the sled motor to move the pickup through to the next track.

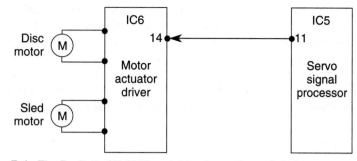

7-6 The Realistic CD-3370 portable player disc and sled motors are controlled by a common actuator motor driver IC6.

The spindle motor is controlled by a constant-linear-velocity (CLV) motor circuit. Because the pits on the disc must be read at a constant rate, the linear velocity of the track must be constant. Therefore, the angular velocity of the disc must be changed, depending on the position of the track being read, in order to maintain a constant linear velocity. So, the angular velocity must increase as the pickup moves toward the center of the disc.

The CLV circuit compares the phase of the RF signal to a reference clock from PCM decode/system control section of digital signal processor (IC3). An output pulse train appears on pin 39 (SPDLO) of IC5. When the motor speed is correct, a 50% duty cycle signal appears; a shorter duty cycle indicates the speed is too high. IC6 amplifies the signal, and uses it as a reference to control the spindle motor speed.

Motor troubles

A defective motor could be dead, intermittent, rotate slowly, or it might be very noisy. An open or "dead" motor can be located with continuity and voltage measurements. After isolating the correct motor function and locating the correct motor, a continuity measurement across the motor winding will indicate if the winding is open (Fig. 7-7). Remember, the resistance measurement across these motors should be practically zero. Likewise, improper voltage measurement across the motor windings can indicate a defective motor or motor circuit.

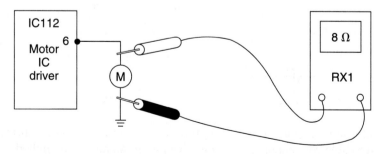

7-7 Check a suspected motor for open windings with the RX1 scale of ohmmeter. Most motors' resistance is below 10 Ω.

Some of the motors are located under the chassis, so it might be difficult to get at the motor terminals. Trace the motor terminals up to the main circuit board. Usually, they are plugged into some sort of socket. Check the suspected socket if the motor is intermittent or no voltage is present at the motor terminals (Fig. 7-8). This type of a socket connection can work loose after many hours of operation. Push the plug down tight. Sometimes the small clamps that dig into the connecting wire make a poor connection. This condition usually shows up after the player has been in use for some time.

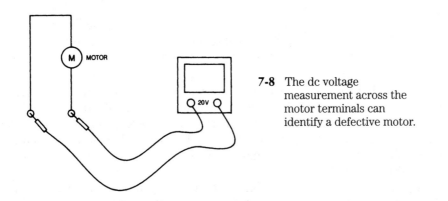

7-8 The dc voltage measurement across the motor terminals can identify a defective motor.

Remember, dc motors can operate in any direction by simply reversing the polarity of the supply voltage. Most CD motors can be checked with a "C" or "D" battery. A suspected motor should operate with 1½ volts applied across the motor terminals (Fig. 7-9). Apply the battery voltage at the motor terminals or make sure you have the correct pair of wires when injecting voltage into a socket. Always remove the socket from the main chassis before applying voltage in case you have the wrong component. The slide or tray motor might not rotate if it is at the end of its operation. Reverse the motor battery terminals or remove the motor for a good test.

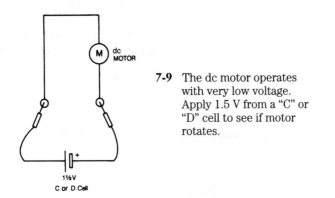

7-9 The dc motor operates with very low voltage. Apply 1.5 V from a "C" or "D" cell to see if motor rotates.

An intermittent motor can result from an intermittent motor control circuit, poor motor cable connections, or a defective motor. Monitor the applied voltage at the motor terminals. Notice if the motor is intermittent but has a constant voltage. If so, replace the defective motor. Suspect a defective motor circuit if the voltage varies when the motor speed acts up. Doublecheck the motor terminal wires at the motor terminals and where they plug into the main circuit board. Service the motor circuits if the voltage is intermittent or absent at the motor terminals.

Gummed-up motor bearings can slow the speed. This does not usually occur until after several years of operation. Clean the motor bearings with alcohol and cotton swab or other cleaning stick. The noisy motor may have worn or dry bearings. Most motors in the CD players are lubricated for the life of the player. Sometimes a drop of light oil on the motor bearing cures a noisy motor. Check for a worn bearing by checking end play and movement of the motor pulley. Replace the motor when the bearings are worn and noisy. All defective motors must be replaced with the original part number.

The tray, loading, or carriage motor

The tray or loading motor, also called the carriage motor, moves the tray in and out for loading and unloading the disc. In most players, this process is activated with a push button (push to open or to close). Usually, the plastic tray is driven by a plastic gear box next to the tray assembly (Fig. 7-10). This same gear assembly might operate a large plastic gear which raises and lowers the clamper assembly. When the tray is out for loading, the clamper (or flapper) assembly raises. As the tray is closing, the clamper provides spring-loaded pressure on the CD, holding it in position.

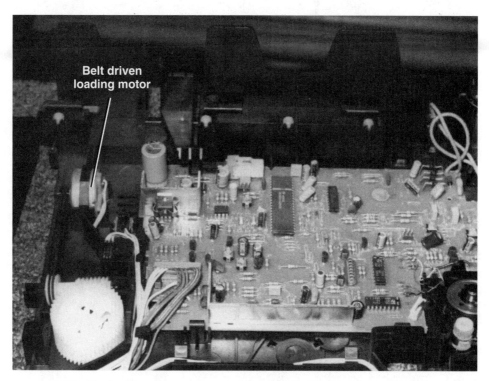

7-10 The loading motor can be mounted close to the driver gears side rails.

A dirty OPEN/CLOSE switch can cause intermittent or erratic tray operation. Inspect the button terminals for poor contact. Check the tray switch by shorting a test clip across the switch terminals. Check interlock switches in the same manner. A test lead with two small alligator clips on each end can do the trick. If the drawer will not open, check all possible mechanical problems first. Make sure the transit screw is removed (or loosened). Visually inspect the drawer gear assembly for foreign objects. Notice if the tray rails or gears are binding. Clean up the area and apply a light coat of lubricant to the sliding areas.

Make sure the small tray motor is stopped when the tray is out. Often a small leaf type switch is engaged by the large plastic drum that raises and lowers the flapper assembly. Dirty or poor contacts of this switch can cause erratic or no operation of the tray assembly. Clean the leaf contacts with contact cleaner. Place a piece of cardboard between the contacts, and holding the leaf contacts tight, move the cardboard back and forth to shine up the contacts.

The loading motor might drive the loading tray and gear box assembly with a small rubber belt. Oil and grease upon the belt can cause erratic tray loading operation. Clean off the belt with alcohol and swab. A broken or stretched belt can prevent the tray from opening or closing (Fig. 7-11). Although phono compound or liquid rosin applied to the motor pulley can help temporarily, the drive belt should be replaced. The slipping compound can be used while you are waiting for the arrival of a new belt.

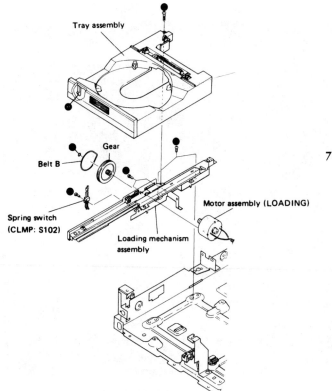

7-11 Here, the loading motor assembly is mounted horizontally and it turns a gear or belt to move the tray assembly in a Pioneer PD-7010 (BK) player.

Stripped gears on the loading pulley or alongside the tray carriage can jam or prevent the tray from opening and closing (Fig. 7-12). Carefully inspect both gear assemblies. These plastic gears might get stripped or broken if someone grabs the tray while loading or if you try to pry it open when it is stuck. Replacing the broken gear part is the only solution.

7-12 Besides opening and closing the tray door, the cam gear raises and lowers the clamper assembly over the loaded disc.

Pioneer PD-9010 carriage servo   The return resistance voltage of the tracking activator current driver final stage is used as the input (Fig. 7-13). The carriage movement drive is done by controlling the current supply in CX2108 with the serial data so that the input is a dc voltage (Fig. 7-14). Because this type of carriage drive system is used, the final stage employs voltage drive. Due to the gain setting, the movement drive is limited at about ± 11 V. Consequently, motor drive is a dc voltage if the unregulated voltage gets too high.

Replacing the tray or loading motor

The loading motor is rather easy to remove in most CD players. The motor usually is bolted to the main chassis. In some units, there might be a separate loading assembly. Locate the loading or carriage motor near the tray and clamper assembly. The bottom cover of the CD player must be removed or the main chassis pulled up if there is no removable cover. Remove the small motor pulley belt. Remove the pulley if the motor won't fit through the chassis hole. Now remove the mounting screws that hold the motor to the chassis base.

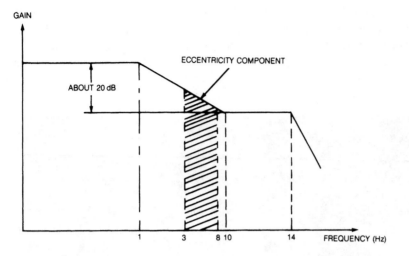

7-13 A carriage servo chart of the carriage motor circuit of a Pioneer PD-7010 model.

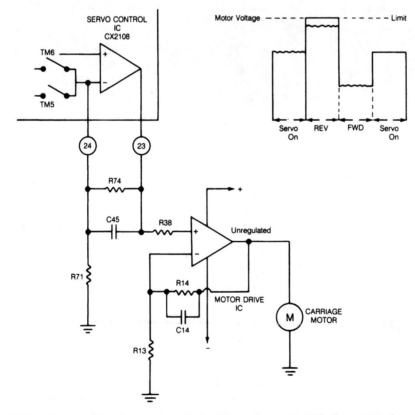

7-14 By controlling the current supply in the servo control IC, the output drive voltage goes to the drive motor IC and carriage motor in a Pioneer PD-9010 CD player.

RCA MCD-141 tray motor drive circuits When the loading motor switch SW-02 is closed, voltage goes to L1D-SW at pin 61 of IC601 (system control microprocessor). The IC601 control signal goes from pin 43 to the tray motor drive IC401 (Fig. 7-15). Here the output control voltage from pins 1 and 2 are tied to both base terminals of Q202 and Q203. A +10-V source goes to the collector terminal of the npn tray-drive transistor Q202, where a −10-V source is tied to the collector terminal of pnp transistor Q203. There should be a zero voltage at both base terminals until a control voltage is applied. The loading motor connects to both emitter terminals, and the other side of the motor is grounded to the chassis.

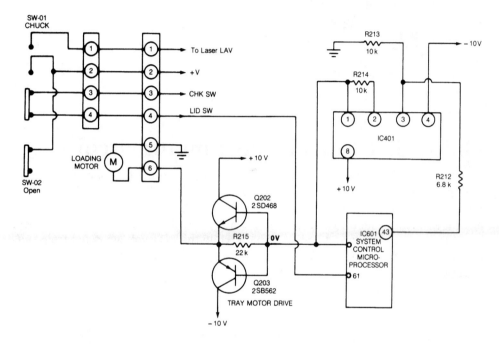

7-15 The tray motor controls drive circuits of an RCA MCD-141 CD player.

Yamaha CD-3 player tray motor In some models, the flapper and cam assembly must be removed before you can get at the motor mounting screws. Remove screw 6 and pull up on the cam assembly. Then, remove the motor pulley and belt. The motor mounting screws can be removed from the top of the main chassis (Fig. 7-16).

Sanyo CP500 loading motor Remove the center screw that holds the plastic cam that raises and lowers the plastic disc pressure lever. Pull the plastic cam off and then remove the idler gear. Now remove the loading drive belt. Remove the two small screws holding the loading motor to the plastic frame. Measure the distance from the top of the motor pull to the end belt of the defective motor so the motor pulley can be installed in the right place on the loading motor. Reverse the procedure when installing a new motor.

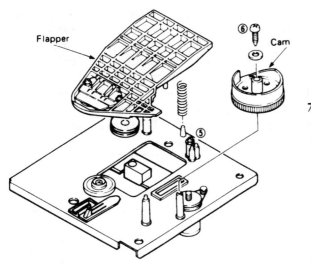

7-16 To remove the tray motor in a Yamaha CD-3 player, the flapper assembly and plastic cam must be removed first.

Onkyo DX-C606 loading motor circuits

The Onkyo loading motor loading circuits are controlled by the open signal from pin 58 of control IC Q202 and the close signal from pin 57. This signal is sent to pins 6 and 7 of motor driver IC (Q206) (Fig. 7-17). The positive and negative voltage for the loading motor is taken from pin 8 of Q206. One side of the loading motor (LD–) is connected to common ground while the LD+ voltage is fed from pin 8. Thus, the tray closes with a positive voltage and opens or pushes out with a negative voltage.

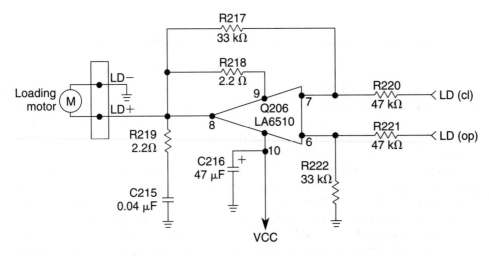

7-17 The loading motor circuit in an Onkyo DX-C606 CD player.

Slide, sled, or feed motor

The slide, sled, or feed motor moves the optical pickup assembly across the disc from the inside to the outside rim of the CD, keeping the object lens constantly in line with the center of the optical axis (Fig. 7-18). The motor is gear-driven to a rotating gear that moves the laser beam down two sliding bars. In some players, the feed motor moves the laser pickup assembly in an arc or radial direction across the CD. The slide motor might have a fast forward and rewinding mode operation.

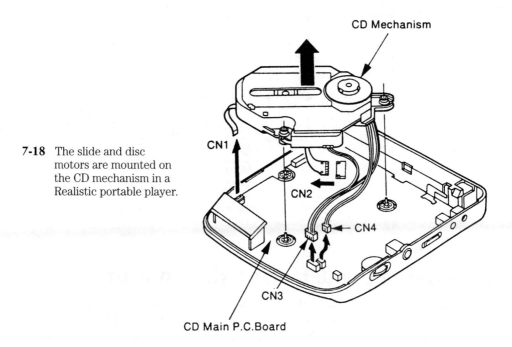

7-18 The slide and disc motors are mounted on the CD mechanism in a Realistic portable player.

Erratic or intermittent operation of the slide motor might be caused by a gummed-up track or poor meshing of the pulley and gears. Check the voltage on the slide motor terminals and note whether the voltage is intermittent. Erratic signal voltage can result from a defective transistor or IC motor circuit. Apply the battery voltage to the motor and note whether the motor and pickup assembly operates intermittently. Do not overlook a defective motor. Often a voltage and continuity measurement across the motor terminals can identify an open feed motor. Some slide motor circuits have a slide voltage test point terminal.

In some models, the slide or carriage motor has a motor pulley that drives a worm pulley to slowly move the pickup assembly with a small motor belt. If the belt is loose or broken, the carriage or optical pickup will not move. Inspect the pulley belt for oil spots when there is erratic movement. Replace the belt if it shows any signs of slipping.

Realistic boom-box slide and disc motors

The Realistic slide and disc motors are controlled by servo control LSI (IC502). This signal is sent to ¼ of IC507 driver IC which controls both legs of the slide motor (Fig. 7-19). IC502 also controls ¼ of IC507 driver IC to operate the disc motor. IC502 has four op amps inside a common component.

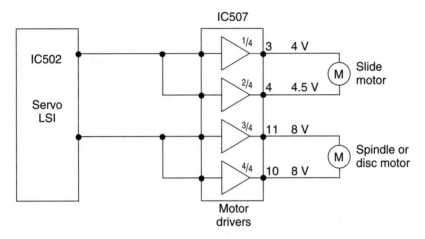

7-19   Servo LSI IC502 controls a four section op amp of IC507 driver for sled and spindle motors of a Realistic CD-3304 player.

Removing the defective slide motor

Locate the slide or feed motor on the main chassis after it is found defective. Usually, the motor is located close to the bar tracks (Fig. 7-20). Two small mounting bolts usually hold the slide motor to the bottom chassis. Remove the gear or pulley so the motor shaft can be pulled through the chassis hole. Observe correct polarity when replacing the slide motor.

In some models, the plastic sled motor assembly must be removed before you can get at the slide motor. Four or more screws must be removed before the plastic assembly can be pulled upward. The two motor-mounting screws can now be removed, releasing the motor. Before replacing the new slide motor, also replace the gear assembly. Measure the distance between the outside gear and the top side of the motor end belt so the gear can be correctly placed on the new slide motor (Fig. 7-21).

RCA MCD-141 feed motor removal

When installing the motor drive pickup assembly, take care not to damage the worm gear of the feed motor assembly. After the installation of the feed motor is completed, check the play between the worm gear and feed gear. Then, move the motor drive pickup assembly outward as shown in Fig. 7-22.

7-20 The slide or sled motor is mounted on a separate section of a Sharp boom-box QT-CD7 (GY).

7-21 Before removing any motor, measure the gear or motor pulley setting from pulley to motor assembly for when replacing the new motor.

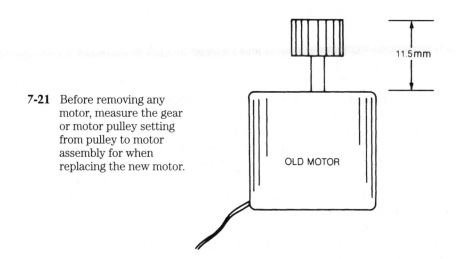

Pioneer PD-7010 (BK) carriage motor removal

You must remove the clamper assembly and mechanism chassis before you can get at the carriage (feed) motor assembly (Fig. 7-23). The carriage motor assembly is mounted on a motor base with a small drive pulley. The carriage motor turns belt A, which in turn rotates the drive worm gear assembly, moving the pickup assembly along the guide bars. Two small motor bolts hold the carriage motor to a motor base plate. Reverse the procedure after installing the new motor.

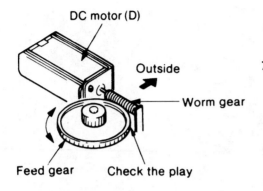

DC motor (D)

Outside

Worm gear

Feed gear   Check the play

7-22 The dc feed motor worm gear assembly should be checked for proper alignment after replacement in the RCA MCD-141 model.

The spindle, disc, or turntable motor

The spindle motor starts to rotate after the disc has been loaded. A small platform that is mounted on the turntable motor shaft spins the CD at a variable speed (Fig. 7-24). The spindle motor is located right under the clamper or flapper assembly. The disc starts out at approximately 500 rpm and slows down as the laser pickup assembly moves toward the outer rim of the CD (approximately 200 rpm).

Check the spindle disc motor with voltage and continuity measurements as the rest of the motors in the CD players. Check the spindle motor drive transistor or IC if the motor tests are normal.

Sylvania Model FDD104 turntable motor In this model, the disc turntable motor is located on the RAFOC (radial and focusing unit). The turntable motor rotates while the radial assembly starts at the beginning of the disc and moves in a radial or arc-type crossing of the CD (Fig. 7-25). To replace the defective turntable motor, decase the frame. Remove the preamplifier PC board, which is fixed to the CD mechanism by four screws. The turntable motor is fixed to the chassis plate by means of three screws. For mounting a new motor, screw A should be replaced first. After mounting the new motor, check the angle disc/light path and height setting of the turntable.

Pioneer Model PD-7010 disc motor When the disc table of the spindle motor is remounted by pressure insertion, always make contact with the stopper below the spindle motor and insert a spacer (Q4MM hexagonal wrench, etc.) to ensure that the gap between the disc table and mechanism chassis is as shown in Fig. 7-26. Apply added pressure from directly above. Always measure the distance between disc table and mechanism chassis before removing the turntable motor so the disc table is of the correct height after installing a new motor.

RCA MCD-141 disc motor removal

1. The top cover, front panel, loading mechanism, and laser assembly must be removed to get at the disc motor (Fig. 7-27).

2. Loosen the hex setscrew and remove the tray stopper along with the disc turntable in the direction of arrow A.

3. Remove the two (2) screws holding the disc turntable motor to the support plate C, then remove.

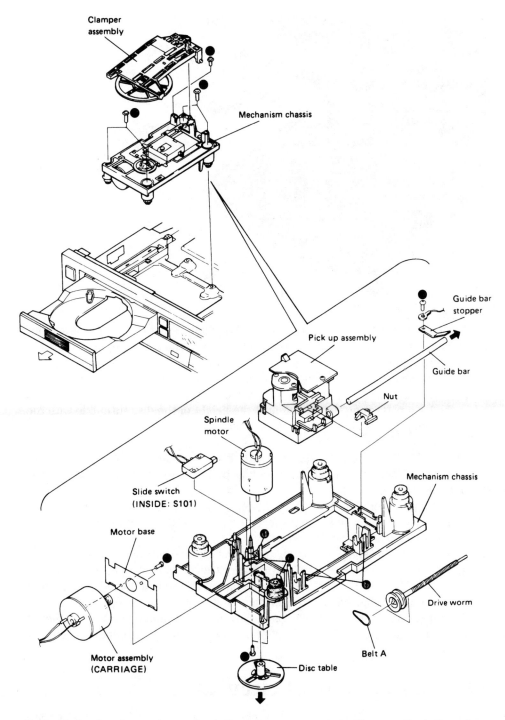

7-23 Notice that the carriage and spindle motors are mounted with respective belts and worm gear in a Pioneer PD-7010 (BK) player.

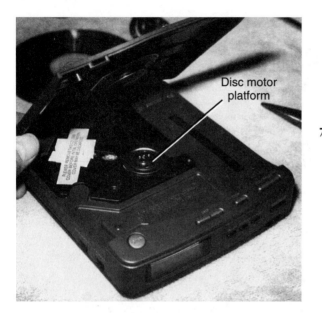

Disc motor
platform

7-24 The small platform in
the middle of an RCA
portable CD player is
connected directly to the
disc motor.

During reinstallation or replacement of the pickup drive (dc) motor assembly, disc turntable motor, coil spring, feed bar, actuator, and the tray stopper, use the following precautions.

When replacing the disc turntable motor, do not apply excessive force in the direction (B) on the unit support plate (C) as shown in Fig. 7-28. This can result in a diminished eye pattern on the disc. Adjust the height of the disc turntable with the turntable height (stock number 176286) and do not apply excessive force to the disc turntable motor shaft.

JVC XL-V400B spindle motor removal First demount the tray assembly. Detach the lever. The lever can be extracted by pulling it upward while pushing the catch in the arrow (Fig. 7-29).

Detach the holder by removing the screw. After the holder has been reinstalled, correctly replace the toggle spring. Now extract the turntable and remove the two screws from the spindle motor assembly.

Reinstall the new spindle motor by replacing the two screws, applying uniform tightening torque pressure. Insert the turntable straight while supporting the motor at its lowest section, and ensure accurate alignment to obtain a height of 12.5 mm ± 0.1 mm from the mechanical base top surface (Fig. 7-30).

After pressure insertion is made, bond the motor shaft and turntable together at the top. Sparingly use the bonding agent of Loclite #460. Keep the bonding agent out of the motor bearings.

Tray motor control circuits

The tray or loading motor is controlled by a loading driver IC or transistors and a signal from the system control IC processor (Fig. 7-31). Usually, a single positive voltage source goes to the balanced transistor circuit. After verifying that the motor itself is

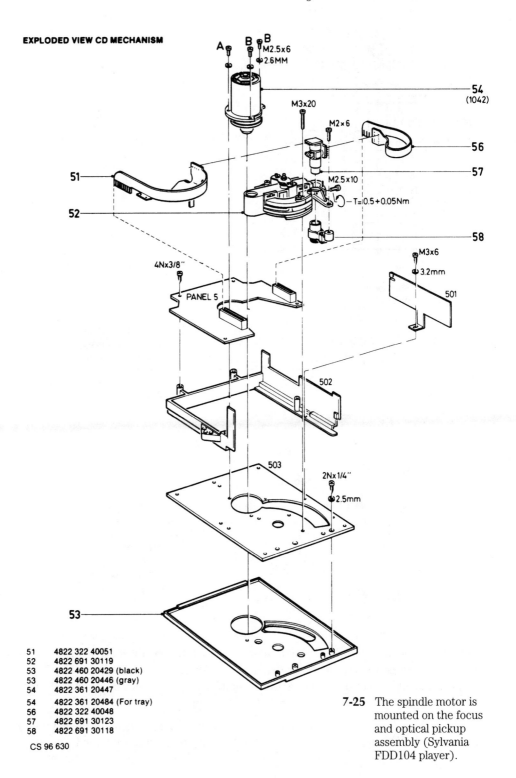

EXPLODED VIEW CD MECHANISM

51	4822 322 40051
52	4822 691 30119
53	4822 460 20429 (black)
53	4822 460 20446 (gray)
54	4822 361 20447
54	4822 361 20484 (For tray)
56	4822 322 40048
57	4822 691 30123
58	4822 691 30118

CS 96 630

7-25 The spindle motor is mounted on the focus and optical pickup assembly (Sylvania FDD104 player).

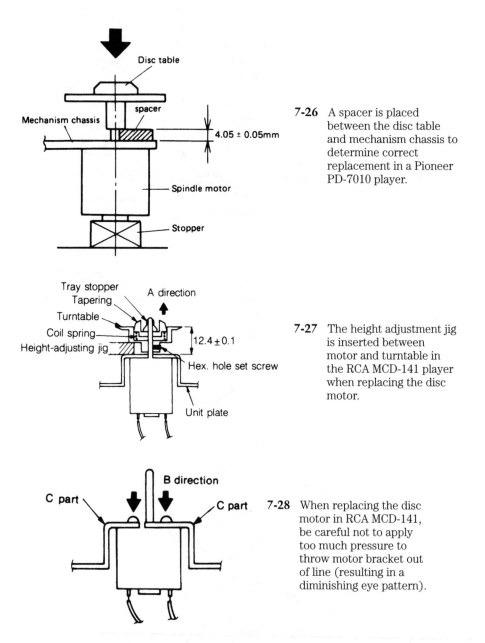

7-26 A spacer is placed between the disc table and mechanism chassis to determine correct replacement in a Pioneer PD-7010 player.

7-27 The height adjustment jig is inserted between motor and turntable in the RCA MCD-141 player when replacing the disc motor.

7-28 When replacing the disc motor in RCA MCD-141, be careful not to apply too much pressure to throw motor bracket out of line (resulting in a diminishing eye pattern).

normal, take accurate voltage measurements on each transistor in the loading motor driver circuit. Test each transistor with a transistor or diode test of a DMM (Fig. 7-32). Suspect a defective control IC processor if the transistor and motor circuit test okay. Do not overlook the possibility of improper voltage at the voltage source.

Yamaha CD-3 loading motor circuit   The loading motor might feed directly from a single IC component. The open/close signal from the processor IC controls the loading motor driving circuit (Fig. 7-33). The loading motor output is taken from

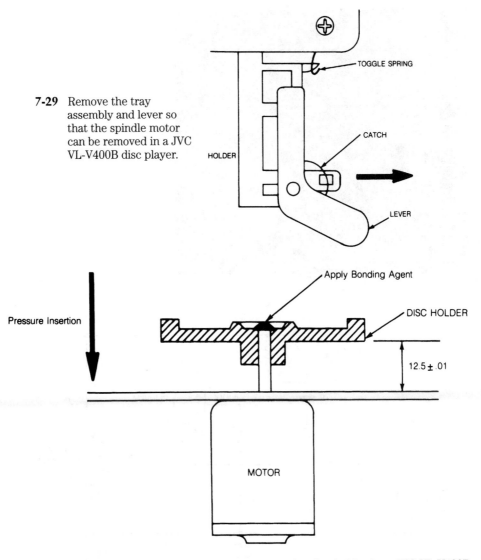

7-29 Remove the tray assembly and lever so that the spindle motor can be removed in a JVC VL-V400B disc player.

7-30 Be careful when applying pressure in replacing the disc holder in a JVC VL-V400B player.

pins 2 and 10 of the loading motor driver IC304. Notice the two different test points on the motor terminals indicating a +5 V close mode. A +15 V power source supplies voltage to pin 8 of IC304.

Onkyo DX-200 tray motor circuit Figure 7-34 shows the circuit used to control disc tray opening and closing operations. Control signals are passed directly from the Q282 microcomputer to pins 2 and 3 of the Q284 tray motor driver. In response, the respective modes are determined by the outputs from pins 7 and 8 as indicated in Fig. 7-35.

7-31 The tray or loading motor might be controlled with an IC or transistors.

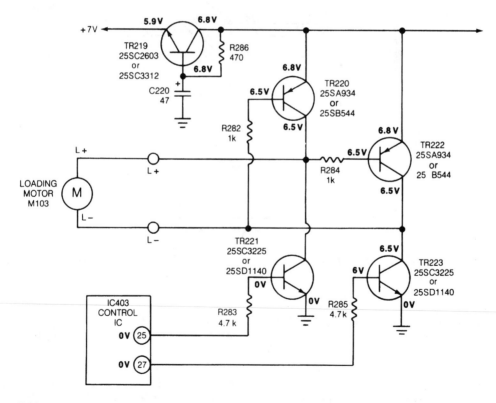

7-32 Take critical voltage and resistance measurements on the motor, loading IC, or transistors when the motor seems to be normal. Test each transistor with an in-circuit transistor tester.

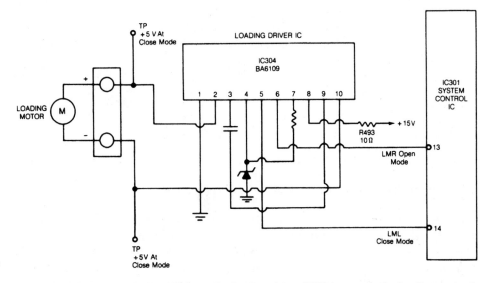

7-33 The control signal from IC301 to the loading driver IC304 controls the loading motor in a Yamaha CD-3 loading motor circuit.

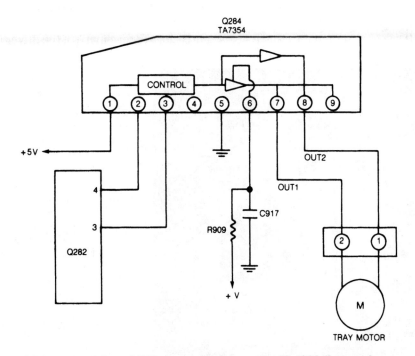

7-34 A signal from Q282 goes to the tray motor IC (Q284) to produce a voltage to rotate the tray motor in the Onkyo DX-200 motor circuit.

IN1	IN2	OUT1	OUT2	MODE
1	1	L	L	Stop
1	0	H	L	Close
0	1	L	H	Open

7-35 The Onkyo DX-200 table of levels for tray operation.

Slide motor control circuits

The slide or feed motor moves the laser pickup assembly from the center to the outside rim of the CD, and is controlled with either a transistor or IC driver circuit (Fig. 7-36). A phase correction IC signal goes from the signal IC with a control signal from the control or servo system processor (Fig. 7-37). Notice a positive and negative 11.3 V is fed to the collector terminals of Q104 and Q103 driver transistors. Also note that Q104 is an npn and Q103 is a pnp transistor. Only a fourth of IC101 is used in the phase correction IC. The slide motor control circuit feeds from terminals 26 and 27 of the servo control IC203.

Pioneer PD-7010 carriage drive circuits The carriage or slide motor in this CD player operates directly from one-half of the driver IC3. The control signal from the servo control IC6 goes from terminals 23 and 24 to pin 4 of IC3 (Fig. 7-38). A positive 10 V goes to terminal 10, and a –10-V source goes to terminal 5 of the driver IC3.

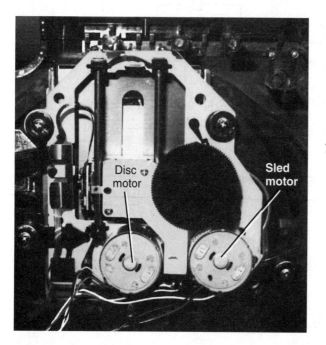

7-36 The slide and disc motors in a portable Sony CD player is operated from one large IC.

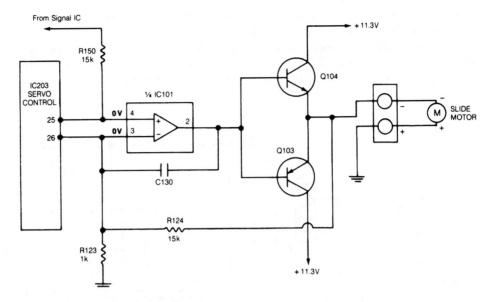

7-37 The signal from servo control IC203 drives motor driver IC101 to two output transistors are used in several slide, sled or carriage motor circuits.

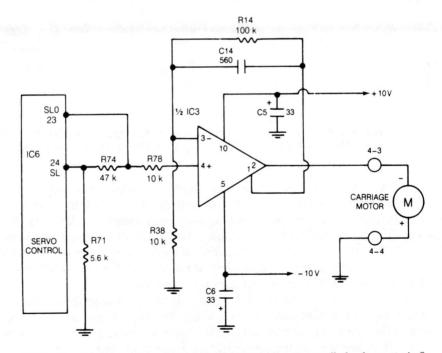

7-38 The signal from the servo control IC6 provides a controlled voltage at pin 2 of motor driver IC3 to the Pioneer PD-7010 carriage motor.

Notice the carriage motor positive (+) connection is at chassis ground. The other half of IC3 feeds the spindle motor circuits.

Onkyo DX-200 slide motor drive circuit The slide motor drive circuit (also called the feed motor servo circuit) is used to move the complete pickup towards the outer edge of the disc, keeping the object lens constantly in line with the center of the optical axis (Fig. 7-39).

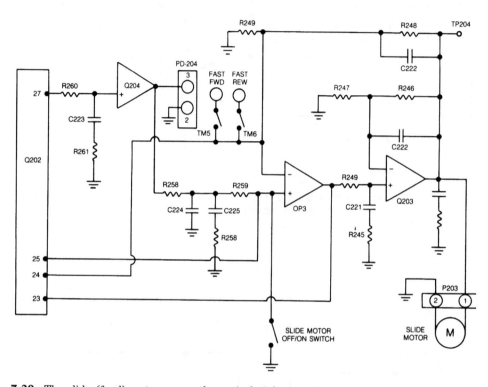

7-39 The slide (feed) motor moves the optical pickup to the edge of compact disc with a control signal from Q204, OP3, and Q203 in an Onkyo DX-200 slide motor circuit.

When the object lens moves toward the edge of the disc while tracing the pit tracks under tracking servo control, the dc voltage at the tracking drive output (TP202) gradually increases. The high-frequency components of this voltage is cut by R258, C224, C225, and R254 before passing from pin 25 of Q202 via OP3 to pin 23 and the Q203 driver to drive the slide motor. TM2 is the slide motor servo ON/OFF switch. Fast forwarding and fast rewinding of the slide motor can be achieved by switching TM5 and TM6 on and off for smoother accessing.

RCA MCD-141 slide motor circuits The slide motor controls the movement of the pickup assembly in the radial direction of the disc. During normal play, the slide motor sets the operating position so that the object lens is aligned with the center axis of the laser beams or so the center (dc component) of the operating voltage of the tracking activator (TAC) is 0 V.

The slide feed signal driving the slide motor is obtained by deriving only the dc component from the tracking activator (TAC) signal through a low-pass filter consisting of C112, C113, R115, and R117 (Fig. 7-40). Whenever the dc average of the TAC signal exceeds the predetermined level or when the operating position of the object lens deviates from the center axis by a predetermined value or more, the slide feed motor signal sets the feed motor and pickup assembly back to its center axis position again.

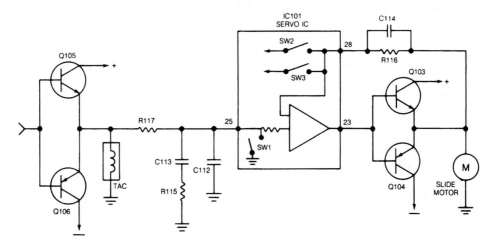

7-40   The controlled dc voltage from the IC101 biases the motor drive transistors Q103 and Q104 to operate the slide motor in the RCA MCD-141 motor circuits.

During high-speed access such as a program search, the feed servo signal is cut off (SW1 is on), and a large drive voltage goes to the slide motor by turning on SW2 (or SW3) so the pickup assembly can be moved at high radial disc speed.

Check the slide motor drive circuits with accurate voltage and resistance measurements. Make sure both positive and negative voltage sources are present at the respective driver transistor or IC components. Take in-circuit transistor tests of each transistor with the diode/transistor test of the DMM. Remember, in erratic or intermittent operations, one of the transistors might be opening only under loaded conditions. Replacement of both driver transistors might be necessary to correct the intermittent operation. Improper voltages on the slide or feed IC driver component can be caused by a leaky driver IC.

Spindle or turntable motor circuits

The spindle, turntable, or disc motor circuit consists of transistors or IC components within the drive motor circuit (Fig. 7-41). The spindle motor drive component is controlled by a PLL and servo processor circuits. The CLV (constant linear velocity) motor circuit might be controlled directly from one large IC processor. In Fig. 7-42, the solid-state disc motor system has two different test points with a motor gain adjustment for the Realistic CD1000 compact disc player.

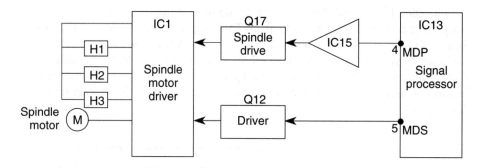

7-41   The spindle motor drive circuits in a Denon DCH-500 CD changer.

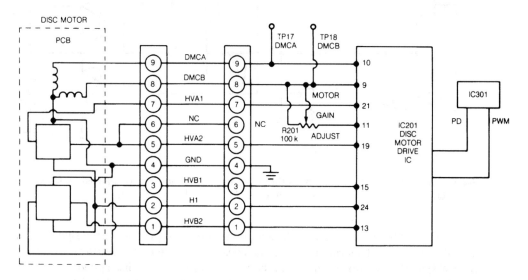

7-42   IC201 operates the CLV (constant linear velocity) circuit in a Realistic CD-1000 player.

After verifying the motor itself is normal, check the voltages on the drive transistors and IC. Test each transistor in-circuit with the transistor tester. If a transistor does not test as it should, remove it and test once again. Check the voltage on each collector and base terminal. Notice Q315 is an npn and Q316 is a pnp transistor (Fig. 7-43). Transistor Q315 is fed with a +5 V and Q316 has a –5 V tied to the collector terminal. If the motor and drive circuits seem normal, check the control signal at the servo controller IC301.

Onkyo DX-200 spindle motor servo circuit   The CD playback is based on a CLV (constant linear velocity) system where different rotational speeds are required at the start and end of the disc. The mechanism used to achieve constant linear velocity consists of a PLL circuit for extracting clock signals from the playback ERM signal and a servo circuit for controlling the motor on the basis of the clock signals.

The spindle motor control outputs come from pins 1 through 4 of Q303 (Fig. 7-44). Pin 1 (FSW) is the spindle motor time-constant selector pin. This pin is

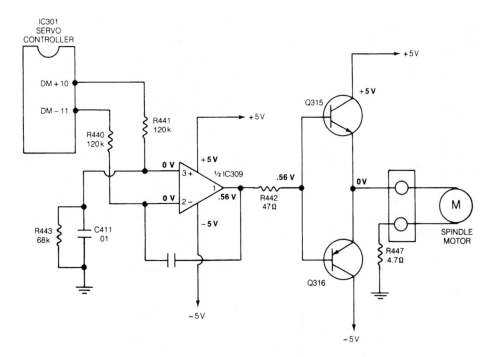

7-43 The spindle motor drive circuits in a JVC XL-V400B player are controlled by the servo controller IC301, IC309, and transistors Q315 and Q316.

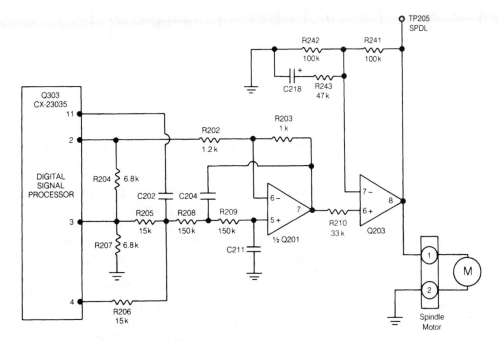

7-44 The CLV spindle motor circuit in an Onkyo DX-200 controlled by Q303, Q201, and Q203.

switched to high impedance when the PLL is locked and to low impedance when unlocked, thereby eliminating high-frequency components.

Pin 2 (MON) is the monitor on/off control output (on when high). Pin 3 (MDP) is the rough servo output when PLL is not locked and is phase control output when the PLL is locked. The output is low in the stop mode. Pin 4 (MDS) is the frequency control output when the PLL is locked and switches to high impedance when PLL is unlocked. The output is low in the stop mode.

RCA MCD-141 disc motor drive circuits The compact disc is recorded at a constant linear velocity. This means the disc rotation must be redirected as the laser pickup tracks towards the disc's outer edge. The revolutions vary from 500 to 200 rpm.

The motor speed is controlled by signals from IC402 (pins 1-4) to IC301 (pins 3 and 5) of the disc motor drive (Fig. 7-45). The signal generated within IC301 is compared with that entering at IC301-6 for phase correction. The correction signals go to the regulated circuitry (Q301 and Q302) and the disc motor.

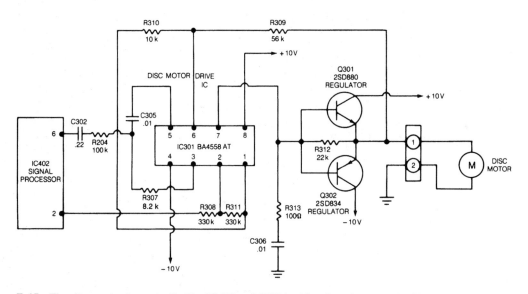

7-45 The disc motor is controlled by IC402 and IC301 with a dc voltage applied to drive transistors Q301 and Q302 in the RCA MCD-141 disc motor circuit.

Onkyo DX-C909 chucking motor circuits The Onkyo six-disc changer chucking motor is controlled by a signal from the servo micro processor (Q202) at pins 56 and 57. This open and close signal is sent to driver IC (Q206). The chucking motor terminals are tied to common ground and the positive terminal connects directly to driver IC pin 2 (Fig. 7-46). Because Q206 is a dual op amp, both loading and chucking motors are driven within the same IC (Fig. 7-47).

Denon DCH-500 elevator motor circuits In the Denon DCH-500 auto changer CD player, the elevator and disc motors are operated with a common IC driver (IC501). The elevator motor terminals are 2 and 10. The disc motor terminals are pins 3 and 10. Motor driver IC501 is controlled from pins 23, 24, and 25 of the system control IC601 (Fig. 7-48). Suspect IC501 when both motors are dead.

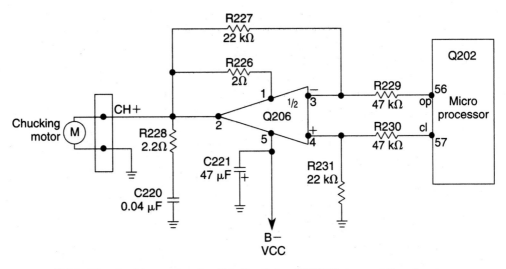

7-46 The chucking motor circuit in the Onkyo DXC909 carousel disc changer.

LA6510 (Motor Drive)

7-47 The motor drive duo-op amp IC (LA6510) provides drive for the loading motor in Onkyo DX-C909 player.

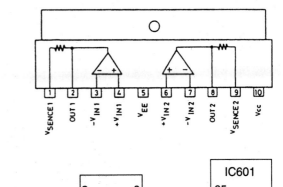

7-48 The system control IC drives the motor driver IC501 for both elevator and disc motors in a Denon DCH-500 player.

Mitsubishi M-C4030 up/down and magazine motors The signal for controlling the up/down and magazine motors is taken from the micro computer control IC301. Both motors are controlled from a dual bidirectional motor driver IC302 (Fig. 7-49). The input control signals from micro computer are fed to pins 4, 5, and 6 of IC302.

The magazine motor can be the same as a loading motor. The output voltage taken from pin 10 of IC302 driver, feeds directly to one side of the magazine motor

IC302: M54649L DUAL BI-DIRECTIONAL MOTOR DRIVER

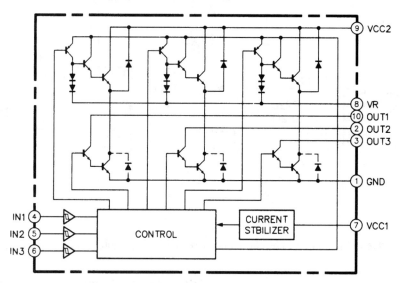

7-49 The internal construction of a dual bi-directional motor driver IC302 for the magazine and an up/down motor in Mitsubishi M-C4030 player.

terminals. The common motor terminals of magazine and up/down motors are pin 10 of driver IC302. The voltage on pin 3 of IC302 drives the magazine motor (Fig. 7-50). The up/down motor drive voltage is found at output pin 2.

7-50 A dual-motor driver (IC302) provides motor voltage for both up/down and magazine motors in a Mitsubishi M-C4030 CD player.

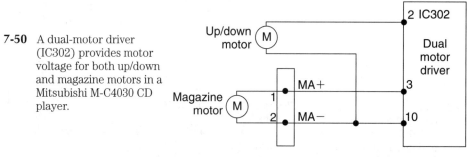

Conclusion

Locate the defective motor on the chassis. Take critical voltage and continuity measurements on the motor terminals. Check the driver transistors and ICs feeding the suspected motor. If the motor is normal, test each transistor with a transistor tester or diode/transistor test of the DMM. If the motor is defective, take extreme care in replacement. Do not apply too much downward pressure to misalign the motor assembly. Always measure the location of motor pulley or gear so it can be correctly replaced on the new motor. Make sure the motor is installed with correct polarity in the circuit.

Chart 7-1 displays the motor troubleshooting chart.

Chart 7-1. CD motor troubleshooting chart.

Motor	Symptom	Defective circuit
Loading motor	Dead	Inspect motor drive belt. Check motor continuity, test voltage applied to motor in operation. Check transistor or drive IC. Check signal applied to motor driver.
	Erratic operation	Inspect drive belt. Inspect area for foreign materials. Check for grease on motor belt. Check for binding track. Suspect erratic motor. Monitor voltage applied to motor terminals. Suspect erratic driver IC.
	Intermittent	Check for poor motor terminals and connections. Inspect motor plugs and jacks. Defective motor. Defective motor driver IC.
Sled–slide or feed motor	Dead	Check motor continuity. Check voltage at motor. Check supply voltage on motor driver IC. Check output voltage at driver IC. Check servo signal from signal processor or control IC.
	Intermittent	Monitor motor voltage. Suspect erratic motor. Inspect motor terminals and plugs. Check for gummed up or dry sliding surfaces on rails.
Disc or spindle motor	Dead	Check motor voltage. Check continuity of motor. Check voltage on motor driver. Measure VCC supply voltage on motor driver IC. Check CLV spindle motor IC. Check signal from servo control IC.
	Comes on shuts down	Notice if all functions are shut down. Check for RF or EFM waveform at RF amp. Check for defective motor circuits if RF or EFM waveform is found at RF amp. Suspect defective CLV spindle motor driver circuits.
Carousel or turn-table motors	Dead	Measure motor continuity. Check voltage at motor. Check voltage at driver. Test for both + and – voltage at driver IC or transistors. Check signal at micro processor IC.
	Intermittent	Monitor motor voltage. Suspect motor. Check motor driver IC.
	Erratic	Check turntable for improper mounting. Check for wires clinging to the bottom of turntable. Inspect start/stop switch. Monitor voltage at motor terminals. Suspect defective motor.

8

The audio circuits

THE TYPICAL COMPACT DISC AUDIO SECTION CONSISTS OF A D/A CONVERTER, sample/hold, low-pass filter network, audio IC amplifiers and headphone circuits. The digital signal is fed into the D/A IC and then it is converted to an audio signal. This stereo signal is connected to separate sample-and-hold circuits that separate the left channel sound for the left channel circuitry and the right channel sound to the right channel circuitry. Each audio signal is then filtered to remove the 44.1 kHz signal from the audio, which is passed on to IC amplifiers. Separate IC audio circuits might be provided for headphone reception; however, some CD players do not have separate headphone circuits (Fig. 8-1).

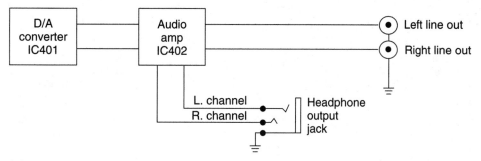

8-1 Block diagram of the stereo audio from D/A converter (IC401) to a dual-audio amp IC402 with stereo line and headphone output in a Mitsubishi M-C4030 CD player.

Boom-box CD-cassette player

The boom-box CD, radio, and cassette player uses the same audio amplifier circuits and speakers (Fig. 8-2). Instead of line output jacks this boom-box combination player has

8-2 The CD player in a Sharp boom-box player uses the same audio amp and speakers.

internal speakers and headphone stereo reception. You might find some units that have both headphone and line output jacks. The output signal from D/A converter can have one IC that amplifies both stereo channels before switching into the regular audio circuits. The CD audio signal is switched by a rotary function switch (Fig. 8-3).

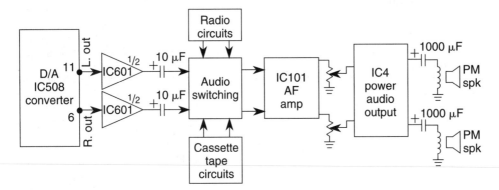

8-3 Block diagram of Sharp's QT-CD7(GY) boom-box audio circuits in CD, radio, and cassette player.

The rotary function switch selects audio signals from the radio, cassette, or compact disc player by simply rotating the function switch. The audio output from this CD player is then coupled by electrolytic capacitors into input AF transistors or one large IC preamp (Fig. 8-4). Usually, one large IC is found in the output circuits driving a heavy duty 4 or 6-inch pm speaker (Fig. 8-5).

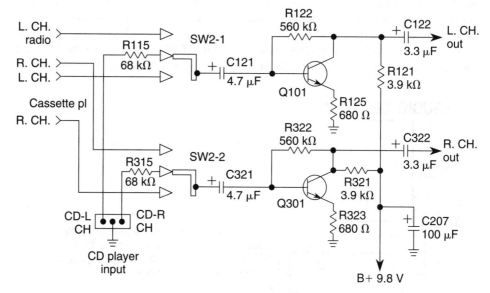

8-4 The different radio, cassette, and CD audio inputs are switched into a transistor AF amp stage in the boom-box CD player.

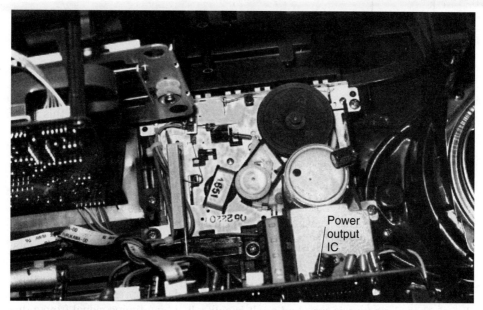

8-5 One large power output IC is found in Sharp's QT-CD7(GY) combination CD, radio, and cassette player.

RCA MCD-141 D/A converter sound circuits The serial data from IC412 is converted from digital to analog (audio) information by IC501 (Fig. 8-6). The audio data is still in the serial format, left information sample followed by right information sample, etc. From IC501 pins 15 and 23, the serial data is then fed to the right and left channel circuitry where a sample-and-hold circuit (IC502R and IC502L) separate the right channel data for the right channel circuitry and the left channel data for the left channel circuitry. The audio is then filtered by CP501R and CP501L to remove the 44.1-kHz signal, is amplified by IC503R and IC503L, and then goes to the system control bus.

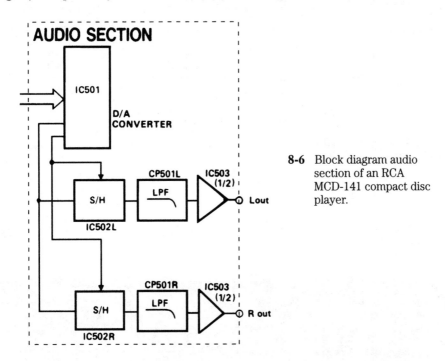

8-6 Block diagram audio section of an RCA MCD-141 compact disc player.

Pioneer Model PD-9010X, PD-7010, PD-5010 sound circuits In this high-end series of models, a digital filter is employed. This digital filter is IC CX23034 (Fig. 8-7). It doubles the sampling frequency to 88.2 kHz (it is a 16-bit, 96-tap FIR filter). By using this filter:

- Group delay near the cutoff frequency is greatly reduced.

- The cutoff characteristics are almost perfect. In addition, high-end distortion is lower and signal transmission performance is improved.

Other audio circuits are basically the same as those of conventional components, except for the top-of-the-line model where de-emphasis switching and muting are performed by transistors and ICs. Also, de-emphasis is switched on during manual search to reduce high-range noise. Muting is provided to suppress noise that is produced when the power is switched on. It is controlled by a timing signal from a discrete circuit.

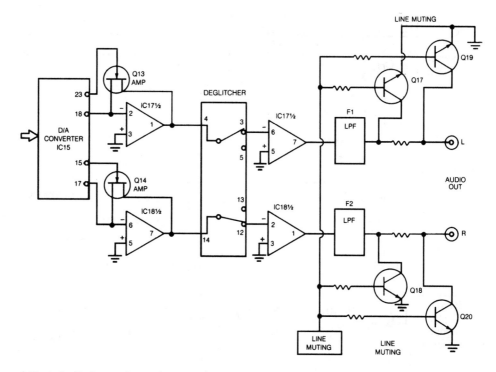

8-7 A deglitcher and transistor muting system is used in a Pioneer PD-5010 (BK) block diagram.

Realistic CD-3370 portable sound circuits

The audio stereo signals in the Realistic portable CD player starts at output IC11 and feeds audio to a line output jack and also to the headphone amplifier. Q12 and Q13 mute transistors are found in the line output J2 (Fig. 8-8). The nominal line output voltage is around 0.65 V, with a ±1.5 dB limit. This small CD portable operates from two AA batteries (3 V).

The D/A converter also feeds a stereo signal to the headphone amp IC1. A dual volume control is found between audio take-off and into the headphone amplifier. This amplified audio signal is fed to headphone output jack J3. Transistors Q10 and Q11 provide audio muting of each stereo channel.

Description of the sound circuits

Signal flow in the audio circuits begins at the output terminal of the D/A converter (Fig. 8-9). Here on pin 17 of IC401, the audio signal goes to the deglitch or sample/hold IC. Next, the signal proceeds to the preamp and the low-pass filter (some models include the preamp in the LPF network). From pin 6 of the low-pass filter network, the signal flows to the audio output IC402 (pin 3). Capacitor (C808) couples the amplified audio signal (pin 1) to the muting switch to the line output jack.

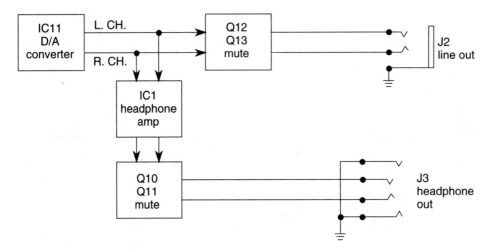

8-8 Block diagram of Realistic CD-3370 portable CD sound circuits.

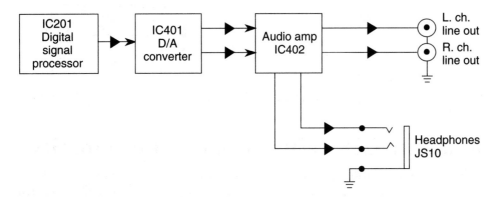

8-9 The arrows indicate the audio signal from IC801 (D/A) through the line output jacks.

The audio signal can be traced as it flows from stage to stage with a scope or external audio amp. The audio signal flow path might have arrows marking its route across the schematic.

D/A converter

The digital/analog converter IC actually changes the digital signal to voltage or audio. The input digital signal from the controller or signal processor is connected to pin 10 of IC401 (Fig. 8-10). In some audio circuits, there might be a digital filter circuit between the digital signal and input terminal of the D/A converter for additional filtering. The stereo audio output signal is taken from pins 1 and 20. The left audio signal (pin 1) is fed to C420 and R432 (pin 2 of IC402) and the right audio signal (pin 20) is connected to C420 and R432. The D/A converter IC internal connections are in Fig. 8-11.

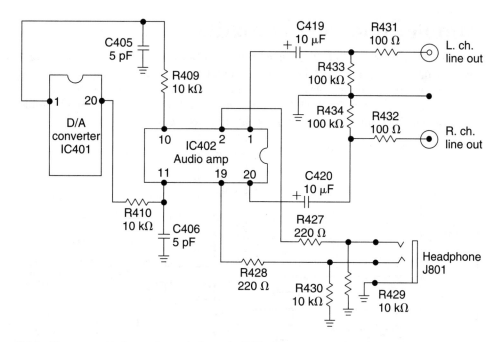

8-10 The separate stereo channels from the D/A converter to audio amp IC402, to stereo line output, and headphone jacks in a Mitsubishi M-C4030 CD changer.

■ **PCM53JP-V-2 (D/A Converter)**

8-11 Here are the internal connections of a D/A converter IC in a JVC XL-V400B compact disc player.

Sample/hold (S.H.) circuits

The sample/hold or deglitch IC is usually located between the D/A converter and low-pass filter network (Fig. 8-12). Some circuits have a channel output level control. The S/H circuit separates the right channel data for the right channel circuitry and the left channel data for the left channel circuitry. When the left channel sample audio passes, the right channel audio is held, and vice-versa.

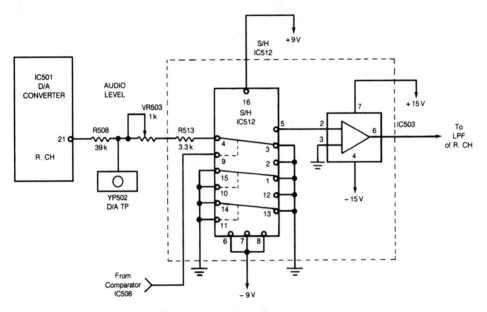

8-12   The sample/hold IC is located between the D/A converter and the audio preamp in a Denon DCH-1800 model.

The S/H circuit samples the analog (audio) waveform at a periodic or fixed rate. The most common rate is 44.1 kHz (sampled 44,100 times each second). Today, some CD players have a double sampling rate of 88.2 kHz, while a few have a 14- or 16-bit oversampling frequency, which is quadruple at 176.4 kHz.

In this sample/hold right channel, the audio signal from pin 21 or IC501 has a right audio output level control. The preset audio signal goes to pin 4 of the S/H IC512. An S/H right-channel capacitor IC ties to pin 9 of IC512. The sample/hold circuit ends with a preamp (IC503) that feeds the audio signal to the low-pass filter network. The internal switching of the S/H IC512 is powered with a positive 9 V at pin 16 and a negative 9 V at pins 6, 7, and 8.

Low-pass filter network

The de-emphasis circuits can be located before or after the low-pass filter (LPF) IC. Usually, the emphasis switching circuit is wired in after the LPF network. Emphasis is switched on when the output level is high. The low-pass filter IC produces a large drop-off between 20 and 25 kHz to eliminate distortion caused by signals above the audio range. The filtered audio signal then goes to the preamp audio ICs.

The input audio signal from the preamp IC goes to terminal 2, and the output comes from pin 6 of the low-pass filter IC504L (Fig. 8-13). A –15 V goes to pin 4 with a +15 V on pin 7. Terminals 1, 3, and 5 are at chassis ground.

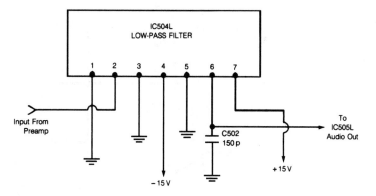

8-13 The low-pass filter eliminates distortion (filters out signals above the audio range). IC504L is found in a Realistic CD-1000 player.

Muting systems

Sound muting is often provided to suppress noise that is produced when the power is turned on. In some players, muting is automatic when the disc stops, during accessing operations, and during PAUSE mode. The sound muting circuits involve relays, transistors, or IC components (Fig. 8-14).

Some units have line muting at both channel output terminals. The same system mutes the signal to the earphone circuits. Muting might be controlled by an automatic muting IC. The control signal operates transistors, ICs, and relay components in the line audio output circuits (Fig. 8-15). Muting often becomes active when the output is at a high level.

Preamp audio line output

The audio line output signal often comes from a preamp that is inside the low-pass filter IC (Fig. 8-16). The input audio signal goes from pin 7 of the sample-and-hold IC17. Capacitor C117 (47 µF) couples the audio signal to the left output line jack through isolation resistors R147 and R146. Line output muting is controlled by a voltage from Q21 to the base terminals of Q17 and Q19. Right and left audio output stages often use separate IC components.

In many of the audio line output circuits, a single IC component serves both channels (Fig. 8-17). Here the audio input signal goes to terminals 4 and 6 of IC214A-B. The audio output signal couples with C269 and C270 through isolation resistors R349 and R350 to the audio line output jack. Transistors TR229 and TR230

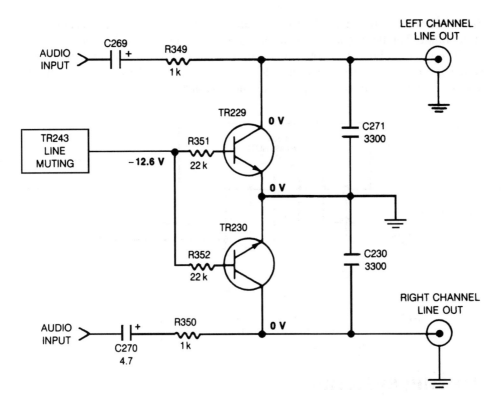

8-14   Transistor line muting of the Yamaha CD-3 player.

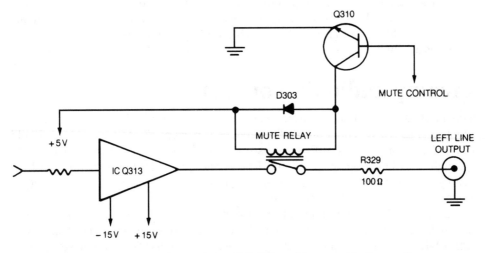

8-15   A relay is used in an Onkyo DX-200 model to provide line muting.

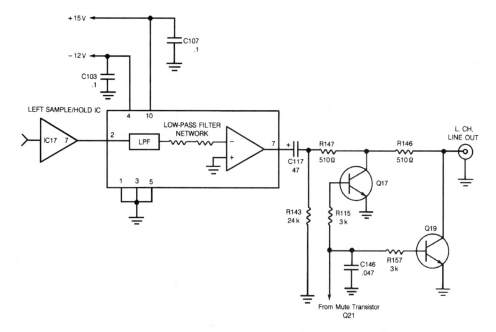

8-16 In the Pioneer PD-7010 model, the line output audio has a preamp circuit inside the LPF network, which has a preamp circuit inside the LPF IC. Transistor muting is found in the line output circuits.

provide line muting. The line muting voltage is applied to transistor Q243. A positive 12 V feeds terminal 9 with a negative 12 V at pin 5 of IC214.

Onkyo DX-C606 audio line output

The audio system in this six CD changer carousel has several stages of amplification. The analog signal is taken from the left channel at pin 13 of D/A converter Q400 and amplified by Q401. This audio signal is coupled to pin 5 of Q405. C439 couples the signal through R411 and R447 before reaching the left line output jack (Fig. 8-18).

The audio signal from the right channel starts at pin 16 of D/A converter and is amplified by Q402 and on to Q406. Again the right channel is amplified and capacity coupled to Q406. C440 couples the amplified audio and ends up at the right channel line output jack through R442 and R448.

The left headphone audio is tapped off the left line to op amp (Q411) with amplified audio applied to the duo-volume control R301. The controlled audio is fed to Q112 and amplified again through two paralleled resistors R304 and R306, to the headphone jack. Likewise the right audio signal is taken from the right line output through Q412 and into the top side of the volume control. R301 (20 kΩ) controls the audio applied to Q411 and through resistor R303 and R305 to the headphone jack JS401.

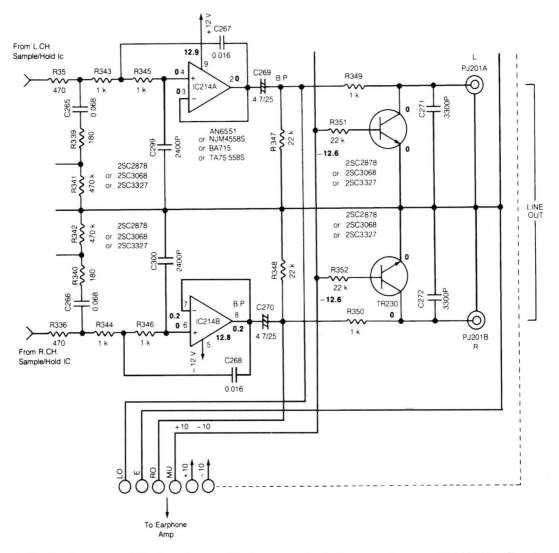

8-17 One large power IC is found in most CD players, serving both stereo channels with IC214 in a Yamaha CD-3 player.

Earphone sound circuits

Some CD players do not have earphone jacks at the rear of the cabinet. Most earphone sound circuits have a dual volume control to adjust the headphone level. The earphone circuits might consist of a dual-sound IC connecting directly to the preamp line output ICs. The audio line entering the earphone circuits is muted in the latest models (Fig. 8-19).

In the Mitsubishi DP-107, the audio signal from C269 and C270 enters the LO and RO terminals on the Operation (3) PC board (Fig. 8-20). Both audio channels are muted with TR405 and TR406. Adjust the headphone volume level by VR401.

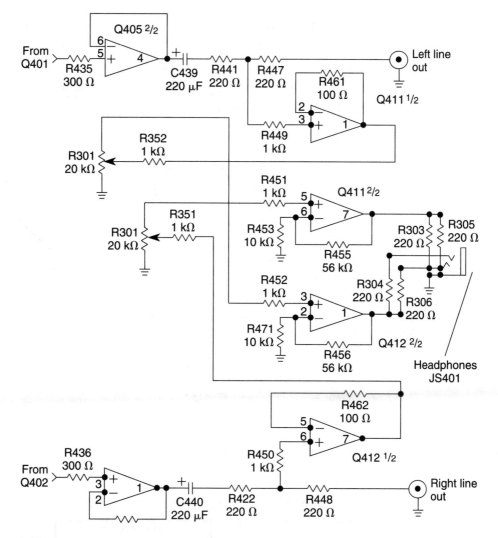

8-18 Several stages of audio amplification are found in the Onkyo DX-C606 carousel CD player.

The audio signal couples with C403 and C404 to the positive (+) terminals 4 and 6 of the earphone IC amp IC404 A and B. The audio output signal is isolated from the earphone jack with resistors R417 and R418. A negative supply voltage goes to pin 5 and a positive voltage goes to pin 1 of IC404.

Realistic 42-5029 headphone circuits

The left channel analog circuit from the digital/analog converter IC11 starts at pin 11 and is capacity coupled by C61 and C48 to the left channel volume control (VR1). VR1 is a dual volume control for both channels. The controlled audio signal is fed to

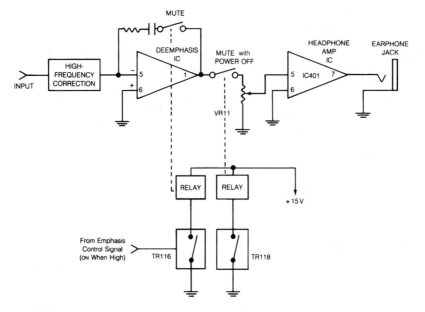

8-19 The headphone audio can be muted in a transistor-relay system ahead of the volume control.

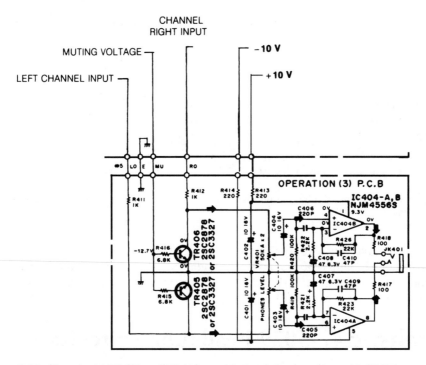

8-20 Transistors TR405 and TR406 provide headphone muting with IC404 as power audio output amp in the headphone circuits of a Mitsubishi DP-107 model.

pin 24 of headphone amplifier IC1. C74 couples the left output audio signal through R63 to headphone jack J3 (Fig. 8-21).

The right audio channel is taken from pin 6 of IC11 and capacity coupled through C88 and C41. The right line output audio is tapped between these two capacitors. Again VR1 controls the headphone right channel audio and connects to pin 3 of IC1. The headphone IC1 amplifies the audio and the output appears at pin 10. C114 couples the audio to the right stereo output jack J3.

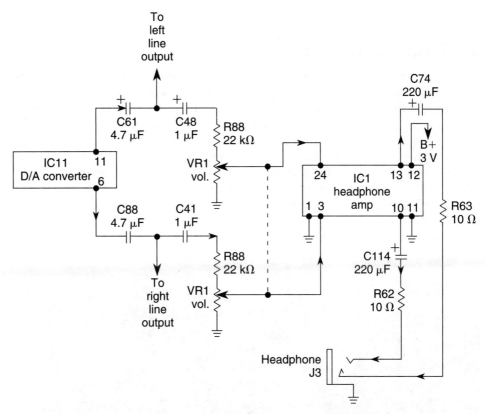

8-21 The headphone circuit of a Radio Shack portable CD player with volume control ahead of input amp IC1.

Audio output voltage

Most CD players have an output voltage of 2 V. This is a fixed voltage if there is no audio level control. CD players with level or adjustable audio outputs should be adjusted to a level of 2 V. Check chapter 9 for audio level adjustment. Some CD players have more than one set of output jacks. Frequently, one set of jacks has a fixed output and the other has an adjustable sound output. The audio frequency response can vary from 2 Hz to 20 kHz, and the output impedance also varies (Fig. 8-22).

Model		Output voltage	Output Impedance
Akai	CD-M88T	2 V	1 kHz
Panasonic	SL-P3610	2 V	330 ohms
Pioneer	PD-7010	2 V	1 kHz
Quasar	CD8975 YW	2 V	330 ohms
Sanyo	CP500	2 V	470 ohms
Yamaha	CD-3	2 V	1 kHz

8-22 Voltage and output impedance of several different CD players.

CD audio hookup

The CD music system is no better than the amplifying system to which it is connected. If hooked up to a low-wattage amplifier and mono speakers, the system will not produce the high-fidelity reproduction the CD can offer. Great music reproduction results when the player is connected to a high-powered amp and quality stereo speakers. Most CD players come with a set of stereo connecting cables (Fig. 8-23). Connect the compact disc player output male plugs to the right and left auxiliary or input CD jacks of the amplifier. Some audio amplifiers have two separate audio input jacks for CD players (like the Sanyo JA540 model). Determine if the output jacks are fixed or variable. Always use the variable output connections when available.

8-23 Even the boom-box and portable CD players have line output jacks at the rear panel for audio amp hookup.

Troubleshooting the sound circuits

A dead, weak, distorted, erratic, or intermittent symptom can exist in one or both channels. Locate a defective audio stage by doing component comparison tests, signal tracing, and individual component checks. Signal tracing the audio circuits with a scope and external amplifier can locate a defective stage or component. Accurate voltage and resistance measurements help locate a defective transistor or IC. You can inject an audio signal from a generator into the audio output circuits to locate a dead or weak stage. The speaker or scope can be used as an indicator. You can also use this method to locate a defective component in the headphone amplifiers.

Troubleshooting CD audio distortion

Check the audio output circuits for a distorted channel. If both channels are distorted, suspect the common audio output IC. Determine which channel is distorted. Very low distortion is difficult to locate, but in a stereo audio circuit the good channel can be compared with the defective channel. Usually distortion is caused by a leaky coupling capacitor, ICs, transistors, defective mute transistors, and broken or cracked resistors.

A sine or square-wave generator can quickly compare the two channels with the duo-trace scope as monitor. Inject the square-wave signal at the volume control and compare each audio channel. Move the audio signal from one stage to the next with scope at headphone or line output jacks.

Inject the signal in one side and on the other of a suspected 44 electrolytic coupling capacitor. Check the signal at the base and collector of AF or preamp transistors. If the square waveform is rounded at the top or is misformed, a distorted condition exists. Locate the defective audio IC with input and output test of the generator and scope of each power output channel (Fig. 8-24).

CD player or amplifier?

Determine if the problem occurs in the CD player or sound amp. It's possible the CD player is fine, but the amp has a defective channel. Interchange the connecting cables to see if the cable is at fault. The cable wires often break right where the wire enters the plugs (Fig. 8-25). A poor solder connection of the tip can cause a dead or intermittent channel.

Check the cable with an ohmmeter. Measure the resistance of the shielded cable from the shielding to the plug. There should be no resistance. Clip the meter leads to the center terminal of the male plug at both ends, and flex the cable to determine if the continuity is broken or erratic. If there is a resistance change at any time during these tests, suspect a broken internal cable lead or plug.

Substitute another amplifier to determine if your amplifier is dead or weak. Usually, both channels of a good amplifier don't fail at once. If a headphone jack is provided, determine whether both channels are okay through those circuits. If so, the problem is in the final amplifier output stages. Check the output cable with a scope or external audio test amp if the CD player is dead or weak.

8-24 Inject a square wave at input terminal of each power IC and check for distortion at headphone jack with the scope for distorted square waveform.

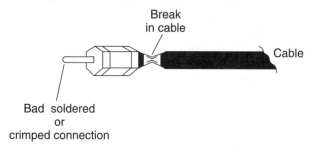

8-25 Often, the connecting line jack cables will break where it connects to the male plug and produce intermittent or dead audio.

How to locate a defective audio channel

With a disc loaded and playing, check for audio at the audio line jack and the output terminal of the D/A converter with a scope to determine if the audio circuits are defective. If an audio signal is found at the output pin terminal of the D/A converter but not at the line jack, suspect defective audio circuits. Improper signal at the D/A converter might indicate a defective D/A or signal processor.

Next, check the low-voltage sources feeding the various audio circuits. Go directly to the power supply voltage sources if all sound circuits are dead. Several different voltage sources might feed the audio stages (Fig. 8-26). Here, the D/A converter is powered with a +5 V, –15 V, and +15 V. The sample/hold IC receives a +9 V and –9 V. A positive and negative 15 V feeds the low-pass filter IC and preamp power audio line amp.

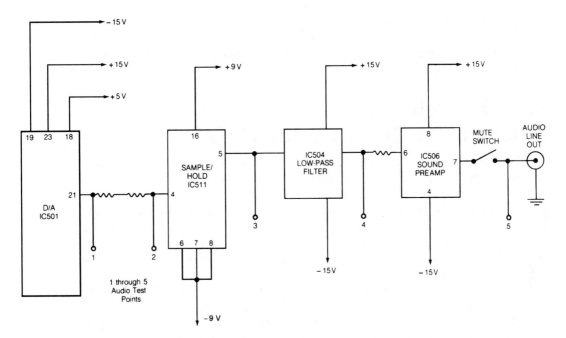

8-26 Check the four different voltage sources feeding the sound circuits first and then signal trace audio at test points 1 through 5 for a defective audio channel.

Signal tracing the sound circuits

Trace the audio circuits with a scope and external audio amp. With the disc playing, check the signal at the output terminal of the D/A converter. If the signal is weak or missing, the trouble is in the D/A converter or before it. Check the signal into the D/A, and take critical voltage measurements.

Proceed to the input terminal of the sample/hold IC and output terminal. Check the preamp and low-pass filter in the same manner. If the signal is normal, proceed to the stereo preamp IC. Distortion often occurs in the preamp line IC. Measure for correct source voltages (both voltages must be present).

Check the input and output signal of each IC. When the signal becomes weak or distorted in the external amp, you have located the defective component. Then conduct voltage measurements on the suspected component to verify whether the component is leaky or open.

Signal tracing with external amp

Just about any audio circuit can be checked with the external audio amplifier. If one stage is weak or distorted check the signal output at the D/A converter with audio amp. If it is normal proceed to the sample-hold IC, through the low-pass filter network. Compare the left and right channel audio at this point. If the line output stereo channels are normal and the headphones are distorted, signal trace the headphone circuits.

Sometimes low audio distortion is difficult to locate with the external amp. Weak and no audio conditions can easily be tested with the external audio amplifier. Of course, extreme distortion can be located with the external amp. Just compare each stage in the normal channel as you proceed through the audio circuits.

Locating defective transistors or ICs with the DMM

A leaky or open transistor and IC component can be located by doing accurate voltage and component tests with the digital multimeter (DMM). Take voltage measurements after locating the defective stage with signal tracing. If a scope or external amp is not available for signal tracing, you probably have to rely on accurate voltage measurements to locate an open or leaky IC or transistor. Identify a defective IC when a normal signal goes in and a poor signal comes out. Then take accurate voltage measurements on the suspected IC. Then, accurate resistance measurements on pins with low voltage can indicate a leaky IC. The same procedure applies to transistors.

The desired voltage measurements are often indicated on the service schematic of most audio components (Fig. 8-27). Note the variety of supply voltages (5, 9, 12, and 15 V) on components in the audio circuits. Both negative and positive voltages go to the D/A converter, low-pass filter, preamp, and audio output ICs.

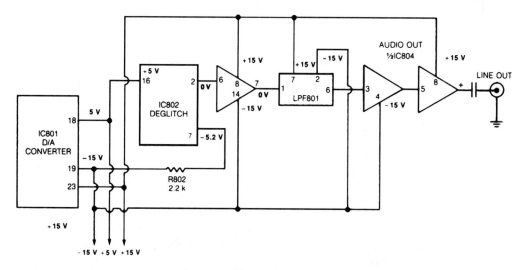

8-27   Take a critical voltage test on each pin terminal when improper sound is found at the D/A converter IC801.

Although most audio circuits use IC components, transistors might be used in the mute-switching and relay circuits. First, test the transistor for open junctions with the positive terminal at the base and negative probe at the emitter terminal, using the diode/transistor test of the DMM. A low resistance measurement of 500 to 950 Ω indicates a normal transistor. Now reverse the test probes; an infinite or very high reading indicates that the transistor is normal. A similar measurement should result with the negative probe at the collector terminal.

A leaky or shorted transistor will have a shorted or low measurement under 1 kΩ in both directions. Doublecheck the emitter-to-collector terminals. Most transistors short between these two elements. Discard the suspected transistor if you get a low measurement in both directions between any two elements. Before removing the transistor when leakage tests are noted, doublecheck the schematic for diodes or other components (or even shorts) in the circuit that might be connecting the two elements being tested. If in doubt, remove the suspected transistor and test it out of the circuit.

IC resistance measurements

After locating an audio IC with lower-than-normal voltage on any terminal, suspect the IC is leaky or an improper low-voltage source. It's possible both the negative *and* positive supply voltages are low when only one IC terminal shows leakage. Compare the various voltage measurements on the IC with the schematic. Always mark down the correct terminal voltage on the schematic after doing the correct repairs.

If a +15-V source at pin 8 is down to 7.5 V, this same voltage could be low at other IC components (Fig. 8-28). Apply power to the CD player and take another measurement. If the voltage remains the same, suspect that the power source or another component is pulling down the voltage. If the voltage returns to a normal +15 V, the IC is likely leaky. Take a resistance measurement between the low pin and common ground. Usually, a leaky IC pin reads under 1 kΩ. A random resistance measurement between each terminal and ground can isolate a leaky IC, but check to be sure there are no low-ohm resistors or diodes in the circuit that would indicate a low reading before removing the suspected IC.

Replacing the transistor or IC components   It's always best to replace transistors and IC components with the original components, but when these compo-

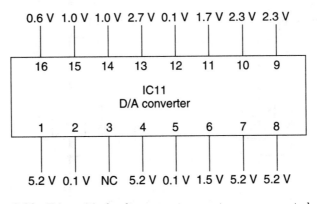

8-28   Take critical voltage measurements on a suspected IC to determine if it is leaky or open.

nents are not available, you must make substitutions. At this stage of development in CD players, the D/A converter and audio output amps might have to be originals. But some of the sample/hold or analog switch/deglitch ICs and op amps are available with universal replacements.

Locating defective
muting relays and transistors

The lower priced CD players might not have any type of muting circuits. The later and higher priced players usually have output muting and operate with transistors or muting relays. Determine if the signal stops at the muting component. A dead or erratic sound can be caused by dirty muting relay points. Defective transistors in the muting line circuits can produce a dead channel. Improper voltage or signal to the relay or transistors can cause the same problem.

If the audio signal is traced to the muting relay switch or transistors, determine what component is defective. Clip a wire across the relay terminals to restore the audio. Peek at the solenoid to see if it is energized. Remove the plastic cap from the relay and push down the flat metal piece that trips the contacts. Suspect a dirty contact if the sound does not appear. Clean the contacts or replace the relay assembly.

Suspect a defective transistor or IC circuit if the solenoid does not energize (Fig. 8-29). Measure the resistance of the solenoid and check it against the good one in the other channel (usually, both relays are not defective at the same time). Check the voltage across the solenoid coil and compare it with the good relay in the emphasis circuits. Suspect a defective transistor or IC if improper voltage is at the relay

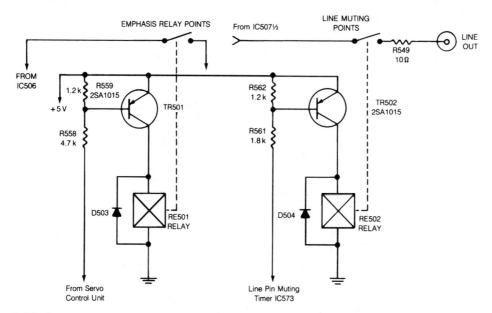

8-29 Suspect a defective IC or transistor when a relay will not energize in the muting circuits.

winding. Do not overlook the possibility of an improper signal coming from the muting control units.

Some of the line output circuits have IC or transistor muting (Fig. 8-30). Accurate voltage and transistor in-circuit tests can often locate the defective muting component. When the power is turned on and the voltage is high, the muting transistors should be at cutoff, and with the power off, the voltage should return to zero.

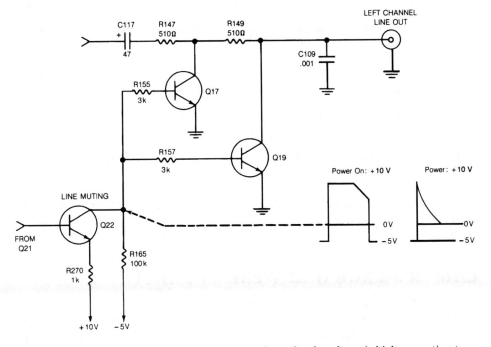

8-30 When the power of the CD player is turned on, the dc voltage is high on muting transistors Q17 and Q19.

If there is no signal at the line output jack, simply remove both collector terminals of each transistor from the muting circuit. The audio should be normal. Measure the voltage at the base terminals of the transistors or the line muting transistor if you get a very low or no voltage. Check each transistor for open or leaky conditions. Determine if the muting system is working if a voltage change can be detected at the collector terminal of the line muting transistor Q21. Take accurate voltage and resistance measurements on the line muting IC.

Dead right or left channel

Either channel can be dead and the other channel normal. For example, if there is no output from the right channel, check the audio signal at the right output line jack with the scope or external amp. Backtrack to the right sound output terminal of the preamp stage (Fig. 8-31). Because the stereo signal splits at the D/A converter output, check each component signal terminal up to the D/A IC or until the channel

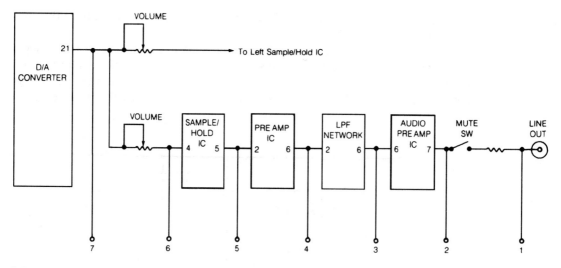

8-31 Start at the line output jack and work towards the D/A converter at the various test points with a scope or external amp while a disc is playing.

comes alive. It's possible to have one dead and one normal channel coming out of a (defective) D/A converter IC. In this case, any component within the bad channel could be defective up to where the signal splits at the D/A IC.

One dead and one weak channel

Any component common to both channels could cause one channel to be weak and the other dead. Because the power supply sources are common to both channels, check each voltage source first. Notice if either the negative voltage is lower than the positive voltage. It's possible both negative and positive voltage sources are off, because they usually come from the same common power supply.

In many of the audio IC components, one half of the same component is used in each channel. This is especially true of the preamp and audio output ICs. When a common audio IC leaks or opens, it can affect both audio channels. Take accurate voltage and resistance measurements on the suspected IC. Signal tracing the audio up to the same IC in both channels can locate the suspected common integrated component.

Distorted channel

Audio distortion in one particular channel can be caused by a leaky or open IC or transistor. Signal trace the audio signal to locate the stage causing the distortion. Take accurate voltage measurements after locating the suspected component. If only one channel is distorted, the problem must exist from where the signal separates after the D/A converter. Check the signal with the scope from D/A through the LPF. Do not overlook the possibility of a distorted speaker system. Interchange the line output cables to determine if the amplifier and speakers are at fault. Check the power supply sources if both channels are distorted.

Troubleshooting the earphone circuits

Go directly to the earphone circuits if the audio line output amp is normal but the earphones are dead or distorted. If no sound is audible at the line output and earphone circuits, suspect trouble in the amp or sample/hold stages. Notice if only one or both channels are dead. Suspect the output audio IC if only one channel is defective in both systems, because one half of the IC could be in the line output and the other in the headphone circuits (Fig. 8-32).

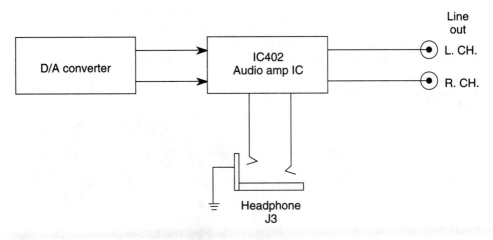

8-32 Suspect a common IC component when both the line output and headphone audio are inoperative.

Substitute another pair of earphones to determine if the headphones are defective. Clip a small 8-Ω speaker to the headphone jack terminals to signal trace the audio output (Fig. 8-33). The auxiliary input with a male headphone plug and cable can serve as a testing source. Signal trace the audio through the headphone circuits with the scope or external amp.

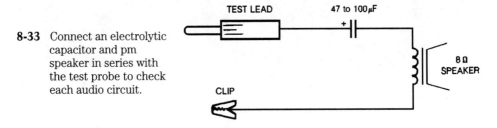

8-33 Connect an electrolytic capacitor and pm speaker in series with the test probe to check each audio circuit.

Cable problems

Check the male plug on the earphone for poor cable connections. Headphone cables often break where the wire enters the male plug or right at the earphone case. Suspect a poor or broken connection if the sound is erratic. Check the resistance between common ground and the outside metal terminal of the headphone plug. Flex the cord and note if the meter jumps. If so, replace the plug or the whole cable. Erratic or intermittent sound can result from a dirty or worn female headphone plug.

Headphone problems

After many hours of playing, jolting, and carrying around the portable CD player, the headphone cable often breaks right where it enters the jack or at the earphone unit (Fig. 8-34). First clean up the jack and plug area with cleaning fluid to eliminate erratic and noisy reception. A squirt of cleaning fluid right into the phone jack area might help the noisy reception. Check inside of earphone jack for intermittent audio. Sometimes a wire can break at the jack terminals. Inspect the jack area for intermittent reception with poor soldered connections at the headphone jack.

8-34 Check for defective headphone reception for a break at the plug and jack where it enters the CD player.

A broken earphone cable right at the plug or at each earphone can cause intermittent or dead audio. Usually, broken wires or cable can be repaired in a few minutes. Replace the headphone plug if it is broken inside the molded male plug. These plugs can be located at electronic stores. Solder and tape all broken wires or cables. Check inside the earphone for broken wires on the small pm speaker or phone.

Weak channel

Notice if the defective channel is normal at the line output amp. If it is weak, suspect a defective IC, capacitor, or poor muting in that channel. Remember, the headphone output muting might be operating from the same line output relays. Signal trace the audio into the headphone IC and out. Don't forget to turn up the headphone volume control.

Distorted channel

Suspect the audio output IC if you have excessive distortion in the headphones. Signal trace the distortion with the scope and external amp. Look for the distortion in the early stages of the audio circuits if the distortion is also detected in one of the line amplifier channels. Do not overlook the possibility of a defective set of headphones.

Many compact disc manufacturers have their own audio troubleshooting methods. Charts 8-1, 8-2, and 8-3 show three different troubleshooting charts.

Chart 8-1. Audio troubleshooting flowchart for the Pioneer PD-7010 CD player.

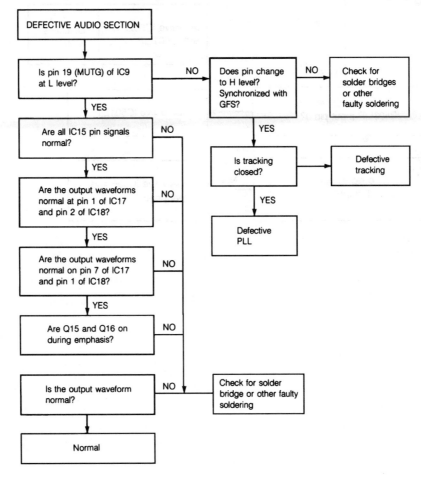

**Chart 8-2. Audio troubleshooting
flowchart for an RCA MCD-141 CD player.**

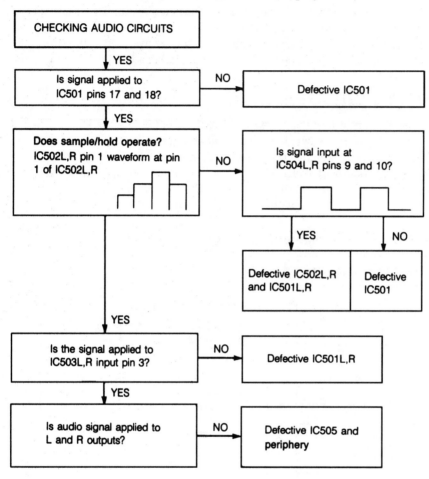

Chart 8-3. Audio troubleshooting flowchart for a Realistic CD-1000 CD player.

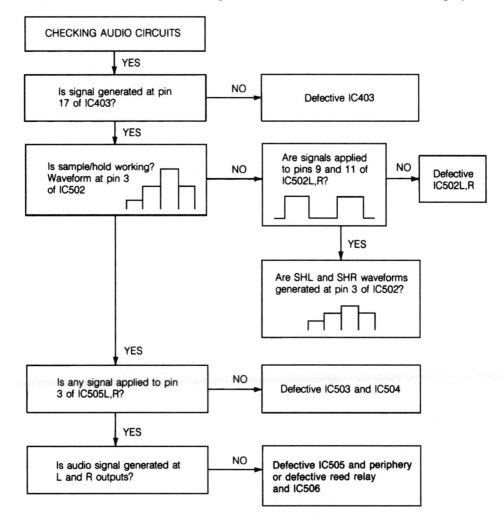

9
Electronic CD player adjustments

THE ELECTRONIC AND MECHANICAL ADJUSTMENTS SHOULD ONLY BE MADE AFTER replacing a critical component or a simple touch-up test. After installing a new pickup head assembly, the E-F balance adjustments should be made. When replacing the disc motor, the disc platform must be adjusted for maximum EFM signal at the preamp IC, if the disc platform is not found on the new motor. Focus or tracking gain adjustments can be touched up after replacing the preamp or servo IC components. Critical waveform adjustments might confirm if that particular circuit is performing (Fig. 9-1). If complete electronic adjustments are to be made, they should be checked in the correct order. Follow the manufacturer's order of adjustments, if different from those above.

Like the radio or TV receiver, adjustment screws do not get out of line by themselves. The same applies to the CD chassis. Do not touch them unless correct adjustment is needed. When the signal is missing on a certain component after you take scope or voltage tests, make sure you don't make any electronic adjustments without the correct test equipment. First, locate the defective component. The laser diode VR adjustments should not be touched because hazardous invisible laser radiation could result. Usually, this adjustment is made at the factory. Do not make any electronic adjustments without the correct test equipment or manufacturer's adjustment procedures.

Required test equipment

The oscilloscope, ac and dc digital voltmeters, audio AF oscillator, frequency counter, test discs, and various scope band-pass filter test homemade circuits are needed for correct CD electronic adjustments. Several manufacturers use special servo gain and conversion connecting cables. You might even want to use two separate scopes. The oscilloscope is used to take waveform adjustments with critical volt-

9-1   Critical waveforms can be taken with the scope and test disc while playing.

age tests made with the DMM. In some tests a two-channel scope is needed for anything over 30 MHz. The frequency counter is used in frequency adjustment of the VCO and PLL circuits.

The commercial laser power meter might help the electronic technician measure the laser output in compact disc players and infrared sources. This instrument can be used in servicing CD players, video disc players, VCRs, remote controls, and other infrared sources (Fig. 9-2). The laser power meter has a built-

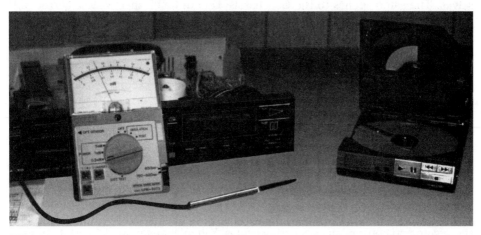

9-2   A new laser power meter to measure the laser output of a CD player and other infrared sources.

in load simulation circuit, required to service many CD players. The range settings are 0.3 mW, 1 mW, and 3 mW with switchable wave length settings of 633 nM and 750 nM–820 nM.

The ordinary CD disc can be used to make most of the electronic adjustments. Some manufacturers use only one test disc for all of the electronic adjustments, while others use several different test discs. The eccentricity, surface oscillation, and scratch test discs are used for checking the results of the electronic adjustments. The various test discs are given with each manufacturer's electronic adjustment procedures. Several manufacturers use special adjusting instruments, adapters, and connectors for their special adjustment procedures. See Chart 9-1.

Chart 9-1.
The different test discs to make
CD adjustments. Most manufacturers use the
YEDS1 or YEDS7 Sony test discs for adjustment.

Test disc	**Use**
800104	For demonstration
400088	
400067	
YEDS1	
YEDS7	For signal characteristics
YEDS18	
Eccentricity disc	Eccentricity width: 200 µM
Surface oscillation disc	Surface oscillation width:400–500 µM
Scratch surface	Black scratch width: 300 µM black line
TCD–784	Type made in A–BEX

Test points

Most CD players have the various test points listed right on the PC board (Fig. 9-3). All test points should be located before trying to take scope waveforms. Besides making correct electronic adjustments, the various test points might determine if that circuit is performing with a correct scope waveform or voltage test. Check for a chassis layout parts location drawing, which usually shows the various test points and IC or LSI components (Fig. 9-4). Be careful not to touch other components or test points with the scope probe. Use a clip-on probe, which might cling tightly to the test point or IC component terminal pins.

Often the different VR adjustment controls are located close together for easy adjustment (Fig. 9-5). Locate the correct control adjustment for the right adjustment procedure. Most manufacturers list these controls separately in the adjustment procedures or are clearly marked on the PC board. In some instances a starting point might be shown of halfway rotation of the adjustment control. The slotted screwdriver adjustments are found in most models.

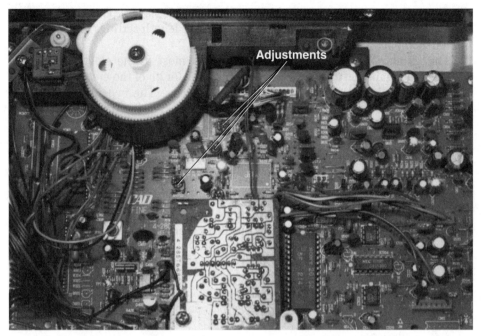

9-3 The various test points and alignment are located in the compact disc chassis.

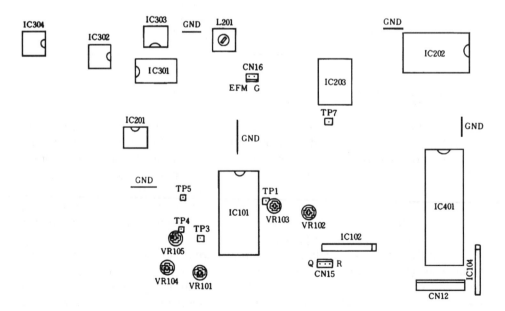

9-4 Locate the manufacturer test points and different control adjustments on the board layout drawing.

9-5 The different adjustments can be quite small and they are often located close together.

Laser power adjustments

Laser power adjustments are made to ensure proper operation of the laser diode. You will know the laser diode is operating correctly with the laser power adjustments. A low EFM output indicates a defective laser diode. In some optical pickup systems, the VR adjustment mounted on the assembly is adjusted at the factory and should not be touched.

Denon DCD-1800R laser power adjustment When you turn the power on, the laser beam is emitted. Be careful not to look at the laser beam directly. Place the laser power meter in contact with the pickup lens (Fig. 9-6). Adjust VR102 on the motor wiring board so that the laser output becomes 0.3 mW ± 0.01 mW.

JVC XL V400B laser adjustment Connect the IC802 pin (1) of the front PC board (EMM-028-2 to ground) and turn the power switch on. Then measure the laser radiation power with the laser power meter. If the indication obtained is less than 0.1 mW, then the service life of the laser diode has expired. When the EFM output is extremely low (it cannot focus enough) the service life of the laser diode has expired.

Magnavox FM1040 laser adjustment Because the light pin is very sensitive to static charges, care should be taken that during measurements and adjustments of the laser power supply the potentials of the aids and yourself equal the potential of the CD mechanism.

The laser simulator PC board NR 2-4822-395-30215 should be used to check the laser. Take the flex PC board out of socket A11 and connect the simulator PC board with the socket. Remove plug A16 and insert it in the socket on the simulator PC

9-6 Using the laser power meter to check if the optical laser beam is adequate.

board. Connect the plug with four wires to socket A16 (Fig. 9-7). Take out plug A17 and insert the plug with one wire in socket A17.

In rest position the current through the laser diode should be 1 mA. To check it, set the switch on the simulator PC board in the OFF position and the main switch in the ON position. Turn the trimming resistor 3180 counterclockwise (minimum to the right) and measure the voltage across resistor 3194. The voltage should be 15 mV.

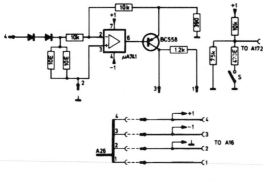

31 966B12

9-7 The laser simulator is used to check the laser power beam in the Magnavox FD1040 laser adjustments.

Check

The laser simulator PCB nr. 2 4822 395 30215 should be used here.
Take the flex PCB out of socket A11 and connect the simulator PCB with the socket.
Remove plug A16 and insert it in the socket on the simulator PCB.
Connect the plug with 4 wires to socket A16. Take out plug A17 and insert the plug with 1 wire in socket A17.

To check the laser supply control, set the switch on the simulator PC board in on position and measure the voltages between points $+V$ and $-V$ on the simulator PC board. Resistor 3180 clockwise (maximum to the right): $U + V - V = 60$ mV $\pm$ 30 mV. R3180 counterclockwise (minimum to the right): $U + V - V = 560$ mV $\pm$ 50 mV. Set resistor 3180 to midposition. This is a preliminary adjustment. After the simulator PC board has been removed, the laser current must be adjusted.

In adjusting the laser supply voltage, place track 1 of test disc 4822-397-30096 (disc without defects). Connect a dc voltmeter across resistor R3308 on the servo PC board (on the emitter of transistor Q6239 and ground). Adjust the laser power supply with resistor 3180 until the voltage across resistor 3308 is 575 $\pm$ 75 mV.

Mitsubishi DP107 laser power check   To confirm the laser output, place the player in the FOCUS-SEARCH mode. Short terminals FD1-R together. With the laser power meter over the optical lens, the correct measurement should be 0.24 mW $\pm$ 0.3 mW. After removing the flapper, adjust the laser output by the laser meter. Apply -9 V $\pm$ 0.5 V to the LB terminal when the pickup head is off the circuit board.

Pioneer PD-7010 laser diode power check   Set to the normal mode. (Normal mode can be set by switching the power off and on again.) Position the optical power meter sensor immediately above the object lens. Press the play key without a disc loaded, and check that the LD (Laser Diode) power reading in the optical power meter is within the specified range (0.26 mW $\pm$ 0.02 mW). Adjust VR1 for the specified rating.

Realistic CD-1000 laser adjustment   Connect the oscilloscope to TP13 (TDET) and TP16, which is grounded on the adjustment board. Load a disc in the player, and set the player to PLAY mode. Adjust R629 (Laser gain adjust) so that the EFM signal level becomes 700 mV.

RCA MCD-141 laser diode output   The laser diode output should not be adjusted unless the laser pickup assembly or circuit is replaced. The laser current can be checked by measuring the voltage across R209. The laser diode current ranges from 40 to 80 mA (0.48 to 0.96 V) across R209. If the current is over 120 mA (1.44 V across R209) the laser diode can be defective.

Connect the oscilloscope to test point TP3 (EFM and test point (TP1) ground). Preset the laser gain control R205 to minimum (counterclockwise). Load the disc and place the player in play mode. With no laser output (control at minimum), increase the laser gain control (R205) and press the power button on and off until the disc rotates several revolutions. Press the play button and adjust the laser gain control until the EFM signal level is 1.3 V p-p + 200 mV (Fig. 9-8).

Sylvania FDD-104 laser adjustment   Same as Magnavox model FD1040.

Yamaha CD-3 confirmation laser output   Place the player in Focus Search mode and short terminals FD1 and R together. Use the laser power meter for a 0.24 mW to 0.3 mW. After removing the flapper assembly, adjust the laser output meter. Apply $- 9$ V $\pm$ 0.5 V to terminal LB when the pickup head is off the circuit board.

9-8   Adjust the laser gain control (R205) in the RCA MCD-141 CD chassis until the EFM signal level is 1.3 V p-p on the oscilloscope.

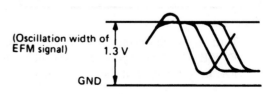

Denon DCD-1800R preadjustments Preadjustments require an adjustment adapter, adjustment disc, oscilloscope, and audio oscillator.

1. Turn off the power. Unload the transparent disc and load the adjustment disc.

2. Connect the oscilloscope to YPHF (Hot), YP552 (GND) on the signal processing board (Fig. 9-9).

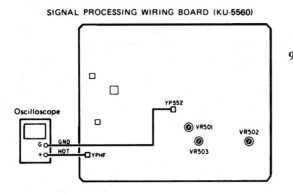

9-9 The scope is connected to test pins YP552 and YPHF on the signal processing board to check the HF waveform within the Denon DCD-1800CD player.

3. Turn on the power.

4. Turn on switches SMSA-1 (Full Torque) and SMSA-2 (Constant Speed) on the adjustment adapter consecutively. When the disc is revolving, turn off SMSA-1.

5. Adjust the pick-up height adjustment screw to obtain an HF (High Frequency) waveform.

6. Set VR101 on the motor wiring board at mechanical center (Fig. 9-10).

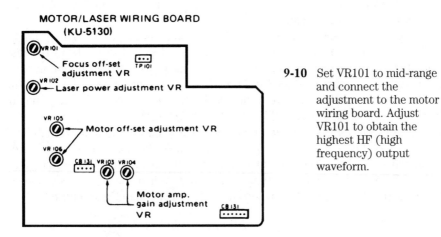

9-10 Set VR101 to mid-range and connect the adjustment to the motor wiring board. Adjust VR101 to obtain the highest HF (high frequency) output waveform.

7. Turn on switch DD on the adjustment adapter. Then turn on switches FSW-A FSW-B, CSW consecutively. Turn off switch SMSA-2. Make sure LEDs for FZC and HSS light. If they do not light, readjust from step 5.

8. Adjust VR101 on the motor wiring board to obtain the highest HF waveform output (Fig. 9-11).

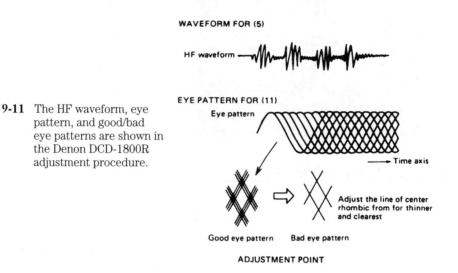

WAVEFORM FOR (5)

HF waveform

EYE PATTERN FOR (11)

9-11 The HF waveform, eye pattern, and good/bad eye patterns are shown in the Denon DCD-1800R adjustment procedure.

Eye pattern

Time axis

Adjust the line of center rhombic from for thinner and clearest

Good eye pattern   Bad eye pattern

ADJUSTMENT POINT

9. Adjust the jitter direction adjustment screw on the pickup to obtain maximum amplitude of the HF waveform.

10. Adjust the radial direction adjustment screw to obtain maximum amplitude to the HF waveform.

11. Turn on switch TSW on the adjustment adapter, then turn switches SSW and CSW consecutively. Check on the oscilloscope that an eye pattern (EFM) signal can be observed (Fig. 9-12).

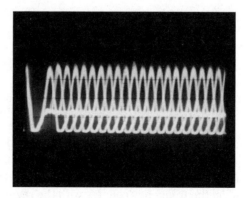

9-12 A typical PLL-VCO waveform at the voltage control oscillator (VCO).

12. Adjust VR101 on the motor wiring board to obtain the clearest eye pattern (Refer to Fig. 9-13). If there is a considerable amount of jitter along the time axis, readjust from step 9.

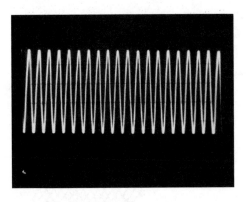

9-13 The oscillator frequency waveform of VCO free-running IC.

PLL-VCO adjustments

The PLL circuit basically consists of an 8.6456-MHz VCO (voltage-controlled oscillator). The VCO oscillator output is divided (4.3218 MHz when locked) where the phase of the signal is compared with the edge of the EFM signal read from the disc. The PLL-VCO (phase-locked loop voltage control oscillator) adjustment is made with the oscilloscope or frequency counter (Fig. 9-14).

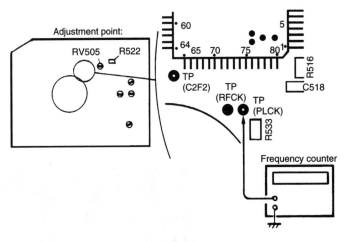

9-14 Adjustment point and frequency meter connection on a Denon DCC-9770 for PLL adjustment.

JVC-XL-V400B PLL free-run adjustment Use the frequency counter as the PLL adjustment instrument. Connect the frequency counter between ENN-028 (TP11) and ground. Short the TP10 and ground. Adjust L301 to 4.32 ± 0.01 MHz indicated on the frequency counter with the regulating rod. Perform this checking adjustment no sooner than switching on the power.

Mitsubishi DP107 VCO adjustments Set the player in STOP mode. Connect the frequency counter to IC207 40 pin (CK) and IC207 8 pin (ERM1) short to ground. Adjust T201 for the correct frequency (FVCO—4.3218 MHz ± 10 kHz).

Onkyo DX-200 CLV-PLL circuit adjustment Required test equipment: Frequency counter, adjusting rod, shorting clip.

1. Turn on power to set.
2. With set in stop position, use shorting clip to drop VC01 (TP-221) to ground.
3. Connect frequency counter to WFCK (TP-283).
4. Turn the oscillator coil L206 to adjust frequency to 7.35 ± 0.01 kHz.
5. Remove shorting clip.

Pioneer PD-7010 VCO free-run frequency adjustment Set the player to test mode. (1) Switch power (S401) on while pressing the test mode switch (S1). (2) Then switch the manual search FWD or REV switch on to activate test mode. (3) Test mode is canceled by switching power off.

1. Set the player to TEST mode.
2. Press the STOP key to switch all servo off.
3. Press the TRACK FWD and PLAY keys in that order to close the focus and spindle servos.
4. Observe the waveform at pin 8 of IC8 (2/2) by oscilloscope at this time (V:0.5 V/div). This waveform can easily be observed at the legs of C47.
5. Write the center value of the waveform at pin 8 of IC8 (2/2).
6. Using the core driver, adjust the VL1 (VCO coil) core so that the center value of the oscilloscope waveform is the same as the previously recorded value when the PAUSE key is pressed to switch the tracking servo on.

Denon DCC-9770 PLL-free-run adjustment

1. Remove the soldering bridge (EFM) from the MD board.
2. Detach R522 from main PC board. (R552) is connected to pin 11 of IC503.
3. Connect the frequency counter to test point (PLCK).
4. Turn the power on and adjust RV505 so that frequency counter reading satisfies the specifications. (Adjustable limits: 4.3118 to 4.3318 MHz).

Realistic CD-3304 PLL (VCC) adjustment

1. Put unit into stop mode.
2. Short circuit test point (ASY) and test point (GND) Both terminal short (TP7).
3. Connect digital frequency counter to test point (PLCK) and test point (GND) TP10 (Fig. 9-15).
4. Adjust VR504 so that the frequency counter reading becomes 4.25 ± 0.01 MHz.

RCA MCD-141 PLL adjustment Observe the following sequence for adjusting the frequency of the phase-locked loop.

1. Connect a frequency counter to TP13 (PLCK) and TP14 (GND).

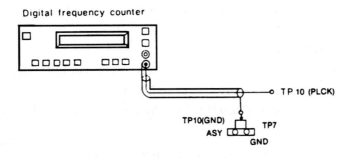

Digital frequency counter

TP 10 (PLCK)

TP10(GND)

ASY

TP7

GND

9-15 Digital frequency counter hookup in a Realistic CD-3304 PLL-VCO adjustment.

2. Connect an oscilloscope to TP9 (GFS) and TP14 (GND).

3. With the player in the stop mode, preset L401 to a frequency of 4500 ± 50 kHz.

4. Place the player in the play mode and adjust L401 until the peak-to-peak output voltage of TP9 is minimum (clockwise). Then adjust L401 until the peak-to-peak output voltage is minimum (counterclockwise).

5. With the player in the STOP mode, note the frequency (F1) at TP13.

6. With the player in the PLAY mode, adjust L401 frequency counterclockwise until the peak-to-peak output voltage is minimum. Then, adjust L401 clockwise until the peak-to-peak voltage is maximum.

7. With the player in the stop mode, note the frequency (F2) at TP13.

8. Then adjust L401 so that the frequency at TP13 is $F_1 + F_2$ times ½.

9. After the preceding adjustments (steps 1 through 8) have been made, operate the player in the PLAY mode to confirm the frequency at TP13 is 4321.8 ± 400 kHz. Check the waveform at TP9 (Fig. 9-16).

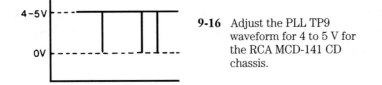

4–5V

0V

9-16 Adjust the PLL TP9 waveform for 4 to 5 V for the RCA MCD-141 CD chassis.

Denon DCD-1800R HF (high frequency) level adjustment Follow these steps to adjust the high-frequency level.

1. Connect the oscilloscope to TP305 HF and GND terminals.

2. Adjust VR303 on the servo wiring board so that the HF level becomes 2.5 V p-p (Fig. 9-17).

Mitsubishi DP107 HF level confirmation Set the player in PLAY mode with a disc and connect the oscilloscope to terminal HS and ground. A standard 1.5 V p-p to 2.5 V p-p should be at the HF level.

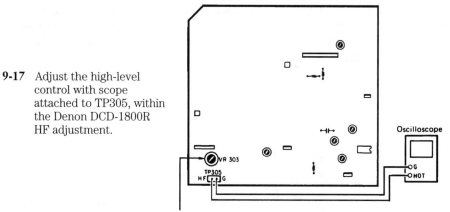

SERVO WIRING BOARD (KU-5550)

Oscilloscope

9-17 Adjust the high-level control with scope attached to TP305, within the Denon DCD-1800R HF adjustment.

HF level adjustment VR

Yamaha CD-3 HF level confirmation Perform the same adjustments as for the Mitsubishi DP107 compact disc player.

RF signal adjustments

In most CD players, the RF and skew adjustments are made for maximum RF (radio frequency) signal waveform at a test point. The radial-tangential screw (mounted under the flapper) is adjusted for the RF waveform on the oscilloscope. The correct adjustment is to make the diamond-shaped area as clear as possible without excessive jitter (Fig. 9-18). A special tool or a simple screwdriver slot are found for the radial screw adjustment.

Mitsubishi DP-107 jitter adjustment Set the player with a disc in the PLAY mode. Connect the oscilloscope to terminal HS and ground. Adjust the head base tilting screw for the best HS (eye pattern) signal. (All lines of the waveform can be observed finely and clearly.)

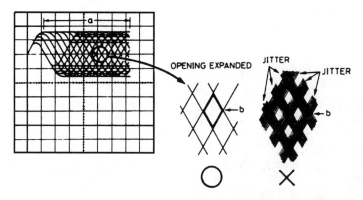

OPENING EXPANDED

JITTER   JITTER

9-18 A typical RF signal waveform found at TP1 on most CD players.

Pioneer PD-7010 tangential adjustment Load the test disc. Set the player to the TEST mode. Using the MANUAL SEARCH FWD key, move the pickup to the disc edge to enable the tangential adjustment screw to be seen from the left-hand side (Fig. 9-19). Press the TRACK FWD, PLAY, and PAUSE keys in that order to close all servos. (The PAUSE indicator will light.)

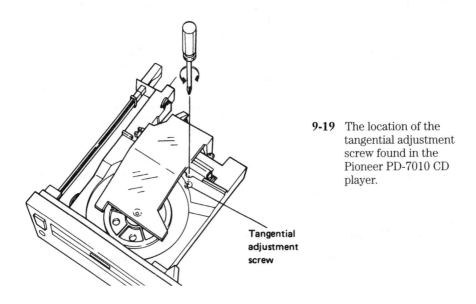

9-19 The location of the tangential adjustment screw found in the Pioneer PD-7010 CD player.

Tangential adjustment screw

Observe the TP2 pin 4 (RF output) in the oscilloscope and adjust the tangential adjustment screw to obtain the clearest eye pattern (Fig. 9-20). The optimum position is the midpoint between the two positions where the eye pattern starts to deteriorate when the tangential adjustment screw is turned clockwise and counterclockwise. In addition to a clear overall waveform, adjust to obtain relatively slender lines where single "diamond" shapes are formed in the eye pattern (Fig.9-21). To make the waveform easier to observe, insert a 10-kΩ resistance in the tip of the probe (or a 5-kΩ resistance if the waveform is hard to see). See Fig. 9-22.

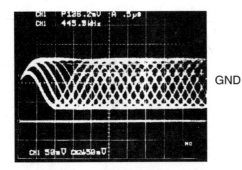

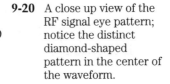

GND

9-20 A close up view of the RF signal eye pattern; notice the distinct diamond-shaped pattern in the center of the waveform.

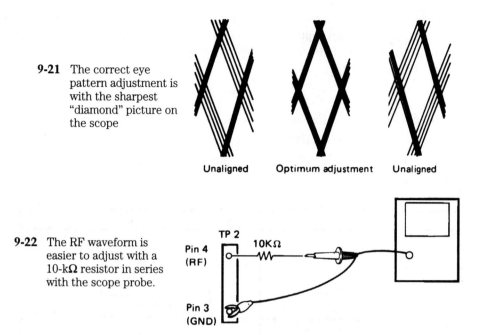

9-21 The correct eye pattern adjustment is with the sharpest "diamond" picture on the scope

Unaligned   Optimum adjustment   Unaligned

9-22 The RF waveform is easier to adjust with a 10-kΩ resistor in series with the scope probe.

Focus and tracking offset adjustments

The focus offset might contain the RF and FE adjustments, one of the same or separate adjustments, in different manufactured CD players. The focus offset adjustments can be called the *jitter* or *eye–pattern* adjustments. The focus offset adjustment is compared to the RF adjustment for less jitter and a clear diamond-shaped opening.

Onkyo DX-C909 RF adjustment   It is not necessary to perform the adjustment of optical pickup. This configuration should be made when replacing the optical pickup.

1. Connect scope to test points RF and VC (Fig. 9-23).
2. Turn the power switch on.
3. Load the test disc YEDS-18 on the tray and press the play button.

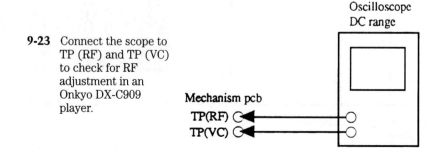

9-23 Connect the scope to TP (RF) and TP (VC) to check for RF adjustment in an Onkyo DX-C909 player.

4. Confirm that the waveform on the scope is optimum eye pattern and optimum level as shown. Optimum means the diamond shape can be clearly distinguished at the center of the waveform.

Denon DCD-2560G focus off-set

1. Push the pause button.
2. Set oscillator to 580 Hz Vp-p (± 0.5 V).
3. Adjust VR103 (Focus Offset) to minimize pattern jitter (Fig. 9-24).

Note: If the focus off-set is not properly adjusted (causing the increase of jitter amount), intermittent sound might occur.

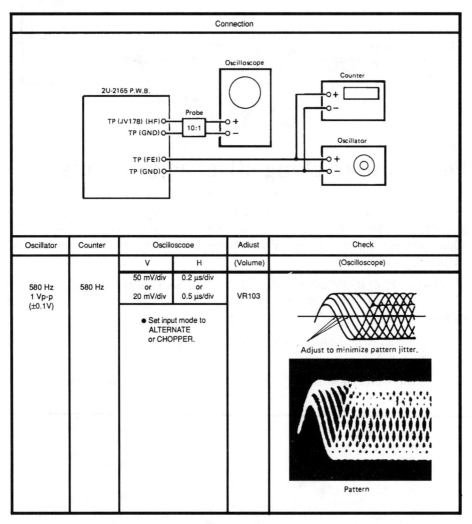

Oscillator	Counter	Oscilloscope		Adjust	Check
		V	H	(Volume)	(Oscilloscope)
580 Hz 1 Vp-p (±0.1V)	580 Hz	50 mV/div or 20 mV/div ● Set input mode to ALTERNATE or CHOPPER.	0.2 µs/div or 0.5 µs/div	VR103	Adjust to minimize pattern jitter. Pattern

9-24 RF adjustment and test instrument connections within the Denon DX-2560G CD player.

Denon DCC-9770 focus off-set adjustment

1. Connect the oscilloscope to test point RF on the MD main board (Fig. 9-25).

2. Load a disc and set mode to play.

3. Adjust RV502 so that the waveform on the scope (eye pattern) is maximum with a good shape. A well-shaped eye pattern means that the mark diamond is clearly distinguished at the center of waveform.

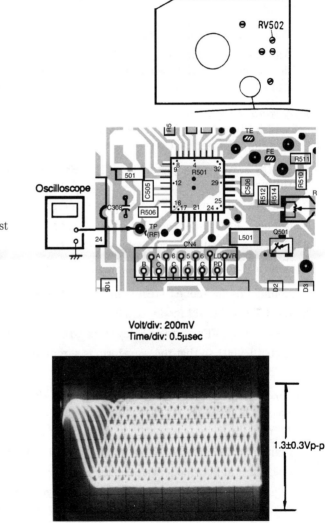

9-25 Connect scope to test point RF and adjust RV502 for sharp eye pattern in a Denon DCD-9770 for focus off-set pattern.

Mitsubishi DP107 focus offset adjustment The focus offset adjustment is about the same as the jitter adjustment. Set the player in PLAY mode with a disc and connect the oscilloscope terminals to HS and ground. Adjust VR101 for the best HS (eye pattern). All lines of the waveform can be observed finely and clearly.

JVC XL-V400B focus offset adjustment The focus offset adjustment is made with the oscilloscope and a normal disc.

1. Connect the oscilloscope between ENN-028 (TP10) and ground.
2. Now play the disc.
3. Adjust VR202 on ENN-023 as the RF signal (waveform on oscilloscope) becomes maximum and the finest waveform.

Onkyo DX-200 focus offset adjustment The manufacturer's special jig is needed.

1. Turn on SW1 of adjustment jig (1).
2. With the meter 2 in the range of 0 ± 0.1 V, adjust R229 for minimum deflection of meter 1. (Note when the deflection of meter 1 is broad, adjust meter 2 to 0 V.)

Panasonic SL-P3610 focus offset adjustment Material relating to Technics Compact Disc Player taken from *Technics Service Manual*, 1985, Matsushita Electric Corporation of America. Used by permission.

1. Set the servo gain adjuster (SZZP1017F) power SW on and the rotary selector switch at "2."
2. Place the unit in the eject mode (tray open).
3. Connect a voltmeter to TJ101 on 03 PC board.
4. Turn power switch on, and adjust VR103 so that the dc voltage is 0 ± 10 mV.

Denon DCC-9770 tracking off-set adjustment

1. Connect oscilloscope to test point TE on the MD main board (Fig. 9-26).
2. Load a disc and set mode to play.
3. Press button FForward or FReverse and observe the traverse waveform.
4. Adjust RV501 so that the waveform is symmetric when centered at the level to be accessed.

Denon DCH-500 CD changer focus off-set adjustment Before starting adjustments, use a YESD-18 test disc and make sure the power supply voltage is 14.4 Vdc (not over 10 A).

1. Connect the oscilloscope to servo board test point RF (Fig. 9-27).
2. Place unit in play mode with the loaded disc.
3. Adjust RV12 so that the scope waveform eye pattern is good. The diamond shape in the center should be clearly distinguished (Fig. 9-28).

Pioneer PD-7010, PD-5010, and PD-9010 tracking offset and focus offset adjustments Set the player to the TEST mode. Adjust the voltage at TP1 pin 9 TR. Adjust RT (Tracking return) to 0 V ± 10 mV by turning VR2 TR-OF (tracking offset) control (Fig. 9-29).

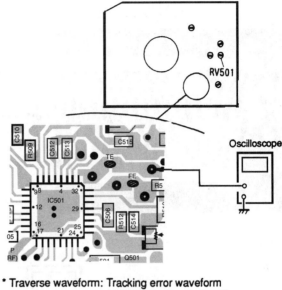

9-26 The tracking off-set adjustment and scope connections in a Denon DCC-9770 player.

* Traverse waveform: Tracking error waveform which is observed when the track is traversed.
Volt/div: 0.5V
Time/div: 2msec
Center: 0V

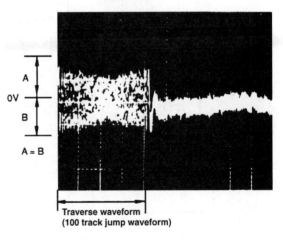

Adjust the voltage at TP1 pin 3 FO.ER (focus error) to 0 V by turning VR6 FO.OF control.

Quasar CD-8975 YW/YE focus offset adjustment Same as for the Panasonic SL-P3610.

Realistic CD-3304 focus off-set adjustment

1. Insert test disc and put unit into play mode.

2. Connect oscilloscope to TP1 (HF GND) (Fig. 9-30).

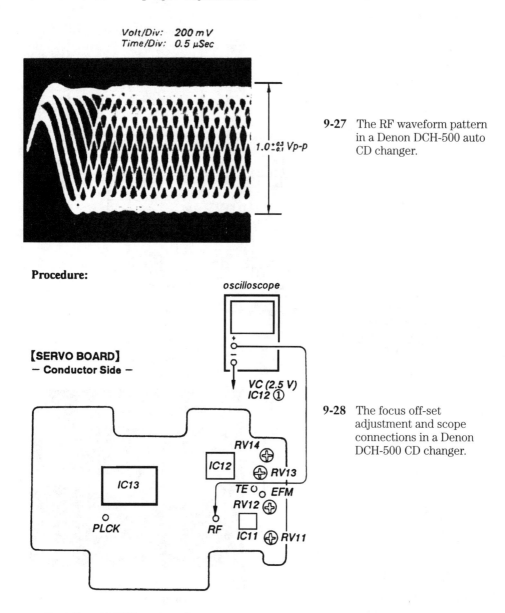

Volt/Div: 200 mV
Time/Div: 0.5 µSec

$1.0^{+0.3}_{-0.1}$ Vp-p

9-27 The RF waveform pattern in a Denon DCH-500 auto CD changer.

Procedure:

oscilloscope

[SERVO BOARD]
— Conductor Side —

VC (2.5 V)
IC12 ①

9-28 The focus off-set adjustment and scope connections in a Denon DCH-500 CD changer.

RV14

IC12   RV13

TE   EFM

RV12

IC13

PLCK   RF   IC11   RV11

3. Adjust VR505 so that the eye pattern becomes clear and waveform (Vp-p) is maximum. When confirming eye pattern, use the 10:1 scope probe (Fig. 9-31).

RCA MCD-141 focus servo offset adjustment

1. Connect the oscilloscope to TP3 (ERM) and TP1 (GND).

2. Preset the AF offset control (R010) to its mechanical center.

3. Load the player with a disc and place the player in the PLAY mode.

4. Adjust the AF offset control (R010) so the EFM signal is set at maximum peak-to-peak volts.

VR6: Focus offset (FO.OF)
VL1: VCO free run (VCO coil)

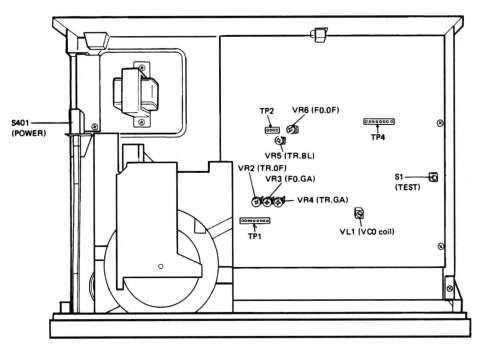

9-29 The adjustment points and controls located on the main PCB in a Pioneer PD-7010, PD5010, and PD-9010 CD player.

5. After the adjustment, measure the dc voltages at the center point (R010) with a dc voltmeter. Make sure the mechanical center of the control (R010) is set to 2.5 V ± 0.5 V.

Yamaha CD-3 focus offset adjustment Set the test disc to PLAY. Make the adjustment at the center of the disc rotation (test disc 35 DHS). Connect the oscilloscope to terminal HS and ground. Adjust VR101 for the best HS (eye pattern) signal. (All lines of the waveform can be observed finely and clearly.)

Tracking offset adjustment of Denon DCD-1800R player Short pins 3 and 4 on the servo wiring board. Turn on TSW (SW 3 to 8 are all on) on the adapter and adjust VR307 so that the slide motor will not drift in either direction. Remove the shorting jumper for pins 3 and 4 after the adjustment is over.

Mitsubishi DP-107 tracking offset adjustment Set the player in the STOP mode. Connect a DCVM meter to terminal Q and ground for measurement. Adjust VR103 to equal $EQ = \pm 50$ mVdc.

JVC XL-V400B tracking offset adjustment Use the oscilloscope with a normal disc. Connect the oscilloscope between ENN-028 (TP1) and ground. Now play the disc. Short test Point TP2 and ground. Adjust VR202 on ENN-023 as making the tracking error signal (waveform on the oscilloscope) that the dc level is 0.

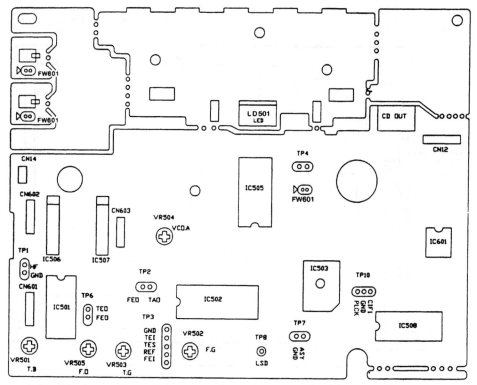

9-30 The focus off-set adjustment and test points in a Realistic CD-3304 CD player.

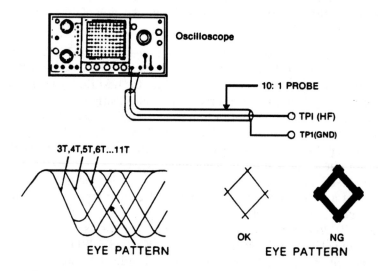

9-31 The scope connections and eye pattern in the Realistic CD-3304 CD player.

Onkyo DX-200 tracking offset adjustment Turn on SW2 of adjustment jig (1). Adjust R226 to minimum (completely counterclockwise). Adjust R114 to bring the deflection meter 2 to the center. Note: When the disc rotates at high speed, make the adjustment while holding down the speed manually. An adjusting tool of insulating material must be used.

Quasar CD8975 YW/YE tracking offset adjustment Material relating to Technics Compact Disc Player taken from *Technics Service Manual* 1985 Matsushita Electric Corporation of America. Used by permission.

1. Set the servo gain adjuster power SW ON and the rotary selector switch at "2."

2. Place the unit in the EJECT mode (tray open).

3. Connect the voltmeter to TJ103 on 03 PC board (optical servo).

4. Turn the power switch ON and adjust VR106 so that the dc voltage is 0 ± 3 mV.

Note: After completing this adjustment, remove the servo gain adjuster and insert the shorting pin into CN103 as it was.

Realistic CD-1000 tracking offset adjustment Connect the oscilloscope leads to TP13 (TDET) and TP16 ground. Load a disc in the player, and set the player to PLAY mode. Adjust R116 so that the EFM signal amplitude becomes maximum (Fig. 9-32).

RCA MCD-141 tracking offset adjustment Connect the dc voltmeter (DVM) to TP7 (TER). Preset the TR offset control (R603) to its mechanical center. Load the

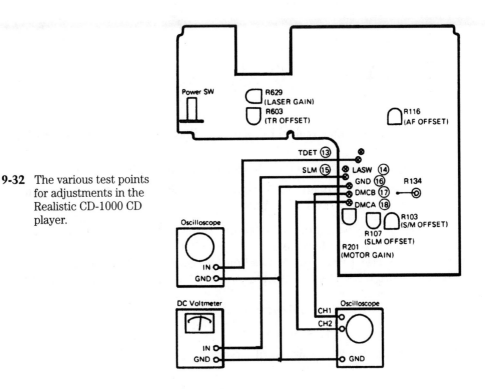

9-32 The various test points for adjustments in the Realistic CD-1000 CD player.

player with a disc and place the player in the PLAY mode. Adjust the TR Offset control (R020) so the dc voltmeter will read +10 mV.

Denon DCD-1800R focus servo gain adjustment Turn on switches 3 to 8 of adjustment adapter.

1. Connect the oscilloscope (X and Y inputs—Lissajous mode) to pins 2 and 4 of TP303 and pin 1, which is ground on the servo wiring board (Fig. 9-33).

9-33 Connect the scope to pin 4 of TP303 with audio oscillator connected to pin 2 for focus servo gain adjustment in the Denon DCD-1800R player.

2. Connect the audio oscillator to pin 2 of TP303 and apply 1.7 kHz, 30 mV p-p sine wave.

3. Turn on switch TSW on the adjustment adapter (SW's 3 to 8: ON).

4. Adjust VR301 so that the X-Y display (Lissajous display) becomes symmetrical in respect to both X and Y axes.

Onkyo DX-200 focus gain adjustment Turn on SW2 of adjustment jig (1). Adjust R232 until the deflection of meter 1 is 0.10 V. (If R232 is turned clockwise, the deflection of meter 1 reduces.) At this time, check to see that meter 2 reads in the range of 0 ± 0.1 V. If meter 2 is outside the range of 0 ± 0.1 V, return to adjustment of the focus offset.

Pioneer PD-7010 focus gain adjustment

1. Set the player to TEST mode.

2. Press the stop key to switch all servos off.

3. Adjust the frequency and output voltage of CH1 of the F.T.G. adjuster (R-878) to 875 Hz and 0.2 V p-p.

Note: If you are adjusting the output voltage by oscilloscope, disconnect the cable from the F.T.G. adjuster circuit board and measure and adjust with the oscilloscope probe in direct contact with pin 3 of the N1 connector (plug). (Because of the hum generated, do not measure at the tip of the cable.)

4. Connect the F.T.G. adjuster.

5. Press the TRACKFWD, PLAY, and PAUSE keys in that order to switch all servos on.

6. Adjust the compact disc player VR3 FO.GA (focus gain) control so that F.T.G. adjuster LED (green) just comes on.

Tracking gain adjustments

In some CD players, the focus gain and tracking gain adjustments are made by taking oscilloscope voltage tests across the coil windings. For the focus gain adjustment, connect the oscilloscope across the focus coil. Play a test disc. Adjust the focus gain control between 500 to 600 mV p-p (Fig. 9-34).

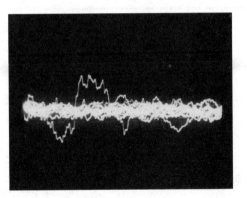

9-34 The typical scope pattern across the focus coil to make focus gain adjustments.

For the tracking gain adjustment, the oscilloscope is connected across the tracking coil. Of course, one side of the tracking and focus coil is grounded, in which the ground lead of the scope is at ground potential. Now play the test disc. Adjust the tracking gain control for a 1.8 to 2.2 V p-p across the tracking coil (Fig. 9-35). Always follow the manufacturer's adjustment procedures.

If the sound jumps when the machine is jolted or bumped, the tracking gain might be set too close or too small. If a test disc with a small scratch is played and the sound jumps, the tracking gain might be set too large.

Denon DCD-1800R tracking servo gain adjustment Use the Denon adjustment adapter in all servo electronic adjustments. (Turn on switches 3 to 8 for tracking gain adjustment.)

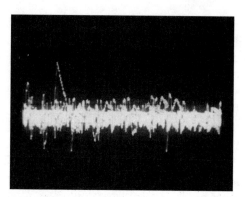

9-35 The typical gain adjustment with scope across tracking coil.

1. Connect the oscilloscope (X and Y inputs—Lissajous mode) to pins 1 and 5 of TP302 on the servo wiring board (pin 3 is ground). See Fig. 9-36.

2. Connect the audio oscillator to pin (1) of TP302 and apply 1.89 kHz, 0.2 V p-p sine wave.

3. Adjust VR302 so that the Lissajous display becomes symmetrical in respect to both X and Y axes.

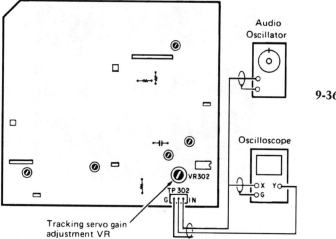

9-36 Use the tracking adapter to make tracking servo gain adjustment in Denon DCD-1800R CD player.

Denon DCC-9770 tracking gain (coarse) adjustment This adjustment is to be performed when replacing the optical pick-up block or RV13. This adjustment should be performed after focus Off-Set and tracking Off-Set adjustments are completed.

1. Connect the oscilloscope to servo board test point (TE). See Fig. 9-37.

2. Put the unit into play mode by loading the disc.

3. Turn servo board RV13 from clockwise stop, then check the oscilloscope waveform disappear (Fig. 9-38).

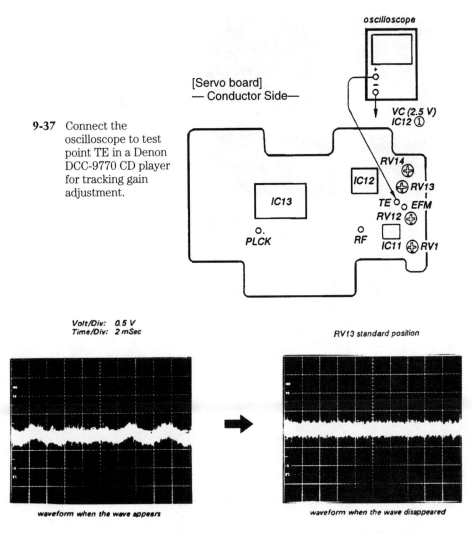

9-37 Connect the oscilloscope to test point TE in a Denon DCC-9770 CD player for tracking gain adjustment.

waveform when the wave appears

waveform when the wave disappeared

9-38 Adjust RV13 where the waveform disappears in the Denon DCC-9700 tracking gain adjustment.

When gain is lower

When selecting by pressing reverse AMS and forward button, brake application is poor because of low tracking gain. Therefore, the traverse waveform is after the 100 jump waveform, then the selection will be located slowly (Fig. 9-39).

When gain is higher

Operation noise is heard due to a scratch or dust, then operation will be unstable. The max and min (high and low gain) setting, when VR contact point is shown in Fig. 9-40.

Panasonic SL-P3610 tracking gain adjustment "Material relating to Technics Compact Disc Player taken from *Technics Service Manual*, 1985, Matsushita Electric Corporation of America. Used by permission."

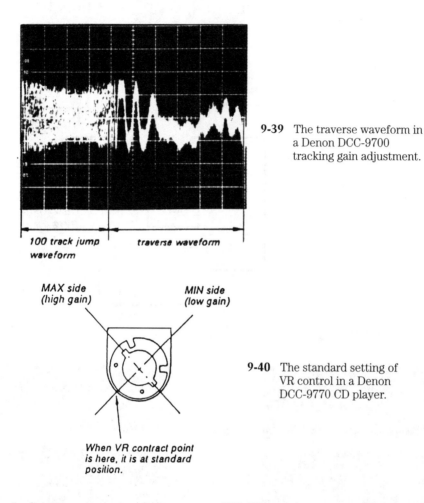

9-39 The traverse waveform in a Denon DCC-9700 tracking gain adjustment.

100 track jump waveform   *traverse waveform*

MAX side (high gain)   MIN side (low gain)

9-40 The standard setting of VR control in a Denon DCC-9770 CD player.

When VR contract point is here, it is at standard position.

1. Set the servo gain adjuster power SW ON and the rotary selector switch to "3."

2. Adjust the low-frequency oscillator to 1.5 kHz and 150 mV p-p output. Connect it to test pin OSC in and GVD of servo gain adjuster.

3. Connect CH1 and CH2 of the oscilloscope to test pins TP1 and TP2 of the servo gain adjuster (TP3 is GND), and place the disc on turntable. Oscilloscope setting: Volt 100 mV (both channels), SWEEP 2 ms, Input ac, Mode Chop.

4. Turn power switch on. When the turntable begins to rotate, 21.5-kHz signal appears on the oscilloscope. Then adjust VR104 so that the waveform amplitude of both channels are equal to each other.

Onkyo DX-C606 focus/tracking gain adjustment Focus/tracking gain determines the pick-up follow-up (vertical and horizontal) relative to mechanical noise and mechanical shock when the 2-axis device operates.

However, as these reciprocate, the adjustment is at the point where both are satisfied.

- When the gain is raised, the noise when the 2-axis device operates increases.
- When gain is lowered, it is more susceptible to mechanical shock and skipping occurs more easily.
- When gain adjustment is off, the symptoms below appear (Chart 9-2).

Chart 9-2.

Symptoms/Gain	Focus	Tracking
• The time until music starts becomes longer for STOP → ▷ PLAY or automatic selection (◄◄ ►► buttons pressed. Normally takes about 2 seconds.)	low	low or high
• Music does not start and disc continues to rotate for STOP → ▷ PLAY or automatic selection (◄◄ ►► buttons pressed.)	–	low
• Disc table opens shortly after STOP → ▷ PLAY.	low or high	–
• Sound is interrupted during PLAY. Or time counter display stops progressing.	–	low
• More poise during 2-axis device operation.	high	high

In a simple procedure:

1. Keep the set horizontal. (If it's not horizontal, this adjustment cannot be performed due to the gravity against the 2-axis device.)
2. Insert disc (YEDS-18) and press play button.
3. Connect the oscilloscope to RF/Servo board TP (FE). See Fig. 9-41.

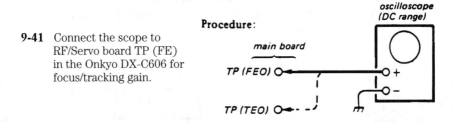

9-41 Connect the scope to RF/Servo board TP (FE) in the Onkyo DX-C606 for focus/tracking gain.

4. Adjust RV102 so that the waveform is as shown in focus gain adjustment (Fig. 9-42).

Radio Shack EF (tracking balance) adjustment

1. Connect the oscilloscope to test point (TE1) in TP3 and REF (Fig. 9-43).
2. Short TES and REF (TP3).
3. Insert the test disc, after play, adjust VR501 (TB) so that the amplitude above and below the zero dc line becomes equal (*Amplitude A = B*).

VOLT/DIV: 100 m
TIME/DIV: 2 mS

—100 mV

—0 V

* Incorrect Examples (dc level changes more than
on adjusted waveform)

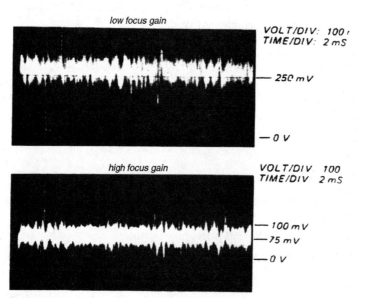

low focus gain

VOLT/DIV: 100 r
TIME/DIV: 2 mS

—250 mV

—0 V

high focus gain

VOLT/DIV 100
TIME/DIV 2 mS

—100 mV
—75 mV
—0 V

9-42   The focus/tracking gain adjustment waveforms in Onkyo DX-
C606 CD player.

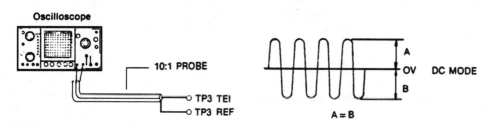

Oscilloscope

10:1 PROBE

TP3 TEI
TP3 REF

A
0V   DC MODE
B

A = B

9-43   Realistic CD-3304 EF tracking balance connections of an oscilloscope.

Yamaha CD-3 tracking servo gain adjustment   Set the player to PLAY mode.
Connect the A.C.V.M. meter to terminals Q and TE. Apply 800 Hz 100 mV n.m.s. signal to TD1 and ground with a 220-kΩ resistor in series from the audio oscillator. Adjust VR104 to the following specifications: ETE = (EQ + 5 dB) ± 1 dB.

Miscellaneous adjustment procedures

The following models require miscellaneous adjustments.

Denon DCD-1800R "Kickvoltage" adjustment Turn off the main switch and remove the adjustment adapter. Connect CH1 (ac mode) of the oscilloscope to TP306 on the servo wiring board (Fig. 9-44). Connect CH2 (dc mode) of the oscilloscope to the cross point of R365 and R366. Set the scope trigger mode at CH2. Play the middle of the program area of the adjustment disc and pause. Press the fast reverse button and adjust VR305 so that the HF envelope waveform becomes symmetrical. Press the FAST FORWARD button and adjust VR305 again so that the HF envelope waveform becomes symmetrical (Fig. 9-45).

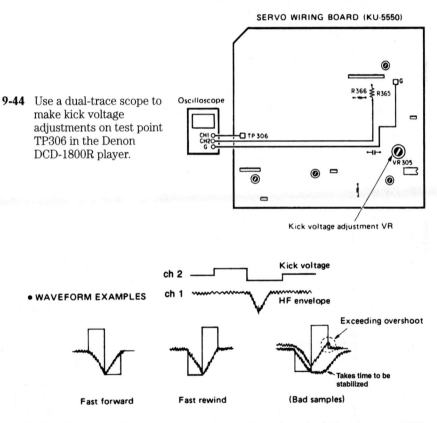

9-44 Use a dual-trace scope to make kick voltage adjustments on test point TP306 in the Denon DCD-1800R player.

9-45 The correct kick voltage waveform exists when the kick voltage and HF envelope are locked in at the same point on the waveform.

Denon DCD-1800R audio output level adjustment Connect a 47-kΩ load resistor across the audio output terminals paralleled with an electronic volt meter. Use the audio test disc Denon Technical CD138C39-7147 and playback 1-kHz signal. Adjust VR502 for L-CH and VR503 for R-CH so that the audio output level becomes 2 V ± 0.3 V (Fig. 9-46).

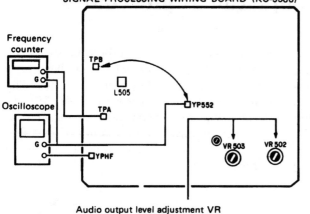

SIGNAL PROCESSING WIRING BOARD (KU-5560)

Audio output level adjustment VR

9-46 Perform the audio output level adjustment of both stereo channels with a test disc and electronic voltmeter in the Denon DCD-1800R CD chassis.

JVC XL-V400B Kick Gain adjustment

Use a two-channel oscilloscope with a normal disc. Connect CH1 of the oscilloscope between ENN-023 TP1 and ground, and CH2 of the oscilloscope between ENN-023 TP5 and ground (Fig. 9-47). Now play the disc. Play back the last number recorded on the disc and press the PAUSE button in midcourse. Observe the oscilloscope and adjust VR301 to obtain the correct waveform (Fig. 9-48). Adjust VR301 so that the fifth peaks (pointed out by the arrow mark in the figure) are tangent to each other. If they are crossing or separate from each other, continue the adjustment to obtain the best results.

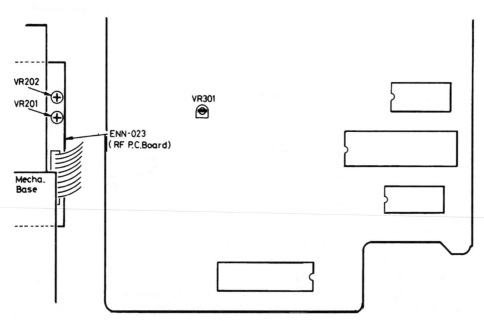

9-47 Use a dual-trace scope with a normal disc to make JVC VL-400B kick gain adjustment at VR301.

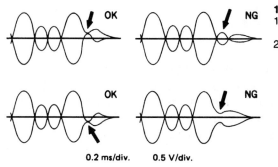

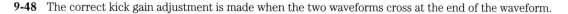

13-(6) Kick gain adjustment
1) Adjustment instrument
Oscilloscopye (2ch), normal disc.
2) Adjustment procedure
1. Connect the ch1 of oscilloscope between **ENN-028** TP 1 and GND, the ch2 of oscilloscope between **ENN-028** TP 5 and GND.
2. Turn the oscilloscope Normal mode with triggered by the ch2.
3. Play the disc.
4. Play back the last number recorded on a disk and press the PAUSE button in mid course At this time, observing an oscilloscope adjust VR301 to obtain the correct waveform as shown in the figure below.

9-48 The correct kick gain adjustment is made when the two waveforms cross at the end of the waveform.

Realistic CD1000 sample/hold offset adjustment

Use the oscilloscope and a defect test disc for this adjustment or a disc to which a black tape approximately 0.5 mm wide is stuck. Connect the oscilloscope to TP13 (TDET) and TP16 (GND). Load the disc in the player and set the player to PLAY mode. Adjust R103 while monitoring the playback sound, so that the track jumping becomes minimum (Fig. 9-49).

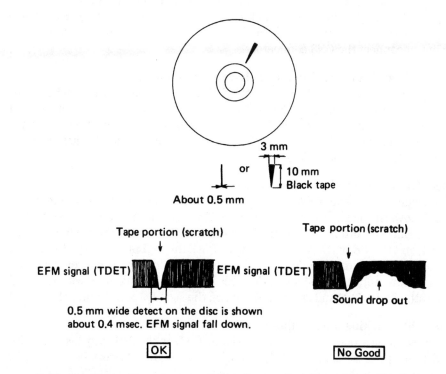

9-49 Use the oscilloscope and a detect disc to adjust the sample/hold adjustment in the Realistic CD-1000.

Auto radio electrical electronic adjustments

The adjustments within the car radio should be made with a 14.4-Vdc supply voltage (more than 2 A). Use a YEDS-1 or YEDS-7 test disc. Connect a two-channel oscilloscope with delayed sweep frequency counter and a light power meter to make the different tests. Practically all of electrical or electronic adjustments are like those found in the home CD player. Locate the test points and various controls on the RF amp PC board.

Pioneer CDX-1 LD power adjustment

While pushing the interlock SW (S11), push the FF button and move the pickup until the power sensor enters. Place the light power sensor on top of the pickup object lens. Push the DISPLAY button, turn on the LD, and check the emitting power.

If it is not within specifications, quickly adjust VF4 so the light power sensor meter will read 0.25 ± 0.01 mW. After the adjustment, push the DISPLAY button again and turn off the laser diode. When replacing the pickup, set VR4 to the minimum (turn completely to the left) and then begin adjustment.

Alpine 5900 RF offset adjustment

Remove the connector (CN3) on the main board. Connect an oscilloscope or digital VOM to the test points (RF and GND) on the RF amp board. Insert the disc (YEDS-1) and press the PLAY/PAUSE button. The disc should eject from the set in a few seconds. Adjust RV651 on the RF amp board so that the digital voltmeter reading is –100 mV ± 10 mV during the time before the disc is ejected (Fig. 9-50). After the adjustment, reconnect the CN3 connector.

Alpine 5900 and Sony CDX-5 focus offset adjustment

Connect the oscilloscope to the test points (RF and GND) on the RF amp board. Insert the disc (YEDS-1) and press PLAY/PAUSE button. Adjust RV653 on the RF amp board so that the oscilloscope waveform eye pattern is good. A good eye pattern is where the diamond in the center of the waveform can be clearly distinguished. Volt/Div: 200 mV Time/Div: 0.54 sec.

Pioneer CDX-1 focus offset adjustment

While pushing the interlock SW (S11), push the TRC button and then the REV button, and move the pickup toward the center of the disc. Insert a test disc and load it with the RELOAD button. Turn on the LD with the DPS button, and push the SCAN, REPEAT, and PAUSE buttons to make it play. Push the FF button and go to the 23rd selection (approximately 23 minutes). The jump operation can be canceled with the PAUSE button. Adjust WR104 so that the RF level is at its maximum with the oscilloscope attached to TP4 and ground, located on the signal processor unit (Fig. 9-51).

Alpine 5900 tracking offset adjustment

Connect the oscilloscope to the test points TE and GND on the RF board. Insert the disc (YEDS-1) and press the PLAY/PAUSE button. Press one of the M sensor buttons or AD1 buttons and observe the oscilloscope waveform for track jump. Adjust RV652 on the RF amp board so that the oscilloscope waveform of 100 track jump is symmetrical above and below, relative to 0 V. Volt/Div: 1 V, Time/Div: 0.2 ms, Center 0 V.

2. ELECTRICAL ADJUSTMENTS

[NOTE ON ADJUSTMENT]

1. The adjustment should be performed with the set placed horizontally.

2. Use YEDS-1 disc unless otherwise specified.

3. Supply voltage: DC 14.4 V (more than 2 A)

[Adjustment Location]

[RF Amp P.C. board] — component side —

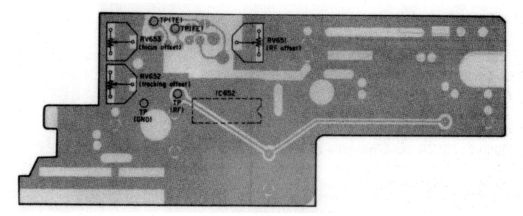

9-50 The RF, TE, and FE test points and controls on RF amp PCB in Alpines 5900 auto CD player.

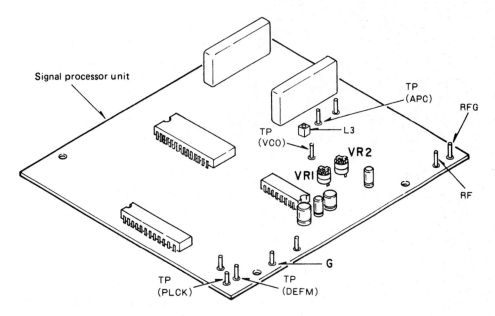

9-51 The correct test points and different adjustment controls of the signal processing board in the Pioneer CDX-1 compact disc auto player.

Pioneer CDX-1 tracking error offset adjustment

Connect the oscilloscope to test point TP37 and ground. Play the disc selection for approximately 14 minutes, with the PAUSE button pushed and the tracking servo open, and adjust VR3 so that the waveform center is 0 volts. (The center zero line of the waveform is in the center of the waveform.) The adjustment is no good if the center zero line is above or below the center of the waveform.

Sony CDX-5 tracking offset adjustment

Use the same procedure as for the Alpine 5900 adjustment.

Alpine 5900 tracking gain adjustment

This adjustment should be performed when replacing the FOP and RV501. The adjustment should be performed after the focus offset and tracking offset adjustments.

Connect the oscilloscope to the test points TE and GND on the RF amp board. Insert the disc (YEDS-1) and press PLAY/PAUSE button. Turn RV501 on the main board clockwise from left side and observe the waveform on the oscilloscope. Adjust RV501 until the fundamental waveform disappears (no large waves) See Fig. 9-52.

Pioneer CDX-1 tracking servo gain adjustment

With the tracking and focus servo gain adjustments, the FTG adjustment jig is used. Turn the selector switch of the jig to number 2. Use the search to find track number 14 on the disc. Connect the yellow wire to TP12, red wire to TP13, and black wire to TP18 (GND). Adjust VR101 to turn J-LED on.

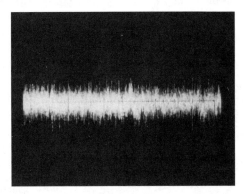

9-52 Adjust RV501 for a nonwaving tracking waveform in Alpines 5900 car CD player.

Alpine 5900 and Sony CDX-5 focus gain adjustment

This adjustment should be performed when replacing the FOP and RV502. Set RV502 on the main board to mechanical center. Check that there is not an abnormal amount of operation noise (white noise) from the two-axis device. If there is, turn RV502 slightly counterclockwise.

Pioneer CDX-1 focus servo gain adjustment

Turn the selector jig to 1. Use the search to locate track #14 of the YEDS-7 test disc. Connect the orange wire to TP15, brown wire to TP17, and black wire to TP18 (GND). Adjust VR105 to turn Y-LED on.

10

Remote and system control circuits

LIKE THE TV AND VCR, THE COMPACT DISC PLAYER CAN BE OPERATED WITH REMOTE control. The system control circuits can be operated with the remote or operated separately with buttons found on the front of the disc players. Usually, the remote-control receiver circuits operate within the control system.

The remote transmitter is constructed like the TV and VCR units. The remote transmitter can be a separate unit or it can be found in a digital command center (Fig. 10-1). Most of the buttons on the remote transmitter are like those found on the front of the CD player. The CD player can be operated from the remote, by itself, or by a combination of the two. The remote transmitter operates within the infrared spectrum.

The RCA Digital Command Center (MCD-141) controls practically all of the functions of the compact disc player. Some of these complex functions are track and index search, memory programming, and programmed playback. Also, when the compact disc player is turned on, the remote-control system automatically turns on the MSR-140 stereo receiver and chooses the compact disc player as the audio source.

Remote control functions

A typical remote-control infrared transmitter has the on/off, open/close, A---B, display, set/check, clear, play, pause/stop, positive +, negative –, fast-forward, and fast-reverse buttons. The more complicated remote might have up to 24 different operations. One large IC with corresponding diodes might control all of the above functions (Fig. 10-2).

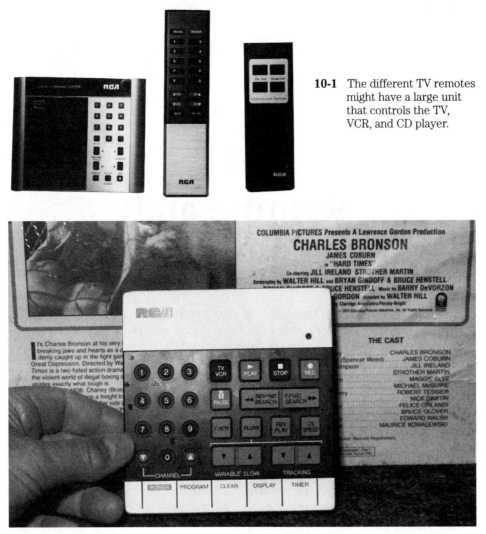

10-1 The different TV remotes might have a large unit that controls the TV, VCR, and CD player.

10-2 One large IC can be found within the TV, VCR, and CD player remote transmitter.

RCA MCD-141 remote functions

There are 17 different CD remote functions with this remote transmitter. When you turn the player on, the MCD-141 stereo receiver will also be turned on (if it is not already on). If the player is on when the button is pressed, the next command is for the player.

PLAY Press the PLAY button to begin playing the disc. If this button is pressed before the disc directory is read (after the CD button is pressed), the command will be rejected. Pressing PLAY also connects the compact disc player to the stereo receiver.

PROGRAM Press the PROGRAM button to enter the programming mode.

STOP Pressing the STOP button stops play. Unlike the manual STOP/CLEAR button, the remote STOP button does not erase memory.

PAUSE The laser pickup is muted when the PAUSE button is pressed. To resume normal play, press the PAUSE or PLAY button again.

REPEAT Press the REPEAT button to repeat the entire disc or selected program.

BAND This button is used to enter the selected track number into memory.

BAND REVERSE Press the BAND REVERSE button to return to the beginning of the track currently playing. Press it again to skip back to the preceding track.

BAND FORWARD Press the BAND FORWARD button to skip to the beginning of the next track. If a program is in memory, then the next track in memory is accessed.

SEEK Press the SEEK button to begin playing the programmed tracks.

CLEAR Press the CLEAR button to begin playing the programmed tracks.

SCAN FORWARD While the SCAN FORWARD button is held down, short passages are played as the laser pickup moves toward the end of the disc.

SCAN REVERSE While the SCAN REVERSE button is held down, short passages are played as the laser pickup moves toward the beginning of the disc.

DIGITS Track and index numbers are selected using these buttons.

MUTE Pressing this button alternately mutes and unmutes the sound. The MUTE function actually addresses the stereo receiver, so when recording from the compact disc player, the sound being recorded will not be affected.

VOLUME UP/DOWN These buttons vary the volume up and down. As with the MUTE, the command is carried out by the stereo receiver.

OFF Press this button to turn the compact disc player off. If no other device is on that requires the stereo receiver to be on, the receiver also turns off.

Auto remote control functions

Operate the remote control unit in the auto while pointing it at the remote control sensor on the in-dash auto player (Fig. 10-3). Usually, the remote control unit can be used up to 6 meters in a straight line from the in-dash player. This distance decreases when the remote control unit is operated at an angle from the remote control sensor.

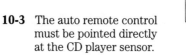

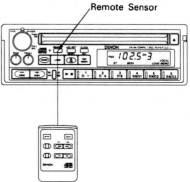

Remote Sensor

10-3 The auto remote control must be pointed directly at the CD player sensor.

Simply point the remote control unit at the remote sensor when operating it. The in-dash player might not function if there are obstacles between the remote control sensor and the remote, so operate the control unit from directly in front of the in-dash CD player.

Do not press the operation button on the in-dash player and the remote control at the same time. This will cause a miss operation. The remote control operation can be impaired if the remote sensor on the in-dash player is exposed to strong light (such as sunlight).

The remote transmitter

The remote transmitter is a hand-operated unit that controls at a distance most operating functions of the compact disc player. Most remote control transmitter circuits are quite simple and revolve around one IC component (Fig. 10-4). The unit is battery-operated from two or three penlight "AA" cell batteries. The infrared-emitting LED (D7) sends out the transmitting signal. Some remote transmitters might have more than one emitting LED. Most transmitters are crystal-controlled (X01). Several diodes are found in the push-button switching network (Fig. 10-5).

REMOTE CONTROL OPERATION

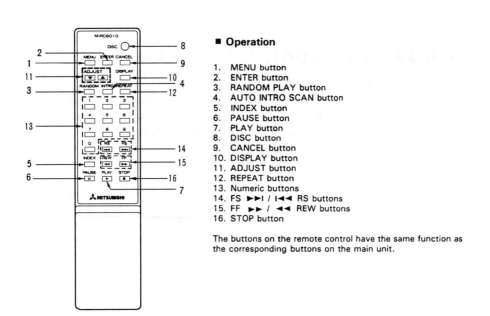

■ **Operation**

1. MENU button
2. ENTER button
3. RANDOM PLAY button
4. AUTO INTRO SCAN button
5. INDEX button
6. PAUSE button
7. PLAY button
8. DISC button
9. CANCEL button
10. DISPLAY button
11. ADJUST button
12. REPEAT button
13. Numeric buttons
14. FS ▶▶I / I◀◀ RS buttons
15. FF ▶▶ / ◀◀ REW buttons
16. STOP button

The buttons on the remote control have the same function as the corresponding buttons on the main unit.

10-4 The remote control transmitter operation within a Mitsubishi M-C4030 automatic CD changer player.

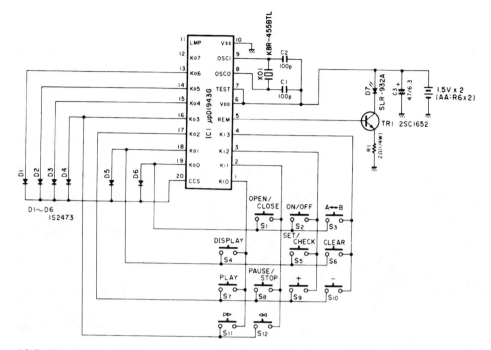

10-5   The Yamaha CD-3 remote transmitter is controlled by one IC1, transistor TR1, and infrared diode D7.

Remote control problems

Often, the remote control problems are quite simple. Defective batteries and broken components cause most remote control problems. First, replace the batteries or test across each battery with the DMM or VOM (Fig. 10-6). Press the ON button while battery voltage tests are made. A weak battery might produce weak or no remote operation. Always replace the batteries with heavy-duty types. Make sure the new batteries are installed correctly for polarity.

Check the battery terminals for poor connection. Inspect each battery terminal spring connector. Clean it off with cleaning spray and cotton swab. If the battery contacts are excessively corroded, clean them off with a pocketknife and sandpaper. Like all contacts, the pencil eraser can clean up dirty battery contacts. Inspect the battery terminals for torn or loose wires.

If the remote control transmitter still does not operate on any given button, suspect a dirty switch button. Remove the bottom cover to get at the transmitter mechanism. The unit can be held together with screws or a plastic clip. Often, the top cover must be removed to get at the switch assembly. Remove the screws or clip and loosen the PC board from the push button assembly. Clean off the switch contacts with cleaning spray or TV tuner lube. Press the plastic tube right down into each switch area. Some of these are difficult to get at if they are sealed buttons (Fig. 10-7).

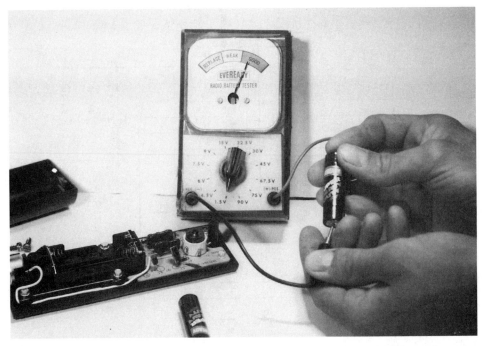

10-6 Check the remote batteries with a battery tester or DMM.

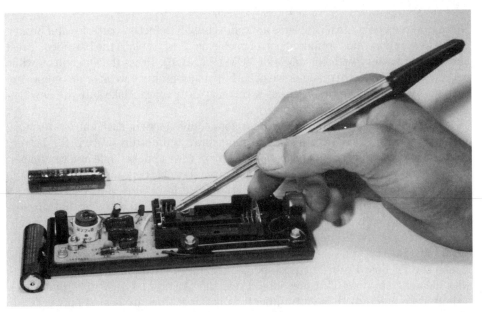

10-7 The inside view of a small remote control transmitter with only a few components.

Rough handling of the remote unit could cause it to be dead or operate intermittently. Sometimes when the remote is dropped or thrown, the PC board or some component might break. Inspect the PC board for broken connections or components. Resolder each connection to locate the intermittent problem. Check each switch and wiring connection with the meter. Inspect the transistor and LED terminals for broken or loose leads.

Remote transmitter or receiver

After battery replacement, the remote transmitter can be checked with a commercial remote transmitter checker or the homemade indicator that checks the laser beam (see chapter 3). The infrared indicator can be taken on house calls to determine if the remote transmitter or receiver is not operating with the CD player, VCR, or TV receivers (Fig. 10-8).

10-8   The infrared indicator can check remote infrared transmitters besides checking the laser diode.

Hold the end of the CD infrared transmitter up close to the infrared indicator. Switch the indicator on. Push down on any button functions and listen for an interrupting tone and LED on the infrared indicator (Fig. 10-9). The infrared photodetector is located at the flat end. Move the remote control around for the loudest signal. Now check out each function button; each one will produce a tone and light when pressed. Suspect a dirty or poor button contact when the tone and light are intermittent. Check the receiver section within the control system of the CD player if the indicator sounds off.

Defective infrared transmitter

After replacing the batteries and checking the infrared transmitter on the indicator with the remote transmitter not operating, suspect a defective transistor, IC, fixed diodes, broken components, or poor wiring of the PC board. Check for 3 volts on terminals 8 and 9 of IC101 (Fig. 10-10). If no voltage, check the battery wire terminals and wiring connections between batteries and the IC pin numbers. Test each transistor and diode with the diode test of the DMM or transistor tester. The infrared-emitting diode can be checked with the fixed diode test. Do not be surprised if the

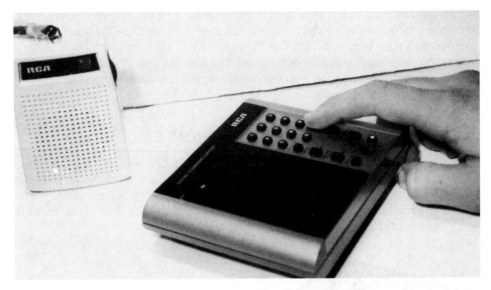

10-9 The small portable radio can be used as an infrared indicator with a tone or buzz each time the button is pressed.

diode resistance is over 1 kΩ. A leaky emitting diode will show leakage in both directions.

To check the IC, take voltage and resistance on the IC terminals to common ground (usually the negative side of the battery). Very low voltage at pins 8 and 9 might indicate a leaky IC component. Very low resistance measurements from each pin to ground might locate a leaky IC. Remove the IC pin with solder wick and take another resistance measurement on the 2-kΩ scale. Often, resistance measurements under 1 kΩ with the pin connection isolated indicate a leaky IC. Check each IC pin number function and compare to the button that is not working for possible trouble (Fig. 10-11). Replace each IC component with the original part number. Also, check each defective switch function and tie them to the respective switch on the schematic diagram (Fig. 10-12).

Like the TV remote control, the CD player remote can be sent in for repair at various service depots. Many of the manufacturer CD player service centers will exchange or repair the remote transmitter. Check the TV module repair and exchange centers if they can repair the defective remote. Sometimes, if the remote is broken or too costly to repair, a new remote transmitter is the only solution.

Universal central control remote

The universal remote control transmitter can operate most TV, VCR, audio and video components, and CD players. The General Electric RRC500 does the work of three remotes, while the RRC600 model does the work of four remotes (Fig. 10-13). The RRC600 controls up to four infrared audio/video products, with over 200 key combinations, program sequencing, LCD display, and low-battery indicator.

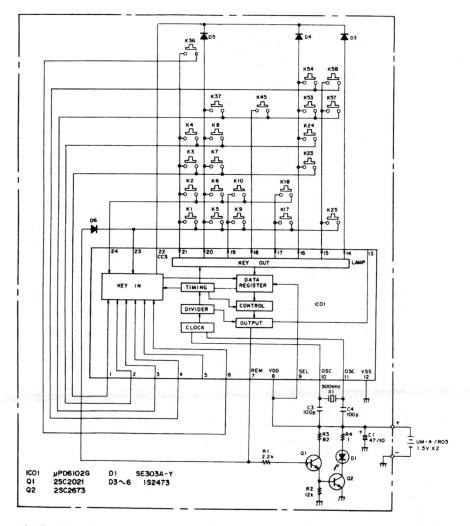

10-10 The infrared remote transmitter can be tested with voltage, resistance, diode, and transistor tests.

This remote, like all other universal control units, can be adjusted to work on all remote control products. These remote control units can be purchased at electronic TV dealers, hardware stores, mall stores, and Radio Shack. The universal remote operates on batteries like other remotes. The remote can be checked like other remotes with the remote tester (discussed in chapter 3 of infrared detector/indicator) or infrared laser tester.

Infrared remote receiver

The remote control receiver sensor is found on the front panel of the CD player. The infrared sensor receives the transmission from the hand-held remote transmitter.

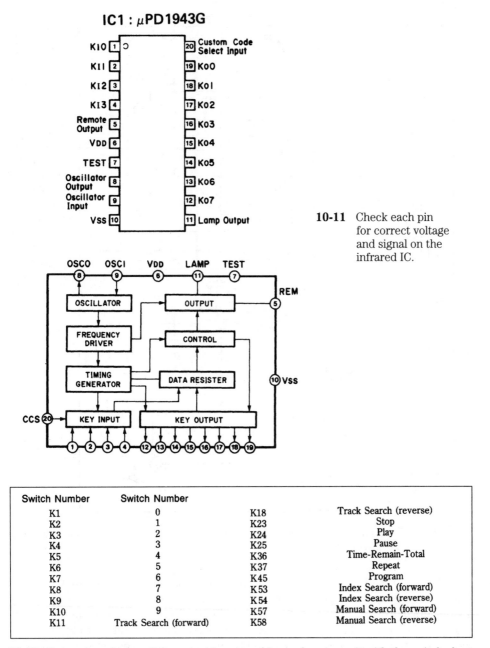

10-11 Check each pin for correct voltage and signal on the infrared IC.

Switch Number	Switch Number		
K1	0	K18	Track Search (reverse)
K2	1	K23	Stop
K3	2	K24	Play
K4	3	K25	Pause
K5	4	K36	Time-Remain-Total
K6	5	K37	Repeat
K7	6	K45	Program
K8	7	K53	Index Search (forward)
K9	8	K54	Index Search (reverse)
K10	9	K57	Manual Search (forward)
K11	Track Search (forward)	K58	Manual Search (reverse)

10-12 Determine which switch contact is not working and compare it with the switch chart of Pioneer PD-7010 CD player.

The weak signal is fed to a preamp stage, decoder, and system control IC (Fig. 10-14). The infrared sensor is usually placed in a shielded container (Fig. 10-15). The remote control light sensor in the Denon DCD-1800R player feeds the remote signal

10-13 A universal control center remote for the TV, VCR, and CD player.

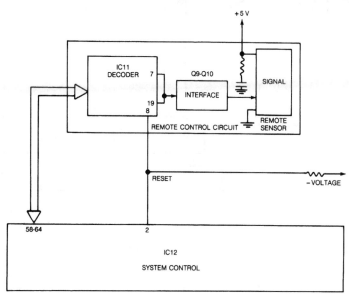

10-14 The remote control transmitter activates the remote sensor and decodes remote circuits in the Pioneer PD-9010 player.

to the remote control Decoder board (Fig. 10-16). IC001 receives both signals from the push-button keys and remote receiver signal in the control system operation.

Onkyo DX-200 remote control circuit After the remote control input from the remote control sensor (photosensitive diode d831) has been synthesized, detected, amplified, and rectified by the remote control circuit, the signal is passed to

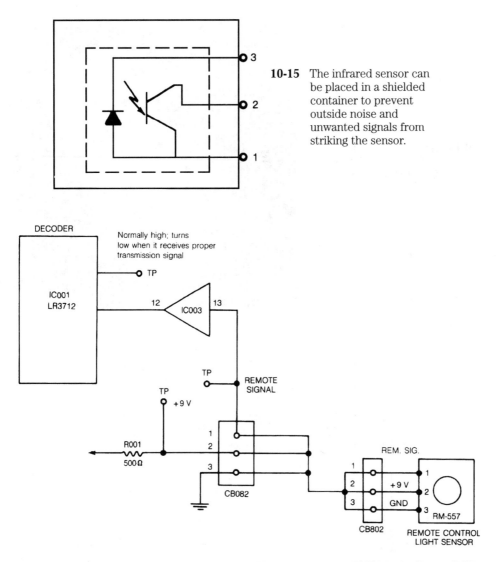

10-15 The infrared sensor can be placed in a shielded container to prevent outside noise and unwanted signals from striking the sensor.

10-16 The remote control light sensor activates IC003 and decoder IC001 in the Denon DCD-1800R remote receiver circuit.

the microcomputer. The remote control circuit is incorporated in the IC BA6340 (Q501) with the synchronizing frequency (38 kHz), gain, and time constants determined by externally connected elements (Fig. 10-17).

The L501 core is adjusted to the point of maximum sensitivity in respect to the remote control input. The output (pin 1 of Q501) is switched to high level (+ 5 V) when there is no input signal, while data output is obtained at CMOS level when a remote control input is applied. The shield around the remote sensor (D831) is very important. If the sensor is not properly shielded, noise might appear at pin 1 output when no input signal is applied, thereby preventing the remote control mechanism

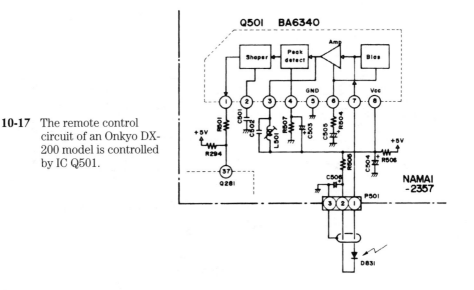

10-17 The remote control circuit of an Onkyo DX-200 model is controlled by IC Q501.

from functioning correctly. The remote control code is decoded by the main micro-computer (Q281).

Onkyo remote control tuned coil adjustment

1. Connect the oscilloscope to IC Q501 pin 3.
2. Continue to press PLAY key of remote control transmitter.
3. Keep a distance between the transmitter and the unit so the peak-to-peak of waveform becomes 0.5 V.
4. Adjust L501 so that the waveform attains maximum output.

Servicing the remote control sensor section

The signal picked up from infrared sensor can be checked, indicating the infrared sensor is operating, with a scope signal waveform. Usually, a test point is found after the infrared sensor or the signal can be scoped after the preamp and detector circuits (Fig. 10-18). The remote control transmitter PLAY key must be pressed down at all times to receive the transmitted signal. Suspect a defective infrared sensor if no scope waveform is found. Check the dc voltage source at the infrared sensor terminals. Sometimes, broken or loose cable connections produce intermittent remote control functions in the receiver circuits. Scope the remote signal and take accurate voltage and resistance measurements on the IC and transistor components to locate the defective component.

System control circuits

The simple system control circuit consists of a decoder control IC, display, and key input boards (Fig. 10-19), while in larger CD players, the system control circuits con-

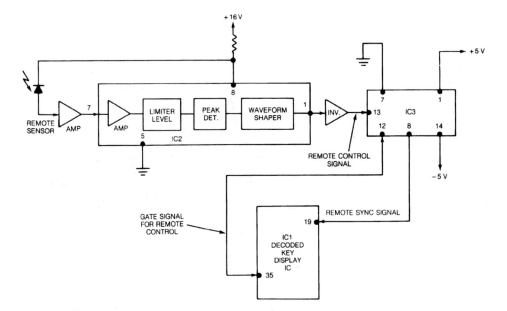

10-18 Check the remote signal after the first remote amp or pin 1 of IC2. The remote signal activates IC3 and decoder IC1.

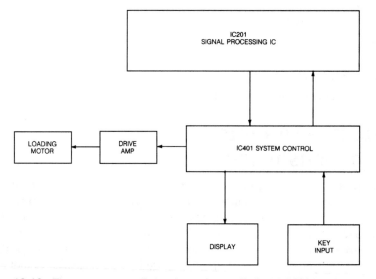

10-19 The system control circuits are controlled with IC201 and system control IC401.

sist of two microprocessors, display, and keyboards. In the RCA MCD-141 player, two microprocessors are in the system control circuits (IC601 and IC901). IC601, the system control microprocessor, is responsible for control of the internal operation of the player (Fig. 10-20). The LMT, LID, and CHK switches inform the microprocessor of the location of the disc tray and the laser pickup assembly. IC601 also outputs

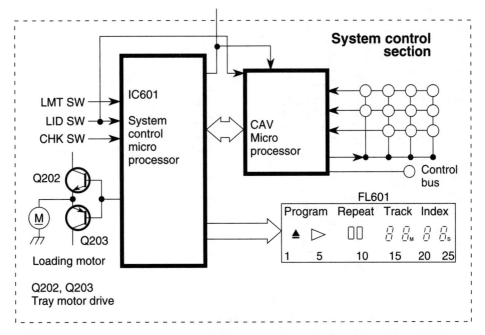

10-20 The keyboard, remote control, CAV microprocessor, and system control (IC601) control the loading motor and fluorescent display in the RCA MCD-141 player.

time shared scan/data information, which consists of keyboard scan signals and fluorescent display data to light the front panel.

The interface microprocessor, IC901, connects the player to the control bus and allows two-way communication between the RCA Audio System MSR140 Stereo Receiver/Amplifier and the compact disc player.

Onkyo DX-200 microcomputer and peripheral circuits The microcomputer actually consists of two 4-kΩ microcomputers—a master (Q281) and a sub (Q282) microcomputer (Fig. 10-21). The master microcomputer (Q281) consists of the display, control, key input processing, remote control, and timer operations. The sub microcomputer (Q282) controls the servo systems, mechanical systems, and subcode decoding operations.

Pioneer PD-9010 control system The system control IC (IC12) governs the remote control circuits, the decoder loading motor (IC1), the servo operations, and the LED and FL display board (Fig. 10-22). The function display board contains the fluorescent display (V201), FL control (IC201), and key matrix function assembly. The function board assembly is located directly behind the front panel assembly (Fig. 10-23).

Realistic CD-1000 system control section The system control section in the Realistic CD-1000 player consists of a 32-pin IC301 system processor (Fig. 10-24). IC301 controls the servo and signal section, loading motor circuits, IC303 fluorescent driver, and display tube. The PK PC board keyboard assembly controls the manual operation of the system processor (IC301).

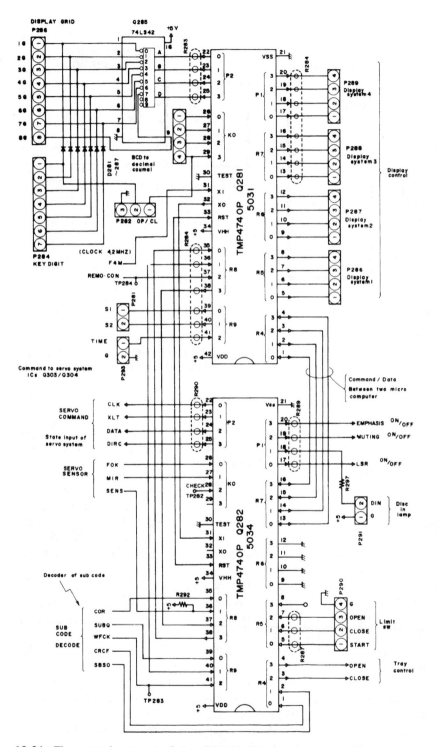

10-21 The control system in Onkyo DX-200 CD player consists of microcomputer chips Q281 and Q282.

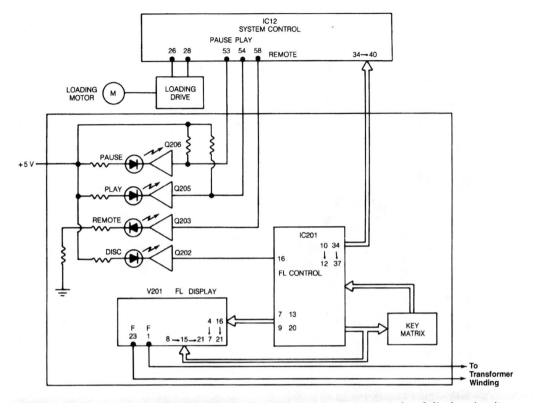

10-22 A block diagram of the Pioneer PD-9010 CD player system control and display circuits.

Mitsubishi M-C4030 display The Mitsubishi M-C4030 remote control operated tabletop automatic changer has a disc set, disc number, track number, elapsed time, reject, program, random, and auto scan indicator with error display. The disc set indicator shows the number of discs in the magazine (Fig. 10-25). The disc number indicator, during playback, shows the number of the current disc. During program entry, the indicator shows the selected track number.

The track indicator, during playback, shows the number of the current track. During program entry, the indicator shows the selected track number.

The elapsed time indicator, during playback, shows the elapsed time in minutes and seconds from the beginning of the current track. The indicator is reset at the beginning of the next track. During program entry, the indicator shows the program number from P-01 to P-20.

The repeat indicator lights up when the repeat playback function is selected and the program indicator is lit during playback. During program entry, the indicator flashes, while the random function is selected. The auto scan indicator lights up when auto intro mode function is selected.

The error (E) display indicates an error in disc loading. Check the disc. The "no disc" display indicates that no disc is in the magazine or turntable.

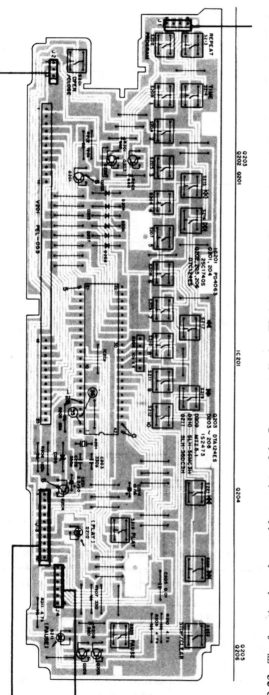

10-23   The function board assembly consists of the fluorescent display, FL driver, LED indicator and transistor drivers of the keyboard in Pioneer's PD-9010 function board.

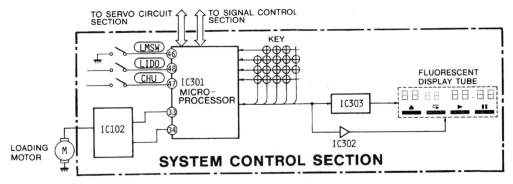

10-24   A block diagram of Realistic CD-1000 system control section.

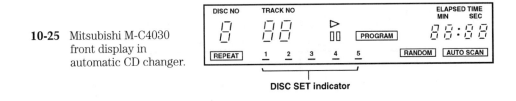

10-25   Mitsubishi M-C4030 front display in automatic CD changer.

The typical microcomputer control processor

The typical microcomputer control processor can provide a gate signal and incoming receiver signal for the remote control circuits. Display output data can be supplied to the fluorescent display board. Data is transferred to and from the servo and signal control section (Fig. 10-26). The control processor can provide loading in and out of the keyboard matrix and display data. The control processor can provide loading in/out and key matrix in from the keyboard. Data transfer in and out is on terminals 1, 33, and 34. The external clock oscillator terminals are 16 and 17. The control processor provides loading motor control data on terminals 9 and 10.

Critical waveforms and voltages on the microcomputer control processor can determine if the IC is leaky or defective. Check for correct supply voltage (+5 V) at terminals 41 and 42. Display the data waveform at pin 25, transfer the data waveform at pin 37, loading the in/out waveform at pins 2 through 8, and the external clock waveform at pin 17 to determine if the control processor IC is working. The complete system control and display circuit of a Sylvania FDD104 CD player is shown in Fig. 10-27. The fluorescent display tube and operational keys usually are found on the same PC board (Fig. 10-28). In the simplest fluorescent display you will find at least 25 terminals. Some of the larger CD players, with many operational functions, have 44 to 54 terminals (Fig. 10-29).

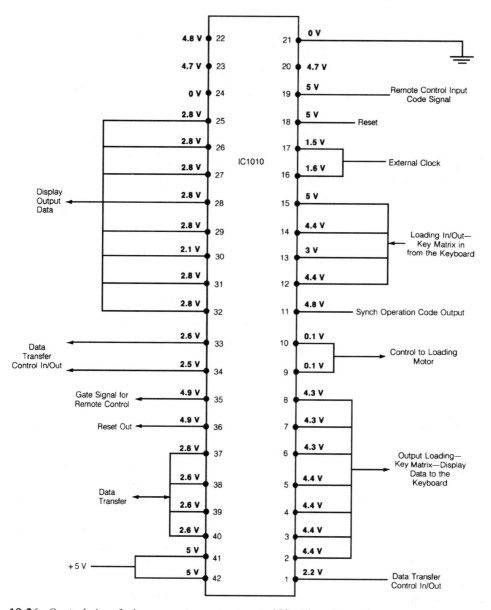

10-26 Control pins of microcomputer system control IC with various voltage measurements.

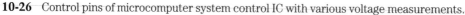

Troubleshooting display functions

Suspect a defective circuit or switch when one function light does not come on within the fluorescent display tube. Very seldom does the fluorescent display cause any service problems. Check for poor button contacts or jamming of the tact switch.

Clean up the switches and replace with original part numbers of any broken front panel components. Inspect the flat or cable wires from chassis to display-key board (Fig. 10-30). Doublecheck socket cable connections. Check for poor or broken soldered bridges around the cable area. Make a continuity check between the chassis terminal and display board for possible break or poor connections.

Separate LED indicators found on the display board can be checked across the LED as any fixed diode with the diode test of the DMM. Measure the voltage across the dead LED. No or low voltage might indicate a defective power source or LED driver transistor (Fig. 10-31). Apply 3 to 5 Vdc across the LED terminals and notice if the light comes on. Test each driver transistor with the transistor tester.

Check the drive voltage and signal applied to the LED drivers and fluorescent control IC from the system control processor. You might assume the system control IC is normal if voltage measurements are okay, the loading motor operates, and the remote control functions are operating. Often this assumption is true, but in some cases one circuit within the system control IC is defective. Inspect all soldered connections and bridges around the system control IC. Accurate voltage resistance and waveform tests on the system control IC should determine if it is defective.

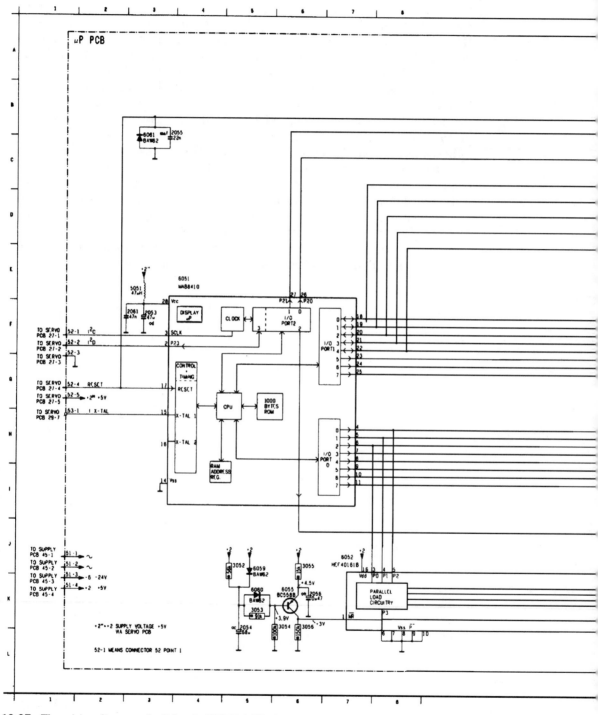

10-27   The wiring diagram of a Sylvania FDD104 CD player control and display system.

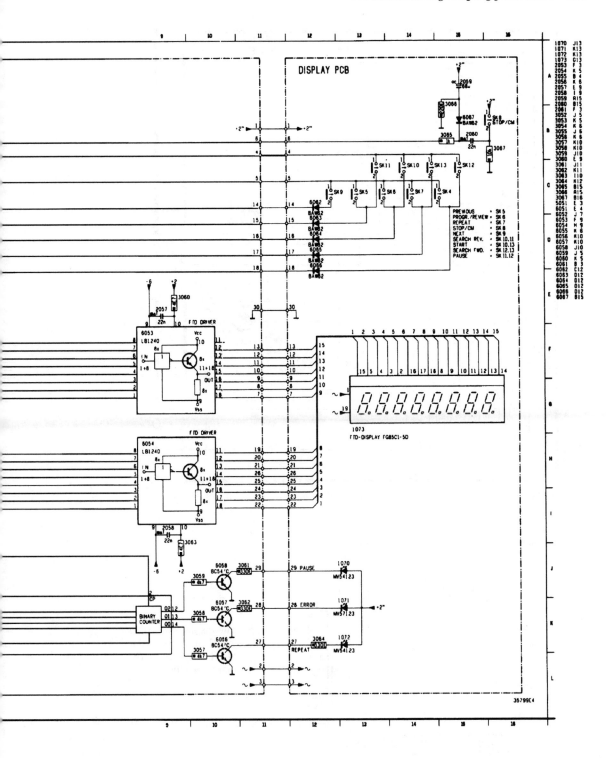

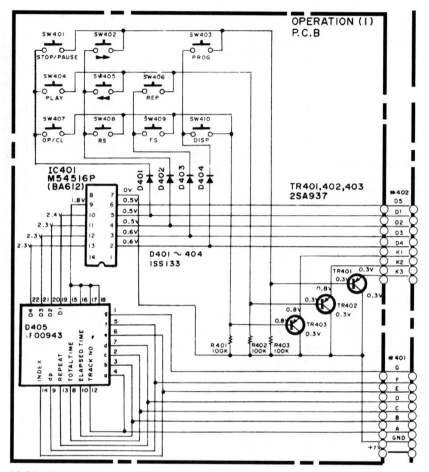

10-28   The fluorescent and key display of the Mitsubishi DP107 compact disc player.

IC701: CXP5014-306Q DISPLAY CONTROLLER

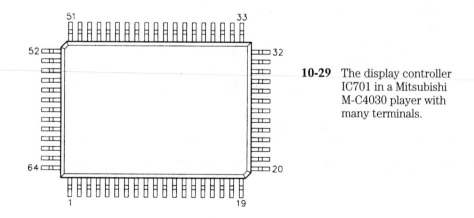

10-29   The display controller IC701 in a Mitsubishi M-C4030 player with many terminals.

10-30 A photo showing the wiring connections and display board of a Sanyo CP500.

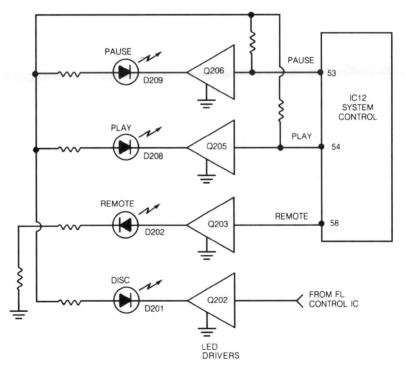

10-31 The pause, play, remote, and disc indicator LEDs, shown with the LED drivers, are controlled by the system control IC12 and located on the key/display board.

11

Servicing the portable
and CD boom-box player

THE PORTABLE CD PLAYER WAS DESIGNED FOR THE ARDENT, ON-THE-GO MUSIC lover. The portable player operates from batteries or a battery pack (Fig. 11-1). Some CD players operate from the ac power supply of a dc power jack. The CD player can be plugged into the power adapter with audio output line jacks. You can listen through a pair of stereo headphones with either battery or ac operation.

Most portable CD players are top loaded, removing the loading motor found in the larger tabletop models. Pushing on the open button makes the cover snap up. After the disc is loaded, push the top cover and it locks in place.

11-1 The compact disc player is only a few inches larger than the disc itself.

Many of the circuits found within the portable CD player are the same as in its big brother. The big difference is space. The parts are smaller in size and they are jammed together on several PC boards. Sometimes the components are hard to get to. Extra patience and slower service methods must be used to prevent damaging and breaking small components. Be careful when trying to repair the portable compact disc player.

The boom-box CD player

Today, the boom-box player can have a compact disc player, besides the cassette player and AM-FM-MPX radio circuits (Fig. 11-2). The boom-box CD player can have preamp circuits that switch into the regular stereo cassette and radio amplifier circuits. The outputs might include internal speakers and separate stereo line output jacks (Fig. 11-3).

11-2   Besides a CD player, the boom-box unit has an AM-FM-MPX radio and cassette player.

Because most CD players' boom-box players are loaded at the top of the plastic cabinet, no loading motor is used. Likewise the CD mechanism can be hung from the top of the cabinet, on a separate PC board (Fig. 11-4). Because both units are mounted in such a small space, surface-mounted devices (SMD) are found on both sides of the PC chassis.

Test equipment and tools

Basically, the same test equipment and tools required for the larger CD players are used. The laser power meter, oscilloscope, and test disc are required test instru-

11-3   The boom-box CD player may have line output jacks and stero speakers.

11-4   Since most boom-box players have top-loading disc, the complete CD player is found at the top of the plastic cabinet.

ments. The eccentric adjustment driver, small screwdriver set, and small point soldering iron are needed for critical adjustments and cover removal (Fig. 11-5). You might find the PC wiring to be very thin, especially at the IC processor connections, where you will need a small point tip on your soldering iron.

11-5 Small screwdrivers are needed to remove those little metal screws from bottom cover.

Safety requirements

The same safety requirements for working around the laser optical system and chassis apply in the larger tabletop CD player. When defeating the top side door interlocks, do not look directly at the laser beam. Remember, the optical lens assembly is open and it points upward under the disc, while in the table CD player the lens assembly is usually covered with the flapper assembly.

A wrist band should be used while servicing the portable CD player on a ground conductive mat. Make sure the soldering iron is also grounded. Less than 10 Ω should be measured between the test equipment, soldering iron, player and common ground wire. Always replace safety marked components with the original parts. The use of substitute replacement parts that do not have the same safety characteristics as specified in the parts list might create shock, fire, and other hazards (Fig 11-6).

Several personal safety precautions should be made while operating the player or when the set is not to be used for an extended period of time. In the latter instance, remove the ac power adapter from the outlet. Do not leave the portable player near a hot radiator or air ducts, and don't place it directly in the hot sun. Keep the player away from excessive dust, rain, or any kind of moisture. Remove the player from the auto or outside temperatures of below 40°F or above 95°F. Keep foreign objects out of the safety slot (interlock) to prevent the laser beam from coming on when the lid is opened. Replace the top cover with the original part number so the interlocks and laser beam will not be harmful to the eyes.

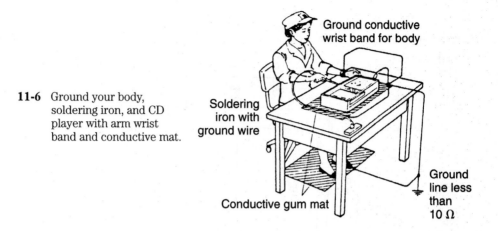

11-6 Ground your body, soldering iron, and CD player with arm wrist band and conductive mat.

Ground conductive wrist band for body

Soldering iron with ground wire

Conductive gum mat

Ground line less than 10 Ω

The block diagram

The block diagram in Fig. 11-7 shows the actual electronic components in the portable CD player. The block diagram ties all of the various components together with a minimum of connecting wires, indicating what IC or transistor component controls certain circuits. Servo IC (Q701) receives the RF signal from the laser pickup and provides the EFM signal to the signal processor, CLV control, RAM processor, and data strobe of Q702.

The CLV control of Q702 controls the disc motor. Q702, servo control signal processor, operates the drive or feed motor. The LCD display and key switch assembly are controlled by the CD bus control of Q702. The tracking coil signal is controlled by the servo status signal processor.

The EFM signal from pin 47 of Q702 goes to pin 29 of Q301. The RAM control signal of Q301 is fed to RAM ICQ302. Pin 40 of Q301 supplies the digital data to pin 7 of DAC (Q501). The left channel sample/hold output (pin 1) feeds the LPF network Z501, while the right channel sample/hold (pin 12) ties to LPF Z502.

The left and right audio signals are amplified and de-emphasized in output ICQ502. The line output jacks are tied to pins 3 and 19. Stereo headphone jack connects to pins 5 and 17 of the output amp Q502. A dual-line level control is located between the line output jacks and input terminals (4 and 18) of Q502. Remember, the block diagram is very useful in locating the defective circuits.

Boom-box CD player block diagram

The boom-box CD circuits consist of an RF amp (IC501) with input signal from the optical laser assembly (Fig. 11-8). IC501 amplifies the weak laser signal and applies an RF and EFM signal to the servo LSI (IC502). Servo IC502 provides digital output signal to the digital signal processing IC503, focus and tracking voltage to the respective coils, and provides signal to operate the disc and sled motors.

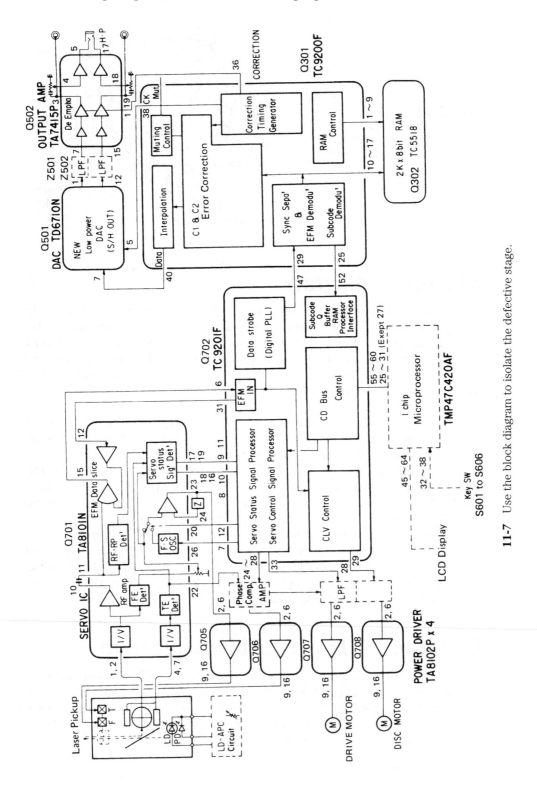

11-7 Use the block diagram to isolate the defective stage.

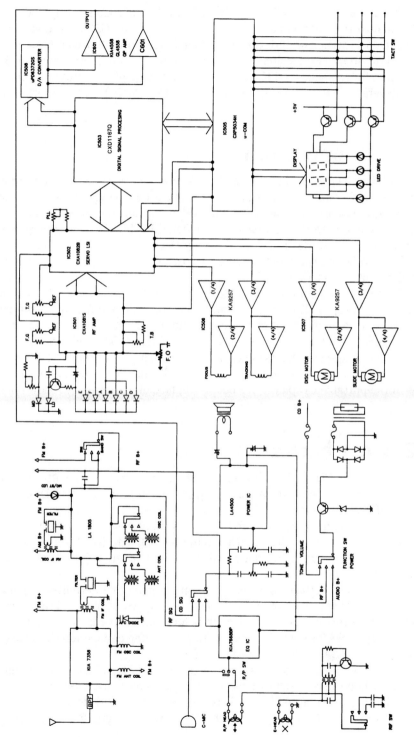

11-8 Block diagram of a boom-box CD, radio, and cassette player.

The digital processing IC provides data to the microcomputer IC505, and digital signal to the digital/analog converter (IC508). At IC508 the digital signal is transferred to analog or audio stereo, which both channels are amplified by IC601 and fed to the function switch or input of boom-box amplifier circuits. IC505 provides data for the servo LSI IC502, IC503, and the display circuits. In some boombox players, separate line output jacks are provided, besides internal speaker operation.

Battery operation

The portable CD player can operate from the house current, energy cells, or alkaline or rechargeable batteries. Most portable compact disc players have a separate battery pack or case to carry the needed batteries. Usually, four or six alkaline "C" batteries are found in the battery pack. The optical EBP-9LC battery case recommends six alkaline "C" batteries to power the Sony D-14 compact disc player. The energy cells last 4.5 hours, while the alkaline batteries can operate for more than 9 hours with intermittent operation.

The nickel-cadmium rechargeable batteries can be inserted in the battery pack for a longer life span. The charging time and battery life of different nickel-cadmium rechargeable batteries might vary. Charging time of the KR-C-F rechargeable batteries in the Sony battery pack is approximately 15 hours. The fully charged batteries allow approximately 2.5 hours of continuous disc play in the Sony D-14 portable disc player. When the batteries become weak, a BATT indicator shows on the display window of the portable CD player. It's best to replace all batteries with new ones when the BATT indicator begins to flicker.

12-V car battery

In some portable CD players, the unit can be powered by the car battery with a special cord. Sony's D-14 player is connected to the car battery with a DCC-120A battery cord that connects the dc 1N9V jack to the cigarette lighter socket of the vehicle. Before connecting, be sure to set the output voltage of the car battery cord to 9 V. Use only the headphones to listen to the compact disc player when it is powered by the car battery. Often, sound through the speakers will be noisy if the player is connected to a car stereo system.

Suspect poor battery connections when skipping or intermittent operation of the portable CD player is noted. First, clean off the dc out plug and the stereo miniplug of the battery case with a dry cloth before connecting it to the player. Inspect the plug and jacks for possible breakage or poor wiring connections. Replace all batteries when the BATT indicator begins to flicker.

Check the battery terminals for corroded or dirty terminals. Always remove all batteries when the compact disc player is not used for a great length of time. Clean off the battery terminals with a pocketknife, sandpaper, and cleaning fluid. Wipe off the battery terminals and battery connections with cleaning fluid. Inspect the battery terminals for broken wire connections. A poorly soldered battery connection might cause no or intermittent operation.

The power supply

Most portable compact disc players have a power pack that operates directly from the house current. The power pack is plugged directly into the back side of the portable player (Fig. 11-9). The ac power supply might contain a 9-V dc output jack with a stereo line output sound jack (Fig. 11-10). Two separate line jacks at the rear of the power supply unit allow the portable compact disc player to be played through a regular stereo amplifier.

11-9 Plug in the small ac power supply when CD portable is operated indoors.

The typical 9-V ac power supply might consist of only a few components: transformer, bridge rectifier, filter capacitor, and a 9-V output jack (Fig. 11-11). Notice that the positive terminal of the power supply is on the inside. The male stereo jack connects directly to the left and right output line jacks (Fig. 11-12).

Within Radio Shack's CD-3000 compact disc player, the ac power supply furnishes a 9- and 5-V source (Fig. 11-13). The power switch can be operated at the power supply (S901) or inside the compact disc player with switch S961. Full-wave rectification is found with diodes D901, D902, D903, and D904. Critical 9- and 5-V regulation is accomplished with Q901, Q902, Q903, and Q904. The ac power supply board is found in the slanted adapter unit (Fig. 11-14).

A voltage IC/transistor regulator circuit is found within Radio Shack's battery pack (Fig. 11-15). Notice three different voltage sources are at J931 (9 V, 5 V, and

11-10 The ac power adapter might include a stereo line jack in addition to the 9-Vdc plug.

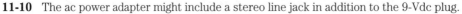

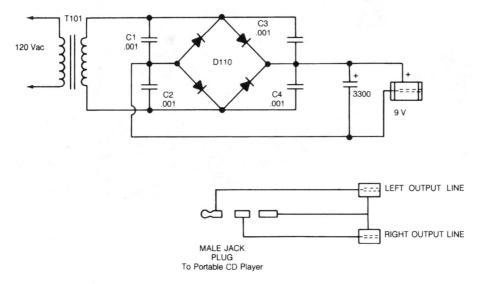

11-11 The 9-V power supply circuit consists of a bridge rectifier, electrolytic capacitor, plug, and transformer.

4 V). A protection thermal switch (S931) is between the battery terminal and dc jack (J932).

Boom-box CD power supply circuits

The boom-box CD player can be operated from batteries or the internal ac power supply. The batteries are switched into the circuit when the ac cord is removed from

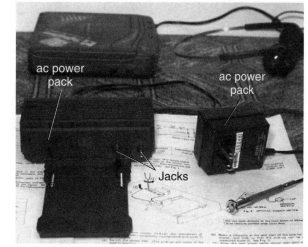

11-12 Two types of ac power adapters to plug the CD player into.

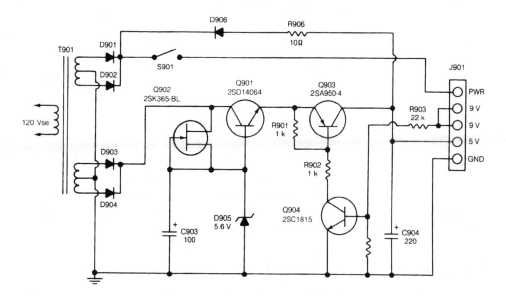

11-13 The ac power supply in a Realistic CD-3000 portable player consists of a full-wave rectification with transistor-regulated 5 and 9 Vdc.

the player. The internal power supply circuits provide dc voltage to the radio, cassette, and CD player. Besides battery and ac operation, external dc source can be applied at J104.

The small ac power supply components can be mounted on a separate chassis with the power transformer (Fig. 11-16). The step-down power transformer voltage is applied to a bridge rectifier circuit. Four separate silicon diodes can be found instead of a regular molded bridge rectifier. C142 (2000 μF) filters the dc voltage when switched from cassette, radio, or CD circuits.

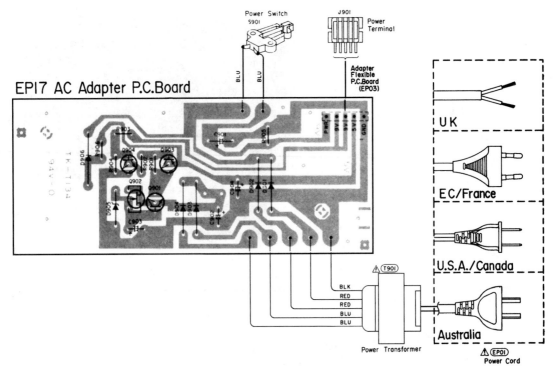

11-14 The ac adapter unit PCB.

Notice fuse protection (F102) appears at the input dc voltage regulated circuits of the CD player dc source (Fig. 11-17). Q253 and D251 provide transistor and diode regulation applied to the CD circuits. A separate motor and power amp circuits have a separate dc regulated source. Notice diode D605 in the battery and external dc source prevents improper polarity of voltage applied.

Phone and line output

The stereo headphone input circuits are taken directly from the low-power filter network (Fig. 11-18). The portable CD player usually is equipped with line output jacks so the player can be connected to a stereo amplifier inside the house (Fig. 11-19). Excessive hum and noise might result when the player is connected to the car amp. These line-output jacks are located within the ac power supply unit. The stereo headphone jack is found at the right side of the CD player.

Headphone output circuits

Often a dual stereo output IC component amplifies the audio for the headphones. A headphone sound level control is available on some players (Fig. 11-20). The audio signal is capacitor-coupled from the LPF network (2501, 2502) to the input termi-

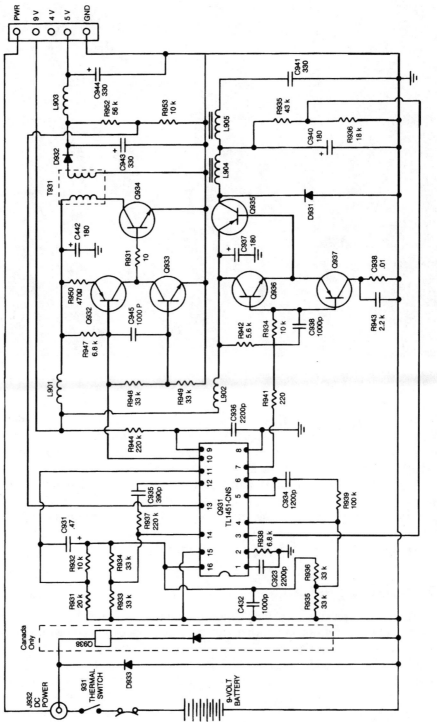

11-15 The regulated battery pack circuit of Realistic CD-3000 model.

11-16 The boom-box ac power supply can be mounted on a separate PC board off of the main chassis.

nals (15 and 7) of IC Q502 (Fig. 11-21). Here the audio is amplified with the right audio taken from pin 19 and the left signal from pin 5. The stereo signal is fed to the top side of the dual volume level control for headphone operation. A tap-off of audio signal is also fed to the line output jacks.

The center tap of the volume control is capacitor-coupled back to pins 4 and 18 to be amplified by Q502. The right audio-controlled signal is capacitor-coupled from pin 19 to the headphone jack. The left audio signal goes from pin 5 through C525 (220) to the headphone jack (J502). Notice R527 and R526 (330 Ω) provides a load on the audio output circuit if the headphones are not plugged in.

Interlock switch

All portable compact disc players have a top lid interlock switch system that provides protection for the operation when the top lid is opened for loading the disc. Remember, the optical lens assembly in portable units shines upward toward your eyes, so the power to the laser diodes must be removed when the top lid is raised. In some models, the start limit and close limit switches are disengaged when the top lid is opened (Fig. 11-22).

The start limit switch consists of a metal pin, which shorts the limit switch contacts with the door closed. The start limit switch is connected to the decoder-opera-

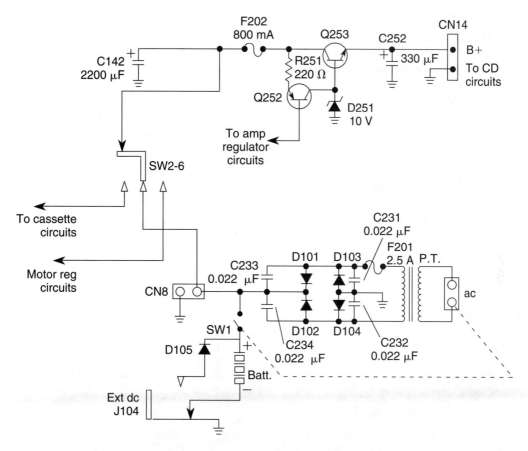

11-17 The boom-box power supply circuit of the Realistic CD-3304 player.

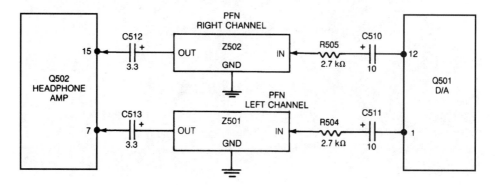

11-18 The stereo headphone audio is taken from Q501 through a power filter network Z501 and Z502 and is capacitor-coupled to the headphone amp (Q502).

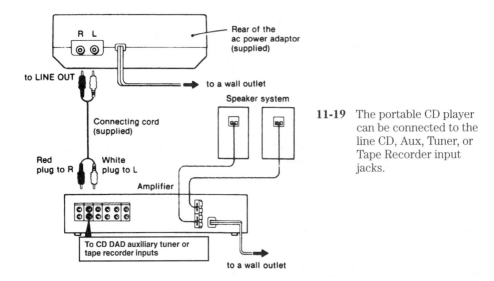

11-19 The portable CD player can be connected to the line CD, Aux, Tuner, or Tape Recorder input jacks.

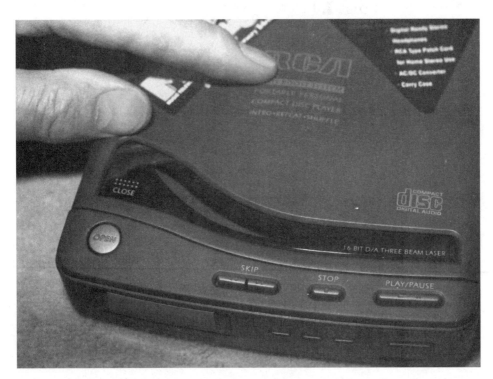

11-20 A separate headphone power level control is found on the front cover of this RCA CD player.

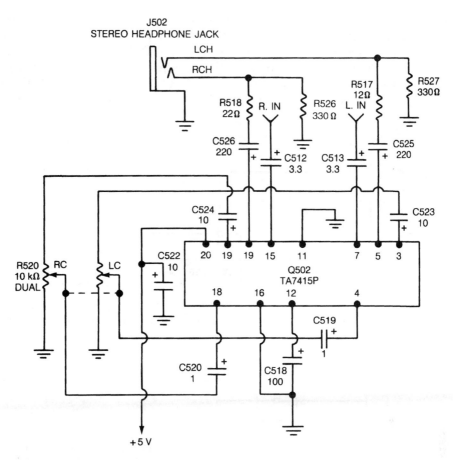

11-21 The stereo headphone amp circuit of Realistic CD-3000 portable CD player.

11-22 When the lid is open, the metal plug and plastic square disengage the interlock.

tion key IC (Fig. 11-23). The close limit switch provides a dc voltage to the APC and laser diode circuits. The square plastic ridge on the top lid pushes the close limit switch contacts together when the lid is closed (Fig. 11-24). To activate the close limit switch, place a piece of plastic down inside the beveled area. A piece of solder or paper clip down inside the start limit switch might defeat the switch (Fig. 11-25). Always keep a piece of metal foil taped over the optical laser assembly while servicing the unit.

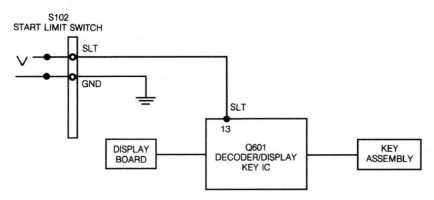

11-23 The start interlock-limit switch is wired to Q601.

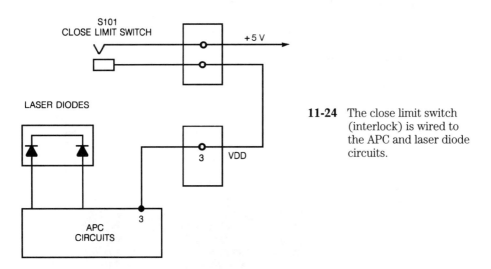

11-24 The close limit switch (interlock) is wired to the APC and laser diode circuits.

The various switches

There are many switches in the small portable compact disc player. Most of these switches are in the OFF position, except a thermostat switch found in some models, which is always ON. Here are several examples:

S101 The close limit switch is turned off when the top lid is open and on with the cover down to play the disc. This switch provides a dc voltage to the laser and APC circuits. The close limit switch is located under the top panel.

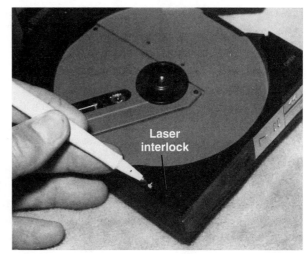

11-25 A piece of solder, paper clip, and a piece of plastic can be used to trip the interlock while servicing player. Keep eyes away from lens area.

S102   The start limit switch is off when the top lid is raised, and it is activated with a metal shorting pin located in the top plastic cover. This switch grounds out the SLT terminal found on the decoder/display IC. The switch is located along S101.

S601 through S605   The PLAY/REPEAT, PAUSE/STOP/MEMORY, TRACK DOWN, TRACK UP, and DISPLAY switches are located on the front panel of the display PC board. These switches are connected directly to the decoder/display IC.

The PLAY/REPEAT button starts the disc to play and repeat the disc-playing action (S601). The PAUSE/STOP switch (S602) stops the disc from playing for a moment or until the PLAY button is pushed again (Fig. 11-26). In some models, a

11-26 The front operation buttons are connected to common ground and IC Q601.

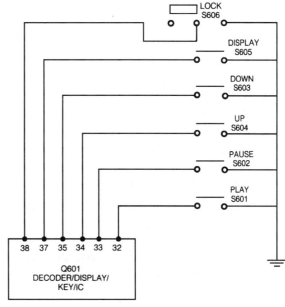

PLAY/PAUSE key does the same functions. The UP (S604) and DOWN (S603) switches search for a particular section of the disc. A MODE or SEARCH button in some models accomplishes the same thing. In other models, the automatic music sensor (AMS) keys or switch is used to locate the beginning of the desired selection in either direction. Sometimes during pause, you can go back or advance faster than during playback.

S901   The adapter power switch is in the OFF position and is located on the ac power supply unit.

S931   The thermostat switch is always on and located on the battery pack PC board of some models.

S961   The power switch controls the dc voltage applied to the portable CD player. The player will stand by and the disc playing will start simply by pressing the PLAY key. The power switch should be turned off after use and when transporting the unit so that the player will not operate even if any of the operation keys or buttons are pressed.

Removing the case

Small side or bottom screws must be removed with a small Phillips or flat screwdriver blade before you can lift off the bottom plate cover. Some of these side screws are very small and short. Place them in a container so you can see them. Be careful not to loosen these small screws in replacement. Often, the mechanism assembly is fastened to the top assembly of the portable CD player.

Realistic CD-3000 mechanism assembly removal   After removing the bottom cover held with four tapping screws, remove the volume control knob screw and knob.

1. Remove the headphone PC board held by three tapping screws. The volume control knob must be removed first before one of the PC board screws can be removed.

2. The main PC board assembly can be removed from the top section by removing four screws holding the assembly to the top section.

3. After removing the mechanism assembly, remove one screw from the display PC board, unhook and remove the display board.

4. When removing the PC boards and mechanism, take care not to damage connections of the flexible PC board.

5. To remove the mechanism assembly from the main PC board, unsolder the flexible cable to the flexible PC board.

Many of the assembly mechanism and display boards are removed in the very same manner. Carefully inspect the PC boards to be removed. Write down what screws and boards you removed so you can replace them correctly. Place all small screws and components in a white container so you can see them. Mark the various leads and cable connections on a separate piece of paper for easy replacement, as they are removed.

Realistic 14-529 boom-box disassembly

1. Open the battery compartment.
2. Remove eight screws (A) holding the front and rear case (Fig. 11-27).
3. Remove two screws (G) holding the cassette deck assembly.
4. Remove four screws (D), (E) holding the CD PC board assembly.
5. Remove two screws (C) holding audio PC board assembly.
6. Remove three screws (F) holding the power PC board assembly.
7. Remove two screws (B) holding the EQ PC board assembly.

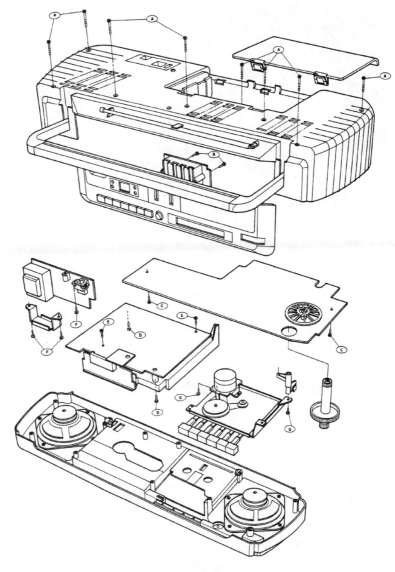

11-27 How to disassemble a Realistic 14-529 boom-box CD player.

The laser head assembly

Before checking the laser assembly, make sure the lens on the disc table is always clean. Do not touch the lens. If you do, the lens might be damaged and the player will not operate properly (Fig. 11-28). Notice the slot in the plastic cover next to the disc turntable. The lens assembly is connected to a worm gear assembly, which is moved outward to the outside disc surface while playing with the feed or slide motor.

11-28 The pen indicates the laser beam assembly, which projects upward to read the disc.

To remove the dust from the lens, blow or brush away the dust with a commercial lens blower. A small camera lens brush and blower will do the job. If anything sticky is on the lens assembly, clean it off with a soft cloth moistened with a mild detergent solution. Be careful when using alcohol as a cleaning agent around plastic parts and cabinets. A dirty lens assembly might cause the player to skip or perform intermittently.

Test equipment required

The following components are necessary or helpful for troubleshooting.

- Laser power meter or infrared indicator
- Oscilloscope
- Test disc (YEDS-7 or equivalent)
- Eccentric adjustment driver and small-tipped screwdrivers

Infrared indicator

The infrared indicator described in chapter 3 can be used to check the presence of the laser lens assembly. The top cover interlocks must be activated before the disc motor will rotate. Hold the photodetector over the lens assembly and push the PLAY button (Fig. 11-29). Move the indicator around until you hear a loud tone from the piezo buzzer. Keep the indicator away from the disc turntable as it rotates. This sound indicates if the laser diode assembly is operating. Be very careful not to let the lens assembly appear outside of the photodetector board.

11-29 Place infrared indicator over the laser lens area to tell if the laser beam circuits are heard with a pulsating tone.

A laser diode mounted inside the pickup is very susceptible to external static electricity. When replacing the laser assembly, use a conductive gum mat and a soldering iron with ground wire to protect the laser diode from damage by static electricity.

Place the laser power meter over the optical lens assembly for weak or defective laser diode tests. Make the correct interlock shorting procedures. Turn the unit on. Notice the power reading in µW. Move the laser meter around the lens assembly for maximum reading of the power meter. Check the measurement with those required upon the CD player. In some units, you will need to adjust the VR control for the correct reading required by the manufacturer.

Realistic CD-3000 laser power coarse adjustment

Perform the following adjustments before installing a new pickup to the mechanism.

1. Connect the main PC board and PU Flexible PC board with two wire leads temporarily (Fig. 11-30). (The shorting pin should be removed from the pickup.)

2. Turn the unit on. Apply the laser power meter sensor over the pickup lens and adjust R109 APC adjustment VR on APC PC board so that the meter indicates 150 µW (Fig. 11-31).

3. After the laser power coarse adjustment is completed, install the pickup on the mechanism and solder the flexible PC board.

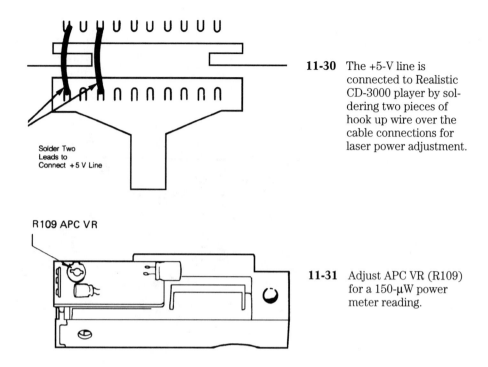

11-30 The +5-V line is connected to Realistic CD-3000 player by soldering two pieces of hook up wire over the cable connections for laser power adjustment.

11-31 Adjust APC VR (R109) for a 150-μW power meter reading.

Realistic CD-3304 RF amp head assembly

In the Realistic boom-box player, the pickup assembly contains the laser diode, monitor diode, and four optical diodes that connects directly to the RF amp (IC501). The focus and tracking coils are found on the same assembly (Fig. 11-32). The spindle and sled motors connect to the same optical board connections. IC501 provides a digital signal to the servo and digital processing IC. The RF and EFM waveform should be checked at the RF amp when the player shuts down at once.

Replacing laser head assembly

Always follow the manufacturer's laser head replacement procedures. Carefully view the laser head assembly for the best removal procedures. Usually, the laser pickup travels down a guide shaft, which is moved by the feed motor gear assembly. The mounting screws at each end of the guide shaft must be removed to get at the pickup assembly. A flexible PC board cable must be unplugged or soldered before the pickup can be removed. Write down all parts that are moved on a separate piece of paper if you do not have the instructions to replace the pickup head assembly.

Realistic CD-3000 pickup replacement   Follow these steps for replacing the pickup assembly.

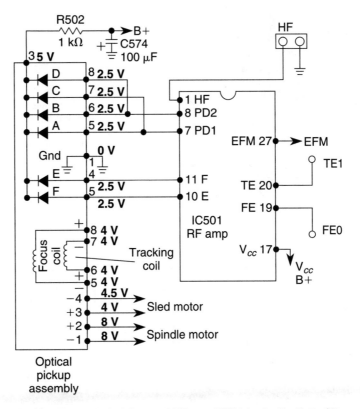

11-32 The optical pickup and RF amp IC501 in the Realistic CD-3304 boom-box player.

1. After removing four screws to remove the bottom plate, secure display PC board with two screws temporarily, so the buttons can be pushed during adjustments.

2. Remove the subgear and main gear assembly by removing the "C" washer (Fig. 11-33).

3. Remove the two screws holding the ends of the fixing guide shaft and unsolder the flexible PC board attached to the pickup. When replacing the pickup and flexible PC board mounted to the drive motor, remove the two screws fixing the pickup motor (Fig. 11-34).

4. Insert the shorting pin, which is one of the repair parts, into pickup to be removed (Fig. 11-35).

5. Lift up the guide shaft side of the pickup slightly and position the pickup height adjusting lever to the mechanism chassis cut out. Then, remove it by pulling it in the guide shaft side (Fig. 11-36).

6. Unsolder terminals of the APC PC board (fixed with double-sided adhesive tape) and remove the PC board. Now remove the rack gear by removing the two screws.

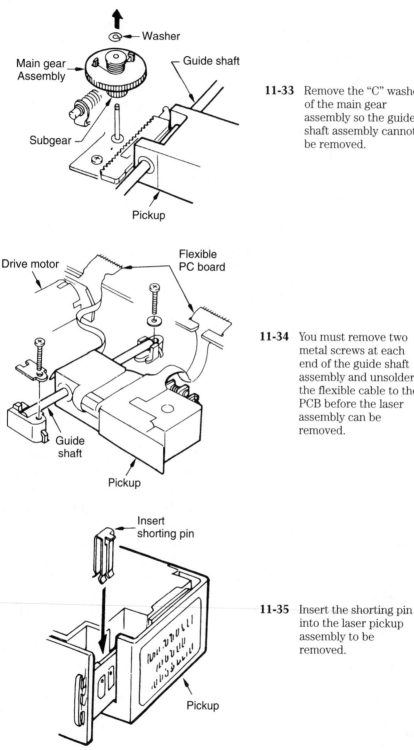

11-33 Remove the "C" washer of the main gear assembly so the guide shaft assembly cannot be removed.

11-34 You must remove two metal screws at each end of the guide shaft assembly and unsolder the flexible cable to the PCB before the laser assembly can be removed.

11-35 Insert the shorting pin into the laser pickup assembly to be removed.

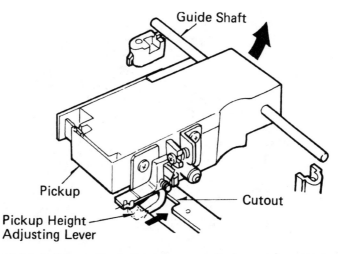

11-36 Pull the guide shaft out to remove the laser pickup assembly.

7. Remove the pickup lever by removing the two screws (Fig. 11-37).

8. Assemble the pickup to the adjustment lever, rack gear, APC PC board, and flexible PC board of APC PC board. After assembling the APC PC board, remove the shorting pin. Now make the required laser adjustments. After the laser power adjustments are completed, install the pickup or mechanism.

Removing Radio Shack boom-box CD assembly

1. Remove CD mechanism by referring to Radio Shack 14-529 disassembly instructions.

2. Remove CD chassis holder and CD mechanism (Fig. 11-38).

3. Remove three screws of fixing gear and shaft clamps (Fig. 11-39).

11-37 Remove two metal screws to remove the pickup adjustment lever.

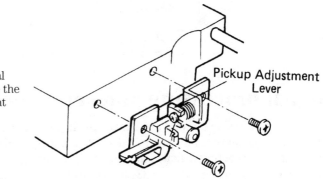

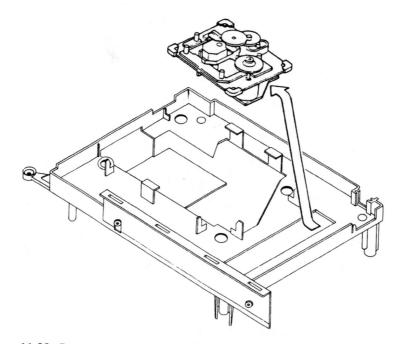

11-38 Remove the CD chassis holder and the CD mechanism in Radio Shack's boom-box CD player.

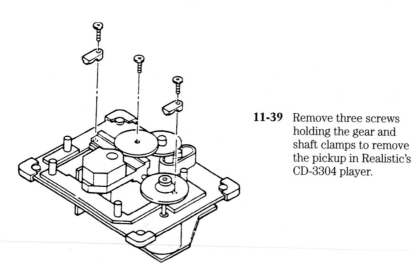

11-39 Remove three screws holding the gear and shaft clamps to remove the pickup in Realistic's CD-3304 player.

Signal processing and servo circuits

The signal-processing circuits are similar to those in any CD player. The photodetector diode signal is fed into terminals 1, 2, 4, and 7 of Q701 (Fig. 11-40). Besides sending the EFM output signal (pin 15) to Q702, the tracking servo amp output (pin 22) and focus servo amp output (23) are controlled by the signal processing circuits.

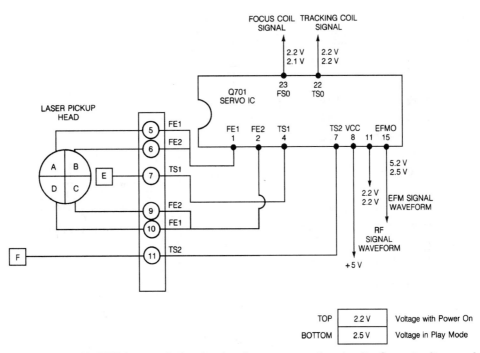

11-40 Servo IC (Q701) controls the signal and servo processing circuits. Correct voltage and waveform tests on Q701 indicate if the IC or laser pickup is defective.

Signal waveforms from pins 11, 15, 22, and 23 can indicate if Q701 circuits are working. Check for correct operating supply voltage at pin 8 (+ 5 V). By taking correct voltage and signal waveforms on Q701, with a normal laser beam, the RF and EFM signal can be signal traced through the signal processing circuits. Do not measure voltage or touch the pin terminals 1, 2, 4, and 7 of Q701 from the laser pickup assembly.

Realistic CD-3370 portable CD pickup circuits The optical pickup assembly is connected directly to the RF amplifier IC4 in the Radio Shack CD player. Besides the RF amp, a laser transistor (Q9) drives the laser diodes within the optical pickup (Fig. 11-41). The photo diodes connect to PD1 (pin 19) and PD2 (pin 20) of IC4. The tracking and focus diodes connect to pins 23 and 22, respectively. IC4 provides an EFM signal to the digital processor (IC3) and servo signal processor IC5.

Focus and tracking coils

The focus coil within the head pickup is controlled directly from Q701. The focus signal is coupled through R716 to the focus driver IC Q705 (Fig. 11-42). Output pins 9 and 16 are applied to the focus coil winding. Input signal at pins 2 and 7 and output waveforms at pins 9 and 16 of Q705 should determine if the focus coil circuits are functioning.

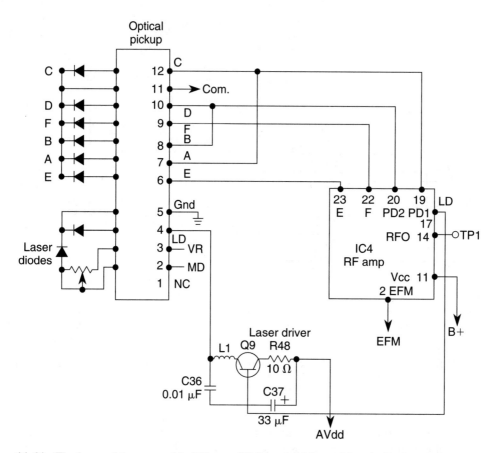

11-41 The laser pickup assembly, RF amp (IC4), and Q9 laser driver in Realistic's CD-3370 portable.

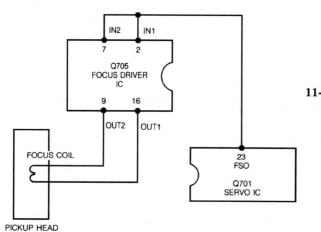

11-42 Focus driver Q705 drives the focus coil from pins 9 and 16. Check the resistance of the focus coil to determine if it is open.

The tracking coil signal from pin 22 of Q701 goes to pin 25 (TESH) of pin 26 of Servo IC Q702 (Fig. 11-43). The tracking error offset signal from pin 26 of Q702 is fed to an op-amp Q703 and then to the tracking coil driver IC Q706. Output terminals 9 and 16 of Q706 are tied directly to the tracking coil within the pickup assembly. Scope waveforms at input pins 7 and 2 and output pins 9 and 16 of Q706 can determine if the signal is reaching the tracking coil.

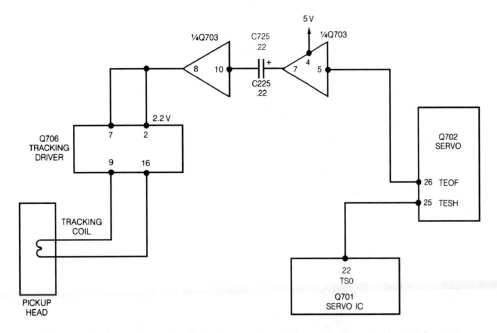

11-43 Tracking driver Q706 drives the tracking coil from pins 9 and 16.

Realistic portable CD-3370 focus, tracking, and motor circuits The focus and tracking coil circuits are controlled by IC6 in the Realistic CD-3370 portable (Fig. 11-44). The focus coil is connected to pins 43 and 44, while the tracking coil connects to pins 41 and 42. The focus coil test points are TP10 (F−) and TP12 (F+).

IC6 also provides drive for the spindle and sled motors. The spindle motor connects to pins 36 and 37 of IC6. The sled motor terminals connect to pins 34 and 35. In this portable CD player the coils and motors are controlled with one IC6 driver.

Realistic boom-box CD-3304 focus, tracking, and motor circuits The boom-box CD assembly is fastened with four screws to the top of the plastic cabinet (Fig. 11-45). Note the slide rails that are mounted to one side of CD assembly. All PC board parts are mounted on top of the PC assembly.

The focus and tracking coils are controlled by IC506. The focus coil is connected to pins 10 and 11 of the driver IC. The tracking coil is connected to pins 3 and 4 of IC506 (Fig. 11-46).

The sled and spindle motors are driven from IC507 (Fig. 11-47). The negative terminal of sled motor (4.5 V) connects to pin 4 and the positive terminal to pin 3 of

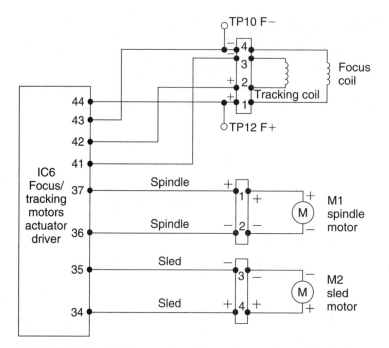

11-44 IC6 drives the focus and tracking coils, spindle, and sled motors from one IC component in a Realistic CD-3370 portable.

11-45 The CD PCB is fastened to the top of the cabinet in a Sharp QT-CD7-3 (GY) boom-box CD player.

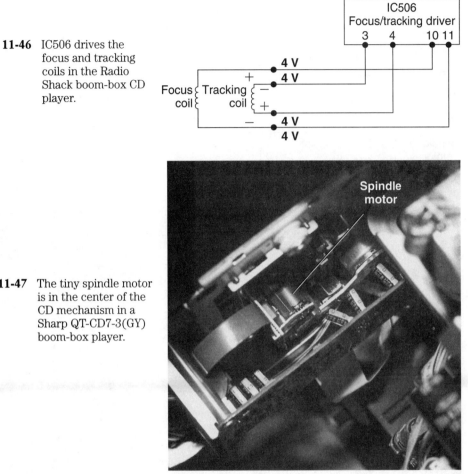

11-46 IC506 drives the focus and tracking coils in the Radio Shack boom-box CD player.

11-47 The tiny spindle motor is in the center of the CD mechanism in a Sharp QT-CD7-3(GY) boom-box player.

IC507. The positive spindle motor terminal connects to pin 11 and negative terminal to pin 10 of motor driver IC507 (Fig. 11-48).

Critical electronic adjustments

Like the table-model portable CD player, adjustments are made after replacing critical components. Tracking error, diffraction grating, focus error, tracking error balance, and APC are the most important adjustments on the portable CD chassis (Fig. 11-49). Always follow the exact manufacturer's adjustment when available. The oscilloscope test disc (YEDS-7), DMM, and small screwdrivers are the most important tools for electronic adjustments.

Realistic CD-3000 electronic adjustments

Although it is impossible to list all the portable compact disc player adjustments in this chapter, the most critical ones were chosen from Realistic's CD-3000 model

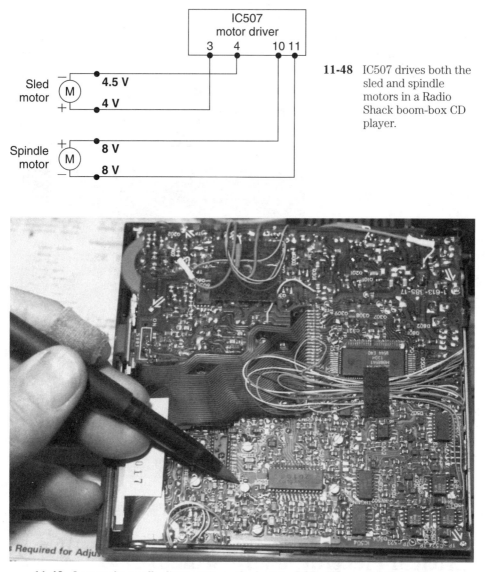

11-48   IC507 drives both the sled and spindle motors in a Radio Shack boom-box CD player.

11-49   Locate the small adjustments on the bottom PCB of the portable CD player.

adjustments. Locate the adjustment screws on the small PC board. Because the chassis might have to be pulled from the power supply to make the electronic adjustment, provision must be made to connect voltage to the chassis. Proceed with batteries if the external battery can be used without tying the dc leads together.

Within the Realistic CD-3000 model, solder lead wires to each pin 3, 11, 22, and 28 of Q701 IC temporarily for easy connection of test equipment (Fig. 11-50). Be careful not to short out the other IC pins. Do not keep the soldering iron too long on each pin. Now, connect the lead wires from the ac adapter to the main PC board (Fig.

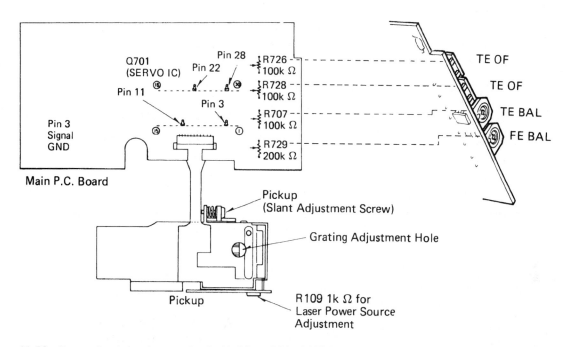

11-50 Correct hookup wires to pins 3, 11, 22, and 28 of Q701 to make easy connections for electronic adjustments in a Realistic CD-3000 chassis. Pin 3 is common ground.

11-51 The ac adapter PCB power lead wires should be connected with the hookup wire to the main PCB when making adjustments.

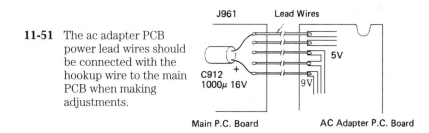

11-51). Make sure the power switch will stay on or short across the terminals with a soldered lead.

Tracking error balance adjustment   Connect the oscilloscope to pins 3 and 22 of Q701 Servo IC (Fig. 11-52). Load test disc YEDS-7 in the tray. Turn the unit on. Hold the pickup motor worm gear (feed motor) to stop its rotation while the unit is searching for music. Push the up key and adjust R707 TE BAL VR so that the tracking error signal waveform becomes ±10 mV. Once the up key is pushed, operation continues for about 20 seconds. If the adjustment is not completed in 20 seconds, push the key again.

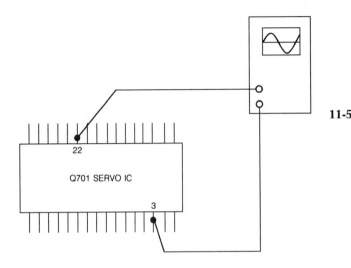

11-52 Connect the scope to terminals 3 and 22 for tracking error balance adjustment.

Pickup slant adjustment

Connect the oscilloscope to pins 3 and 11 of Q701 IC (Fig. 11-53). Play test disc YEDS-7. Adjust the pickup slant adjustment screw so that the center part of RF pattern (eye) is clear (Fig. 11-54). Now, lock the slant adjustment screw.

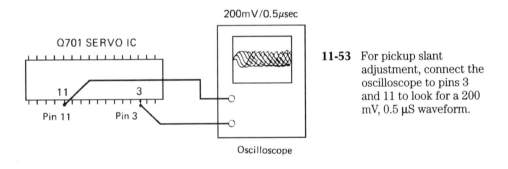

11-53 For pickup slant adjustment, connect the oscilloscope to pins 3 and 11 to look for a 200 mV, 0.5 μS waveform.

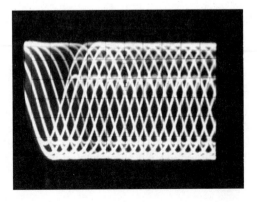

11-54 The RF adjustment should be made so an eye diamond shape is clear in the center of the waveform.

Focus error balance adjustment   Connect the oscilloscope to pins 3 and 11 of Q701 (Fig. 11-55). Play the test disc YEDS-7 and adjust FE BAL (R729) so the RF eye pattern is clear.

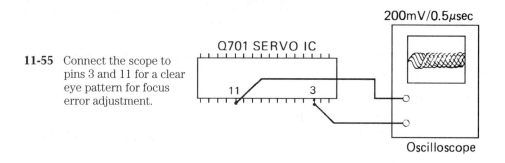

11-55 Connect the scope to pins 3 and 11 for a clear eye pattern for focus error adjustment.

Realistic CD-3304 PLL-VCO adjustment

1. Put unit into stop mode (Fig. 11-56).
2. Short-circuit test point (ASY) and test point (GND).
3. Connect digital frequency counter to the test point (TP10) and test point (GND).
4. Adjust VR504 so that the frequency counter becomes 4.25 ± 0.01 MHz.

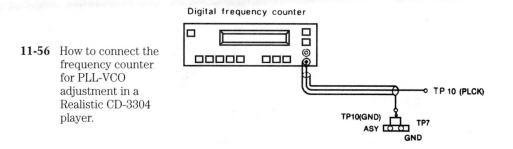

11-56 How to connect the frequency counter for PLL-VCO adjustment in a Realistic CD-3304 player.

Optimus CD-3370 EF balance adjustment

1. Connect an oscilloscope to TP2 (TE) and TP8 (VC) through filter A. Note that TP8 must be connected to ground on the scope (Fig. 11-57).
2. Switch on the power in the test mode and push play button.
3. Next, switch on the P mode until LCD displays "ON TR SL;" then, switch off and on again to display "OFF TR SL". During these displays, turn potentiometer P1 so that the waveform becomes vertically symmetrical with the VC level at center.
4. At this time, adjust potentiometer P1 so that TP2 (TE) voltage becomes ± 20 mV.

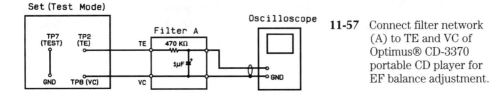

11-57 Connect filter network (A) to TE and VC of Optimus® CD-3370 portable CD player for EF balance adjustment.

Realistic CD-3304 focus offset adjustment This focus offset adjustment is made without a jitter meter.

1. Insert test disc and put into play mode (Fig. 11-58).
2. Connect oscilloscope to TP1 (HF, GND).
3. Adjust VR505 so that the eye pattern becomes clear and waveform (VP-P) is maximum.

Note: When confirming eye pattern, use a 10-1 probe.

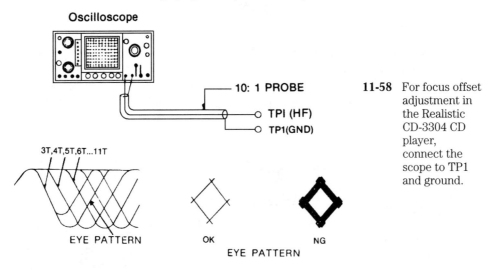

11-58 For focus offset adjustment in the Realistic CD-3304 CD player, connect the scope to TP1 and ground.

Optimus® CD-3370 focus gain adjustment

1. Connect an oscilloscope to TP4 (FE), TP5, and TP8 (VC) through filter B. Note that TP8 must be connected to ground on the scope (Fig. 11-59).
2. Cancel the test mode, switch on the power, load the test disc, and push the FF button. Play the fifth track.
3. Input 1.3 kHz at 50 mV from the oscillator to TP5 and observe the signal output to TP4. Then, adjust potentiometer P3 to produce a level that is the same as the input lead.

Optimus® CD-3370 tracking gain adjustment

1. Connect the scope to TP2 (TE), TP3, and TP8 (VC) through filter B. Note that TP8 must be connected to ground on the oscilloscope (Fig. 11-60).

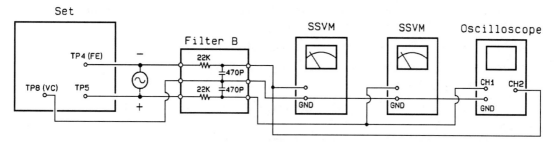

11-59 How to set up test instruments for focus gain adjustments in the Optimus® CD-3370 portable CD player.

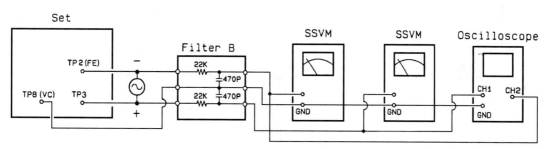

11-60 Connect test instruments to filter B and to TP2 (TE) and TP3 for tracking gain adjustment in the Optimus® CD-3370 player.

2. Cancel the test mode, switch on the power, load the disc, and push the FF button. Play the fifth track.

3. Input 1.7 kHz at 50 mV from the oscillator to TP3 and observe the signal level output to TP2; then adjust potentiometer P4 to produce a level that is the same as the input level.

Realistic CD-3304 focus gain adjust with jig

1. Connect gain adjustment jig to TP3 and TP6 on the main PC board pin to pin.

2. Connect audio frequency counter to the AF OSC terminal and GND on the gain adjustment jig (Fig. 11-61).

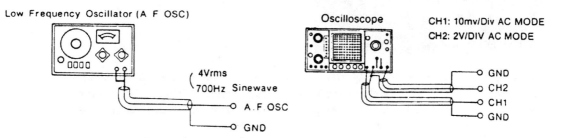

11-61 To make focus gain adjustment with a jig in a Realistic CD-3304 player, connect the oscillator to AF OSC and ground, and the scope to channel 1 and 2.

3. Connect an oscilloscope to CH1, CH2 and GND on the gain jig and put scope into X-Y mode.

4. Insert with test disc and put unit into play mode.

5. Set switch SW2 on the gain adjustment jig to the position of "IF."

6. Set switch SW1 to on.

7. Adjust VR502 so that waveform on the scope becomes like Fig. 11-62.

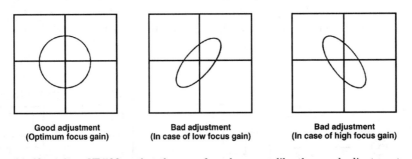

| Good adjustment (Optimum focus gain) | Bad adjustment (In case of low focus gain) | Bad adjustment (In case of high focus gain) |

11-62 Adjust VR502 so that the waveform becomes like the good adjustment in Realistic CD-3304 player.

Realistic CD-3304 focus gain adjustment without test jig

1. Insert the test disc and put unit into play mode (YEDS-43).

2. Connect the oscilloscope to IC506 pin #2 and pin 11.

3. Adjust VR502 so that the waveform on the scope becomes like Fig. 11-63.

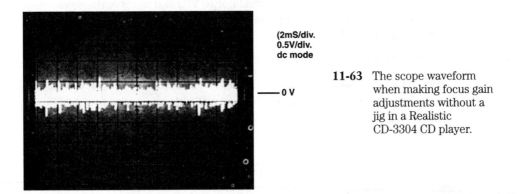

(2mS/div.
0.5V/div.
dc mode

— 0 V

11-63 The scope waveform when making focus gain adjustments without a jig in a Realistic CD-3304 CD player.

Realistic CD-3370 portable CD troubleshooting flowchart When troubleshooting the Realistic portable CD player use the flowchart (Chart 11-1). After completing a particular branch section, go through the main flowchart again to be sure there are no other irregularities.

Realistic CD-3304 boom-box troubleshooting flowcharts A typical boom-box troubleshooting guide is shown in Chart 11-2. If the display LED lighting is not normal see Chart 11-3. If the initial reading is not carried out (with disc) start with Chart 11-4. Check the audio circuits of the boom-box player with Chart 11-5.

Chart 11-1. Troubleshooting flowchart on the Realistic CD-3304 CD player.

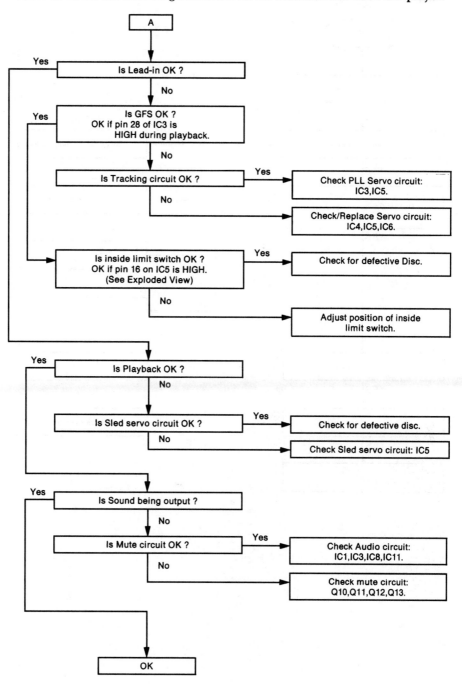

Chart 11-2. A typical troubleshooting guide in the Realistic CD-3304 CD player.

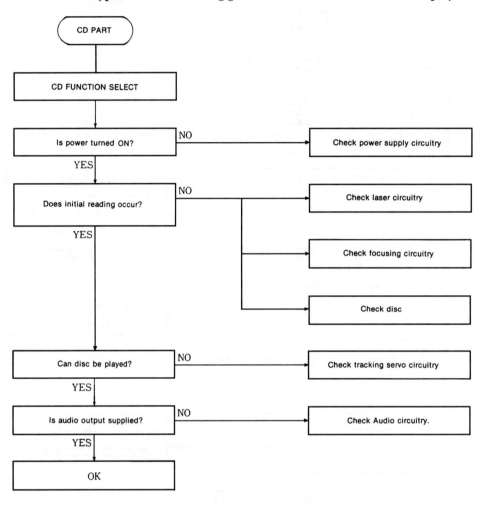

Chart 11-3. A troubleshooting display flowchart.

If display LED lighting is not normal.

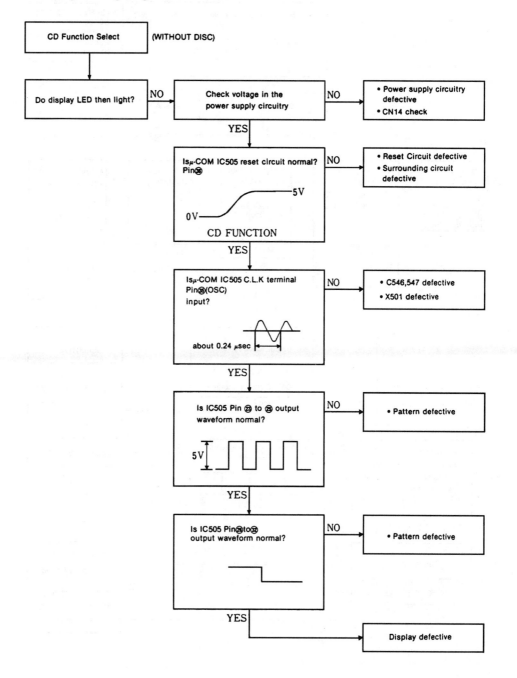

Chart 11-4. If initial reading is not carried out (with disc) in the Realistic CD-3304 troubleshooting flowchart.

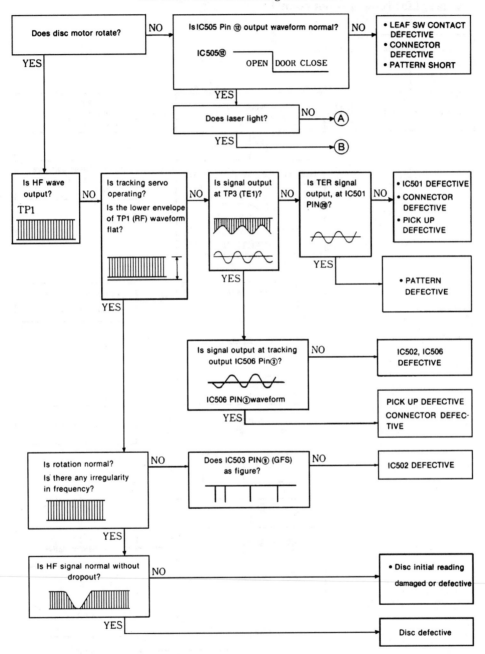

Chart 11-4. Continued.

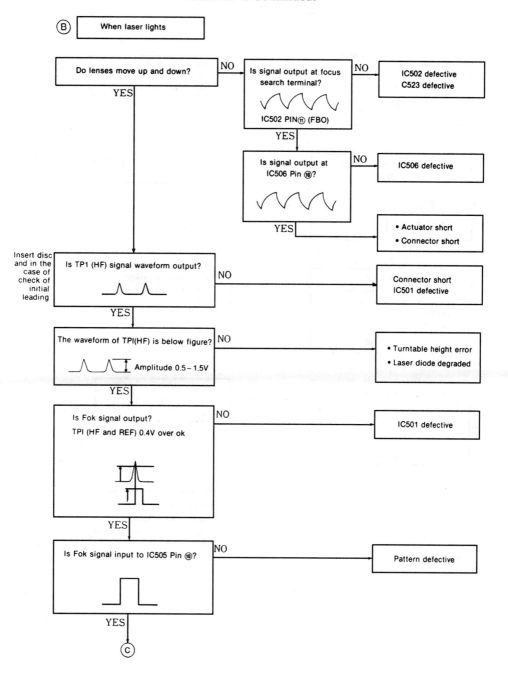

Chart 11-4. Continued.

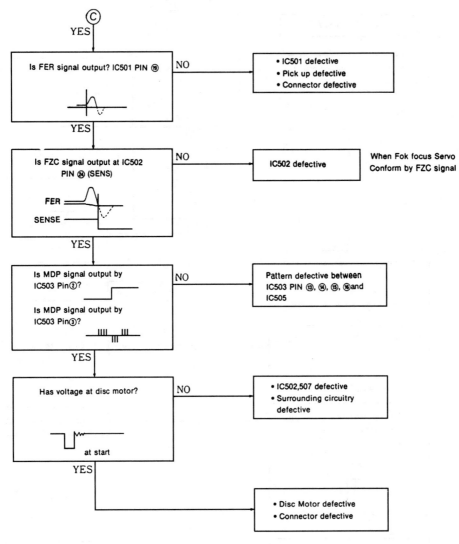

Chart 11-4. Continued.

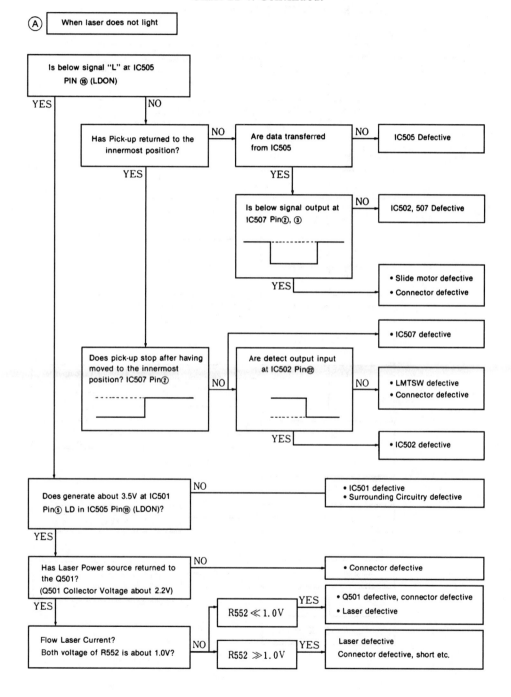

Chart 11-5. The audio check flowchart
in the Realistic CD-3304 compact disc player.

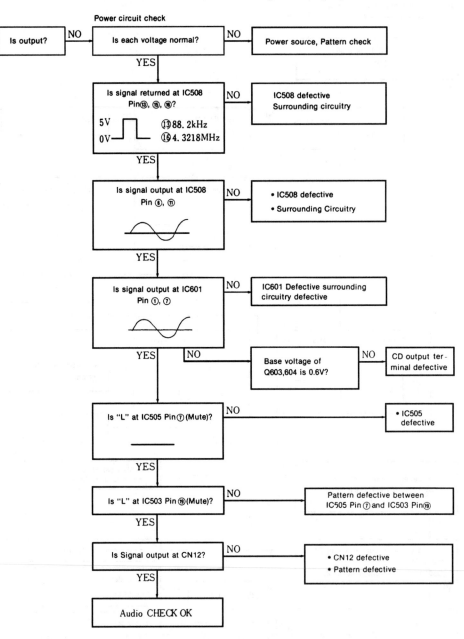

12
The auto CD player

MOST AUTO COMPACT DISC PLAYER CIRCUITS ARE QUITE SIMILAR TO THE TABLETOP player. The same service precautions must be followed to protect the eyes from the laser beam during servicing procedures. The same test equipment, tools, and test discs are used to service both machines. Of course, the auto disc players are all front loaded. The big difference between the auto and the home CD player is the power supply and the physical size.

Naturally, the auto disc player operates from the dc car battery instead of the ac power line. The power supply in the auto player employs a dc- to -dc converter and isolated regulator circuits. The auto power supply is in a separate hideaway unit cabled to the main front-loaded player. In some players, automatic loading of five different discs can be done by placing the unit in the car trunk area.

The big difference between the auto and home players is the physical size of each player. Because most components are placed in one container, several different PC boards are layered together. Like the auto radio, most components are jammed or fit tightly together so that all the parts will fit inside one metal cabinet. Because space is a premium, you might find chip components involving resistors, capacitors, diode, transistors, and ICs. Although servicing the auto disc player might take a little more time to remove PC boards to locate the correct component, the reproduction of music is much greater than the FM radio or cassette player.

Specifications for five auto CD players

Here are five different auto CD players listed alphabetically with their specifications.

Denon DCC-9770 auto compact disc player
(Chart 12-1 depicts a flowchart for removing each section of this unit.)

Chart 12-1. How to remove each section of the Denon DCC-9770 CD player.

REMOVAL OF EACH SECTION
According to the flow chart to remove screws to disaasemble part.

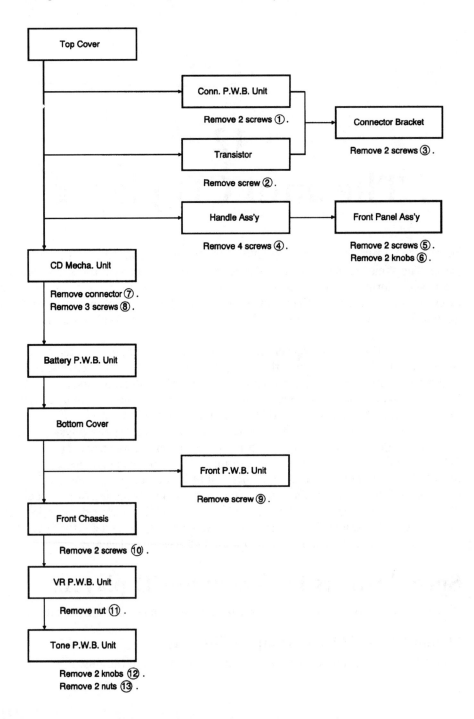

Sampling Frequency	44.1 kHz
Quantization	16-bit linear
Transfer Bit Rate	4.3218 Megabits/sec.
Frequency Response	5 kHz–20 kHz ± 1.0 dB
Dynamic Range	96 dB
Signal to Noise Ratio	96 dB
Harmonic Distortion	0.005%
Wow and Flutter	Below a measurable level
Output Voltage	1 V/10 kΩ

Denon DCH-500 auto CD changer

Laser diode	GaAlAs 780 mW wavelength.
Laser output power	Less than 40.0 µW
Frequency Response	5–20,000 Hz ± 1 dB
Dynamic Range	90 dB
Distortion	0.005%
Wow and Flutter	Below measurable limit
Outputs	Line output
Current drain	800 mA and 1.5 A during disc loading or eject

Pioneer model CDX-1 CD player

Disc diameter	120 nm; thickness 1.2 nm
Laser	Semiconductor; wavelength = 780 nm
Signal format	Sampling frequency = 44.1 kHz; 16-bit linear
Power requirements	14.4 Vdc (10.8 to 15.6 V possible); consumption = 18 W
Frequency characteristics	5 to 20,000 Hz (± 1 dB)
Signal-to-noise ratio	90 dB (1 kHz)
Dynamic range	90 dB (1 kHz)
Wow and Flutter	Below measurable range
Distortion factor	0.005% (1 kHz, 0 dB)
Number of channels	2
Output voltage	280 mV (when level switching high); 140 mV (when level switching low)

Sony CDX-5 CD player

Laser	Semiconductor laser; wavelength = 780 nm
Number of channels	2
D/A conversion	16-bit linear
Frequency response	5 to 20,000 Hz (± 1.0 dB)
Harmonic distortion	0.005% (1 kHz)
Dynamic range	90 dB
Signal-to-noise ratio	90 dB
Channel separation	85 dB

Wow and Flutter	Below measurable limit
Sampling frequency	44.1 kHz
Quantization	16-bit linear
Power requirements	12 Vdc battery; negative ground
Current drain	840 mA playback,
	2 A (disc loading or eject)

Yamaha YCD-1000 CD player

System	Car audio compact disc player with CD cartridge system
Optical pickup	3-beam laser
Number of channels	2
Frequency response	20 to 20,000 Hz (+ 0/–3 dB)
Harmonic distortion	less than 0.05% (1 kHz)
Dynamic range	92 dB
Wow and Flutter	Unmeasurable
Channel separation	75 dB (1 kHz)
Output voltage	2 V at 330 Ω
Operating voltage	14.4 Vdc (10.8–16.0 V allowable)
Grounding system	negative type
Power consumption	14 W

Auto CD precautions

- Check the reset button with a ballpoint pen before starting the unit for the first time or after replacing the car battery.

- All auto CD players made in USA use a negative ground when mounted in the auto.

- Replace the blown fuse with the same amperage as shown on the fuse holder. If a fuse blows more than once, check electrical connections and the CD player.

- In extremely hot weather, let the car's interior cool down before turning on the CD player. Let the air circulate.

- Keep all foreign objects from entering the disc slot because the precision mechanism and disc could be damaged.

- Be sure to remove any discs from the CD player before removing the unit. Moving the unit with a disc in it could damage the disc and the unit.

- Some units will not play in extremely hot weather. Many of these units have a display that indicates that the temperature is too high and the unit will shut down.

- On cold days, condensation might form. Let the CD player set 30 minutes before playing.

- Sometimes a strong road shock will cause the laser head to skip.

Disassembly of Denon DCH-500 auto CD changer

1. Remove bracket (R) and (L) (Fig. 12-1).
2. Remove upper case and front assembly (Fig. 12-2).

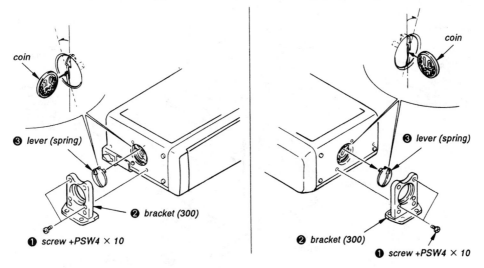

12-1 Remove the brackets from the Denon DCH-500 CD changer.

CASE (UPPER) AND FRONT PANEL ASS'Y

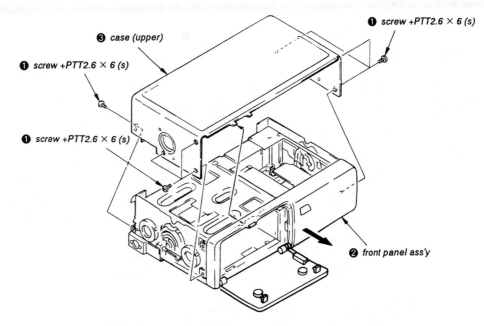

12-2 Remove the upper case and front panel assembly.

3. Remove lower case (Fig. 12-3).
4. Remove servo board and optical device (Fig. 12-4).

CASE (LOWER)

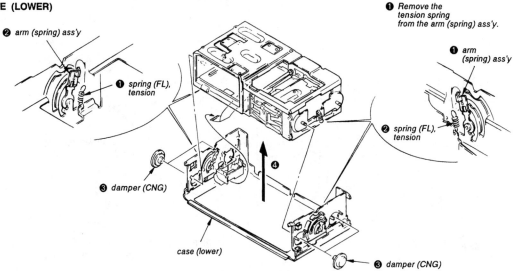

12-3   Remove the lower case of the Denon auto CD changer.

SERVO BOARD AND OPTICAL DEVICE (KSM-310A)

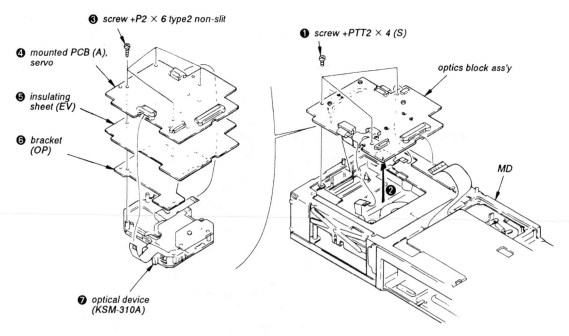

12-4   Remove the servo board and optical device.

5. Remove the main board (Fig. 12-5).
6. Remove the cover (MD) assembly and escutcheon (Fig. 12-6).
7. Remove the EV chassis assembly (Fig. 12-7).
8. Remove the MZ chassis (Fig. 12-8).
9. Remove the lower roller assembly (Fig. 12-9).
10. Remove the DPT board and arm assembly (Fig. 12-10).

The block diagram

The block diagram is useful in locating the defective section of the auto CD player. The auto RF and servo IC circuits are like those found in the tabletop CD player. The RF signal from the pickup photodiodes go to a large RF AM signal processor IC. The servo IC might include the RAM, clock regeneration, data compensation, digital filter, and *VCD* circuits, in addition to controlling the focus, tracking, and various motor circuits. A separate D/A converter IC might follow and feed the stereo signal to the sample/hold and de-emphasis IC. Separate tone and audio output ICs are in the left and right output audio channels (Fig. 12-11).

Pioneer CDX-1 block diagram   The FE (focus error) signal and the TE (tracking error) signals are derived from the RF signal generated at the pickup unit (Fig. 12-12). The FE signal controls the focus actuator, which focuses the pickup unit. The TE signal controls the tracking actuator that accurately traces the tracks on the

MAIN BOARD

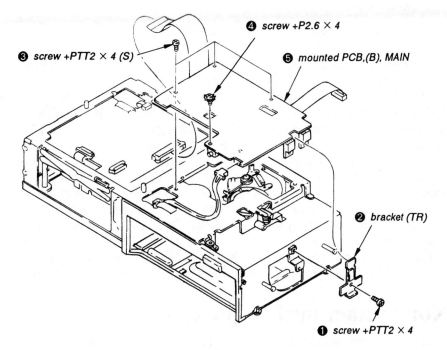

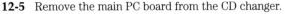

12-5   Remove the main PC board from the CD changer.

COVER (MD) ASS'Y AND ESCUTCHEON

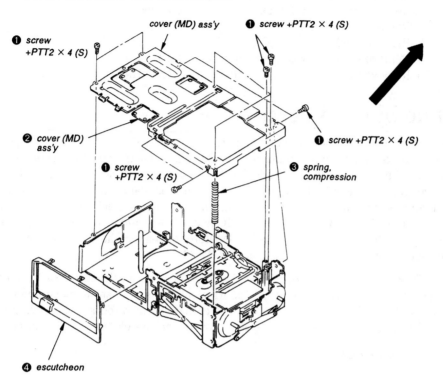

12-6 Remove the cover of MD assembly of the DCH-500 player.

disk surface. A microcomputer controls these signals: the carriage motor, which moves the pickup unit, and the spindle motor, which turns the disc.

The RF signal feeds the demodulation and signal processing IC. The audio stereo signal is taken from the D/A conversion stage feeding the LPF circuits. The IC16 amplifier includes a de-emphasis circuit. The audio signal goes through IC17 isolator circuit with a maximum audio signal of 281 mV to outputs L and R.

Yamaha YCD-1000 block diagram The RF signal is taken from the laser head and goes to the preamp circuits inside IC201 (Fig. 12-13). IC201 also develops the tracking and focus error signals. The RF signal is sent to IC205, which controls the servo and digital data circuits. IC215 converts the digital signal to audio, and a stereo signal goes to the sample/hold and de-emphasis IC206. A volume and balance control is located between left and right tone IC212A and 212B. Q220 and Q225 provide audio muting before audio IC218A and 218B. Q210 and Q211 provide audio muting at the left and right audio output terminals. A separate CD power unit is shown at the bottom.

Noncontact optical pickup

A light laser beam generated by the optical pickup strikes the signal surface of the disc. The reflected beam is then sent to a photodiode, which reads the digital signals

EV CHASSIS ASS'Y

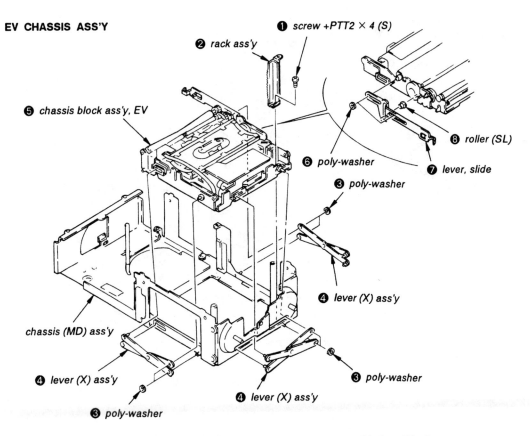

❶ *screw +PTT2 × 4 (S)*
❷ *rack ass'y*
❺ *chassis block ass'y, EV*
❻ *poly-washer*
❽ *roller (SL)*
❼ *lever, slide*
❽ *poly-washer*
❹ *lever (X) ass'y*
chassis (MD) ass'y
❹ *lever (X) ass'y*
❹ *lever (X) ass'y*
❽ *poly-washer*
❽ *poly-washer*

12-7   Remove the EV chassis from the main chassis assembly in a CD player.

picked up from the disc. Because signals are read without contacting the surface of the medium, needle-generated friction as in conventional phonograph systems and the accompanying hiss are eliminated. Also, because the disc itself is coated with clear plastic, the signal surface is protected from the effects of dust, finger smudges, and dirt.

Laser optical pickup assembly

The laser pickup assembly consists of the laser diode, collimator lens, beam splitter, critical-angle prism, four-segment photodiode, reflection prism, quarter wavelength plate, objective lens, and TE and FE diodes (Fig. 12-14).

A diffused laser beam is emitted from the laser diode (LD), and is then made parallel by a collimator lens. This parallel beam is sent through a beam splitter, a reflection prism, and then a quarter-wavelength plate. The object lens then focuses the beam to the disc surface.

The beam is flashed onto a row of pits on the disc surface, and then reflected back through the objective lens. Then it passes through the quarter-wavelength plate, the reflection prism, and finally the beam splitter again. The LD emits a

CHASSIS (MZ)

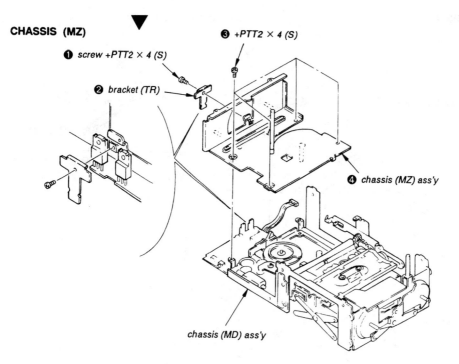

12-8 Remove the MZ chassis of the Denon DCH-500 player.

ROLLER (LOWER)

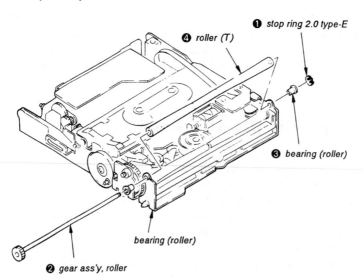

12-9 Remove the lower roller assembly of a CD changer.

DPT BOARD AND ARM (R) ASS'Y

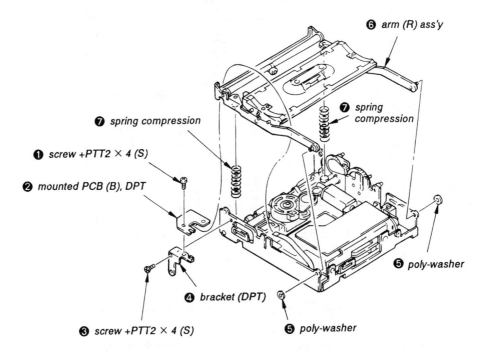

12-10 Remove the DPT board and arm assembly (R) from the Denon DCH-500 CD changer.

straight polarized beam, which is then changed to a circular, polarized beam by passing through the quarter-wavelength plate. After the beam is reflected off the disc plane, it goes back through the quarter-wavelength plate and is changed back into a straight polarized beam.

The polarity of the returning beam is 90 degrees out of phase with the outgoing beam. The beam is reflected off the disc plane, goes back through the quarter-wavelength plate, and is reflected off the beam splitters. It then goes through a critical-angle prism and finally reaches the four-segment PD (photodetector).

The preamplifier

The preamplifier amplifies the weak RF signal from the photodiodes within the laser pickup assembly. Usually, the preamp generates the RF, TE, and FE signals by amplifying and adding or subtracting the output from the pickup unit of the four photodiode detectors. The laser diode within the Sony CDX-5 auto CD player is furnished a voltage from a –5.2-V and +5.2-V power source with transistor regulation (Fig. 12-15). The tracking error (E) and focus error (F) diodes' output go to IC652 and then to the focus/tracking/sled servo IC504.

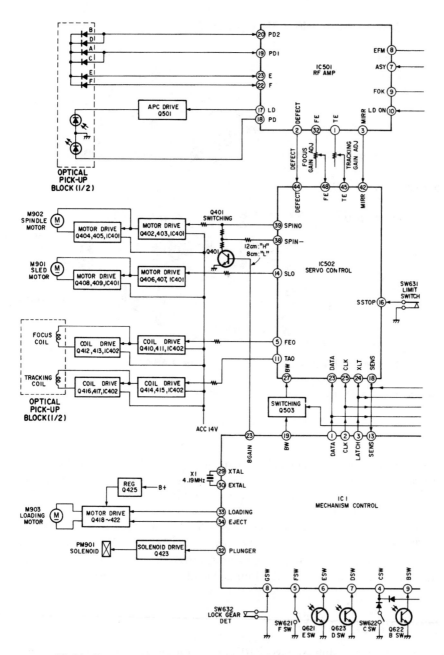

12-11   Front-end block diagram of the Denon DCC-9770 CD player.

Denon DCH-500 CD RF circuits

The optical PD1 and PD2 diodes are coupled to pins 19 and 20 of the RF amp IC11 (Fig. 12-16). The error and focus diodes are connected to pins 22 and 23 of RF amp. Transistor Q11 provides laser drive for the laser diodes in the optical assembly. RF

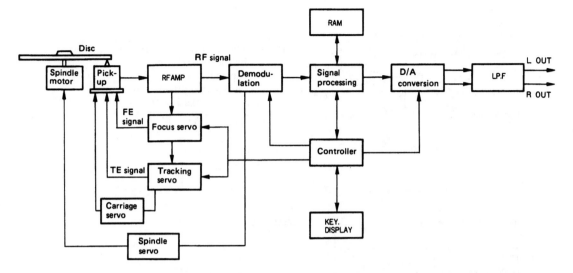

12-12 Here is a block diagram of Pioneer's CDX-1 auto CD player.

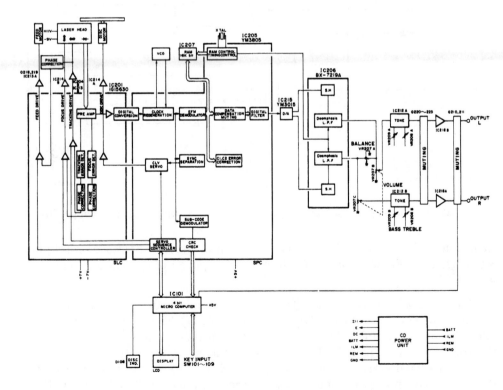

12-13 Block diagram of a Yamaha YCD-1000 CD player.

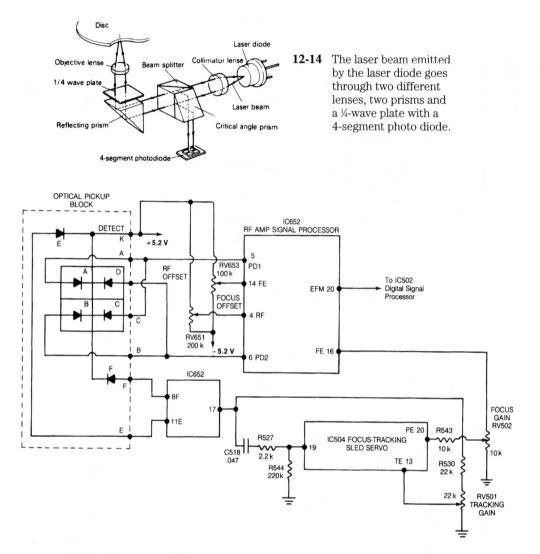

12-14 The laser beam emitted by the laser diode goes through two different lenses, two prisms and a ¼-wave plate with a 4-segment photo diode.

12-15 The photo diode signal is fed to RF amp IC652 with EFM output at pin 20.

signal can be checked at the RF test point from pin 14 and the EFM waveform at pin 8 of IC11. The EFM waveform is fed from pin 8 to pin 24 of the signal processing IC13.

Pioneer CDX-1 preamplifier The output current from the four-segment PD in the pickup unit is converted to voltage by IC1 (Fig. 12-17). Then, the FE signal is obtained by computing $(PD_2 + PD_3) - (PD_1 + PD_4)$. When the objective lens is closer to the disc than the focal point is, the FE signal generates negative output. If the lens is farther from the disc than the focal point, the FE signal generates positive output. IC2 performs the necessary computations and amplification for these functions. The preamplifier IC1 provides an RF, TE, and FE signal output.

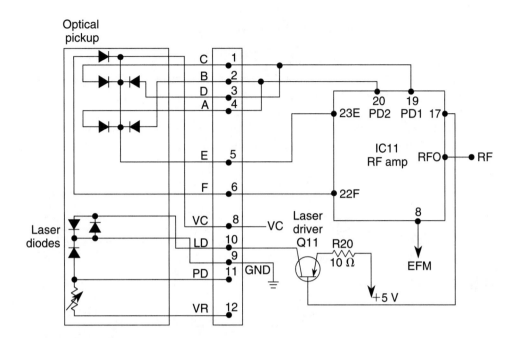

12-16 The photo diode signal PD1 and PD2 are fed from the optical assembly to RF amp IC11 of a Denon DCH-500 CD changer.

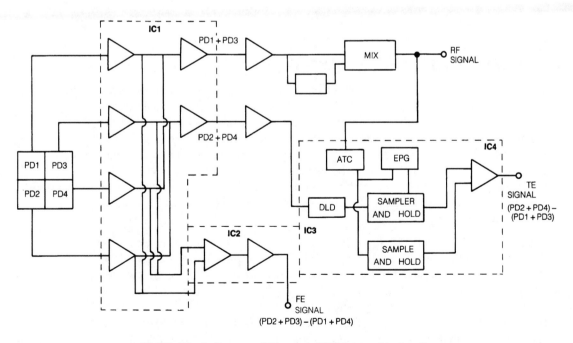

12-17 Block diagram of Pioneer's CDX-1 preamp circuits.

Denon DCH-500 changer signal path

The photo diodes of the optical assembly picks up the digital signal from the compact disc and applies it to pins PD1 (19) and PD2 (20) of RF amp IC11 (Fig. 12-18). IC11 amplifies the weak digital signal. The EFM signal is fed from pin 8 to pin 24 of the signal power IC13. The digital audio signal is sent to pin 10 of the digital/analog IC301.

The right stereo signal is taken from pin 25 and fed to pin 3 of IC101. The left stereo audio is fed to the other half of IC101 on pin 5. The amplified audio signal is capacity-coupled to the right and left output, to be fed to the audio radio amplifier.

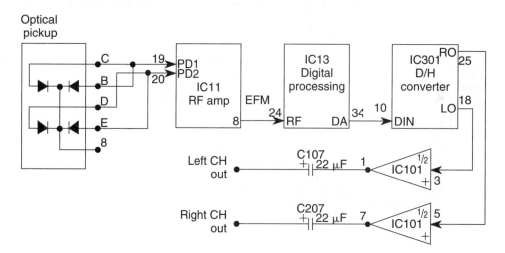

12-18   The signal path in the Denon DCH-500 CD auto changer.

Focus/tracking/sled servo

Often one large servo IC controls the focus and tracking coils, in addition to operating the sled or carriage motor. Within Alpine's 5900 CD player, a MIRR signal is fed to pin 11, FE focus gain at pin 20, and tracking gain signal at pin 13 (Fig. 12-19). Both the focus error and tracking error signal have a gain control in each error leg. The focus error output from pin 21 controls the focus driver Q505, Q506 and on the focus coil. The tracking drive signal from pin 27 feeds tracking drive transistors Q503 and Q504 to the tracking coil located within the optical pickup block. The sled motor control signal is fed to sled amp (IC506) and driver transistors (Q508–Q511), then to the sled motor (M901).

Pioneer CDX-1 focus control   A lead or lag in the FE signal that is generated by the preamplifier is compensated for by IC104 (½) after passing VR105 (gain level control). This signal operates the focus activator (objective lens) in the pickup unit with the current drive circuit made up of IC104, Q38, and Q39 (Fig. 12-20). Focus offset level control VR104 adjusts the shifting of the focus within the optical system or the circuitry of the preamplifier. When the power of the CD unit is turned on, the focus servo opens and the spring-supported objective lens is positioned at the mechanical center.

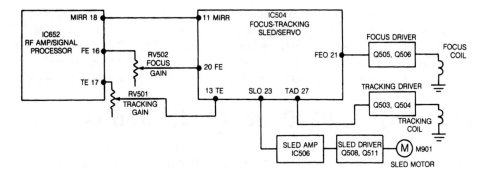

12-19 A block diagram of the focus/tracking Alpine S900 player.

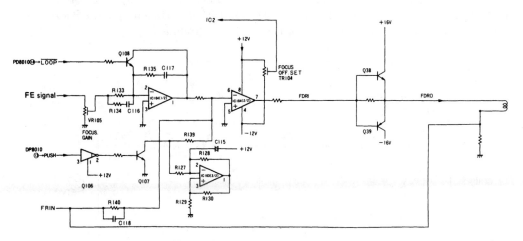

12-20 The focus control circuits of Pioneer's CDX-1 auto CD player.

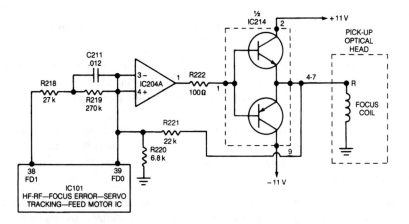

12-21 The focus control signal is fed from IC101 to focus driver (IC204A) and to the base of output driver IC214 to the focus coil in a Yamaha CD-1000 model.

After receiving a command to activate the focus servo circuit, the lens is first pulled back and then pushed outward. When the lens passes by the focal point, an RF signal is generated. This activates the focus servo circuit. The FT (focus trigger) signal determines whether or not the focus servo circuit is properly activated. If this circuit is not activated within a certain period of time, the disc is automatically ejected.

Denon DCC-9770 focus coil circuits

The focus coil circuits of Denon's DC-9770 auto CD player is taken from pin 5 (FEO) of the servo IC502. This signal is sent to the amplifier and driver IC402 (Fig. 12-22). Transistors Q410 and Q411 are found between the two op amps of IC402. The output voltage signal is taken from transistors Q412 and Q413 to the positive terminal of the focus coil. The negative terminal focus coil lead ties in from output transistors Q410 and Q411. The collector terminals of Q412 and Q410 are taken from the B+ 14-V source. Both Q413 and Q411 collector terminals are grounded.

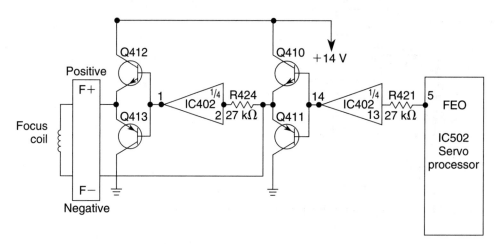

12-22   The focus coil circuits in a Denon DCC-9770 car CD changer.

If the tracking activator starts to vibrate, activation could become impossible. In order to avoid this, the tracking servo is designed to close only when the relative crossover speed is low. It does so by detecting the disc movement with the RF and TE signals. See Charts 12-2 and 12-3.

The tracking servo circuit is activated after the focus servo circuit is activated. The tracking servo circuit activation, however, is controlled to reduce the pickup speed relative to the movement of the disc surface. There is also a jump circuit that accesses tracks randomly.

Pioneer CDX-1 servo circuit   The TE signal generated by the preamplifier is sent to IC102 (½) through the analog switch, IC102 (½). There are equalizers there for phase lead compensation (poles 570 Hz, 10.5 kHz) made up of C103, R101, and R102, and for phase log compensation (poles 4.9 Hz, 59 Hz, 465 Hz) made up of

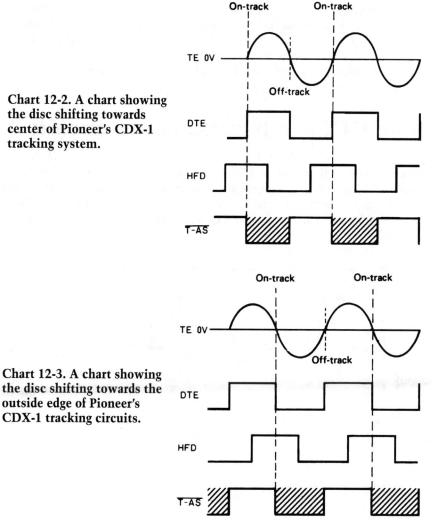

Chart 12-2. A chart showing the disc shifting towards center of Pioneer's CDX-1 tracking system.

Chart 12-3. A chart showing the disc shifting towards the outside edge of Pioneer's CDX-1 tracking circuits.

C106, R109, and R110. This output is then sent to IC102 (½). There are also equalizers for second-stage phase log compensation (10 Hz, 52 Hz, 4.4 kHz when the pole band is narrow, and 8.6 Hz, 264 Hz when the band is wide) and second-stage phase lead compensation (poles 1.1 kHz, 1.8 kHz).

The analog switch IC101 is set up by input to IC102 (½) to open and close the servo loop. When the T-AS signal is "H," and Q103 is off, the analog switch impedance becomes high and the loop opens.

After VR101 has adjusted the phase compensated TE signal, that signal undergoes current conversion at IC103 (½). Q36 and Q37 operate the activator. Feedback circuit IC103 contains C107 and R124; it reduces audible noise (16 kHz or more) created by the activator.

The second-stage equalizer switches bands as follows: the band is divided into two stages, wide and narrow. The bands are switched according to the conditions. The wide band is used during tracking servo circuit activation or jump operations, and the narrow band is used during normal playing.

VR103 functions to cut off the offset voltage generated inside the circuit and sets the activator drive current to zero when the tracking is open.

Denon DCC-9770 tracking coil circuits

The tracking coil (TAO) signal is taken from pin 11 and fed to IC402 (Fig. 12-23). IC402 contains four different op amps in one component. Q414 and Q415 receive the TAO signal and feed it from the emitter through R434 and IC402. The output signal on pin 7 couples directly to the base of Q416 and Q417. The positive tracking coil voltage at both emitters is fed to the tracking coil. The negative coil terminal ties in at the emitters of Q414 and Q415.

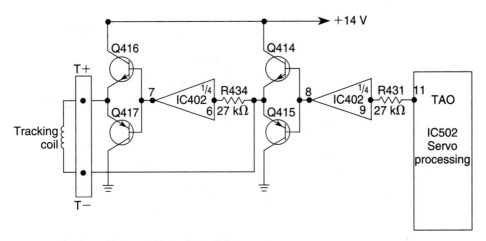

12-23   The tracking coil circuits in a Denon DCC-9770 auto CD changer.

Sony CDX-5 tracking coil circuits   The tracking coil found in the optical pickup block is driven directly by Q504 and Q503 (Fig. 12-24). The collector of Q504 is tied to the +8-V source, while the collector terminal of Q503 connects to the –8- V source. The common base terminals connect directly to pin 27 of the focus/tracking/sled servo (IC504), which has an internal tracking amp.

Hideaway units

Remember, the auto CD player might be in two different sections. The player section might be mounted in the dash and a "hideaway" unit might be mounted against the firewall. The two units are cabled together. In the Pioneer CDX-1 disc player, the player section consists of all operating motors, optical pickup assembly, display key control, display unit, and all IC and transistor components tied to the main unit. The

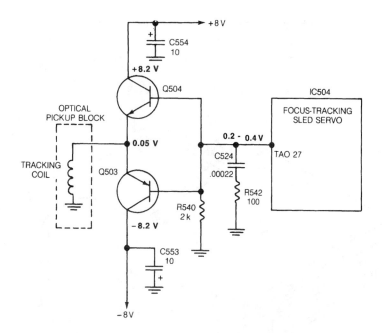

12-24   IC504 provides the focus coil control signal to the base of Q504 and Q505 in Sony's CDX-5 tracking coil circuits.

hideaway section contains the signal processor and servo units (Fig. 12-25). A red and black cable connects the two units together. However, some auto CD players are contained in one main unit.

Troubleshooting the RF and servo sections

If the player comes on and ejects the compact disc within a few seconds, suspect defective focus and tracking circuits or the eject system. Notice if the disc motor is rotating. Quickly check for correct focus and tracking signal at the input terminals of the servo IC. Check the EFM waveform from the RF amp IC. Suspect trouble within the RF preamp or optical pickup block assembly if no EFM, TE, or FO waveforms are found at the output terminals of the RF preamp IC (Fig. 12-26). Measure the B+ and B– voltages fed from the power supply to the RF preamp circuits. Improper TE and FO signals at the servo IC can indicate a defective RF IC or circuits.

If the tracking error and focus error signals are found at the input terminals of the servo IC, suspect a defective servo IC or drive circuits. The tracking and focus activator should search up, down, and sideways when it is first turned on. Make sure the tracking or focus signal is coming from the servo IC to each driving circuit.

The focus and tracking coil can be checked by taking a continuity measurement of the coil. If the coils seem normal, place a 1½-volt flashlight battery across the coil terminals. Remove the ungrounded lead from the coil before applying the battery

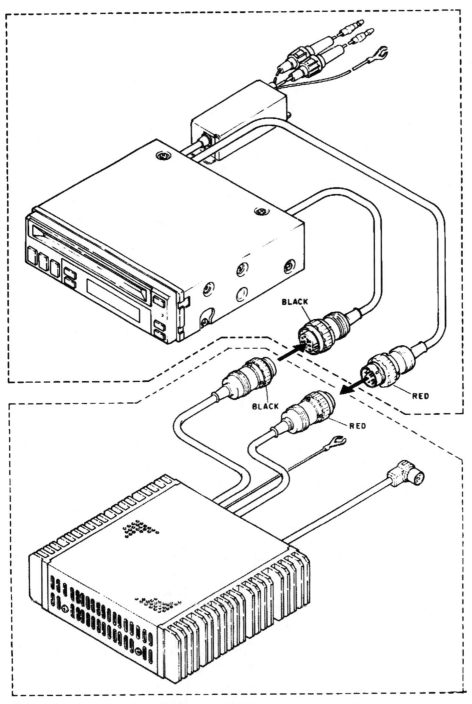

12-25 The hideaway unit in the Pioneer CDX-1 CD player connected to the player section.

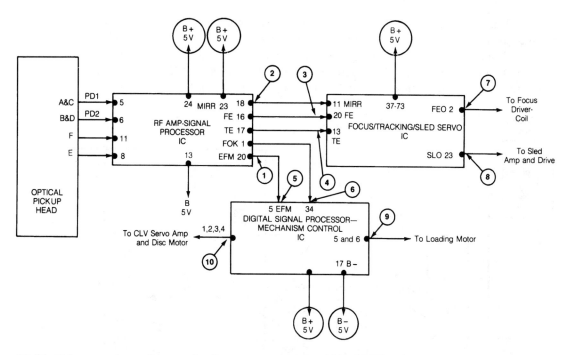

12-26 Take correct waveforms and voltage measurements within the RF and servo sections to help locate a defective component.

voltage. The focus activator should start to move either up or down. Reverse the battery leads. The activator should go in the opposite direction. Do the same to the tracking coil to check its movement.

Measure the voltages on the transistor or IC driver component. Notice a positive and negative voltage is fed to the collector terminals. Check each transistor with a transistor tester or meter. Suspect a poor coil or board connection and an intermittent driver transistor or IC if either system is erratic or intermittent.

The APC circuits

In some of the auto CD players, the output characteristics of the laser diode are greatly affected by changes in temperature. This is especially true in the automobile where a variety of weather conditions could affect the CD player. The beam output must be kept constant at all temperatures in order to accurately read the information recorded on the disc. A monitor diode has been built into the pickup to monitor the quantity of beam output. The beam output from the laser diode is kept constant by applying negative feedback from the current (detected by the MD) to the LD drive circuit.

Pioneer CDX-1 APC circuits The current detected by the MD is input into the IC5 (⅔) inverted input terminal after being converted into voltage by R61 and then amplified 40 times by IC5 (½). The voltage, after being divided by R65 and VR4, is input into the IC5 (⅔) noninverted input terminal as the standard voltage (Fig. 12-27). Circuit IC5 amplifies the difference between the two input voltages and that output current is then amplified by Q15 to activate the LD (laser diode). VR4 controls the beam intensity, which is adjusted to 0.25 mW and projected into the objective lens.

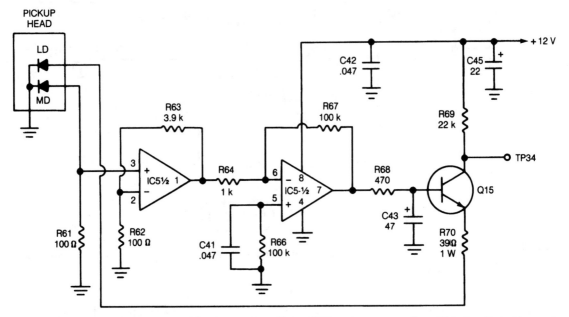

12-27 The laser diode is protected by the monitor diode (MD) and corresponding APC circuits in Pioneer's CDX-1 player.

The APC circuit is controlled by a microcomputer, and when the microcomputer LD signal is "H," the current stops flowing to the LD. The LD can easily be damaged by surge currents or static electricity. To protect the LD, C45 to C48 have been placed on the power supply line, and a diode and capacitor have been inserted into the pickup unit.

Interlock circuits

Interlocks are supplied to protect you while operating the auto compact disc player. Interlocks can be added so when a cover is removed the CD player will not operate. Most interlocks are provided to prevent radiation from the laser beam of striking the eyes of the operator or electronic technician. Take extra safety precautions when the interlock is shunted around or defeated so the player can be serviced. Interlocks should not be defeated and left in that position after the CD player has been repaired.

Yamaha YCD-1000 interlock operation The car compact disc player reads the disc signals by laser beam operation. The human body must not be directly exposed to the laser beam. This unit is therefore equipped with an interlock to prevent the unwanted and unnecessary laser output.

The laser outputs are controlled by the injection or cutoff of the constant voltage source to the laser diode at pin 30 (LS) of IC101 (Fig. 12-28) and also by an automatic laser power control circuit. When pin 30 is in "H" (high) level, the laser emits the beam. When pin 30 is in the "L" (low) level, the laser does not emit the beam.

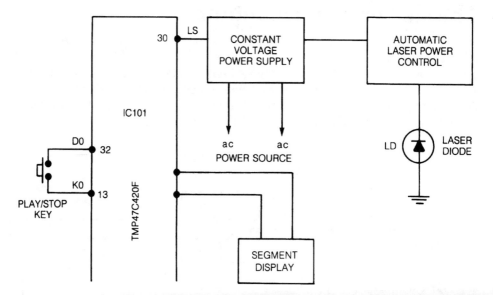

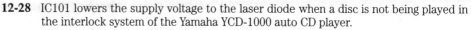

12-28 IC101 lowers the supply voltage to the laser diode when a disc is not being played in the interlock system of the Yamaha YCD-1000 auto CD player.

Pin 30 is set in "H" level when the unit is loaded with the disc and it reads the index signals or when the unit is set in the PLAY mode. When the unit reads the index signals and the following two conditions are met, the laser emits the beam.

- When the CD cartridge is inserted into the cartridge door.
- When the pickup is located at the area of the minimum internal circumference.

After these conditions are met and the index signals have been read, the laser emits the beam when the following two conditions are met.

- When the PLAY/STOP key is pressed.
- When the 0:00 display is on.

Motor operations

The sled or carriage motor, disc or turntable motor, and loading motor can be controlled by the focus/tracking servo, a mechanism control, or a master control IC, or a combination of these. All of the motors within Alpine's 5900 and Sony's CDX-5 CD auto player are operated from the same circuits. In the Yamaha YCD-1000 player, the feed and disc motor is operated from the HF preamp/tracking/focus IC101. In Pioneer's CDX-1 model, the carriage motor is controlled by IC7, Q31, Q32, and Q33 in the servo unit. The disc or spindle motor is controlled by IC9 and the loading motor IC7 in the main unit. Some auto players have an eject solenoid system instead of a loading motor.

The sled or carriage motor

The carriage or sled motor moves the optical laser pickup from the center to the outside while playing. Within Alpine's 5900 and Sony's CDX-5 audio CD players, the sled motor is controlled by the focus/tracking/sled servo IC504 (Fig. 12-29). The SLO signal from pin 23 of IC504 is fed to the sled amp (IC506), then to the sled driver transistors Q508, Q509, Q510, and Q511. The output voltage from the emitter terminals of Q508 and Q511 drive the sled motor M901.

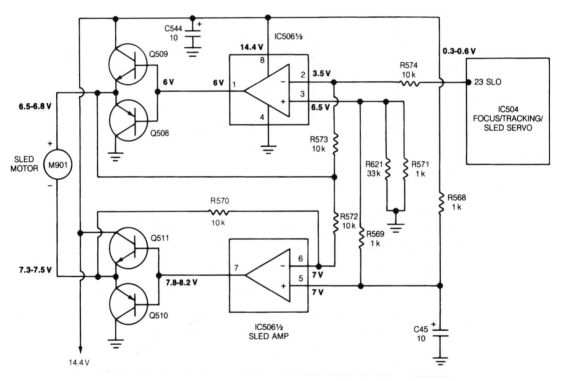

12-29 The sled motor is controlled by IC504 in Alpine's 5900 and Sony's CDX-5 auto CD player.

Denon DCH-500 changer sled motor circuits

In this CD changer the sled motor is controlled by the tracking, focus and motor drive IC14. IC14 is controlled by servo IC12 (Fig. 12-30). The negative motor terminal of sled motor connects to pin 1 and the positive terminal to pin 2 of IC14. IC14 controls the drive voltage for the sled motor, tracking, and focus coils.

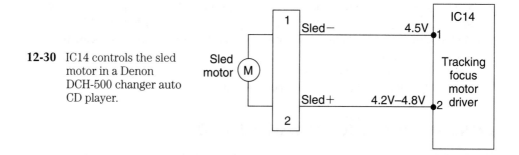

12-30 IC14 controls the sled motor in a Denon DCH-500 changer auto CD player.

Pioneer CDX-1 carriage motor control circuits The carriage control circuit moves the pickup inward and outward in the radial direction on the disc servo. For normal playing, the beam moves outward and traces the tracks on the disc surface. The activator, however, can only move about 0.4 mm. When the drive current of the activator increases, this circuit causes the carriage motor to start the pickup moving outward to reduce the drive current of the activator.

The TDRO terminal converts the tracking activator drive current to voltage; the voltage is then amplified by IC7 and IC8. When the eccentricity of a disc is great, the activator requires a larger drive current. This increase in the drive current of the activator affects the carriage motor and causes it to turn, but because the carriage motor is slower to respond to a high-frequency current, this could damage the tracking servo operation. Because disc eccentricity increases the activator drive current, the carriage servo control circuit gain must be kept low. The IC7 (½) equalizer circuit performs this operation (Fig. 12-31). The equalizer consists of C16, C17, C18, R75, and R76. The poles are 0.014 Hz, 0.62 Hz, and 136 Hz.

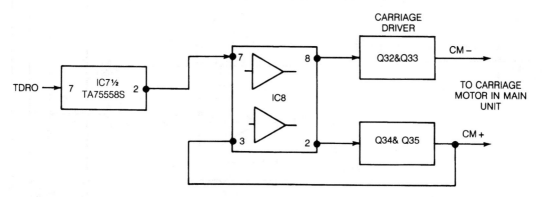

12-31 Pioneer's CDX-1 carriage motor is controlled by IC7, IC8, and carriage drive transistors Q32, Q33, Q34, and Q35.

When the carriage is shifted at high speeds, such as during scanning operation, the microcomputer TOC signal becomes "H" (high). Transistors Q29, Q30, and Q31 also turn on the IC7 (½) and gain is set to zero. As a result, the carriage servo loops open.

Next, the R-OC signal becomes "L" (Low) and the F/R signal selects the carriage movement direction. For example, when the F/R signal is "L," Q26 and Q27 turn off, IC6 pin 5 becomes "L," and pin 13 becomes "H." This connects the analog switch between pins 1 and 2, and 12 V is input to IC8 (⅔) via R68 and R82. In this case, the R-OC signal connects the analog switch between IC6 pins 10 and 11. A voltage of approximately 6 V is applied to the carriage motor.

Disc or spindle motor circuits

The disc or spindle motors rotate the disc, while the carriage or sled motor pulls the optical pickup head toward the outside edge of the disc. The disc motor found in the Alpine 5900 and Sony CDX-5 auto players is controlled by the digital signal processor/CLV Servo IC502 (Fig. 12-32). The servo control signals from IC502 pins 1 through 4 are fed to a CLV servo control amp IC301 (½) and to the CLV disc motor.

In the Pioneer CDX-1 auto player, the spindle motor is controlled by IC9 (Fig. 12-33). A positive 16 V is applied to terminal 3. The spindle motor (CXM-405) is located approximately in the center of the main unit. Only two mounting screws hold the spindle motor assembly in place. When replacing the spindle motor, take care

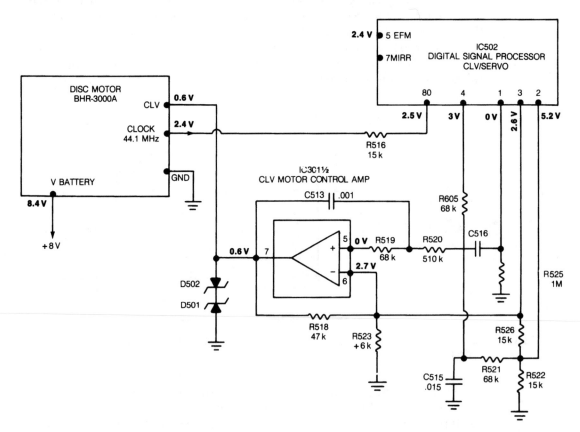

12-32 Alpine's 5900 disc motor is controlled by IC502 which is fed to the CLV motor control amp IC301.

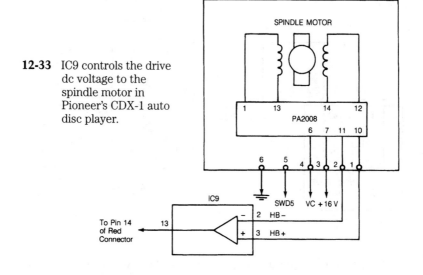

12-33 IC9 controls the drive dc voltage to the spindle motor in Pioneer's CDX-1 auto disc player.

not to let the spindle motor flywheel shaft become scratched or dirty (Fig. 12-34). Always replace motors with the original part number.

The disc motor in the Yamaha YCD-1000 auto CD player is controlled by IC101 (Fig. 12-35). A disc drive amp located inside the IC101 feeds to the drive output IC214 (½). The positive terminal of the motor is fed from pin 10 of IC214, and the grounded side of the disc motor is fed through resistor R230 (2.2 Ω). When the disc motor will not rotate always check if R230 is open.

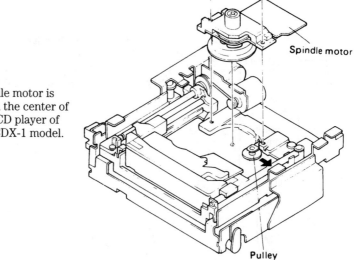

12-34 The spindle motor is located in the center of the auto CD player of Pioneer CDX-1 model.

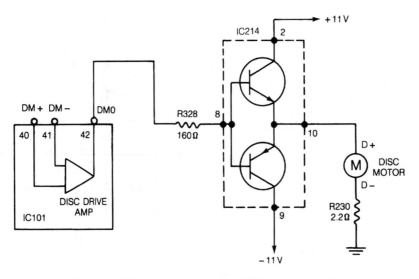

12-35   IC101 drives IC214 from pin 42 and IC214 drives the disc motor in a Yamaha YCD-1000 player.

Denon DCH-500 spindle motor circuits

The spindle motor drive signal is controlled by the signal processing IC13 (Fig. 12-36). The signal is taken from pin 4 and fed to pin 3 of spindle driver IC15. Pin 1 is directly coupled to the base terminal of Q17. The output emitter signal is fed to pin 8 of spindle motor IC1. IC1 and the spindle motor are found mounted on the optical assembly.

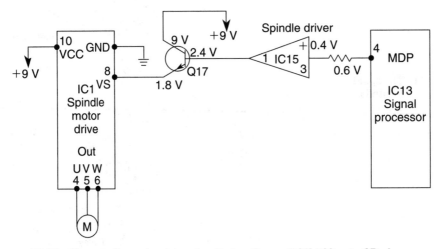

12-36   The spindle motor drive circuits in a Denon DCH-500 auto CD player.

The loading motor circuits

The loading motor circuits within Sony's CDX-5 player are controlled by mechanical control IC508 and in turn power the forward-reverse rotation drive IC507 (Fig. 12-37).

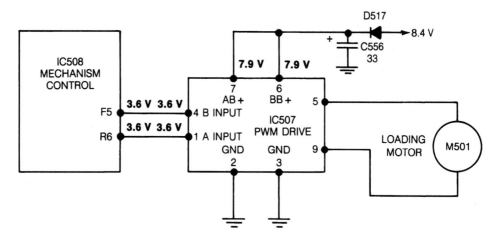

12-37   IC508 controls the loading motor driver IC507 in a Sony CDX-5 auto CD player.

Alpine's 5900 player uses the same method. The loading motor is mounted horizontally with plastic pulley gears (Fig. 12-38). The loading motor in the Pioneer CDX-1 player is controlled from the display key control IC6. The eject and load terminals (2 and 3) go to terminals 4 and 7 of the drive IC7 (Fig. 12-39). Output terminals 3 and 8 from IC7 are fed directly to the disc loading motor (M3). Removing only one metal screw frees the loading motor (Fig. 12-40). When replacing any of the motors with belts or a plastic pulley, make sure all grease is wiped off. Do not twist the belts on motor belt-driven pulleys.

Troubleshooting the motor circuits

The suspected motor can quickly be checked by taking accurate voltage measurements across the motor terminals. This voltage measurement is rather low (1 to 10 V); for example, the Pioneer carriage motor operates at 6 Vdc. If voltage is found across the motor terminals and there is no motor rotating, take a continuity measurement of the motor field coils. The resistance measurement can be less than 1 Ω across the motor terminals. If in doubt, clip a 1½-V flashlight battery across the motor terminals. Always remove the motor plug or leads so that you do not damage other components. Do not apply outside voltage across the input motor board terminal of a PLV solid-state type motor assembly. If the motor appears normal, check the drive signal at the servo IC. Then check the applied voltage to the power drive transistors or IC component. Test each transistor with the transistor tester or a meter. Open or leaky transistors and IC components might produce improper or no voltage to the motor terminals. Make sure both positive and negative voltages are applied to the drive transistors.

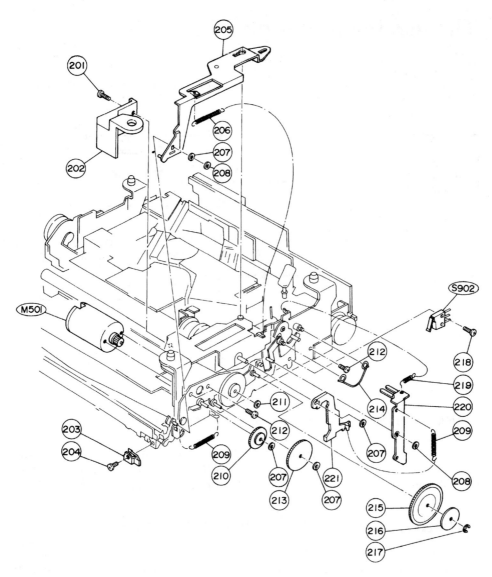

12-38 The loading motor lays horizontally in Alpine's 5900 CD player.

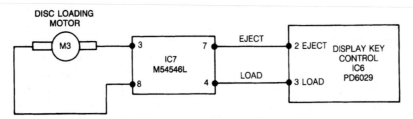

12-39 IC6 controls the motor drive IC7 to the disc loading motor in Pioneer's CDX-1 auto CD player.

• Removing the Carriage Motor

1. Remove the two screws (M2.6 x 4) labeled "Y."
2. Remove the belt.

• Removing the Loading Motor

1. Remove the two screws (M2.3 x 4) labeled "Z."

NOTE:
Before attaching the belt, make sure that it is not soiled with grease and not twisted.

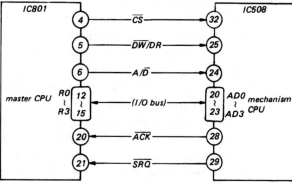

12-40 Both carriage and loading motors lay horizontally in Pioneer's CDX-1 auto player.

Sony's CDX-5 master CPU and mechanism CPU

This unit uses a master CPU (IC801) that controls the system and a mechanism CPU (IC508) that controls the mechanism (Fig. 12-41). The master CPU (IC801) com-

12-41 The master CPU (IC801) controls the system while CPU (IC508) controls the mechanism in Sony's CDX-5 auto CD player.

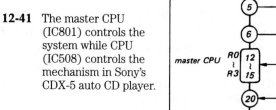

municates with the mechanism CPU (IC508) to get information and command the mechanism to control the system with the following signals:

Chip select (CS) This signal is sent out from the master CPU to command the mechanism CPU.

Data write/data read (DW/DR) The signal that indicates if the master CPU should write or read the data of the mechanism CPU.

Address/data (A/D) Indicates if the signal on the bus line is an address signal or a data signal.

I/O bus Four-bit bus line between the master CPU and the mechanism CPU.

Acknowledge (ACK) The signal that indicates to the master CPU that the mechanism CPU has received a C5 signal and has executed the command.

Service request (SRQ) The signal that indicates to the master CPU that data should be read out because a change has occurred.

Power hookup

Usually, there are at least two different fused "A" leads to the auto CD player: one for the memory and the other to the main player unit. The audio line output connects to the CD input terminals of the cassette-receiver component. In some auto CD players with two separate units, the cables must be connected tightly between the main player and hideaway unit. The CD player can be controlled by the power switch of the cassette-tuner receiver.

Denon DCC-9770 power hookup The Denon CD player connects power to the unit at the battery and ground cable (Fig. 12-42). This AM-FM CD player operates from the 14.4-V car battery. The orange and white wires connect to the light switch and the red wire (ACC) connects to the ignition power supply wire. A CD auto changer can be connected to the CD changer cable (such as DCH-500 model). Two separate stereo power amps connect to rear and front external amplifiers.

Pioneer's CDX-1 power hookup Within this CD auto player, there are three different power supply connections (Fig. 12-43). The hideaway unit is connected to the player with the red and black connector cables. Three different ground connections must be connected to the metal part of the car body. The external line output is cabled to the existing cassette tape deck (Fig. 12-44). Follow these guidelines.

- Before making final connections, make temporary connections and operate the unit to check for any connecting cord problems.
- Connect the red and black connectors of the player to the respective red and black connectors of the hideaway unit, and securely tighten the retaining rings.
- Refer to the instruction manual for details on connecting the various cords of the deck and main amp, then make connections correctly.
- Be sure to correctly connect the memory power supply lead (orange) and main power supply lead (red), as specified. If the connections are made incorrectly or forgotten, this unit will not work at all.
- Don't pass the memory power supply lead through a hole into the engine compartment to connect to the battery. This will damage the lead insulation and cause a very dangerous short.

CONNECTIONS

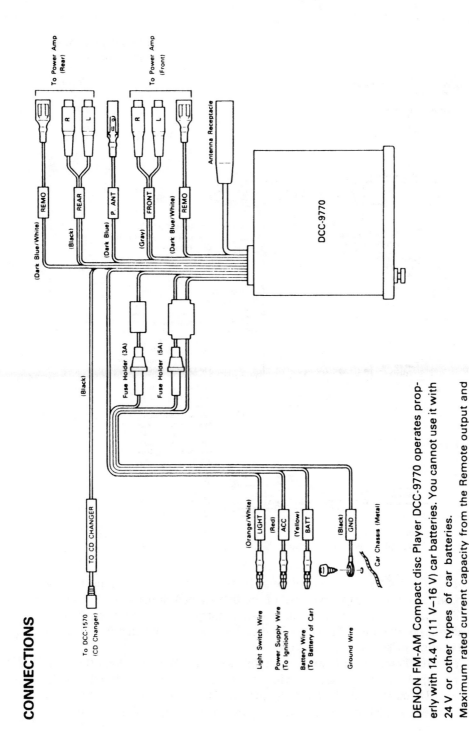

DENON FM-AM Compact disc Player DCC-9770 operates properly with 14.4 V (11 V–16 V) car batteries. You cannot use it with 24 V or other types of car batteries.

Maximum rated current capacity from the Remote output and the Power antenna output is 500 mA.

12-42   The power hookup of a Denon DCC-9770 CD auto player.

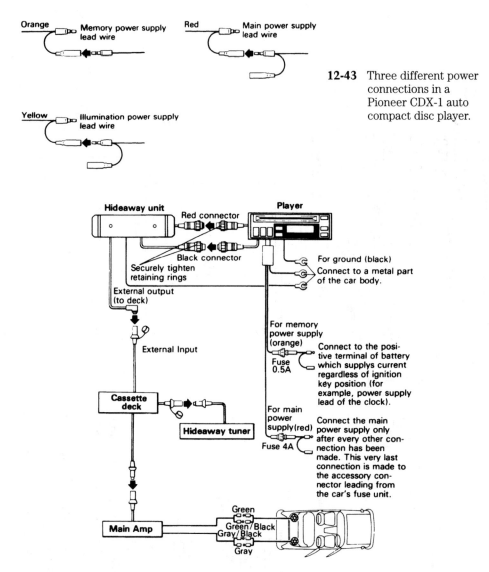

12-43 Three different power connections in a Pioneer CDX-1 auto compact disc player.

12-44 A power hookup of Pioneer's CDX-1 CD player.

Yamaha YCD-1000 power connections Make sure you have disconnected the negative lead from the negative terminal of the battery before installing YCD-1000 (Fig. 12-45). This prevents any accidental short circuitry during installation. The ignition lead is a positive input. It should be connected to a circuit that is turned on when the ignition switch is in the ACC position.

The YCD-1000 connected to an in-dash unit with no CD control lead (brown), will not interrupt the radio or cassette when you turn the CD player on. When connecting the YCD-1000 to in-dash units that have no CD input jack, CDA-10 should be connected. After completion of the connection and installation, be sure to press the

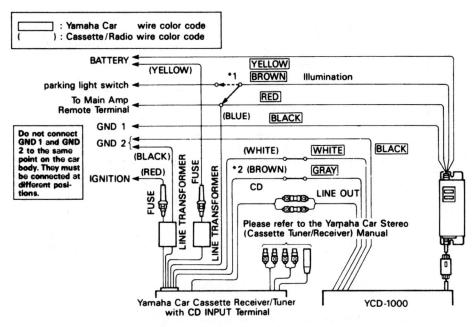

12-45 The power hookup connections with the Yamaha YCD-1000 auto CD player.

reset button for a few seconds to initialize the unit. The leads are identified as follows:

White CD control input   When the function selector of the cassette/tuner/receiver is set to TAPE or TUNER position, the CD play stops.

Gray CD control output   When the YCD-1000 is set to PLAY mode, the function mode of the cassette tuner/receiver is automatically set to CD.

Red remote power on/off input   The power of the YCD-1000 can be controlled by the power switch of the cassette tuner/receiver. This lead should be connected after completion, of other connections. When the cassette tuner/receiver is not used, connect this lead to the line that passes the ignition key.

Brown illumination   For illuminating the front panel.

Yellow power lead   Connect to the positive battery terminal of the battery.

Black ground   To a metal point on the car.

The power supply

Most auto CD players contain a dc-to-dc converter unit connected to the 14.4-V power "A" lead connection. The converter is controlled by an IC oscillator and two high-powered input transistors (Fig. 12-46). The output transformer (T1) produces several voltages on the secondary windings. Full-wave bridge and diode rectification are found in the secondary of T1.

Several transistor switching and voltage regulation circuits combined with zener diodes are found in the many different power supplies. A +30-V power supply is fed

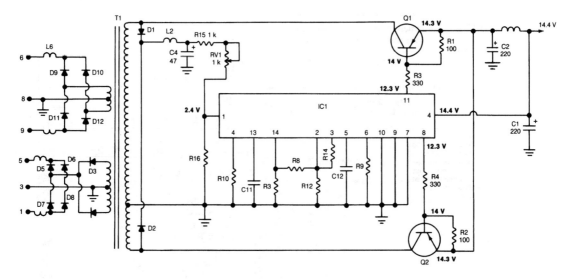

12-46 The dc to dc converter power supply in Sony's CDX-5 player.

to the display tube/drive/decoder IC802 in a Sony CDX-5 player (Fig. 12-47). The voltage is taken directly from full-wave rectifier D4 and D3. The Sony CDX-5 power supply circuits generate +30 V, ±14 V, ±8 V, and ±5 V.

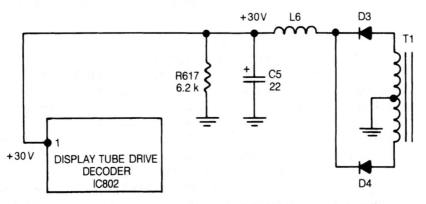

12-47 A +30-V supply feeds the display tube driver IC802 in Sony's CDX-5 model.

The dc-to-dc converter power supply in Pioneer CDX-1 auto player has four different regulator ICs for the different power sources (Fig. 12-48). Two separate secondary windings provide ±16-V, ±12-V, and ±5-V power sources. Notice the ± 16-V taps are taken before IC regulation. Check the auto regulator circuits like any voltage regulated circuit.

Accurate voltage measurements and scope waveforms of the IC to transformer dc-to-dc converter solve most power supply problems. Always check the output voltage from the IC or transistor regulator circuits that tie to the section that is not operating. Disconnect the voltage output terminal of the regulator of the power supply

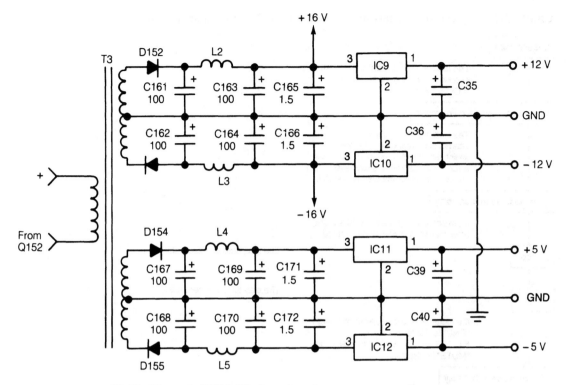

12-48 Pioneer's CDX-1 CD player transformer power supply sources.

to see if the overload is in the power supply or connecting circuits with low voltages. Suspect components within the power supply when the low voltage exists with the power source lead disconnected. Troubleshoot the connecting circuits when the voltage is normal at the output terminal of voltage regulator.

Denon DCC-9770 test mode

1. Press reset key while simultaneously pressing 1, 2, 3, and 4 keys.
2. Press timer switch and insert disc.
3. When disc is inserted, the following actions should be performed in Chart 12-4.

Denon DCC-9770 PLL-Free run adjustment

1. Remove the soldering bridge (EFM) from the MD main board (Fig. 12-49).
2. Detach R522 from the main PC board (R522 is connected to pin 11 of IC503).
3. Connect the frequency counter to test point (PLCK).
4. Turn the power on and adjust RV505 so that the frequency counter recording satisfies the specifications.

Adjustable limits: 4.3118 to 4.3318 MHz.

Chart 12-4. The test mode chart of a Denon DCC-9770 auto disc player.

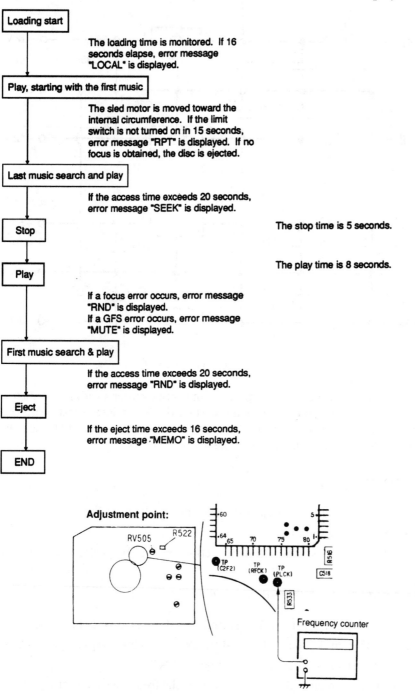

Loading start

The loading time is monitored. If 16 seconds elapse, error message "LOCAL" is displayed.

Play, starting with the first music

The sled motor is moved toward the internal circumference. If the limit switch is not turned on in 15 seconds, error message "RPT" is displayed. If no focus is obtained, the disc is ejected.

Last music search and play

If the access time exceeds 20 seconds, error message "SEEK" is displayed.

Stop

The stop time is 5 seconds.

Play

The play time is 8 seconds.

If a focus error occurs, error message "RND" is displayed.
If a GFS error occurs, error message "MUTE" is displayed.

First music search & play

If the access time exceeds 20 seconds, error message "RND" is displayed.

Eject

If the eject time exceeds 16 seconds, error message "MEMO" is displayed.

END

Adjustment point:

Frequency counter

12-49 The PLL-Free running frequency counter adjustment in a Denon DCC-9770 auto changer.

Denon DCH-500 focus offset adjustment

1. Connect oscilloscope to Servo board test point RF (Fig. 12-50).

2. Put the set into play mode by loading disc.

3. Adjust (servo) board RV12 so that the scope waveform eye pattern is good. A good eye pattern means the diamond shape in center can be clearly distinguished.

Procedure:

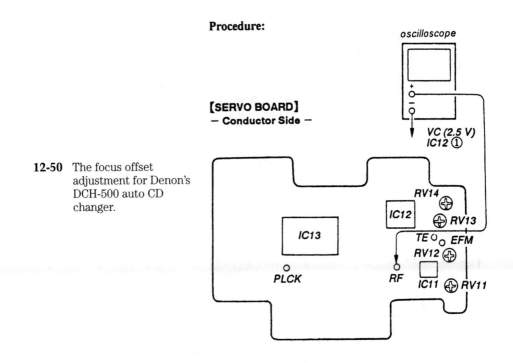

12-50 The focus offset adjustment for Denon's DCH-500 auto CD changer.

Denon DCH-500 focus gain adjustment The coarse focus gain adjustment is performed when replacing the optical assembly block or RV14.

1. Set RV14 (servo board) to the standard position (Fig. 12-51).

2. Check that there is not an abnormal amount of operation noise (white noise) from the 2-axis device. If there is, turn RV14 slightly clockwise.

When the gain is higher, the set does not play because of the lack of focus operation; if operation noise is heard due to a scratch or dust, operation will be unstable.

Denon DCC-9770 tracking offset adjustment

1. Connect oscilloscope to test point TE on the main board (Fig. 12-52).

2. Load a disc and set mode to play.

3. Press FForward and FReverse and observe traverse waveform.

4. Adjust RV501 so that the waveform is symmetric when centered at the level to be accessed.

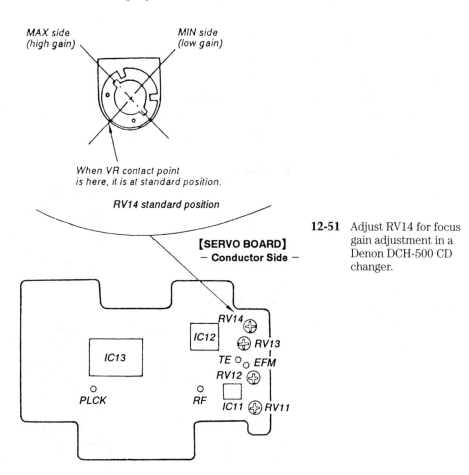

12-51   Adjust RV14 for focus gain adjustment in a Denon DCH-500 CD changer.

Denon DCH-500 tracking gain adjustment This coarse gain adjustment is made when replacing the optical pickup block and RV13. Also, adjustment should be made after focus and tracking offset adjustments are completed.

1. Connect the scope to servo board test point TE (Fig. 12-53).

2. Put the set into play mode by loading disc.

3. Turn servo board RV13 from clockwise stop, then check scope waveform. Fix RV13 at the position where the waveform disappears (Fig. 12-54).

Adjustment point: MD main board

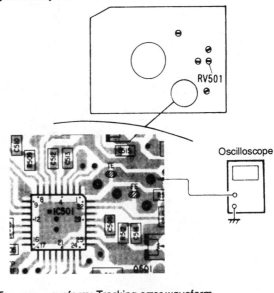

* Traverse waveform: Tracking error waveform
which is observed when the
track is traversed.
Volt/div: 0.5V
Time/div: 2msec
Center: 0V

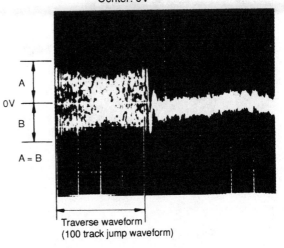

12-52　Tracking offset adjustment in the Denon DCC-
9770 CD player.

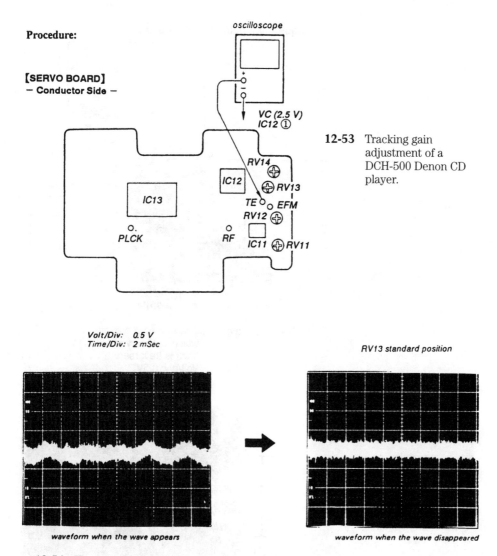

12-53 Tracking gain adjustment of a DCH-500 Denon CD player.

12-54 The waveforms when wave appears and adjustment for waveform to disappear.

13
Troubleshooting methods and service hints

TROUBLESHOOTING THE COMPACT DISC PLAYER IS NOT AS DIFFICULT AS IT MIGHT seem. Simply isolate the various symptoms on the block diagram and apply them to the schematic to locate the defective section. A good schematic diagram is a must in servicing the compact disc player (Fig. 13-1). Of course, locating problems in the power supply and audio circuits could be easily done without the schematic. Always have the schematic handy when servicing the RF path, focus, and servo circuits.

Critical waveforms

Besides taking correct voltage and resistance measurements, critical waveforms are needed in most CD circuits. You will find actual waveforms and voltage charts in the service literature of each CD player. The service literature can be obtained from the local CD distributor, manufacturer's distributor, service depot, or the manufacturer itself. If you are doing warranty work for certain brands of TVs and compact disc players, subscribe to the CD service literature.

You can follow the RF or EFM signal path with critical scope waveforms (Fig. 13-2). Just by taking input and output waveforms on the critical servo and focus IC components, you can determine if the component is defective. Often, each processor or IC is isolated with critical waveforms. If you are working only on a couple of brands of CD players, take the critical waveforms of a working model and mark them on the service diagram for future reference. Always mark on the outside area of the schematic the defective components and voltages found in locating a defective part.

A static wristband should be used while servicing the CD chassis to keep your body at the same potential as the compact disc player (Fig. 13-3). Clip the ground clip to the CD chassis from the static wristband. Extreme care should be exercised in attaching test equipment and taking voltage measurements and scope waveforms on the compact disc chassis to not damage the fragile processors and IC components.

13-1 The schematic diagram is a must item when servicing the CD player.

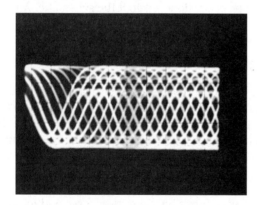

13-2 Observe the eye pattern (EFM) to see if the laser and preamp or RF amp are normal.

The most common problems

Many of the problems related to the compact disc failures are common to any player. These troubles can be listed as nuisance or simple failures brought on by the operator. Knowing how to operate the player can solve a lot of nuisance problems. Read the operating manual several times. This might also apply to the service technician who repairs many different brands of CD players. Knowing how they operate saves valuable service time.

Check the transit screws located at the bottom side of the player when the unit will not operate. These screws should be removed before the player is fired up. They

INCORRECT

CORRECT

Ground conductive wristband
for body

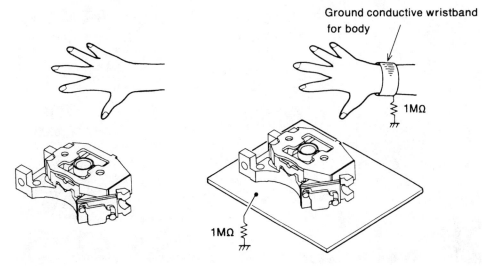

1MΩ

1MΩ

13-3 Wear a ground conductive wrist strap to ground yourself when servicing the CD player.

should be in place when the player is moved from the shop to the home or vice versa, preventing damage to the laser optical assembly. The player might not turn on, start to play, and stop without removing the transit screws. In some players, the transit screws are removed entirely; in others they are loosened and still remain with the player.

Scratched or dirty discs make the player operate for a few minutes and then suddenly stop. Deep scratches in the disc can prevent the disc from playing. Small scratches or dirty areas on the disc can cause sound dropout. The machine might not even begin to operate with a warped disc. Always inspect the disc for defects and make sure the disc is loaded correctly. The label side should always be up with the rainbow side downward.

A dirty optical lens might let the player begin and shut off suddenly. Clean up the optical lens with regular camera lens cleaning equipment. Because the optical assembly is down under the flapper a loading device very seldom is cleaned. Always clean the optical lens when the player comes in for repair.

Broken components or a cracked PC board often occur when the CD player is knocked off the stand or in shipment. Look for breakage around the heavy components, such as power transformers, mounting screw holes, and optical lens assembly. Carefully inspect the PC board when the service card indicates the unit has been dropped. Small breaks on the PC board can be repaired with bare hookup wire. Replacing the whole PC board is possible, but rather costly. Look for broken boards that can be mounted separately on the metal chassis support tabs (Fig. 13-4).

Intermittent operation can be caused by improper connections from the cables of the CD player to the input jacks of the stereo amplifier. The player might become intermittent or appear dead with poor contacts at the various plugs on the main electronic board. Make sure all plugs are pushed down tightly. Move the plugs to locate

13-4 A small, separately mounted board can be easily broken during servicing, shipment, or if the player is dropped.

the intermittent connection. The optical laser assembly, most motors, display assembly, and the power transformer might plug into the PC board.

Many of the manufacturers have flowcharts at the rear of their service manuals. Sometimes these charts do not actually locate the defective component, but they do point you in the right direction. This is another reason you should have the manufacturer's service manual. A simple troubleshooting chart of a Pioneer PD-7010 CD player is shown in Chart 13-1.

Realistic CD-3370 portable flowchart

Use the following flowchart to troubleshoot most portable CD players (Chart 13-2). After completing a particular branch section, go through the main flowchart again to make sure there are no other irregularities. By following this basic flowchart, you can apply it to any portable player. Use Fig. 13-5 to correspond with chart and the various circuits.

Symptom: No power (defective power supply)

Suspect a blown fuse or the player is not plugged properly into the power outlet if the display will not light up with the power switch pressed on. Do not forget to check the timer setting found on some CD players. You might find that some CD player low-voltage circuits are not protected by a fuse. Inspect the power switch for breakage or poor contacts. If 120 Vac is measured across the power switch with the switch on, suspect an open switch. Dirty switch contacts can cause intermittent turn on.

Chart 13-1. A troubleshooting flowchart of Pioneer's PD-7010 CD player.

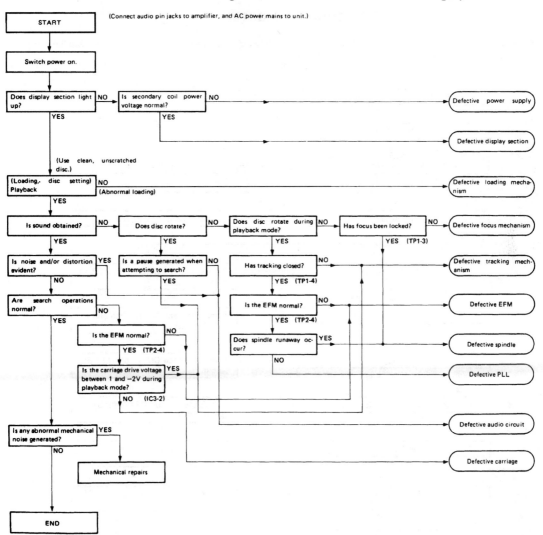

Turn the player off at once if you hear a loud groan from the transformer with the power switch on (Fig. 13-6). Remove the plug and check the low-voltage power supply for a shorted condition. Often, when several diodes short out, the primary winding of the power transformer might open up. Check the primary winding with the low ohm scale of the ohmmeter. The bridge rectifier might be in one unit or there might be separate silicon diodes (Fig. 13-7).

Many electronic technicians go directly to the low-voltage power supply when voltage is missing in a certain section of the TV or CD player. Because the power supply furnishes critical voltage to the various circuits, test each voltage source for correct voltage. You might find the low-voltage power supply is at fault instead of suspected

Chart 13-2. Realistic CD-3370 portable CD player troubleshooting flowchart.

TROUBLESHOOTING

Use the following flowcharts when troubleshooting. After completing a particular branch section, go through the main flow again to be sure there are no other irregularities.

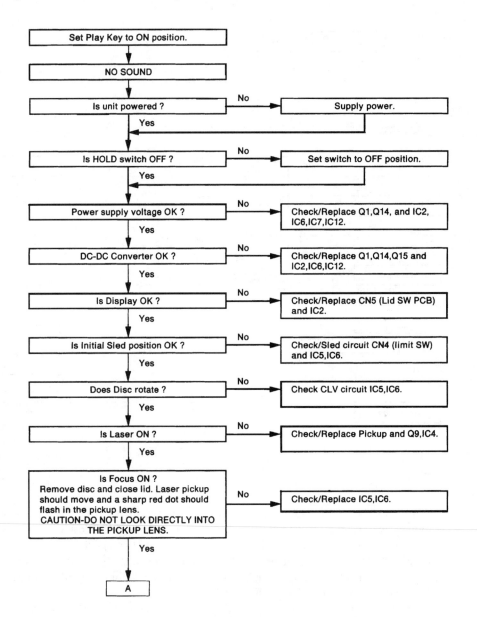

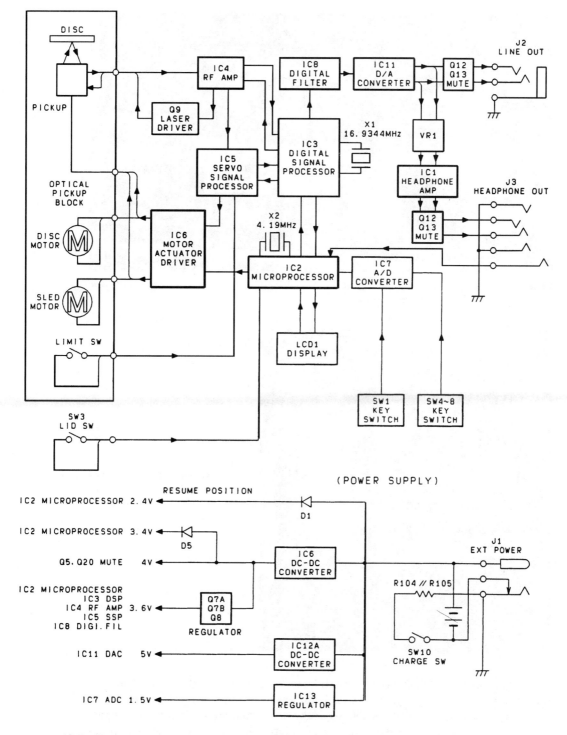

13-5 Block diagram of a Realistic CD-3370 portable CD player to go with flowchart 13-2.

13-6 A loud hum from the power transformer could indicate a shorted component in the power supply or leaky transformer.

13-7 You might find separate silicon diodes instead of a bridge rectifier part in the low-voltage power supply.

components in the CD circuits. It's wise to take stop and play mode voltages on each transistor or IC component when servicing only one or two brands of CD players.

Leaky low-voltage and zener diodes, leaky or shorted voltage transistor regulators, and dried up filter and decoupling electrolytic capacitors produce most problems in the low-voltage power supplies. Remove one end of each diode for correct leakage tests. It's best to remove the regulator transistors if suspected of leakage. Test the transistor out of the circuit with the DMM or transistor tester. Check the suspected electrolytic capacitors in and out of the circuit with a digital capacitance meter (Fig. 13-8). For more on power supply troubles, refer to chapter 4.

13-8 The digital capacitor tester is ideal to check open or leaky capacitors in CD players.

Dead nothing-Sanyo CP500

No pilot light or display symptoms in this Sanyo CP500 compact disc player. A quick voltage measurement on the +14 V and +9 V bridge rectifiers indicated no dc voltage source. In fact, diodes D601 and D602 showed leakage. ac voltage measurement across the transformer secondary at pins 10 and 11 indicated no voltage.

The ac plug was pulled and a resistance measurement across the ac power plug indicated an open circuit. S901 tested normal. The primary winding across 1 and 5 were open, indicating transformer replacement (Fig. 13-9). Replacing diodes D601 and D602, and the power transformer (PT) with original part numbers restored the CD player (4-300T-95200).

Dead Sylvania FDD104 CD player

The display would light up in the Sylvania CD player, but it would not accept any operation. Because the servo and decoder circuits were dead, the low voltage (12 V) was checked in the low-voltage power supply. A −12 V was measured, but there wasn't a +12 V.

Checking the schematic, a +18 V was measured at the bridge rectifier circuits. Only a fraction of the proper voltage was found at IC voltage regulator (MC78-M12CT) pin terminal 3 (Fig. 13-10). The diode BAX18 tied to pin 3 was normal. Replacing the IC regulator (6451) solved the dead compact disc player.

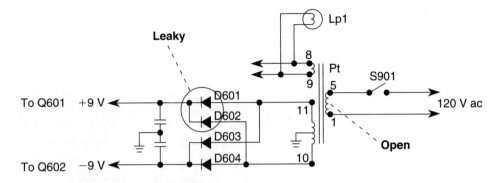

13-9 Leaky and shorted D601 and D602 opened the primary winding in the power transformer in a Sanyo CP500 CD player.

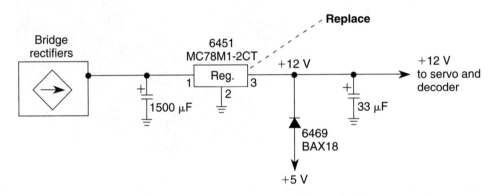

13-10 The dead Sylvania FDD104 CD player was caused by a defective regulator transistor (6451) in the +12-V source.

Defective loading circuits

When the power switch is turned on, the display panel lights come to life. In some models, the CPU RESET and MANUAL SEARCH key must be on before the OPEN/CLOSE button is pressed. When the tray is open, lower voltage is applied to the laser circuit causing the laser not to emit light.

In some models, a leaf tray loading switch is engaged when the door is open reversing polarity voltage to the loading motor. The disc is loaded into the tray. Push the close switch and the loading motor pulls the tray so the disc is loaded on the spindle or disc platform. The laser beam is lighted. Now the disc will start to rotate when the play button is pushed. If no disc is loaded in the tray, the disc motor will not play music with an interlock governed by a phototransistor LED circuit.

In some models, IC components govern the opening and closing functions of loading the disc. When the OPEN button is pressed, the tray should start to move out because one of the pins on the IC control is low. The loading motor rotates. While the tray is open, one pin is low and the other is high. The disc is loaded. Press the close key or button and the low pin goes high and the loading motor rotates, pulling the door closed.

Drawer or tray does not move

Listen quietly to hear if the loading motor is trying to rotate. A damaged or jammed gear track can keep the motor from operating. If someone grabs the drawer during operation, it can strip or jam the plastic slide gear assembly. Go directly to the motor drive transistors and check the positive and negative voltage applied to the drive transistor collector terminals (Fig. 13-11).

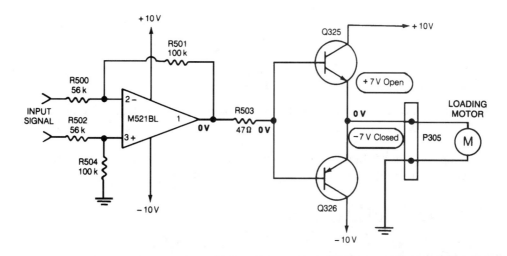

13-11 Critical voltage measurements on the loading motor drive transistor and motor terminals can locate a defective motor or transistor.

The dc voltage applied to the collector terminal of Q325 is +10 V with –10 V on the collector terminal of Q326 in a JVC XL-400B loading motor drive circuit. When the tray is open, the emitter terminals of Q325 and Q326 measure about –7 V, and when the tray is closed, +7 V are measured there. Check the voltage at the motor terminals. No voltage might indicate a poor connection at the motor or plug-in connections (P305). Normal voltage at the motor terminals indicate a dead motor.

Remove one end of R503 from the base terminals of Q325 and Q326. Now, measure the voltage at pin 1 of the servo controller (IC301). You should have about –7.5 V when the tray is open and +7.5 V when tray is closed. If not, suspect a defective IC301 or IC802.

No loading—Goldstar GCD-616 CD player

The loading tray would not move out or in. When the tray or loading box was pressed, the sound of the loading motor operating or tray movement could not be heard. No voltage was measured on the loading motor terminals (M603). The motor leads were traced back to loading motor drive IC104. Voltage measurements on IC104 were taken with a 7-V supply on pin 6 (Fig. 13-12). Controlled voltage was

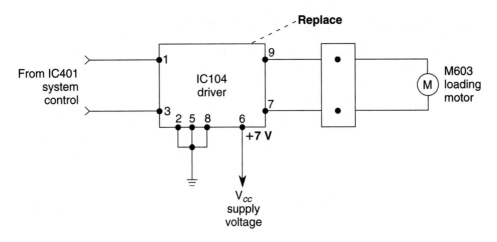

13-12 Replacing loading motor driver IC104 in a Goldstar GCD-616 CD player solved the no-load problem.

found on pins 1 and 3, but not on pins 7 and 9. Replacing IC104 (BA61218) with original part number 668-680A solved the no loading problem.

Erratic loading in a Magnavox COC552 CD changer

In this Magnavox COC552 CD changer the large carousel unit would sometimes catch and not move all the way out (Fig. 13-13). The drawer would not fully extend by about two inches. The large carousel track was inspected and seemed normal.

The motor belt was tight, but showed some signs of slippage. After cleaning up the motor pulley and belt, the unit still would not come all the way out consistently. Removing the large tray revealed a long connecting wire was loose and sometimes would catch on the tray assembly and hold it back. The unit had been worked on before and the bunch of wires and cables laying in the bottom chassis area were not tied down.

Homemade battery box

Most motors found in the CD player can be checked with a dc voltage applied to the motor terminals. Remove the motor wire or plug from the motor drive circuit. Apply voltage from a battery to the motor terminals. If the loading motor is at one extreme end of rotation, the motor might groan and start to rotate. Quickly remove the battery terminals and notice if the motor starts to operate. When using a variable battery voltage, always start at zero and slowly raise the dc voltage. You can make an adjustable battery box to test motors, focus coils, and tracking coils (Fig. 13-14). Here either a positive or negative voltage can be applied to the motor terminals by just flipping a three-position DPDT toggle switch (Fig. 13-15). A rheostat or control is used to vary the voltage applied to the motor terminals with voltage monitor jacks

13-13 Erratic loading in a Magnavox COC552 changer was caused by loose wires holding the carousel back before opening.

13-14 A battery box constructed from a few components to determine if the motor is defective.

indicating on a DMM how much voltage is applied to the motor terminals. Add another battery or two if the motors run at a higher voltage. Of course, some motors might not rotate as fast in normal operation but they will indicate that the motor is rotating. The parts list follows. The numbers denote Radio Shack parts identification.

1 two "C" cell holder (270-385)
SW1 DPDT with center off position switch (275-1533)
2 Micro test clips (270-372)
R1 1 kΩ linear control (wirewound, if possible)
2 male banana plugs
4 banana female jacks (274-725)
1 plastic project case—6" × 3" × 1.84" (270-223)
Misc. 2 "C" cells, 2 feet of test lead wire, solder, etc.

13-15 A DPDT three-position toggle switch reverses polarity voltage applied to the suspected motor. At the center, the polarity switch is off.

Only twelve parts are needed to build the small battery motor box (Fig. 13-16). The "C" batteries are placed in a battery holder for easy replacement. A DPDT toggle switch with center-off position was chosen to quickly reverse the polarity to the motors and turn off the voltage at center position. It's best to use a linear 1 kΩ wire-wound control for R1, if possible. The voltage monitor and output terminals are regular banana jacks. Choose or make up flexible test leads with small clip-on type terminals to go over the small plug pins or motor terminals.

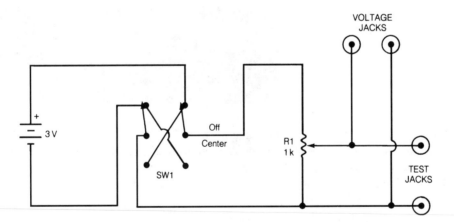

13-16 Only 12 parts are used to build the battery box.

All holes in the top plastic cover can be drilled or fashioned with the tip of the soldering iron. Remove the burr or raised plastic areas around the holes with a pocketknife when using the soldering iron tip to make the mounting holes. No special mounting of components is required. The "C" battery holder was fastened to the bottom side of the cabinet with silicone rubber cement. Use a DMM or VOM with center zero scale to monitor the voltage applied to the suspected motor. Components can be obtained at Radio Shack or electronic part stores.

Tray will not open

Suspect a broken motor or sliding gear when the motor is rotating and the tray will not move outward. Inspect the sliding gear for broken spots or a dry surface. Do not overlook a damaged or broken tray open/close (loading switch). This switch is usually found close to the tray or plastic clapper gear (Fig. 13-17). A damaged or frozen tray or teeth missing from the plastic clamper gear might prevent the tray from moving (Fig. 13-18).

13-17 A tray end-gear switch assembly reverses the direction of the loading motor. Check for poor contacts with loading problems.

13-18 The loading tray might not move if the gears are broken or jammed.

Tray will not close

Inspect the rail-tooth gear slide assembly for broken teeth. Suspect dirty contacts on the close/open loading switch. Clean up the contacts with a thin piece of cardboard. Hold the contacts together and push-pull the cardboard between the contacts to clean them up. Make sure correct voltage is applied to the motor for the closing position. Also check for broken motor belts, missing pulleys, and broken plastic motor gears. (Check chapter 7 on motor circuits for additional troubleshooting methods.)

Defective display section

Check the wiring or a poorly seated socket when the display section will not light up when the player is operating. Inspect the display PC board for possible poor connections for intermittent or dead conditions. The wiring can be checked with the low ohm range of the ohmmeter. Check the small pin soldered or clamped section around each wire cable. Notice if the flat cable has been inserted correctly.

Suspect a defective LED or lead wire when only one operation light is out that should be on. The LEDs and diodes can be checked like any LED with the diode test of the DMM. Check for soldered bridges or connections going to a specific light. Measure the voltage across the suspected diode. Poor seating of a button or switch jamming can prevent operation. Sometimes a switch can be held up when plastic binds against a plastic switch. Often, a drop of cleaning spray solves the binding problem.

Measure the dc voltage applied to the LED driver transistor or IC components. Do not overlook the ac or dc voltage applied to the fluorescent tube or LCD display. In some models, ac is applied from a power transformer winding.

A defective reset circuit section can prevent the display from lighting up. Check the dc voltage source from the power supply. Check for pulses at the pins on the control IC, which controls the display section. The fluorescent display should light up the minute the player is turned on. If not, check voltages on the IC that controls it. Inspect the FL PC board for poorly soldered connections. Check the external clock waveform found in some models of the display data IC, which might indicate the IC is operating.

Onkyo DX-200—No display

This CD player seemed to operate without any display features. Often, the display circuits operate from the negative voltage source from the low-voltage power supply. A quick voltage measurement on the fluorescent tube indicated that the negative voltage was missing.

The negative voltage regulator Q907 was located with D905 wired in reverse of positive voltage power supply. The collector terminal had a negative 40.7 V with no voltage found on the emitter terminal. Q907 was found open (Fig. 13-19). Replacing Q907 enabled the display to light up again.

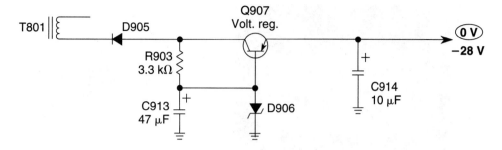

13-19   Open regulator transistor Q907 prevented the display to light up in an Onkyo DX-200 CD player.

Defective EFM or signal section

Sometimes players start to operate and then shut down. Sometimes they make a second focus attempt and then stop. Improper or no EFM signal can prevent CD operation. Remember, the EFM signal must be present to send an FE and TE signal to the focus, tracking, and sled servo section. The EFM signal is sent to the digital control, CLV servo, and signal path to provide audio at the line output jacks (Fig. 13-20).

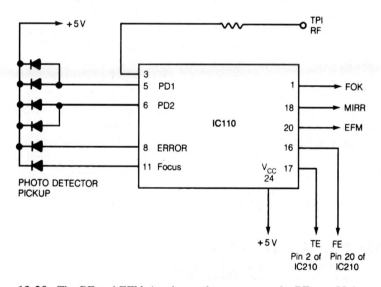

13-20   The RF and EFM signal must be present at the RF amp IC for correct tracking, focus, and servo operations.

You might assume the EFM signal is present from the preamp and RF IC when the disc continues to rotate. If not, take a quick RF waveform test at TP1 and pin 20 of IC110 (Fig. 13-21). Suspect a defective IC110 or no signal from the laser optical diodes. Improper laser voltage or a defective laser diode can result in low or no RF signal at the RF transistor IC.

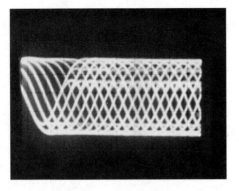

13-21 Take the RF or eye pattern signal at TP1 of most CD players RF amp circuits.

Laser diode not lit

The laser diode can be checked with the external power meter or indication tester. Critical voltage of the laser test will indicate if the laser beam is present. (Check chapter 3 for additional laser diode tests and procedures.) If an RF signal is found at TP1, the optical laser assembly is working. No EFM signal at pin 20 of IC110 or focus and tracking error signals at pins 16 and 17 might indicate a defective RF IC110.

Before replacing IC110, check each terminal voltage and compare them to the schematic. Make sure the supply source voltage pin 24 is normal. You can assume the RF preamp transistor or IC component is defective with RF signal in and no signal out with correct applied voltages. By taking critical waveform and voltages on each stage, you might be able to find the defective component. If the EFM level is greatly reduced when tracking is closed, grating adjustment should be made.

In addition to providing FE and TE signal to the focus, tracking sled servo section, the EFM signal is applied to the digital signal control/CLV servo IC. The EFM waveform at pin 20 goes to the signal processing IC. Suspect a defective IC110 if RF at TP1 and the FE and TE signals are normal without an EFM waveform at pin 20. Of course without the EFM signal applied to the CLV servo control IC, the disc will not rotate. The EFM signal might be affected if proper adjustment is not made of the grating, focus offset, and tangential adjustments. A quick touchup of these adjustments might help the level of EFM signal.

No laser indication— Sanyo CP660 CD player

In a Sanyo CD CP660 player, the laser diode showed no signal of infrared power on the laser power meter (Fig. 13-22). At first the laser interlock photo-diode was suspected, but it turned out normal. The laser power IC121 terminals were checked for voltage with no results. According to the diagram, a –9 V feeds the laser power IC.

Checking the wiring and voltage source indicated a –9 V was applied to R631, with no voltage at transistor regulator Q631. Q631 was tested and found open. Replacing the regulator transistor solved the no-laser power symptom (Fig. 13-23).

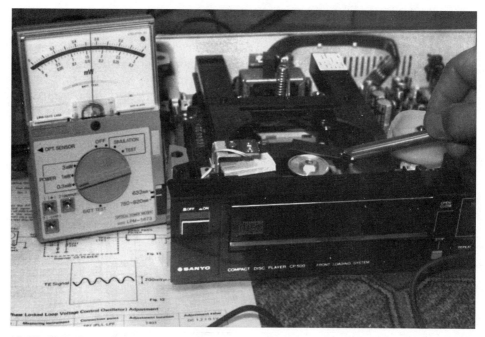

13-22 No indication on a laser power meter indicated problems within the laser driver circuit in a Sanyo CP660 CD player.

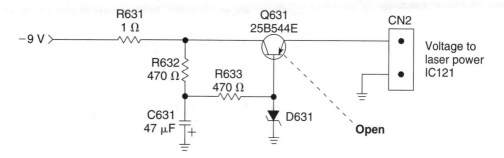

13-23 The laser driver (Q631) was found open providing no voltage to the laser diode.

Troubleshooting optical shutdown circuits

The most difficult shutdown problems occur in the optical or digital signal processing circuits. The disc starts to rotate and within a few seconds the whole unit shuts down and the disc stops. Each time the player is started, the unit begins to start and then stops. If the EFM signal is not sent to the signal processing IC or data sent to the servo IC, the player will shut down. Also it's possible to have trouble within the servo circuits.

Notice if the tracking and focus coils begin to hunt when the unit is first turned on. Actually, there is not much time to get waveforms. Clip the scope to the circuits to be tested and start up the player each time. You might have to start the player several times before all the waveforms and voltage measurements are taken. A defective optical assembly, RF amp, and voltage sources can cause the chassis to shut down.

Place the laser diode cable over the laser lens to measure the infrared signal and if the laser diode is emitting power to the compact disc (Step 1). In some players the interlock must have tape put over the LED to take the place of a disc, before unit will turn on. In battery CD players, the small lid interlock has to be defeated by placing a paper clip or toothpick into interlock area. Keep your eyes away from the lens area while taking power measurements.

Turn on the laser meter and compact disc player. Notice if the disc or turntable is rotating. This usually occurs a few seconds before shutdown. If the laser meter indication is good, go to Step 2 (Fig. 13-24). If not, check the voltage applied to the laser diode from a laser driver or dc source. When the voltage is applied to the transistor or IC laser driver, check the voltage at the LD terminal. If no voltage, check out the laser driver transistor or the voltage regulator circuits feeding the laser voltage.

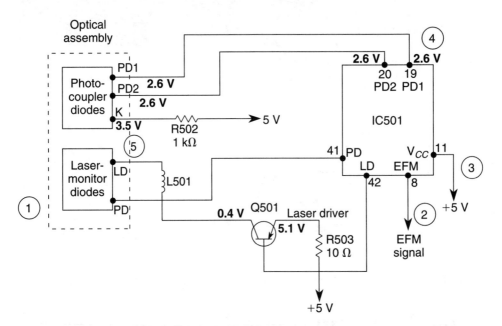

13-24   Check by the numbers to troubleshoot the RF amp, laser driver, and photo diodes optical system.

Proceed to Step 2, when the laser diode power meter indicator is normal. Scope for EFM waveform at the RF amp (eye pattern). In some portable players, the RF amp and signal processing circuits might be in one large IC. If the EFM signal is present for only a few seconds, you can assume the circuits up to this point are normal.

When no EFM signal is present at the RF amp, suspect a defective RF IC, RF transistor, optical photo diodes, and low-voltage source (*VCC*). Check the voltage at supply pin (*VCC*) 11 of IC501. If the voltage is missing or low, proceed to optical supply pin (K). Often this voltage is supplied from a +5-V source.

Step 3. When the voltage is normal at the photo diodes and at PD1 and PD2, with no EFM signal at pin 8, replace IC501. Be very careful when replacing this RF amp. Do not apply too much heat to the IC. If after replacement, no EFM waveform or signal are present, suspect a defective optical assembly. Make sure the IC was not damaged when it was replaced; try installing another one. Check out the cost of a new laser pickup assembly because they are quite costly.

Shutdown on JVC XL-V400B CD player

The disc would start to rotate and then shut down in a JVC CD player. Often when this happens, improper RF or EFM signal is not found at the RF amp. The laser power meter indicated the laser diode emitted infrared light when the unit first came on. You cannot see the laser lens light up because the infrared signal is invisible. Keep your eyes away from the lens area.

In these RF circuits, two RF transistors are found with EFM signal from the laser photo diodes. No EFM signal or waveform was found at the signal processor or off Q201 and Q202. These measurements must be made quickly; several attempts must usually be made because the player shuts down. Q202 was found leaky and replaced.

Defective focus mechanism

Improper or no focus action can shut down the CD player. Does the lens actuator move up and down when the disc platter is closed by pressing the OPEN/CLOSE button? The optical lens assembly might be covered with a flapper or clamper assembly, and it must be removed to check the actuator assembly. If the disc will not operate with the clamper assembly removed, check for an open interlock circuit. Sometimes the lens actuator mechanism can be seen with a reflective mirror when the disc is removed.

Focus lock is not achieved if the focus actuator does not move. Check for foreign or excessive dirt blocking the focus actuator. Clean up the lens assembly at the same time. Quickly see if the EFM waveform is found at the RF signal processing IC. Now check for a focus error waveform at the same IC. The focus error signal at IC110 should look somewhat like the waveform in Fig. 13-25. Often an FE test point is found for this quick test (TP2). Doublecheck the FE signal where it enters the focus/tracking/sled servo IC (pin 20).

When an FE signal is applied to the focus servo IC, you should be able to check the waveform right up to the focus coil. The defective focus IC or component will indicate no waveform, only a white line at the focus driver stages and coil assembly (Fig. 13-26). If the focus circuits are performing, you should be able to take a waveform at pin 21 of IC211 and the emitter terminals of Q203 and Q202 (Fig. 13-27). The noisy looking waveform is not present when the FE signal is missing.

You can assume IC211 is defective when an FE signal is entering at pin 20 and no waveform at pin 21 (Fig. 13-28). Check the supply voltage feeding IC211. Often

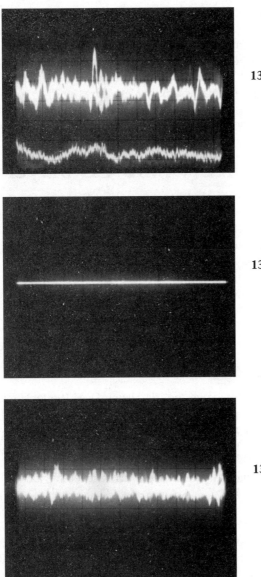

13-25 The focus error waveform taken from TP2 and IC110.

13-26 Horizontal white line on the scope at any test point means that no signal is present.

13-27 A focus waveform at pin 21 of IC211 and the emitter terminals of Q203 and Q202.

the same voltage (+5 V) feeding IC211 also supplies power to the RF signal processing IC110. If IC110 EFM signal is normal, the same voltage should be applied to IC211. You might want to check all voltages at the low-voltage power supply before troubleshooting the CD circuits. Many electronic technicians check these low voltages first.

If you find a good FE waveform at pin 21 or IC211 and not at the focus coil (5), check collector voltages at Q202 and Q203. One of the voltages might be low with a leaky driver transistor. If one of the voltages is missing, go directly to the same source in the low-voltage power supply. Test each transistor in the circuit with a

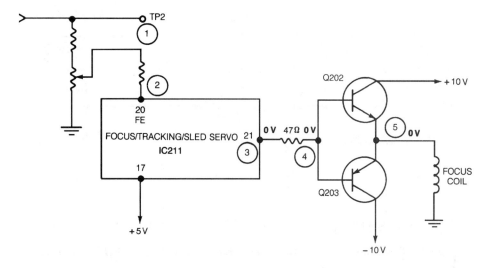

13-28   A waveform at TP2 and pin 20 of IC211 and no waveform or voltage at pin 21 can indicate a defective IC211 or improper supply voltage.

transistor tester. If in doubt, remove and test it out of the circuit. A typical focus troubleshooting chart of a Pioneer PD-7010 model is shown in Chart 13-3. See Fig. 13-29.

Defective tracking mechanism

The tracking and focus circuits can be checked in the reverse procedures if the player is shutting down without any actuator movement. Measure the resistance or take a continuity reading across the tracking coil. Some tracking coil circuits have a test point at this connection. Take another resistance measurement from both emitter tracking transistors or IC pin-to-ground to ensure there is not a bad socket or wiring connection between the drive component and the coil (Fig. 13-30).

Attach the scope test probe to the tracking coil offset terminal feeding the tracking drive coil transistors. Now push the play button. Notice if for a few seconds a noisy type of waveform is found at this terminal (Fig. 13-31). A noisy type of waveform might indicate the tracking servo IC is performing. Go to the TE input terminal of the tracking IC (13) if only a white horizontal line is found at pin 27. No TE signal is present with a horizontal white line.

Remember, the tracking/focus/sled servo IC must have a signal from the EFM-RF IC before either will operate. Often, if a focus error signal is found at IC211, the tracking error signal should be found at terminal 13 or test point TP4. The TE signal at TP3 is greater than that found at TP4 (Fig. 13-32). Of course, this waveform will be determined by the tracking error offset or gain control. A quick waveform test at terminal (TE17) of IC210, TP3, TP4, and TAO-27 will indicate the trouble lies in the tracking coil drive transistor or IC.

You might find an IC or several transistors as tracking driver components. Some have two driven transistors within an IC component (Fig. 13-33). Check each com-

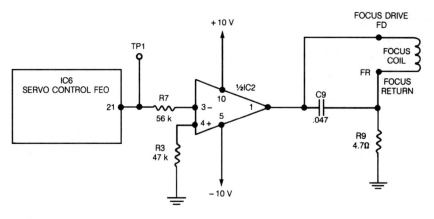

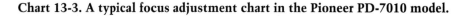

13-29 A corresponding focus drive circuit of Pioneer PD-7010 player with Chart 13-3.

Chart 13-3. A typical focus adjustment chart in the Pioneer PD-7010 model.

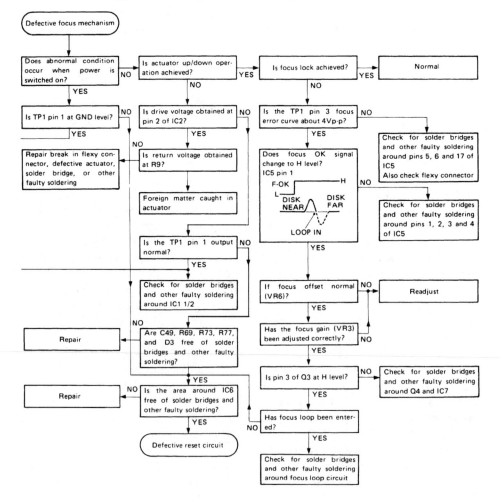

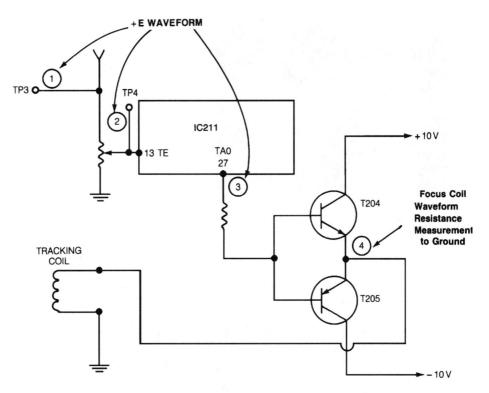

13-30 A waveform taken at TP3 and TP4 (pin 27) of IC211 and emitter terminal of T204 and T205 might locate the defective tracking coil.

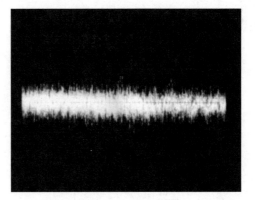

13-31 A tracking error waveform taken at pin 27 of IC211 in Fig. 13-30.

ponent in the same manner as all driving stages. Take a quick voltage measurement on each terminal and compare it to the schematic. Note that the 10-V supply voltage is higher without a load. Zero voltage is found at the emitter terminals until a tracking signal is applied. A typical tracking servo troubleshooting chart of a JVC XL-V400B player is shown with corresponding servo drive circuits in Fig. 13-34 and Chart 13-4.

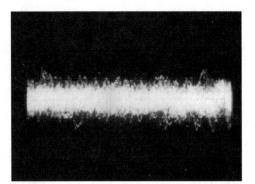

13-32   A tracking error waveform taken at TP4 in Fig. 13-30.

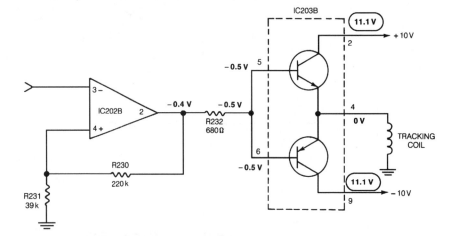

13-33   Here two ICs are found as tracking coil drivers in a Mitsubishi PD107 CD player.

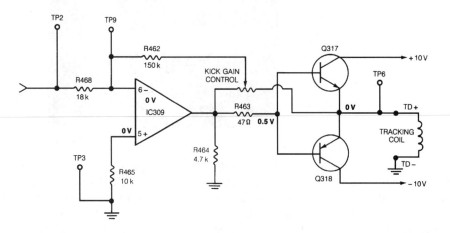

13-34   A corresponding tracking driver circuit of the JVC XL-V400B (compare to Chart 13-4).

Chart 13-4. A typical tracking servo troubleshooting chart in the JVC XL-V400B CD player.

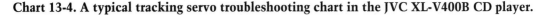

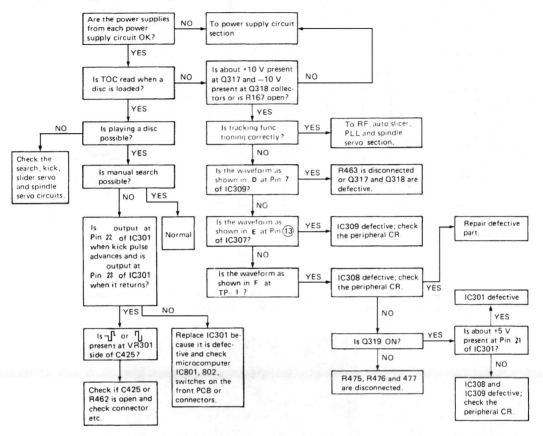

Do not overlook breaks in wiring or board connections where the tracking and focus actuator takes off from the PC board. Check the flexible actuator leads for breaks or intermittent wiring. Look for broken or cracked bridge wiring. Especially check the actuator lead sockets on the servo PC board. Doublecheck the wiring with resistance measurements.

Defective carriage, slide, or sled operation

The carriage or sled motor operates from the same focus/tracking or servo control IC. The sled signal is taken from pin 23 of IC6 (Fig. 13-35). The SLO control signal might be fed to another IC amp and drive transistors, or it might be fed directly to the drive transistors and slide motor. Scope waveforms can be taken up to the slide motor terminals. The horizontal sled waveform will move up and down when operating (Fig. 13-36).

Notice if the carriage motor is moving the optical assembly. If not, check for a broken or slipping belt or gear train at the motor pulley. Check the motor for an open

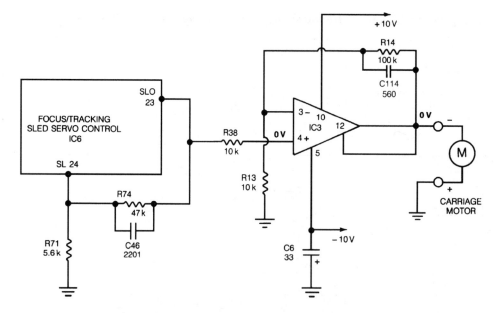

13-35   The sled, slide, or carriage signal is taken from pin 23 of IC106. Correct waveforms and critical voltage measurements might locate defective parts in the slide motor circuits.

13-36   A slide motor waveform taken while motor is operating across motor terminals.

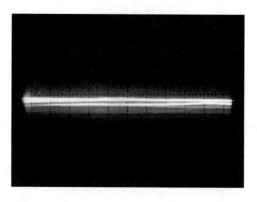

winding. To check the motor, inject dc voltage from the battery motor box. Always remove the ungrounded lead from the motor terminals.

Check for normal voltage on IC211, Q104, and Q103. Suspect an improper voltage power source or a leaky driver transistor when one of the collector terminal voltages is missing or is low. Improper carriage motor polarity voltage can cause the motor not to move in the right direction. In many of the carriage motors, forward direction is with a negative voltage applied from the driver transistors. Check for a defective inside switch, mechanism or soldered connections when the carriage does not continue after reaching the inside track. Notice the voltage changes on the carriage motor terminals in Chart 13-5.

In STOP mode, the voltages at pin 2 of IC3 and pin 23 of IC6 are "0." When the carriage mode (outer tracks) is in the FORWARD mode, the voltage on pin 2 of IC3

**Chart 13-5. The playback modes and voltage
measurements on pin 2 of IC3 and pin 23 of IC6
in schematic 13-35.**

Mode \ Point	IC3 2 Pin	IC6 23 Pin
Playback	+1 ~ −2V	+0.09 ~ −0.18V
Forward (outer tracks)	−9 ~ −11V	−0.8 ~ −1V
Reverse (inner tracks)	+9 ~ +11V	+0.8 ~ 1V
Stop	0V	0V

or at the carriage motor terminal is –9 to –11 V. The voltage at pin 23 of IC6 in FOR-
WARD mode is –0.8 to –1 V. In REVERSE mode (inner tracks), pin 2 of IC3 varies between +9 and +11 V with pin 23 of IC6 at +0.8 to 1 V. Suspect the motor terminals
are reversed if the carriage or slide motor was replaced and is going in the reverse
direction with +9 V at the motor terminals. A typical carriage motor flowchart of a Pioneer PD-7010 player is shown in Chart 13-6.

Chart 13-6. A typical carriage or slide motor flowchart in a Pioneer PD-7010 model.

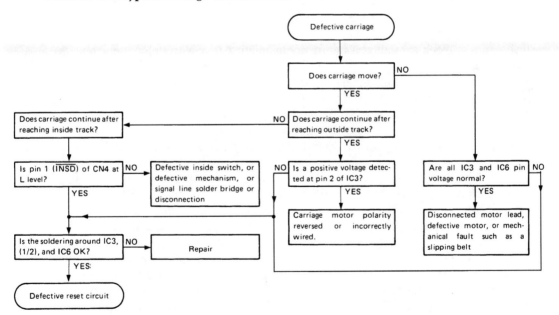

Player skips

Touch up all tracking-related adjustments to the CD circuits. Especially check the
tracking balance for skipping or improper tracking. Make sure the RF PLL is accu-

rate. Next, determine if the skipping is caused by a mechanical problem at the slide or sled motor. Try holding the optical assembly and check the play between the motor gear and sliding track assembly. Too much friction in the slide track assembly can cause the optical assembly to jump or skip. Clean up the slide rods and assembly.

When a normal disc is being played and the optical pickup assembly skips, especially at the outside area of the disc, or if the pickup stops playing and resets to the beginning of the disc, suspect a defective carriage or slide motor. Sometimes a clicking noise is heard while the mechanism is moving. First check the motor belt for slippage. Replace the belt if it shows signs of slipping. Inspect the pickup assembly where it rides on the base and pickup guide rails. Check the lubrication on the guide base and rail assembly.

Monitor the tracking error signal at test point (TE) with the scope. Look for a change in signal when the skip occurs to determine if the trouble is electronically controlled. If there is no tracking error connection, you might assume the trouble is mechanical. Remember, tracking gain can be set to close or small causing the sound to jump when the machine is bumped.

Defective spindle or disc operation

The defective turntable spindle or disc motor might be dead or not running at the correct speed. The disc motor is locked in with a correction signal from the CLV circuitry. The RF PLL and write frame clock (WFCK) must be accurate for CLV control. Touch up the RF PLL adjustment to ensure the disc motor will operate with the optical block assembly. If not, dropout might occur with defects on the disc surfaces.

The EFM and focus signal must be present before the disc motor will operate. In some players, the disc will begin to rotate when the on button is pushed and then it stops. When the play button is pressed, the disc should begin to rotate. If the disc starts to run and then the unit shuts down, suspect improper or missing EFM (eye pattern) or focus okay (FOK) signal. You must have an RF or EFM signal to get the disc to rotate.

To get the RF or eye pattern, the laser must be emitting and the focus servo circuitry working. Check the RF at the RF preamp and the EFM signal feeding the CLV motor control IC with the scope (Fig. 13-37). If these signals are found at the CLV disc motor control IC, suspect a defective motor control or disc motor assembly.

The spindle motor can be controlled with a separate IC and transistor driver circuits. In some circuits, the disc or spindle motor is controlled by two transistor drivers fed directly from the large IC servo controller. The dead disc motor can be checked by starting at the motor and working toward the servo circuits. The quickest method is to check the voltage at the collector terminals of the disc drive transistors. If one of the positive or negative voltages is missing, check the low-voltage source at the power supply. A vibrating or unstable eye pattern can be caused by a poor turntable or disc motor.

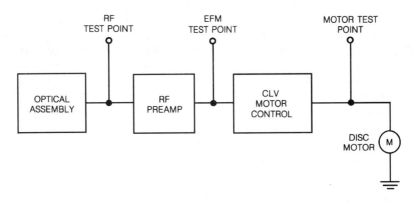

13-37 The RF and EFM signal must be present for the CLV disc to operate.

Spindle motor won't stop

The collector voltage at Q315 is +10 V, and –10 V at Q316 (Fig. 13-38). If not, check the power supply. Zero voltage should be found at the emitter and motor terminals in stop mode. If the spindle motor does not stop in STOP mode, suspect higher voltage at pin 1 of servo IC308. If not, replace or test both driver transistors Q315 and Q316. A very high voltage at pin 1 of IC308 can indicate a leaky IC308 or IC301.

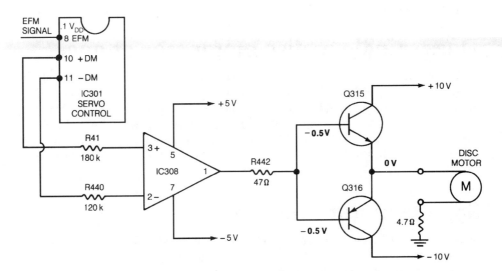

13-38 Very high voltage at pin 1 of IC308 could indicate a leaky IC308 or IC301.

Disc does not start after loading

Measure the emitter voltage at Q315 and Q316; +6 V should be found there. In some players the disc motor voltage is 2 to 5 V at the beginning of disc playing. Normal motor drive voltage at the motor terminals might indicate a defective motor. Check the motor winding with the low range of the ohmmeter. Inject disc motor voltage from the battery motor box and see if the motor rotates. Some motors will operate at 2.5 Vdc and between 1.5 and 3.7 V at 600 rpm. Inspect the motor harness and connections for poor wiring. Replace the motor if it will not rotate with dc voltage applied to the terminals.

No voltage at the emitter terminals might indicate a defective servo controller IC301. If +2.5 V or more are found at pin 1 of IC308 and the motor does not rotate, suspect Q315 or Q316 open. Replace IC308 if pin 10 is set to "H" without motor control voltage. Doublecheck IC301 with no control signal.

No rotation of turntable in Mitsubishi M-C4030 player

The turntable or disc would not rotate in a Mitsubishi M-C4030 CD player. In the changer, the turntable motor sets up on the edge of the chassis and drives a worm gear assembly. At first, the motor assembly was suspected of a binding gear assembly. Two small screws were removed to drop the motor down, to see if it was damaged. The DMM was clipped to motor terminals to determine if motor or circuits were normal. A voltage measurement of 10.7 V was found on the motor terminals, with turntable operation, except no motor rotating. The motor was replaced with exact part number L945D501G01.

Does spindle or disc motor stop at once?

The spindle motor should stop at once when the STOP mode is set if all circuits are operating. If not, measure for about –6 V at the emitter terminals of Q315 and Q316 in the STOP mode. The spindle motor might be defective if it does not stop with negative voltage present. Check pin 11 of IC301 with a low negative voltage at IC308. If over –3 V is present at pin 7 of IC308 in the stop mode, check Q315 or Q316 for open conditions. A typical spindle motor troubleshooting chart of a JVC XL-V400B player corresponds with Fig. 13-34 and Chart 13-7.

Spindle motor runaway

Suspect poor pin connections around IC8 and IC9 if the spindle or disc motor starts in high speed (Fig. 13-39). Test pin 2 of IC8 for ground potential. Check for faulty bridges of wiring or pattern breaks. Rotate the spindle motor by hand and notice if it feels normal in rotation. A defective motor can cause high-speed problems. Are pins 5 and 6 of IC9 normal (EFM and ASY)? Check pin 7 (MIRR input) for a repeatedly "H" and "L" level waveform.

Remember, the spindle or disc motor must turn in a positive or clockwise motion. The laser beam must be lit and the FOK (focus) at high level. A normal eye pattern must be present with normal tracking and focus servo systems. Usually, the ungrounded side of the motor has a negative voltage for forward direction and a pos-

Chart 13-7. A typical troubleshooting spindle or disc motor chart for the JVC XL-V400B player.

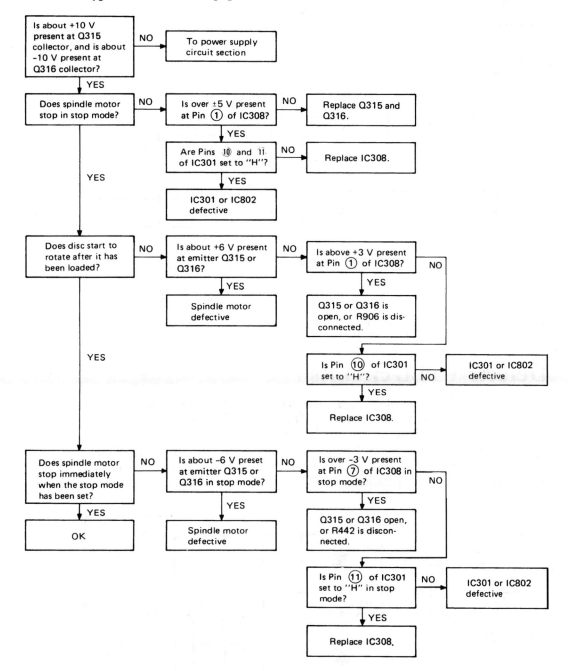

itive voltage for reverse direction. In some motors, 2 to 5 Vdc are found at the start while in others it varies between 5 and 6 V. Do not overlook R15 and R11 of open conditions with a dead spindle motor.

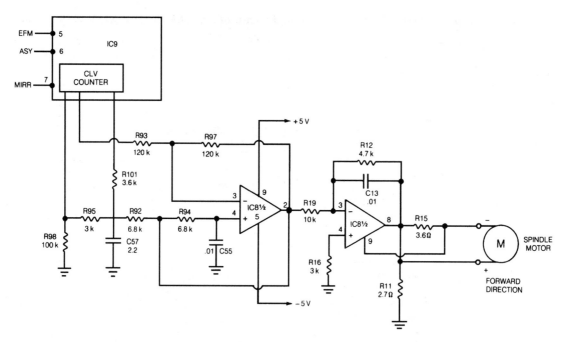

13-39 Suspect poor pin connections of IC8 and IC9 when the spindle motor runs at high speed. Do not overlook a defective spindle motor.

Defective PLL circuits

The 4.3218-MHz frequency of the VCO-PLL circuits must be very accurate to ensure correct recover of disc dropout conditions (Fig. 13-40). Proper adjustment of the PLL frequency is needed so the disc motor follows the optical lens assembly and responds to dropouts caused by scratches or defects on the disc. The VCO PLL circuits can be part of the digital control/CLV servo IC411. Here a scope waveform at TP7 indicates the PLL circuit is operating (Fig. 13-41).

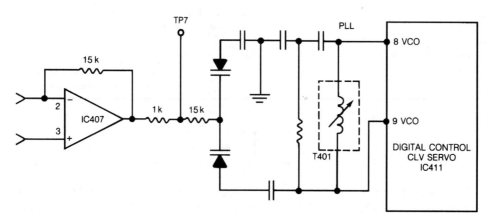

13-40 Adjustment of coil T401 in the VCO PLL circuit can correct disc dropout conditions.

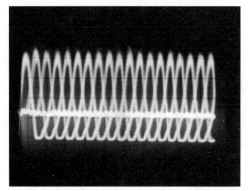

13-41 A scope waveform of the PLL circuit in a Sanyo CP500 model is taken at test point TP7.

The PLL waveform is used for correct VCO-PLL output signal adjustment. A typical adjustment of coil T401 is for a 1.2-Vdc waveform; if a digital voltmeter is used at TP7, adjust for 1.4 Vdc. A frequency counter can be used to check the PLL frequency. Check the manufacturer's literature for correct adjustment of the VCO-PLL circuits. This waveform can be taken with the player on or in pause mode. Correct waveforms and accurate voltage measurements on IC411 should find the defective component in the PLL circuits. The eye pattern is fairly stable if PLL is in lock and turntable loop is controlling correctly.

Defective audio circuits

The audio signal path begins at the left and right output terminals of the D/A IC (Fig. 13-42). Start at the audio output terminals and work back toward the D/A IC305. If the left channel is weak or dead, compare the sound level with the good right channel or vice versa. Are all dc voltages normal on IC305, IC311, and IC312? If not, check the dc power source in the power supply.

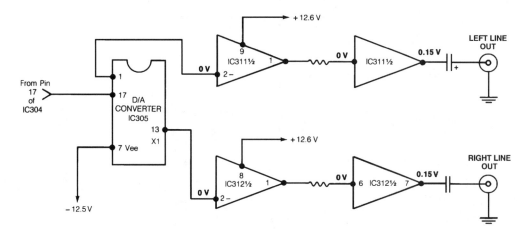

13-42 Here the analog or audio signal begins at pin 1 for the left and pin 13 of the right channel of the D/A converter IC305.

Check for audio signal at pin 1 of IC311 and IC312. If audio is normal at the right channel and not at pin 1 of IC312, suspect IC312 or IC305. Check the audio signal at pin 13 of IC305. If the signal is normal at pin 1 of IC305 and not at pin 13, suspect IC312 loading down the circuit or a defective IC305. It's possible to have some circuits defective and some normal in the same IC component.

Do not overlook the muting circuits; usually audio muting is found in the audio output line circuits. If the audio is good up to the last audio IC or transistor, suspect improper muting at the line output. Disconnect the mute transistor emitter or collector terminal that is tied to the audio line and notice if the sound appears. If the sound returns to normal, check the mute transistor, voltage, and other components tied to the muting circuits. For further sound problems, refer to chapter 8. A typical sound flowchart is shown in Chart 13-8.

Chart 13-8. Typical sound signal processing chart in the JVC XL-V400B CD player.

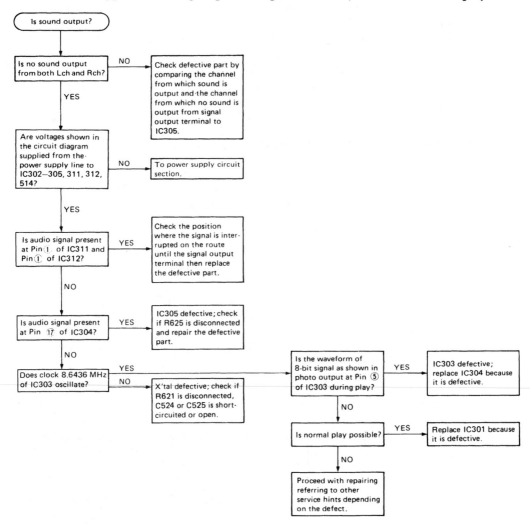

Sound check

The sound output of the CD player can be checked with a sound-noise distortion meter. Total harmonic distortion (THD) and intermodulation distortion also can be checked with the same hookup. Connect a filter between line output channel of CD player and distortion meter (Fig. 13-43).

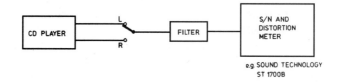

13-43 Connect an S/N distortion meter to the line outputs of the left and right channels to check distortion and signal-to-noise ratio.

Intermittent sound— Denon DCD-2560 player

Sometimes, the symptom in a Denon DCD-2560 CD player had intermittent sound. Then again it might play okay. At first the D/A converter or audio amps were suspected. The audio circuits were monitored with an external amp. In another CD player, we found excessive jitter with intermittent sound. Because both the left and right channels were intermittent, the focus offset can cause this problem.

If the focus offset is a little off, intermittent sound and excessive jitter might occur. The audio oscillator was set to 580 Hz with the frequency counter connected for monitor. VR103 was adjusted to minimize pattern jitter on the eye pattern (Fig. 13-44).

13-44 Intermittent sound can be corrected in a Denon DCD-2560 player with a correct focus offset adjustment. Adjust VR103 for less jitter of eye pattern.

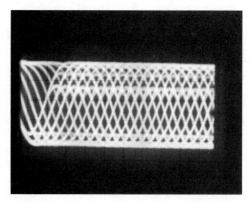

Major waveforms

It is wise to take waveforms on critical IC components and mark them on the schematic diagram when servicing only a couple of different brands of CD players. These normal waveforms might in time point out a defective IC or transistor when all voltages and other waveforms on the IC are normal. You might find many different waveforms on some manufacturer's CD schematics, while in others there are only a very few. This also applies to actual voltage measurements.

Following are a number of major waveforms that are critical in troubleshooting the CD player, along with a few that might not be found in the service manual. The RF or EFM signal found on the RF amp IC (Fig. 13-45); the focus coil waveform taken across focus coil winding (Fig. 13-46); the tracking coil waveform taken across tracking coil (Fig. 13-47); the focus error waveform fed to the focus coil (Fig. 13-48); the 8.4672 MHz crystal waveform on pin 53 of Sanyo CP500 player (Fig. 13-49); the input data waveform from the digital control/CLV servo IC at pin 10 (DIN) of the D/A converter IC (Fig. 13-50); the WLCK input waveform at pin 8 of the D/A converter (Fig. 13-51); the right output waveform of the D/A converter pin 8 (Fig. 13-52); the left audio waveform on pin 13 of the switching audio IC504 (Fig. 13-53).

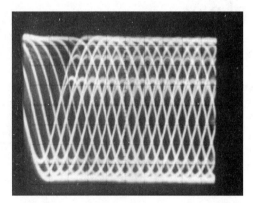

13-45   The important RF or EFM eye pattern signal waveform at the RF IC amp.

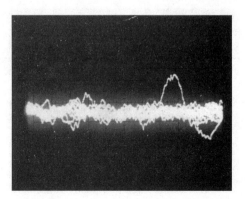

13-46   The focus coil waveform taken across the focus coil winding.

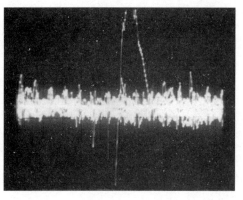

13-47 The tracking coil waveform (TE) fed to the tracking coil.

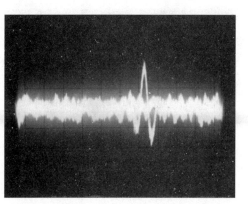

13-48 The focus error (FE) waveform.

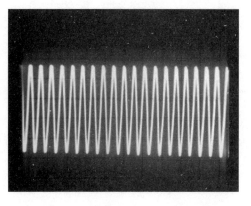

13-49 The 8.4672 MHz crystal waveform on pin 53 of Sanyo CP500 player.

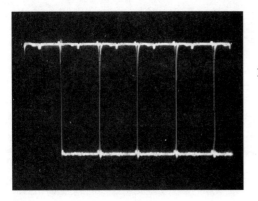

13-50   The input data waveform from the digital control/CLV servo IC at pin 10 (Din) of the D/A converter IC.

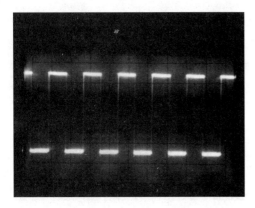

13-51   The WCLK clock input waveform at pin 8 of the D/A converter IC.

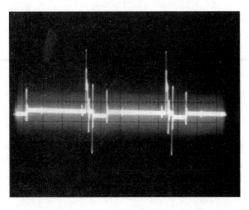

13-52   The right output waveform of the D/A converter pin 17.

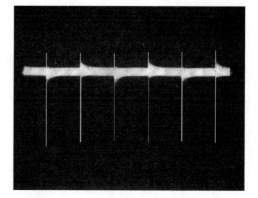

13-53 The left audio waveform on pin 13 of the switching audio IC504.

Service notes

- Sound blasts might occur with disc scratches when the focus gain control is set too large. Most focus gain controls increase in a clockwise rotation.
- The focus pickup might fail if the focus gain control is set too small. Too small of an adjustment might offer low resistance to vibration.
- If the focus offset adjustment is too far from the 0-V level, focus pickup failure will occur readily. Also, if the RF signal jitter is extremely large, the audio output is distorted.
- When tracking gain is too large, track jumping can occur easily due to a disc scratch. Also, during operation the mechanical noise becomes large.
- When the tracking gain is too small, sound blast might occur when using a large eccentricity disc. Also, head take out is delayed and there is low resistance to vibration.
- If the tracking offset adjustment is too far from 0-V level (particularly in the case of an eccentric disc), the possibility of continuous sound blast occurring during performance exists, and sound blast occurs easily due to disc scratches.
- Always put a soft cloth under the unit to prevent the plastic and case from bench scratches, especially in packing the unit for shipment.
- Make sure the lock or transport screws are fastened before shipping or delivering the CD player for any long distance.
- Service bulletins and a change of part lists are often produced by the manufacturer. Subscribe to or ask for these bulletin changes.
- When replacing the pickup assembly, place paint over the lock screws so they will not loosen up.
- It is very important to select a ground point as close as possible to the test point in taking voltage measurements or waveforms.
- Irregular working of the display when the set is opened and playing might have been caused by incidental body effect in the region of the crystal oscillators. Switching off and on the main voltage might eliminate this effect.

- If the eye pattern is present, you might conclude that the laser is working, the laser is in focus, and the turntable motor is running.
- General checkpoints before servicing:
  Make sure the disc is clean and not damaged.
  Check all clock frequency waveforms.
  Measure all low-voltage power supply sources.
  Make sure the mute circuit is inactive.
- Make sure that the CD player and all test equipment has warmed up before attempting to make adjustments.
- The laser beam can be disconnected when servicing circuits that do not require RF or EFM signal to protect the eyes.
- Keep a disc on the turntable or spindle at all times to prevent damage to your eyes or from touching the laser while servicing the CD player. Remember, you cannot see the laser beam. Your eyes are more important than fixing any CD player.

14
Schematics

THIS CHAPTER CONTAINS CD SCHEMATICS AND DIAGRAMS OF ALPINE'S 5900 CAR CD player (Fig. 14-1), a block diagram of the Denon DCC-9770 AM-FM-MPX auto changer (Fig. 14-2), and FM/AM tuner pack (Fig. 14-3), Denon CDH-500 auto changer block diagram (Fig. 14-4), Mitsubishi automatic tabletop changer M-C4030 (Fig. 14-5), Onkyo CD Carousel CD changer DX-C909 and DX-C606 (Fig. 14-6), Realistic CD-3370 portable CD player (Fig. 14-7), and Realistic boom-box CD audio circuits (Fig. 14-8) and CDP circuits (Fig. 14-9).

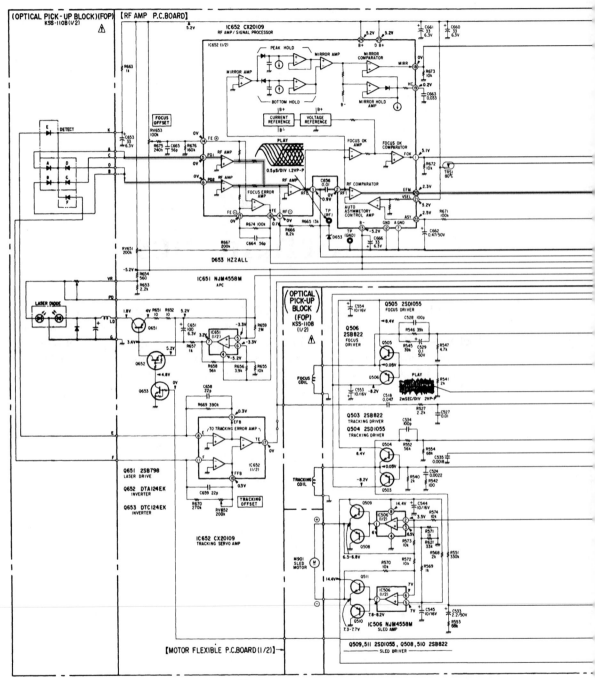

14-1 The schematic diagram of Alpine's car CD player.

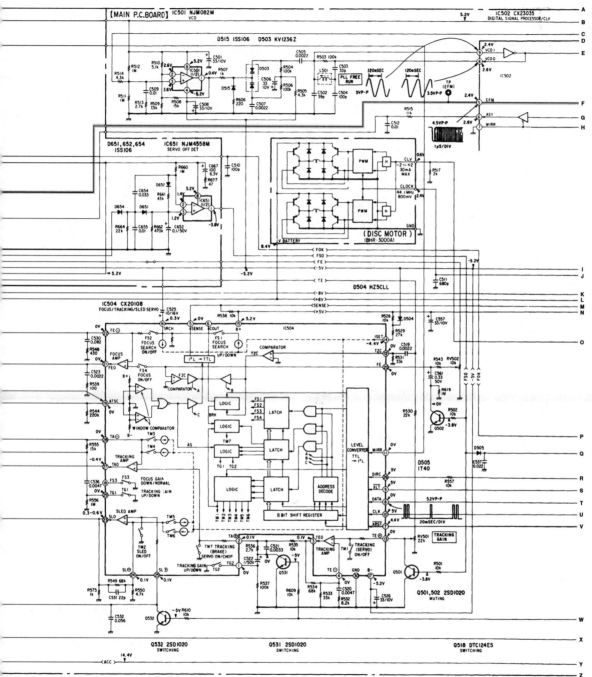

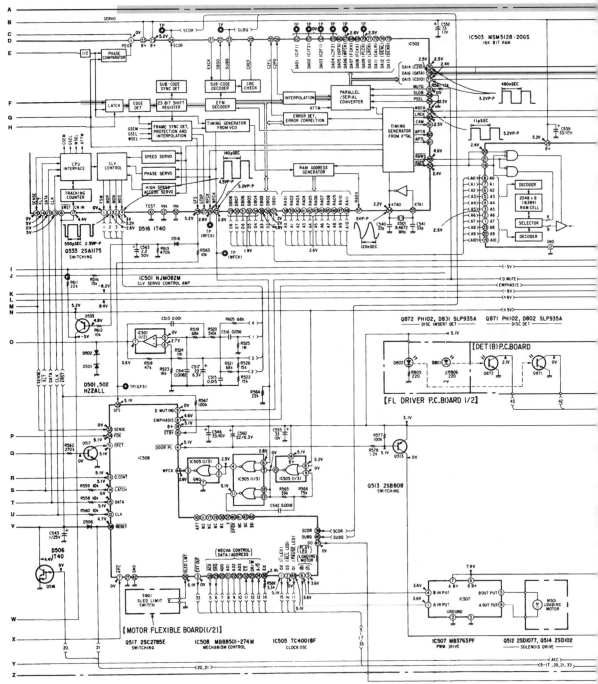

14-1 Continued.

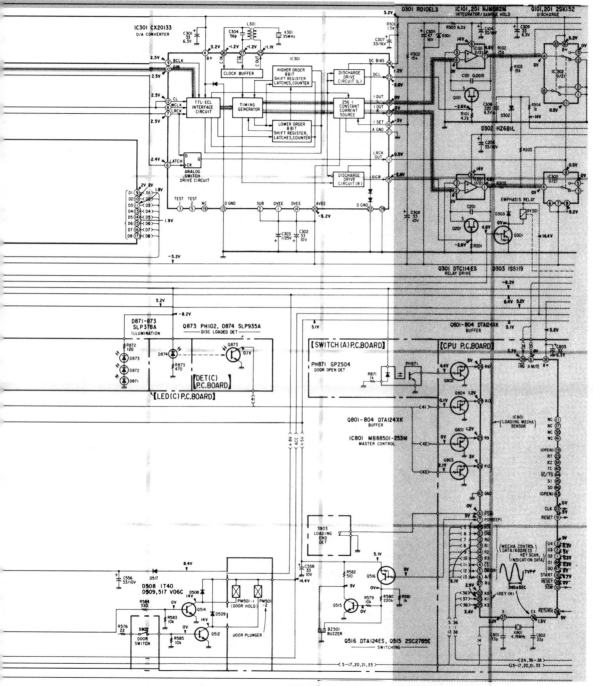

NOTES:
1. All resistance values are in ohms. K — 1,000
2. All capacitance values are in microfarads. P = $\dfrac{1}{1,000,000}$

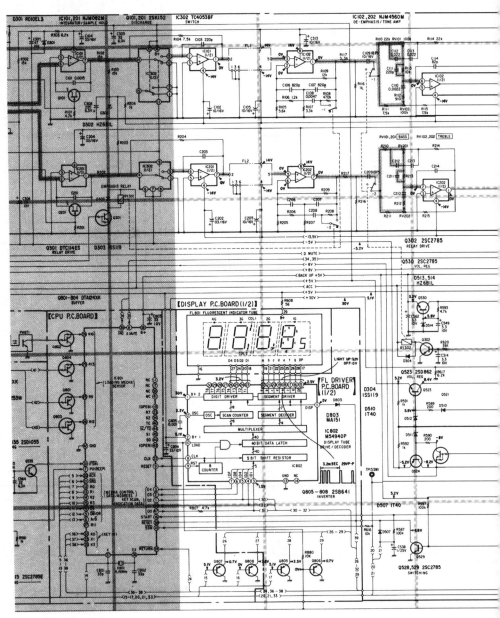

14-1 Continued.

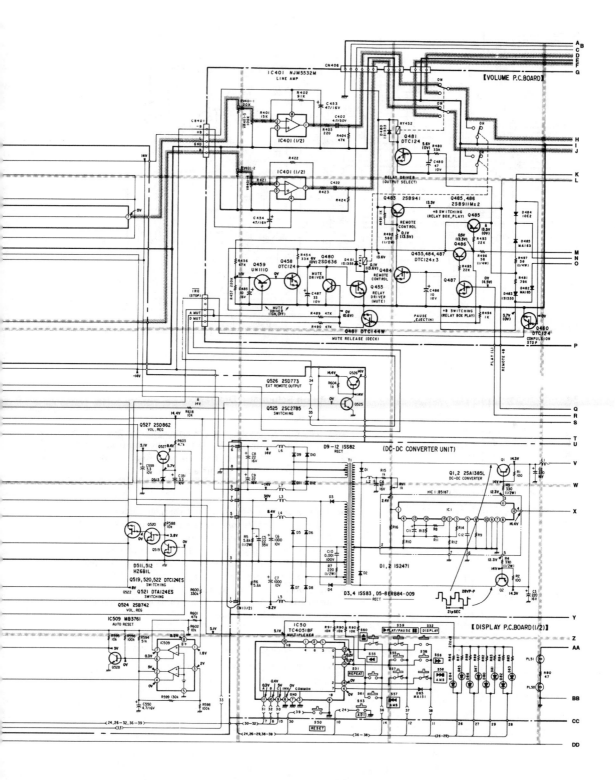

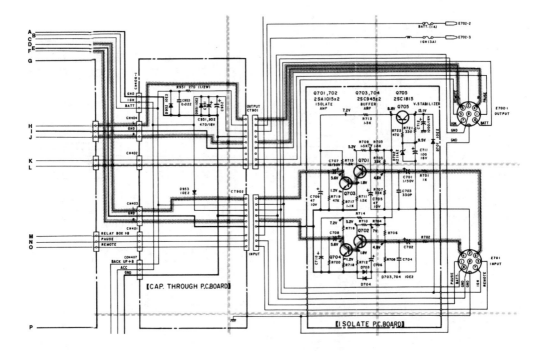

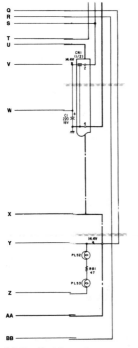

● Note on Schematic Diagram.

● ➡ : signal path.

> **Note: The components identified by shading and mark ⚠ are critical for safety. Replace only with part number specified.**

● Components for right channel have same values as for left channel. Reference numbers are coded from 200 and 420.

● Power voltage is 14.4V and fed with DC voltage regulator from ACC and BACK UP. Voltages are dc with respect to ground in CD playing mode. Voltage variations may be noted due to normal production tolerances.

● Waveforms are taken to ground in CD playing mode by using oscilloscope. Voltage variations may be noted due to normal production tolerances.

NOTES:

1. All resistance values are in ohms. K = 1,000
2. All capacitance values are in microfarads. $P = \dfrac{1}{1,000,000}$

14-1 Continued.

FM/AM TUNER PACK   Part No. 216 0080 007

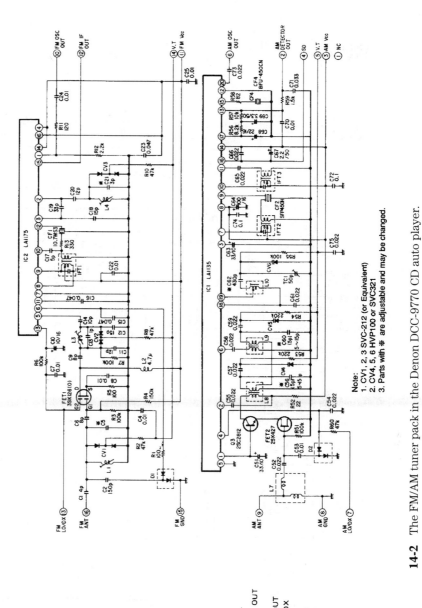

Note:
1. CV1, 2, 3 SVC-212 (or Equivalent)
2. CV4, 5, 6 HVP100 or SVC321
3. Parts with ✳ are adjustable and may be changed.

14-2 The FM/AM tuner pack in the Denon DCC-9770 CD auto player.

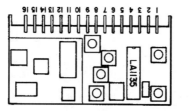

Terminal No.

1. NC	9. AM ANT
2. AM·DET OUT	10. FM OSC OUT
3. AM +B	11. FM +B
4. AM SD	12. FM IF OUT
5. AM VT	13. FM LO/DX
6. AM OSC OUT	14. FM VT
7. AM LO/DX	15. FM GND
8. AM GND	16. FM ANT

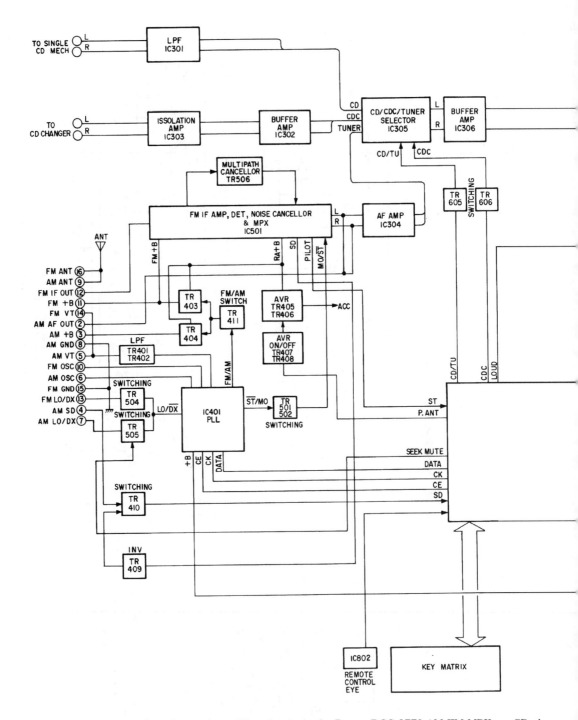

14-3 Block diagram of receiver and amplifier circuits in the Denon DCC-9770 AM-FM-MPX car CD player.

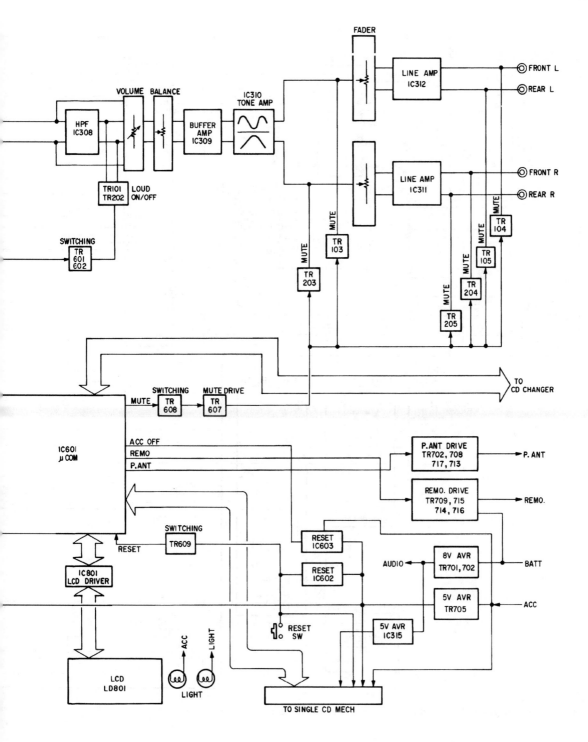

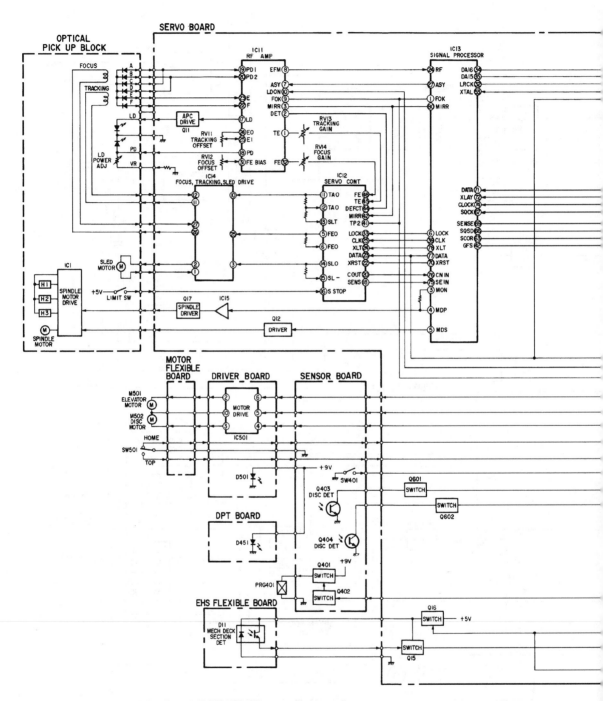

14-4   Block diagram of the Denon DCH-500 CD auto changer player.

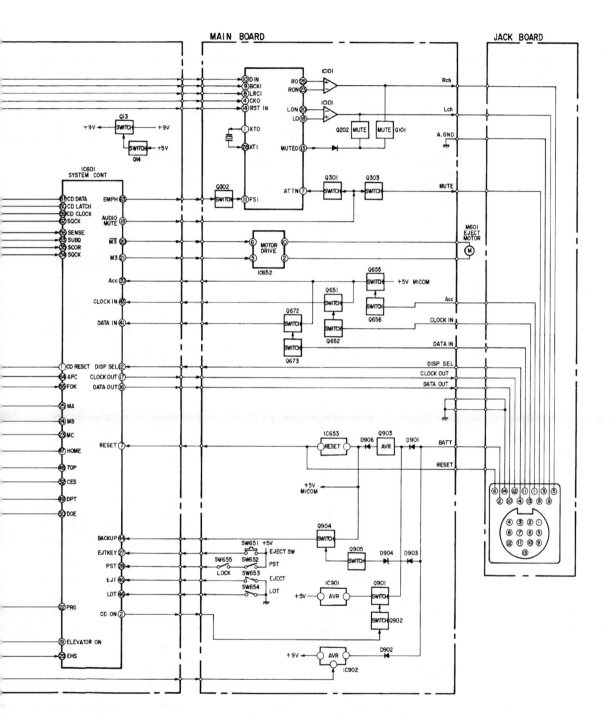

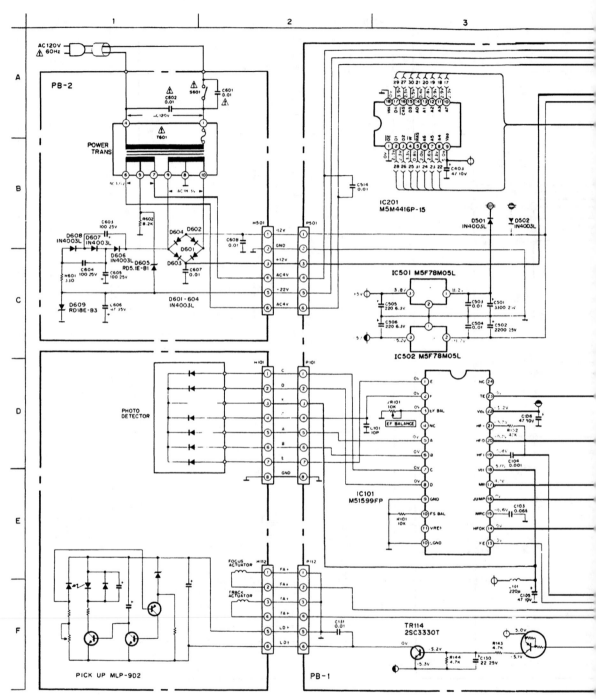

14-5 Schematic of a Mitsubishi M-C4030 automatic tabletop CD changer.

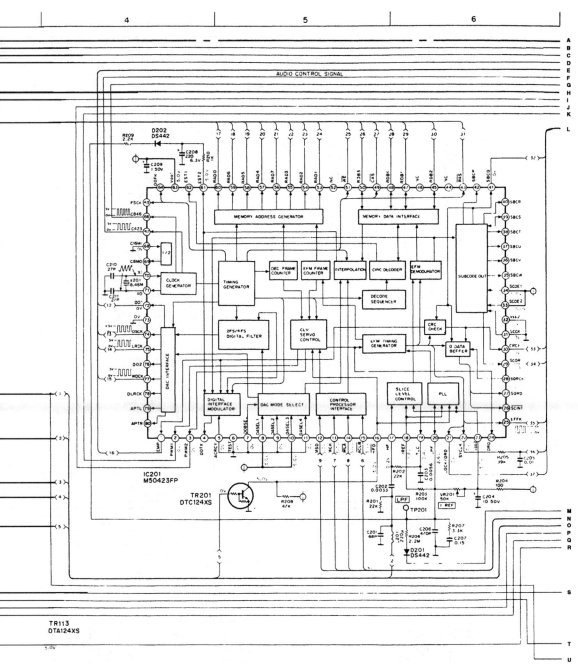

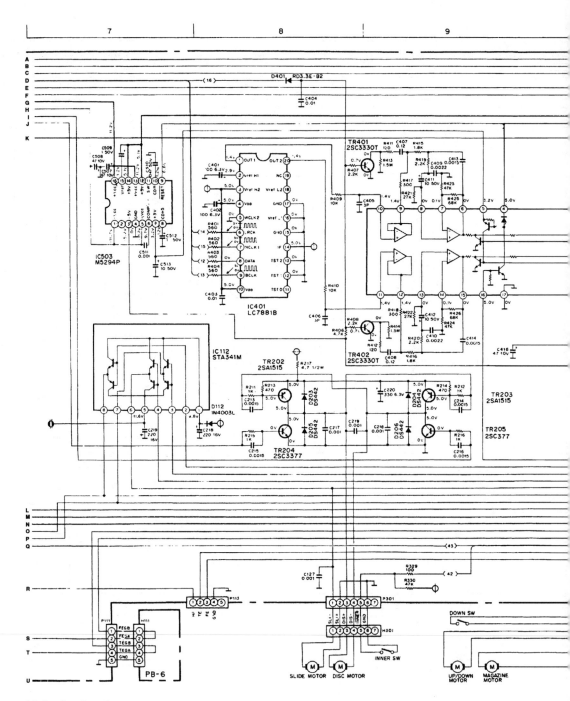

14-5 Continued.

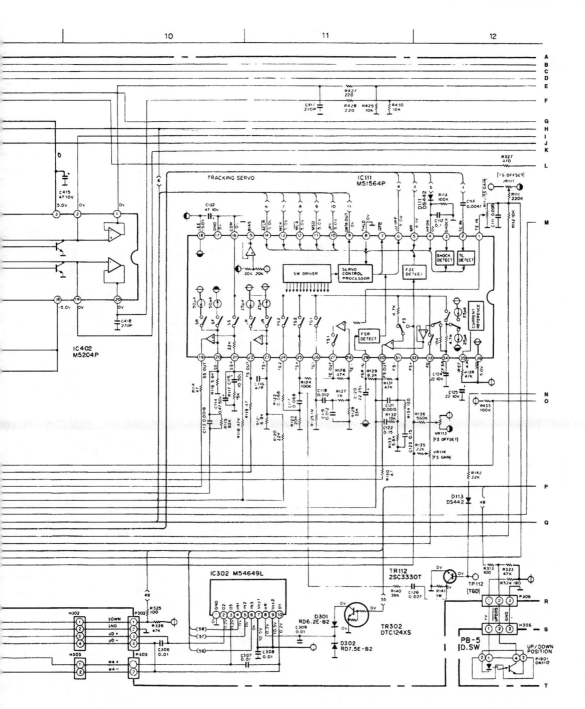

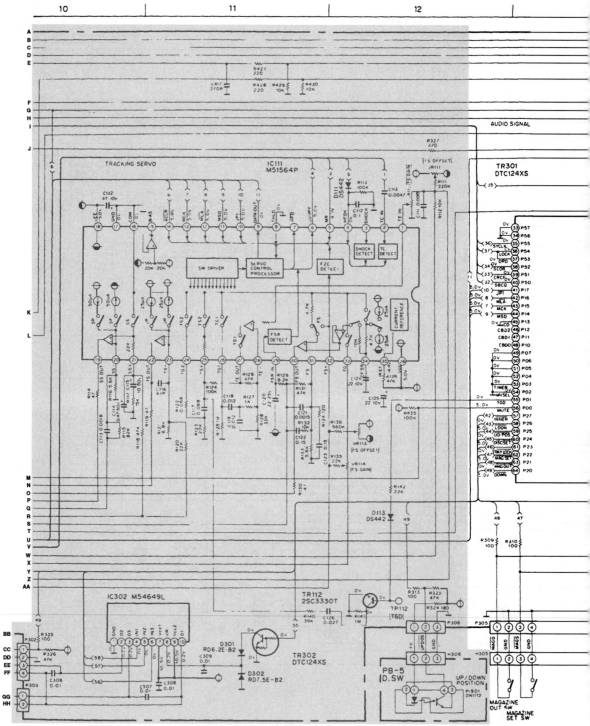

Duplicated from page 443

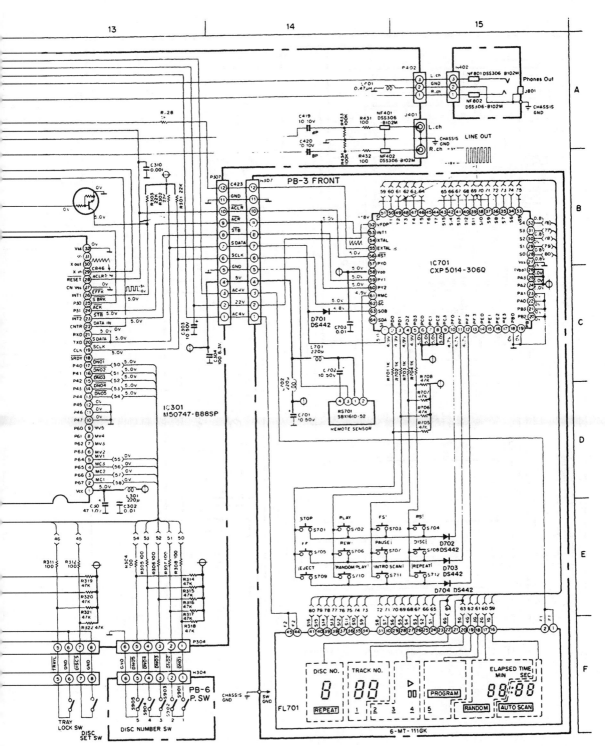

14-5 Continued.

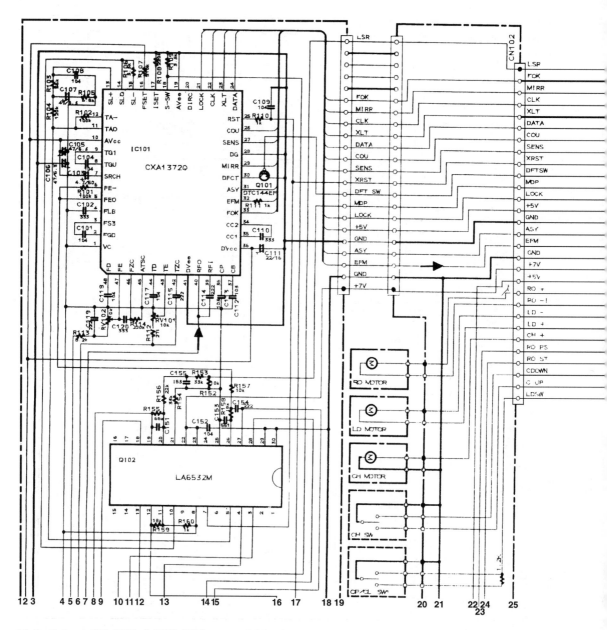

14-6 Onkyo's DX-C909 and DX-C606 carousel CD schematic.

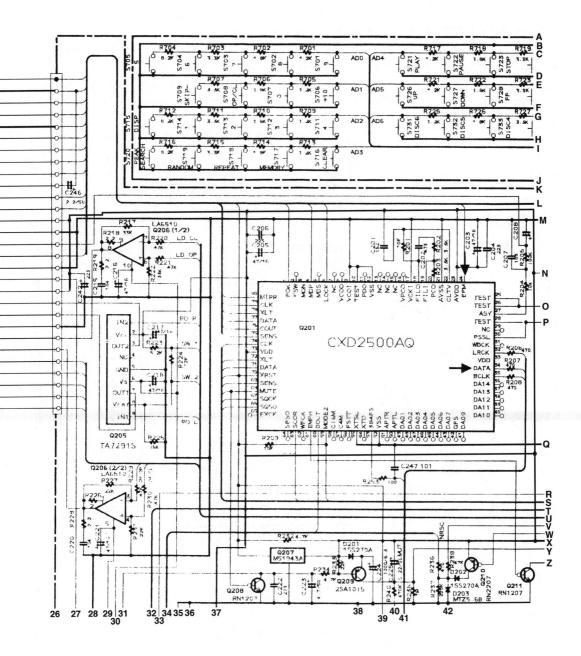

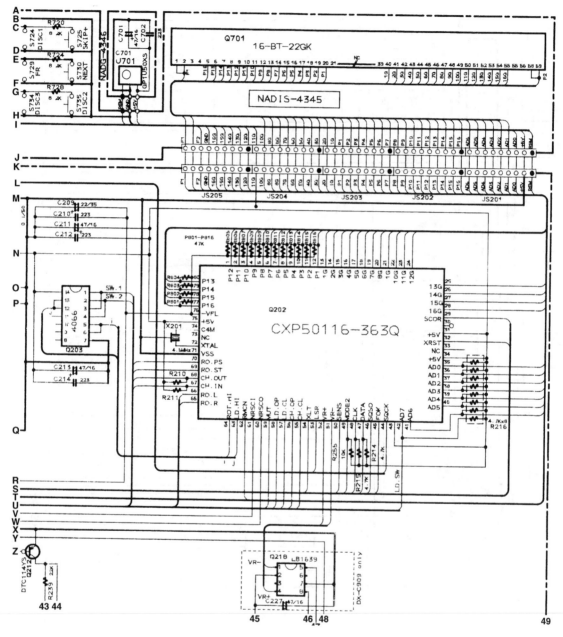

14-6 Continued.

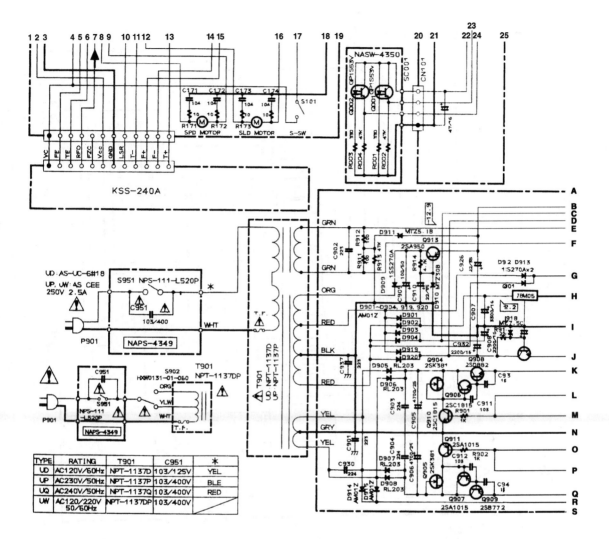

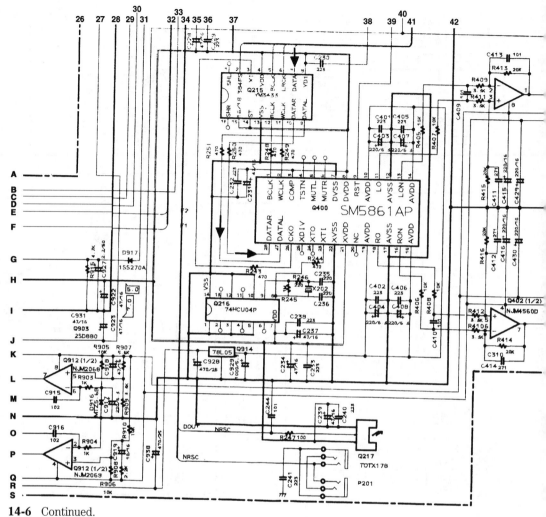

14-6 Continued.

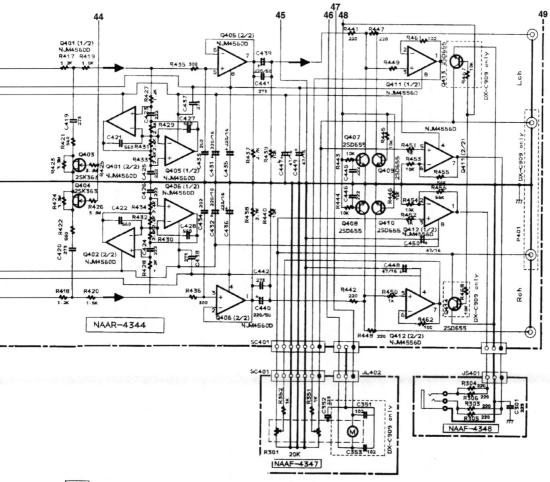

NOTE

- THE COMPONENTS IDENTIFIED BY MARK ⚠ ARE CRITICAL FOR SAFETY.
  REPLACE ONLY WITH PART NUMBER SPECIFIED.
- VOLTAGE (MEASURED WITH VOLTMETER) IS DC VOLTAGE.
- ALL PNP TRANSISTORS ARE EQUIVALENT TO 2SA1015-GR UNLESS
  OTHERWISE NOTED.
- ALL NPN TRANSISTORS ARE EQUIVALENT TO 2SC1815-GR UNLESS
  OTHERWISE NOTED.
- ALL DIODES ARE EQUIVALENT TO 1SS270A UNLESS OTHERWISE NOTED.
- ELECTROLYTIC CAPACITORS (⊞) ARE IN μF/WV.
- ALL CAPACITORS ARE IN pF/50WV UNLESS OTHERWISE NOTED.
  EX) 3pF→030, 33pF→330, 330pF→331, 0, 033μF→333
- ALL RESISTORS ARE IN OHMS 1/4 WATTS UNLESS OTHERWISE NOTED.
- THE THICK LINES IN PC BOARD ARE THE PRINTING SIDE OF THE PARTS.
  EX) ▬▬ PRINTING SIDE
- CIRCUIT IS SUBJECT TO CHANGE FOR IMPROVEMENT.

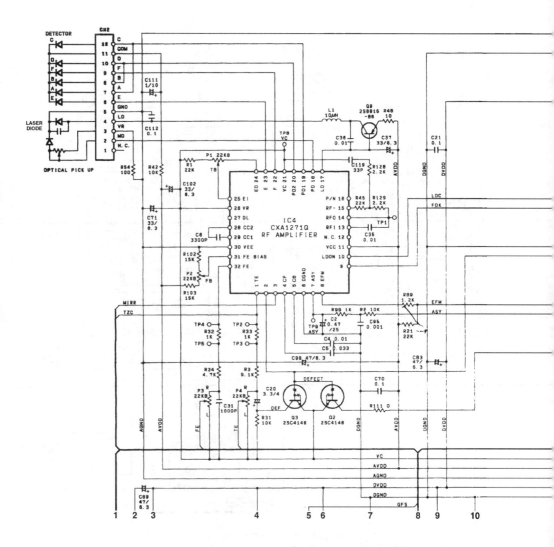

14-7 Diagram of a Realistic CD-3370 portable CD player.

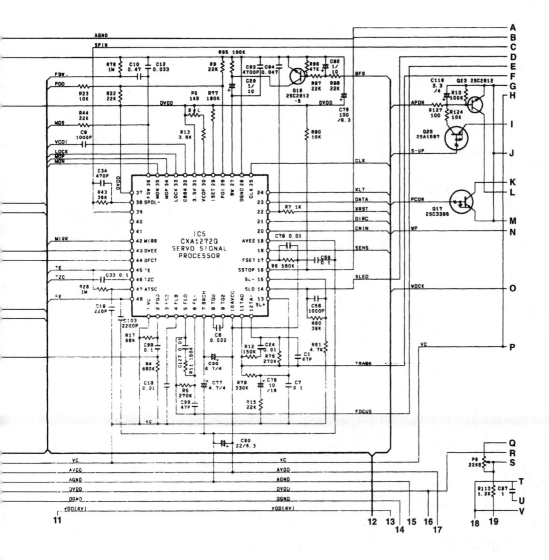

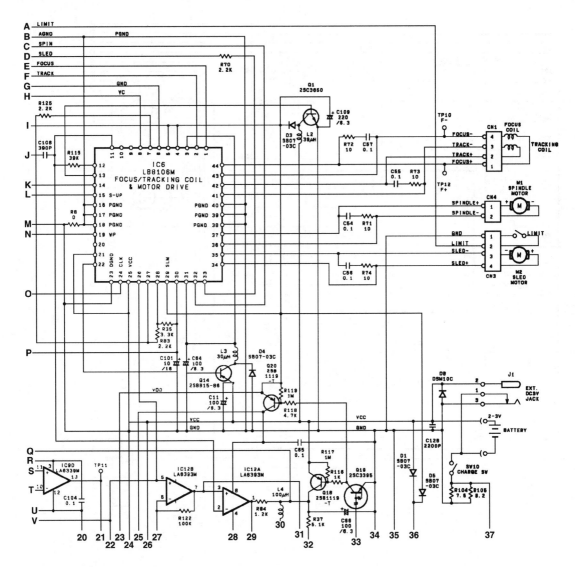

14-7 Continued.

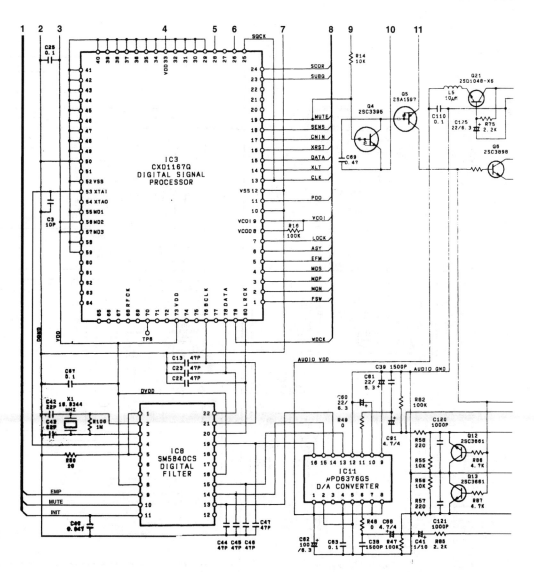

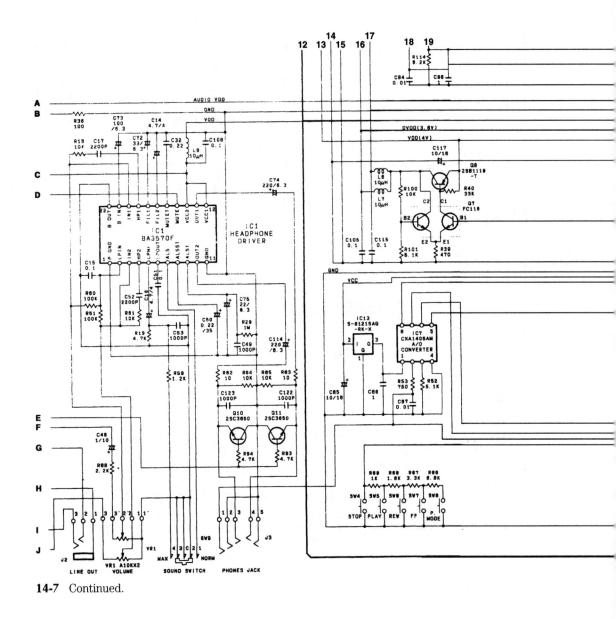

14-7 Continued.

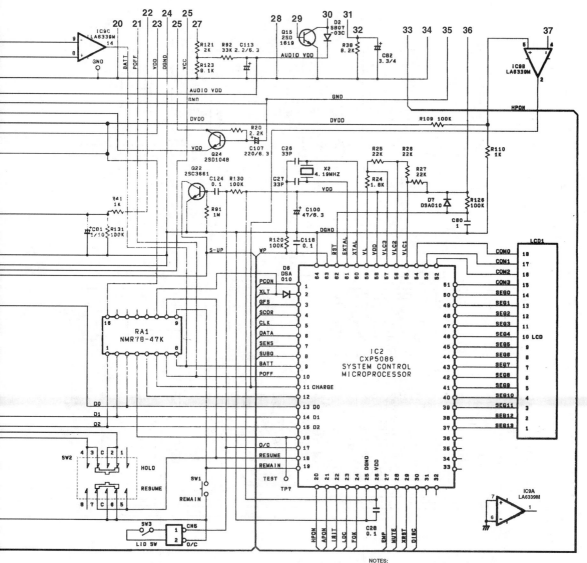

NOTES:
1. ALL RESISTANCE VALUES ARE IN Ω, K = 1000 Ω M = 1000 KΩ
2. ALL CAPACITANCE VALUES ARE IN μF, P = 10⁻⁶μF

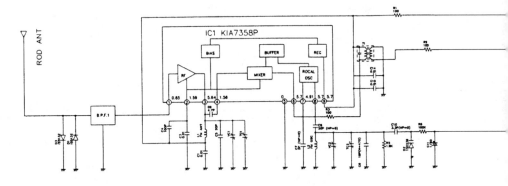

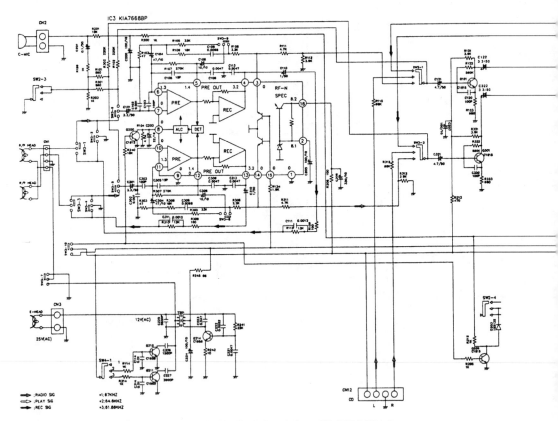

14-8 Audio and radio amp circuits of a Realistic boom-box CD-3304 CD player.

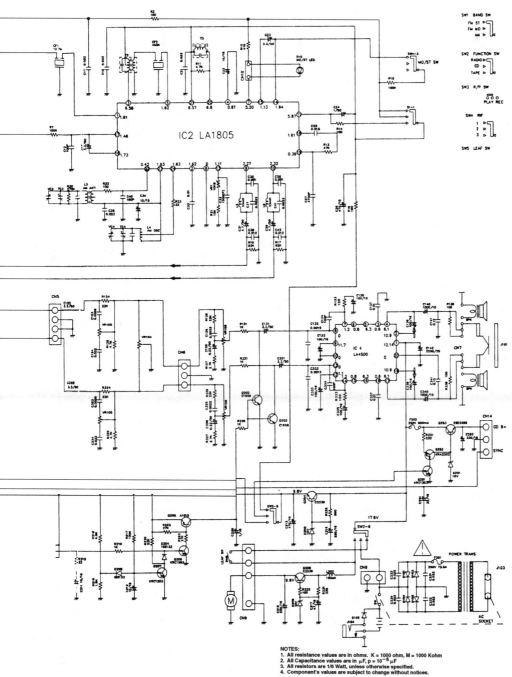

NOTES:
1. All resistance values are in ohms. K = 1000 ohm, M = 1000 Kohm
2. All Capacitance values are in μF, p = 10^{-6} μF
3. All resistors are 1/6 Watt, unless otherwise specified.
4. Component's values are subject to change without notices.

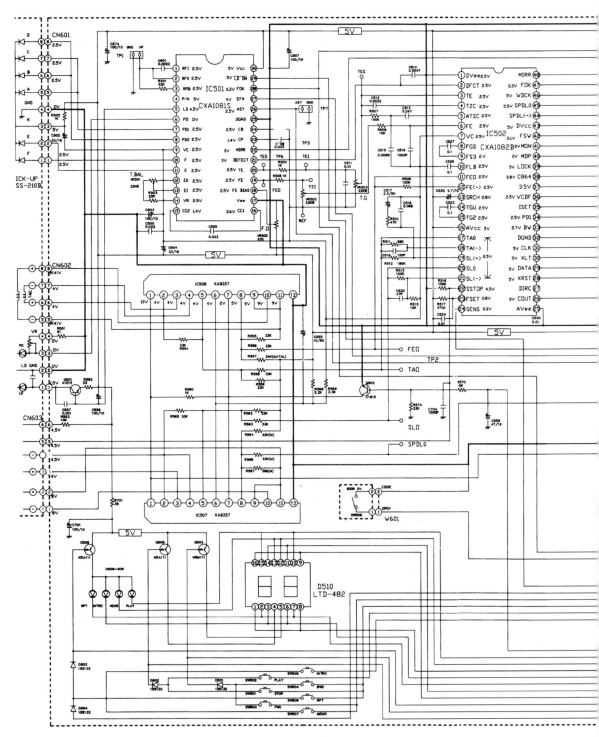

14-9 Schematic of the Realistic boom-box CD-3304 CDP circuits.

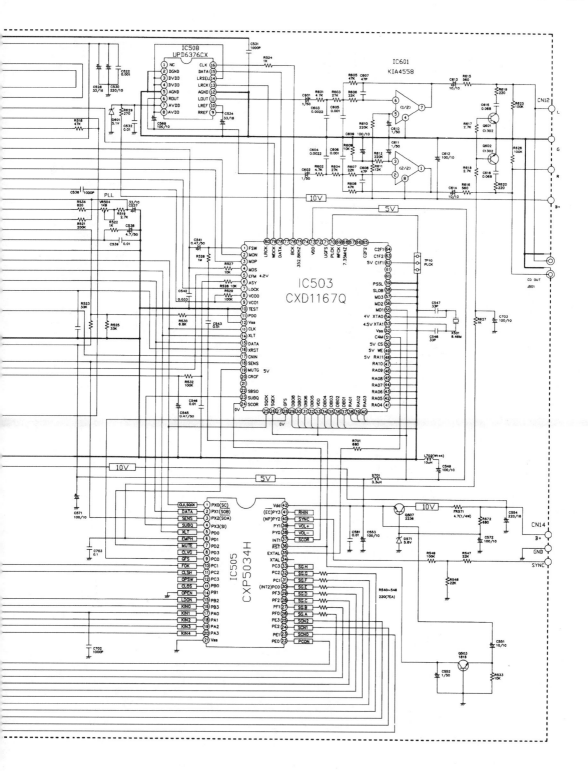

Appendix

A tracking signal lead code detector
ABUS audio bus
AF LPF audio focus error low-pass filter
AF OFFSET auto focus offset
AL ELECT aluminum electrolytic
A0-A10 address line
APCG APC ground
BC-CON semiconductor ceramic
B1-B4 output from ¼ divides detectors used to detect RF and focus signals
BCLK bit clock
BMBK brake signal of disc motor
CA-DR carriage drive
CAV system control
CBI bus input
CBO bus output
CDP control and display p code
Chip BC chip semiconductor ceramic
Chip TAN chip tantal capacitor
CHU chuck
CKEXT clock external
CLK clock
CLMP clamp of disc tray
CLVH constant linear velocity high
CM clear memory
CMCLS signal showing that disc tray is completely closed
C1F1 error flag indicating when decoder LSI is correcting errors
C1F2 error flag indicating when decoder LSI is correcting errors

C2F1   error flag indicating when decoder LSI is correcting errors
CF2   error flag indicating when decoder LSI is correcting errors
CRCF   subcode Q error detection result output
CS   chip select
D1-D8   RAM data fine
Data   data playback signal
D Con   dc line on
DEMP   de-emphasis
DIRC   direct
DMSW   disc motor switch
DMF   disc motor frequency
Elect   electrolytic capacitor
EXCK   external clock
FE   focus error signal
FER   focus error
FFER   focus error output signal
FG DW   focus gain down
FO-DR   focus drive
FO-ER   focus error
FO-IN   focus loop in
FOK   focus OK
fOK   frequency OK
FO-UT   focus loop out
FO-RT   focus
FP Carbon   flameproof carbon resistor
FUD   focus up/down
GFS   GFS frame sync lock status output
GND   ground
HLT   halt
1D1   data 1
1D1-1   data 2
1D4-1   data 4
1D8-1   data 8
INSD   inside
INT   interrupt
JPF   jump to forward
JPFS   jump forward signal
JPR   jump to reverse
KD1   key data 1
KD2   key data 2
KD3   key data 3
KD4   key data 4
KD5   key data 5
KD6   key data 6
KD0   key data 0
KS   key st. (output indicating that key has been pressed)

LAMP VOLT   lamp voltage
LAS1   laser switch
LASW   laser switch
L1DO   lid open
L-IN   loading in
L-OUT   loading out
LD-ON   laser diode
LDM   loading motor drive terminal
LOAD +   loading motor drive voltage output
LOAD –   loading motor drive voltage output
LMSW   limit switch
LRCK   LR clock
MDET   mirror surface detect terminal
MEDET   mirror surface envelope detect terminal
MIRR   mirror (mirror surface)
MR1H   mirror inhibit
MU1   mute 1
MU3   mute 3
MUTE   muting
OPEN   open (disc tray is open)
OSC1   oscillator 1
OSC2   oscillator 2
PCB   printed-circuit board
PDET   pit surface detect terminal
PEDET   pit surface envelope detect terminal
PPCON   polymopylene capacitor
RADOC   radial and focusing unit
RAOV   RAM overflow
RES   reset
RESET   reset
RF   radio frequency
RFCK   read frame clock
R-LPF   tracking error of low-pass filter
RMKS   remote control key
ROT   rotation
SBSO   subcode serial output
SC   scan
SCK   serial clock
SCLK   system clock
SCOR   subcode sync
SD   serial data
SENS   detector output bus
SLM   slide motor gain
SLM GAIN IN   slide motor gain in
SLM GAIN OUT   slide motor gain
SLM NF   slide motor negative feedback

SLR   slide reverse
SP-DR   spindle drive
SP-RT   spindle return
SRES   serial reset
STS   status
SUBD   subcode Q
T GAIN   tracking signal detect terminal
TER   tracking error
TEST   test
TOC   tray open/close
TOK   tracking OK
TR   tracking
TR CK   tracks clock
TR-DR   tracking drive
TR-ER   tracking error
TR-IN   tracking loop in
TR-NF   tracking negative feedback
TR-OT   tracking loop out
TR-RT   tracking return
TSW   tracking switch
WCLK   digital filter 88.2 kHz strobe input signal
WDCK   clock (88.2 kHz)
VR   variable resistor
XCK   clock signal
XLT   servo and decode IC serial latch clock pulse signal

Glossary

amplitude The strength of a waveform, expressed in height. Can be either negative or positive.

analog filter A filter system in the CD player that reduces and cancels out noise. The analog filter is before and after the D/A converter in some players.

APC (automatic power control) This circuit keeps the laser-diode optical output at a constant level.

auto focus (AF) The focus servo that moves the objective lens up and down to correct the focus of the beam.

balance The control in the stereo amp that equalizes channel output.

bit A binary number. A group of bits makes a word. There are 16 bits in most CD players.

block diagram A drawing or diagram showing the different sections or stages of the compact disc player.

chip devices Examples used in the various CD players are the thick-film chip resistor, multilayer ceramic chip capacitor, mini-mold chip transistor, mini-mold chip diode, and mini-mold chip IC.

clamper assembly The clamper assembly fits over the compact disc after loading. The clamper assembly must be removed to get to the laser pickup assembly.

CLEAR buttons The button that erases the last digit entered or the complete program if pressed immediately after the BAND button on some CD players.

clipping Clipping can occur if a stage is distorted or with too much volume. Clipping can be observed on the scope.

clock An electronic circuit that provides correct timing in the CD player.

CLV servo An electronic system that provides proper constant-linear velocity during disc playback. The CLV servo circuits control the spindle, turntable, or disc motor.

collimator   A special lens in the CD optical system that makes the beam rays parallel.

compact disc (CD)   The compact disc player plays a small record or disc of digitally enclosed music. The compact disc provides noiseless high-fidelity music on one side of a rainbow-like surface.

constant-linear velocity (CLV)   The constant speed of the disc with reference to the radius of the CD disc. The disc turns approximately 500 rpm at the center and 200 rpm at the outer surface.

CPU   A computer-type processor used in the master and mechanism circuits of the CD player.

crosstalk   When the right channel and left channel are mixed together. Crosstalk is less in the CD player compared to the stereo tape player. Crosstalk is leakage of one channel into the other.

cylindrical lens   A special lens in the optical system of the laser pickup assembly in the CD player.

D/A converter   A special stage that separates the audio signal from the digital signal. The audio signal can be detected after the D/A converter.

decibel (dB)   A measure of gain; the ratio of the output power voltage with respect to the input, expressed in log units.

de-emphasis   The de-emphasis circuit is automatically engaged in the compact disc player when the discs with pre-emphasis are being played. The de-emphasis stage follows the D/A converter.

digital   Information expressed in binary terms.

digital filter   A low-pass filtering network.

disc holder   The disc holder or turntable that sits directly on top of the motor shaft in a compact disc player.

dither   A very low-level noise added to a digitized signal to reduce high distortion caused by quantizing low-level audio signals. Quantization can be found in the motor control IC of the CD player.

dropout   Dropouts are caused by dirt, scratches, and foreign material on the disc. The optical system cannot read the digital information with this type of substance.

dynamic range   The ratio between the maximum signal level and minimum level expressed in decibels (dB). The full dynamic range of the human ear can be recorded on the compact disc.

E-F balance   After changing the optical laser pickup assembly, the balance of the E-F diodes must be adjusted for tracking error detection in the CD player.

eight-to-fourteen modulation (EFM)   A very complex encoding scheme used to transform the digital data to a form that can be placed on the disc. This information is modulated by EFM. The EFM signal goes into the signal processing LSI. The EFM signal must be present or most CD players will automatically shut down if focus and tracking error is missing.

equalization (EQ)   Alteration of the frequency response so that the frequency balance of the output equals the frequency balance of the input. Equalization is also used to correct response deficiencies with speakers.

eye pattern The RF signal waveform at the RF amplifier in the CD player. The waveform is adjusted so the diamond shapes in the eye pattern are clear and distinct.

fast forward (FF) Push the fast-forward button to advance quickly to another program.

filter A circuit that selectively passes certain frequencies but no others, such as the low-pass filters in the CD player. The large electrolytic capacitors in the low-voltage power supplies are sometimes called filter capacitors.

flutter A change in speed of the disc turntable. Practically no flutter exists in the CD player.

focus coil A coil at the end of the focus drive transistor or IC that moves the object or actuator assembly up and down to maintain accurate focus at all times.

focus error (FE) The output from four optosensing elements are supplied to the error signal amp and a zero output is produced. The error amp corrects the signal voltage and goes to the servo IC to correct the focus in the CD player.

focus offset adjustment The offset adjustment made at the RF amp with a test disc. The eye pattern is monitored with the scope. A good eye pattern means that the diamond shape in the center of the waveform is clear.

focus OK circuit (FOK) The circuit that generates a signal used to determine when the laser spot is on the reflecting surface of the disc. The FOK signal is high when the laser is in focus of the CD player.

focus servo The servo IC controls the correct focus applied to the focus driving circuits. The focus servo IC detects the errors and corrects them.

frequency response The range of frequencies a given piece of equipment can pass to the listener. The ideal frequency response of a given amplifier is (practically) 20 Hz to 20 kHz. It is often defined with decibel variation over a flat specified frequency range.

FZC circuit (focus zero cross) The circuit that detects when the FE signal reaches 0 V. It is used together with the FOK circuit to determine the focus adjustment timing in the CD player.

ground A point of zero voltage or the common voltage return for the components within a circuit, sometimes referred to as *earth ground*. The common ground can be a metal chassis in the CD player. All test equipment should be connected to one common ground when servicing the CD player.

harmonic A multiple of a given frequency.

harmonic distortion The addition of harmonics not present in the original recording. Harmonic distortion should be less than 1%.

hertz (Hz) The unit expressing cycles per second (cps), the unit of frequency.

high frequency (HF) The RF signal that carries the EFM signal data to the various circuits in the preamp signal circuits of the CD player.

hiss The annoying high-frequency background noise found in tape, record, and CD players. Hiss can be caused by or confused with a "frying" sound made by a defective IC or transistor in the audio circuit.

hum A type of noise that originates from the 60-cycle power line, due mainly to poor filtering in the low-voltage power supply. Hum can be picked up from CD player and sent to the amplifier input jack. Hum and vibrating noise might be audible in a power transformer or motor with loose particles or laminations.

impedance The degree of resistance (in ohms) that an electrical current encounters in a given circuit or component.

index search When using a disc with index coding, press track forward or track reverse until the desired number appears in the display. If the track or index does not exist on the disc, the player will search to the end of the disc and then stop.

integrated circuit (IC) A single component that contains many diodes, transistors, resistors, etc. The LSI and CPU are forms of integrated circuits.

interlock A safety circuit in some CD players that activates when loading the disc. The interlock circuit lowers the supply voltage to the laser optical assembly while the loading tray is out, and it raises the voltage to enable the laser assembly after the disc is loaded. Interlocks are placed in the circuits to protect the operator.

intermodulation distortion (IMD) The presence of unwanted frequencies that are the sum and differences of the test signals. Blurring or smearing of sound is the result of IMD. These levels should be below 0.1%.

jack The CD player might have two line output jacks at the rear so the external amp can be attached. Some CD players have a headphone jack for quiet listening.

kHz 1000 Hz or 1000 cycles per second.

land The flat areas between pits on the rainbow surface of the compact disc.

laser assembly The assembly that contains the laser diodes, photodiodes, correction diodes, focus coils, and tracking coils. The laser assembly is also known as the optical assembly or pickup head.

laser diode A semiconductor laser diode in the pickup head assembly. The laser diode emits the beam that reads the coded information from the disc.

LED (light-emitting diode) The low-power diodes used for optical readouts and display in electronic equipment. They are available in many colors.

level The strength of a signal. The turntable or disc motor assembly should be leveled in some CD players.

line-line output jacks (left and right) They are at the rear of the CD player and connect to the external amplifier.

loading motor The motor in the CD player that moves the loading tray out and pulls the loaded disc and tray back into play position.

LSI (large scale integrated) Includes the processors, ICs, and CPUs found in the compact disc player.

memory The program memory of a CD player. Some program memories can play up to 15 selected tracks. The tracks can be entered in any sequence or the same track can be repeated several times.

MHz (megahertz) One million hertz or one million cycles per second.

microprocessor An integrated circuit that serves many different functions. The microprocessor might be used in the control and mechanism systems.

MIR (mirror detector circuit) The circuits used for detection of the mirror portion of the disc between tracks and outside the lead-out track and also in the detection of disc flaws.

modulation The way in which one signal modifies or controls another signal for the purpose of carrying information.

monitor diode A special photodiode for monitoring the light output of the laser to a correction circuit.

music search A feature that finds the beginning of each song automatically.

mute switch An electronic device that controls the muting of the output line audio circuits in the compact disc player.

noise Any unwanted signal that is unrelated to the desired signal. Noise can be generated during the rewind or playback of the disc.

optical lens The lens assembly in the laser pickup. The optical lens should be cleaned by wiping with a lint-free cleaning paper or camera lens cleaning products.

oversampling When the digital data derived from the disc is sampled at a rate higher than normal.

peak The level of power or signal. A peak indicator light shows the highest signal levels.

phase Sound waves that are in sync with one another. Expressed in degrees. Speakers are wired together so the cones go in and out together, or in *phase*.

phone plug The headphone plug where you can plug in a pair of headphones for private listening.

photodiode A light-sensitive device used in the laser assembly to bring the RF signal to the preamp stages of the CD player.

pickup The laser or optical assembly might be called the pickup assembly. This unit contains the laser diode, photodiodes, lenses, and other optical components.

pickup motor The motor used to move the pickup assembly towards the outer edge of the disc. Also called *sled, slide, or feed motor.*

pit A tiny impression on the surface of the disc that carries the digital data.

PLL (phase locked loop) An accurate system used in the digital control processor of the compact disc player. The PLL circuit must be accurate for CLV motor control.

preamp The preamp amplifies the weak RF signal from the photodiodes in the pickup head. The preamp provides EFM, FE, and TE signals.

quantization The number of possible values available to represent various levels of amplitude of a digital audio system. The resolution of quantization is 16 bits in the compact disc player. Quantization takes place within the RAM and control system processor.

radial arm The radial arm consists of a motor and pickup head assembly that moves the head in an arc across the disc.

RAM (random access memory) Used to store information and audio data in the CD player. REPEAT button-push to replay the same track of music on the compact disc player.

RF (radio frequency) The RF signal from the phototransistor diodes are fed to the preamp stages within the CD player.

sample/hold (SH) The circuits in each stereo channel that sample incoming data and hold it momentarily.

sampling frequency   The rate or the number of times a signal is sampled in digital audio. The sampling rate of a disc player is 44.1 kHz.

separation   The complete separation of two audio signals in stereo channels.

servo   Refers to the servo control or tracking circuits that keep the laser pickup in the grooves at all times. Most servo components in the CD players are IC processors.

servo control   Refers to the servo control IC that controls the focus and tracking coils in addition to maintaining accurate tracking.

signal   Any form of detectable electronic information.

signal processing   In the compact disc player, converting the laser beam signals to audio with preamp and signal processors.

signal-to-noise (S/N)   The ratio of the loudest signal to that of hiss or noise. The higher the signal-to-noise ratio, the better the sound.

skip   Certain compact discs have index points that allow different movements or parts of pieces of music, such as symphonies, to be selected. To set the index number, press the skip or track index number button.

slide   See *pickup motor*.

spindle motor   The spindle motor can be called the turntable or disc motor. The spindle motor rotates the disc at a variable rate from the beginning to the end of the disc. Also called the *turntable* or *disc motor*.

test disc   A compact disc used to make alignment and adjustments on the compact disc player.

total harmonic distortion (THD)   A percentage of harmonic distortion found in components. To measure how accurate an amp is, for example, a signal is fed in and the harmonics are measured at the output. The lower the percentage, the less the distortion.

track   One lane of spiral pits on the surface of a compact disc.

tracking coil   A coil located with the tracking driver transistor or ICs that moves the lens back and forth across the disc for accurate tracking.

tracking servo   The IC processor that keeps the laser beam in correct focus and tracking.

track kick circuit   The circuit used when the laser beam skips to a relatively close track during accessing and cue/record operations. Skipping is achieved by applying kick and brake pulses to the tracking coil with the tracking servo loop open.

tray   The loading tray or drawer in which the CD disc to be played is placed.

wow   Variation in speed of a reproducing system. Practically no wow is found in the CD player. Can be called *flutter*.

Index

U

V

About the Author

Homer L. Davidson worked as an electrician and small appliance repair technician in his own repair shop for 38 years. He is the author of more than 30 how-to books for TAB/McGraw-Hill. His first magazine article was printed in *Radio Craft* in 1940; since that time, Davidson has had over 1000 articles printed in 48 different magazines.

Other Bestsellers of Related Interest

Troubleshooting and Repairing Consumer Electronics Without a Schematic
—Homer L. Davidson
Indispensable for electronics technicians, students, and advanced hobbyists, this hands-on guide comes to the rescue for all those times when no schematic diagram is available.
ISBN 0-07-015650-6 $22.95 Paper
ISBN 0-07-015649-2 $34.95 Hard

Troubleshooting & Repairing Audio & Video Cassette Players & Recorders
—Homer L. Davidson
This is an all-in-one, illustrated guide for consumers and hobbyists—covering everything from microcassettes, portables, and stereo/auto cassettes and compact disks to VCRs, camcorders, and digital audio tape. One of the world's best known electronics how-to authors, Davidson's coverage ranges from basic cleaning and maintenance to performing repairs.
ISBN 0-8306-4258-7 $19.95 Paper

Troubleshooting and Repairing PC Drives and Memory Systems
—Stephen J. Bigelow
Professional diagnostic techniques for IBM-compatible hard and floppy drives, tape backups, memory chips, solid-state memory cards, and optical drives (including CD-ROMS). Covers new tools, test equipment, and diagnostic software.
ISBN 0-8306-4551-9 $22.95 Paper
ISBN 0-8306-4550-0 $39.95 Hard

Troubleshooting and Repairing Solid-State TVs, 2nd Edition
—*Homer L. Davidson*
A complete workbench reference for electronics technicians and students. Packed
with case study examples, troubleshooting photos, and diagrams for every kind of
TV circuit, this popular guide is just what technicians need to diagnose and repair
virtually any TV malfunction.
ISBN 0-8306-3893-8 $24.95 Paper
ISBN 0-8306-3894-6 $36.95 Hard